Emotions and
Psychopathology

Emotions and Psychopathology

Edited by

Manfred Clynes
University of Melbourne
Victoria, Australia

and

Jaak Panksepp
Bowling Green State University
Bowling Green, Ohio

Plenum Press • New York and London

Library of Congress Cataloging in Publication Data

Emotions and psychopathology / edited by Manfred Clynes and Jaak Panksepp.
    p.   cm.
    "Proceedings of a symposium on emotions and psychopathology, held September
26–27, 1986, at Bowling Green State University, Bowling Green, Ohio" — T.p. verso.
    Includes bibliographies and indexes.
    ISBN 0-306-42916-0
    1. Psychology, Pathological — Congresses. 2. Emotions — Congresses. 3. Neuroim-
munology — Congresses. I. Clynes, Manfred, 1925–   . II. Panksepp, Jaak,
1943–   .
    [DNLM: 1. Emotions — physiology — congresses. 2. Mental Disorders — physio-
pathology — congresses. 3. Psychophysiology — congresses. WL103 E54 1986]
RC480.5.E46   1988
616.89 — dc19
DNLM/DLC   88-12508
for Library of Congress   CIP

Based on a symposium on Emotions and Psychopathology,
held September 26–27, 1986, at Bowling Green State University,
Bowling Green, Ohio

© 1988 Plenum Press, New York
A Division of Plenum Publishing Corporation
233 Spring Street, New York, N.Y. 10013

Printed in the United States of America

PREFACE

This book summarises the proceedings of a symposium on "Emotions and Psychopathology" which was held by the Department of Psychology of Bowling Green State University from September 26-27, 1986. It is coming to be realized that to understand the underlying structure and dynamics of many psychopathologies, it is essential to understand the nature of emotions. The aim of this symposium was to gather a group of investigators and thinkers who would have valuable and unique perspectives on the nature of emotions and on their relationship to psychic disorders. The main participants were Manfred Clynes, Helen Block Lewis, Michael Liebowitz, Marvin Minsky, Robert Plutchik, John Paul Scott and Jaak Panksepp. Ted Melnechuk chaired the half-day of round table discussion on the day following the symposium, and Gail Zivin and Larry Stettner presented informal position statements on ethological approaches during the round table. On the evening before the symposium, Elliot Valenstein of The University of Michigan presented a pre-symposium colloquium entitled "Great and Desperate Cures" which summarized his most recent contribution to the Psychosurgery debate. We should like to refer you to his excellent book on the subject, with the same title, (Basic Books,1986), which can help forewarn us of possible future worries in the application of biological technologies. Paul Byers who did not attend the meeting was invited to write a chapter summarizing cultural and societal issues which were not formally covered at the meeting. Other topics of importance to understanding emotions which could not be covered at such a short meeting may be found well presented in several other recent collected works on the topic (e.g. Plutchik & Kellerman (Eds.) *Emotions: Theory, Research & Experience* in four volumes, Academic Press, 1980-1988, Scherer & Ekman (Eds.) *Approaches to Emotion; Erlbann*, 1984, Izard, Kagan & Zajonc (Eds.) *Emotion, Cognition, and Behavior*, Cambridge Univ. Press, 1984; Izard & Read (Eds.) *Measuring Emotions in Infants and Children*, Cambridge Univ. Press, 1986. We think that the present collection adds dimensions which are not well represented in those contributions.

The idea for this symposium was triggered by the appointment of Manfred Clynes as Visiting Distinguished Professor of Psychology for the Fall semester of 1987, under a new program that was instituted by the president of BGSU, Paul Olscamp. The symposium was planned by a committee consisting of Robert Conner, Harold Johnson, Donald Kausch, Stuart Keeley, who were gathered for this purpose by Panksepp. The nuts-and-bolts organization of the symposium was greatly facilitated by several energetic graduate students, especially Loring Crepeau, Meg Dwyer, Barbie Johnson and Kelly Morton. Sharyn Steller and Jaak Panksepp transcribed the round table discussion and many thanks to Ted Melnechuk for the final skilled editing of that segment of the book.   Karen Miklosovic provided meticulous editorial assistance in the final composition of the book at BGSU as did Pat Vann and Kim Doman at Plenum Press. Funding for the meeting was obtained from an Academic Challenge Grant to the Bowling Green Department of Psychology from the State of Ohio, as well as via support from Dean Kenneth Baker of the Graduate College and Research Services Office headed by Chris Dunn. Joyce Kepke facilitated keeping essential details in mind, and Panksepp served as the central depository for all head-aches involved in getting the symposium realized. The main part of the symposium was held at the BGSU Planetarium, which was graciously made available for this purposed by Dale Smith. The planetarium provided an intimately rounded environment for the symposium. The meeting stimulated fertile interchange of ideas in this new and important area of inquiry. We encouraged participants to expand on their spoken thoughts in their final written contributions, but the final chapters well reflect the tenor of the meeting. We thank everyone involved for helping put this event and project together.

Jaak Panksepp. May 1987

FOREWORD

No-one yet knows where an accurate scientific analysis of emotions will take us, but we believe that such knowledge will have to be the foundation on which a scientific understanding of major psycho-pathologies will eventually have to be constructed. Obviously, the very nature of emotions is also integrally intertwined with the issue of values. Without emotions, we would have no intrinsic rationale for deciding how we should behave, and we would not be able to experience the highest joys nor the lowest despairs of life. It is remarkable that it has taken so long to begin probing scientifically and in earnest, the mystery of emotions.

For the first time in the history of Western science, it is being recognized that emotions are entities. We are beginning to see that there is a precise meaning to the concept of pure emotions - of pure anger, of pure fear, or pure joy - in the same sense as we may speak of pure oxygen, or better, pure red or blue or green. The unique experience of "pure color" is elicited by stimulation of retinal receptors, but such experiences can also be elicited through electrical stimulation of higher areas of the brain in the absence of external light stimulation. As can basic colors, certain basic emotions can be stimulated from specific neuronal networks. These circuits do not interface the external world directly, however, as do receptors for red. Rather, they have internal receptor sites in the brain and, perhaps the body, which are activated by neurotransmitters, some of which surely include some of the newly discovered peptides. Further, as secondary colors are experienced because of the concurrent influence of pure 'receptors', emotions too can be experienced not only in their pure forms, but also in 'mixtures', derived from their combined actions. It is the task of psychobiology and neuropsychology to delineate these specific circuits for emotions and to find the internal receptors and transmitting agents.

The experience of emotion is more, however, and different than the experience of red or green in a number of important ways that are biologically determined, and have evolved integrally with emotional circuits. First of all, each emotional entity links directly and reciprocally to the motor system, and this link provides the faculties of emotional expression and the possibility of direct communication of emotions. By their nature, emotions are social as well as individual. They generate communication between individuals as well as within the individual. It is one of nature's marvels that emotional communication is symbiotically programmed by the genetic apparatus so that for each specific motor form of expression there is a faculty of reception. The coding and decoding of emotional communication are coordinated by the design of the nervous system. While these input and output functions are initiated by entirely different neuronal and bodily structures, the central essence of both functions may be a single harmoniously operating neuronal system which is the primal source of social emotional interaction.

A second significant function of emotions that goes beyond perceptual qualities, such as red, is their greater inherent link to cognitive function. This link may be specific and different for each emotion. It is a task of clinical, cognitive and neuropsychology to delineate the specific ways in which each emotion affects cognitive functions, thereby narrowing the gap between what has been called 'instinctive behavior' and 'learned behavior'. This inherent, biologically-given link between specific emotions and cognitive function will surely be one of the most important aspects of research in the years to come.

A third aspect of the function of emotions that distinguishes it from such experiences as red is that it can be 'suppressed'. There is an inherent need for expression, and if prevented through voluntary control, the emotion may continue to exist in a subterranian and tyrannous way, that is, 'subconsciously' awaiting a future opportunity to be released and expressed. The cognitive and bodily aspects of such suppressed emotions are particularly unresearched, though very significant. More and more we see that the inherent relation between specific emotions and cognitive functions underlies the gamut of all social possibilities as well as problems. Appropriate and enlightened planning of societies is impossible without understanding these. Once the inherent link between the specific emotions and cognitive functions have been clarified, we may understand man's nature sufficiently to begin sensibly building a better society and provide a real possibility of improved lives for individuals.

A key relationship between specific emotions and cognitive functions is in the realm of the arts. Emotion and meaning combine in special ways. Freed from the necessity of action, emotion steps out of the constraints of a person's life-line. Time is no longer the time of a person - it is an impersonal time in which music and dance happens, a time in which individuals forget or transform their own cares and temporal pressures. In the arts, it is possible to play with the emotions. What does this mean? Neuroscience is just coming to grips with this question.

In this volume there is a consideration of play in animals - a play circuit is proposed which is activated characteristically when animals play - an important and hitherto unexplored brain function. To what extent do human joy and creativity emerge from this primal substrate, to guide the developmental competence we call maturation? Surely, the play circuit leads to a blossoming of various human possibilities, and it can come to be used deliberately and consciously as an investment in one's emotional vigor and health. And thus we also describe herein an art form of touch through which persons can practice to play with emotions - in the same way in which a musician plays with emotion when he improvises or composes.

The word "play" describes an activity which we all think we know rather well. But what are the real entities described by this word - how accurate is this word, or for that matter, are the words anger, joy, love and so on? This difficult and important search leads us to discover "basic" emotions - for which there may be no unambiguous, clear words. Words may be helpful in considering the qualities of experience, but also they are often woefully inadequate, missing or misleading. In most languages, there are no words to describe the time course of experiences, even when they denote the quality itself clearly. Grammatically, even related languages differ greatly in their handling of emotions. For example, in German one says "ich freue mich uber..." or "ich argere mich uber..." which literally translates as "I joy myself over..." or "I anger myself over..." In English 'joy' cannot be a verb.

Thus animals, not having words to contend with, can be especially helpful for approaching the problem of 'basic' emotions. It is likely however, that man has developed a number of emotions that are not shared with animals. Laughter appears to be one of these. The cognitive relations of the emotions of laughter are of a high order. In the moment before laughter erupts, an extraordinary conflux of thought takes place, and the attitude of play (or detachment) is called upon. This cognitive attitude laughter has in common with the arts, and with play itself.

Imagination and emotion are entwined. For example, fear thrives on imagination but also limits imagination. Looked at closer, all emotions appear to depend on imagination. In a life situation, imaginative realization of the implications of the situation fires the emotions. The less imagination, the less emotion. But also the more comprehensive the imagination, the more altered the scope of the emotion. This appears to apply both in play and non-play situations.

Thus it is all the more surprising for traditional psychology that one finds that emotions are capable of also being generated without any images, in the conventional sense, merely by the expression of the underlying motoric plan. This concept, called 'generalized emotion' is a new one for psychology. Musicians and dancers have known this in their own way for a very long time. They use the communication of emotions devoid of any generating 'cause'. Precise forms of emotional communication, disembodied of real life 'causes', in various sensory modalities can and do generate emotions - contagion of emotion occurs. Contagion can happen with joy, anger, grief, sex, love and other emotions. It cannot happen with jealousy. Why not? We must look at the cognitive functions attached to that emotion.

The cognitive aspects of emotions are clearly marked in the emotions of shame and guilt. Helen Block Lewis, in this volume, looks at these and also attempts to relate them to neuronal circuits such as those investigated by Panksepp. These circuits are those of fear, expectancy, separation distress and play. There is discussion of how Freudian censorship may function in this perspective.

More generally, Marvin Minsky discusses the working of emotion, personality and mind from a perspective gained by considering the problems that artificial intelligence would have to solve to model the mind.and its interaction with the body. His discussion of the interrelation of emotion and cognition and of the nature of emotions are tied to his theories described in his recent book "The Society of Mind". He describes mental function as a multiplicity of separate agents operating autonomously, each with their own quasi-Freudian censor. The multiplicity of unconscious processes forms a society as well as a heirarchy of operations. Conscious knowledge of some of these is only the tip of the iceberg. His theories, contrary to Freud, question the validity of the concept of a single self or personality. His contributions are a challenge for research on understanding the relationship between emotion and cognition.

At the most fundamental level of considering what are basic emotions, we must consider what is encoded in the genome. John Paul Scott, a pioneer in this field of behavior genetics, considers such sources of differences in emotional temperaments and also provides a general overview of the types of issues we need to consider when we seek therapeutic change of emotional problems, especially those related to attachment processes, which he has studied extensively in dogs.

The time is approaching when basic research will help guide the therapeutic enterprise which hopes to reachieve emotional homeostasis. Robert Plutchik is one of the pioneer investigators of human emotions and his most recent efforts have been devoted to translating this knowledge into therapeutic practice. In the present chapter, Plutchik focuses his extensive experience in the area toward providing a systematic analysis of how emotional and therapeutic issues may interrelate.

Playing with emotions can also have an effect on mental health - this is described in the chapter on Sentic Cycles (Clynes). Behavioral and biological considerations converge when we consider the intrinsic motor patterns which accompany and express emotions. The exercise of such motor patterns may have profound influences on the central circuits which can also be influenced directly through chemical means. Clynes summarizes some of the considerable data he has collected concerning the responses of people to exercising Sentic Cycles.

Liebowitz describes a new generation of therapeutic applications of pharmacological strategies to emotional problems which, until recently, were exclusively the purview of the psychotherapist. Such chemical treatments suggest that there are different forms of anxiety and he describes how emotions can be freed from the necessity of the chain of cause and effect in the life circumstances of a person. When brain chemistries are changed directly, individuals can experience a new freedom to behave in ways that they long wished but had not been ready options for them because of their emotional distress.

The brain circuits of emotionality need to be unravelled and the pioneering work of Panksepp provides a rationale for why this long neglected area of brain research must be opened up if there is to be a substantive biological science of emotionality. Panksepp takes the position that a knowledge of the underlying brain circuitries must be a foundation pillar for understanding the nature of psychopathologies.

The activities of emotional circuits have widespread ramifications for the health of the organism—not only psychic but also somatic. Melnechuck, who has long been a promoter and observer of progress in this field, brings his broad perspective to bear on the topic with a synopsis of what is happening in the exciting new field of psychoimmunology and interfaces between medicine and psychology which will soon have to deal much more forthrightly with how the nervous system organizes emotions.

Through all this, careful observation of human feelings and human behaviors remains essential to every recipe to acquire knowledge. The newly developing area of human ethology should provide the scientific rigor to help us understand the flow of human behavior from moment to moment as well as other scales of time. The amount of emotional information that can pass across the human face and body is presently not describable, and the only field that is trying to deal with it forthrightly is human ethology.

Zivin and Stettner provided selected perspectives on such issues during the round-table discussion.

Finally, emotions have to be considered within the life-line of individuals and societies. Paul Byers brings his anthropological and philosophical perspective to discuss the rhythms involved in human speech interaction that also involves emotion.

Obviously, we are only on the near shore of knowledge in this area. It is only recently that medical therapeutic disciplines are beginning to take the issue of emotionality seriously - as an essential part of psychological and bodily health. There has been an increasing recognition that emotions have to be studied at fundamental scientific levels and that such knowledge should have direct consequences on how we view psychological health as well as cultural health. The understanding of emotions, more than any other area, will have to consist of an interplay between psychological and biological perspectives, with a progressively decreasing amount of dualism in their scientific dance.

How much, then, do chemicals contribute to our emotional life and how much to our mental activity? Which controls which? Clearly, it is a 'circle' in which each has a reciprocal effect on the other. The 'circle' however, is not evenhanded or simple. Favored directions occur, become cultivated, but most importantly, both the chemical and mental influences are hierarchial - with both independent and interdependent heirarchies for each. Thus, the problem of mental health encompasses double interacting hierarchies.

Play and laughter may be at a nexus of interaction of such seemingly irreconciliable dualities. Obviously, playing with emotions can have a profound effect on mental health. It is only recently that a playful perspective has entered the therapeutic field through the recognition of the healing and opening - up properties of laughter. But we would also use the concept of play in a broader sense. Even as adults, we can voluntarily play through vigorous work to help regenerate health through sport, dance, music and the exercise of other dynamic movements. Chemically playing with emotions, too, can be beneficial, if we know what we are doing. Many emotions can now be selectively stimulated or inhibited by different drugs, to the benefit (but also occassionally but too often to the harm) of emotionally ailing individuals, and psychodynamically and behaviorally oriented therapists have to remain open to the new possibilities in this realm, as opposed to closing the doors to knowledge because of human and cultural fears. Indeed, the behavioral ways in which we can modify emotions are truly neurochemical ways. Perhaps the clearest example is sexuality, which is so clearly a kind of chemical play with feelings which involves external stimuli. Sexual needs, as all other bodily drives, undoubtedly arise from neurochemical circuits - although we do not yet know these very well. Specific neurotransmitter substances for specific emotions could allow some such chemical kind of play to take place. How shall we preserve such play from tyranny or from addiction? How do we open up such modes of neurochemical play for the emotionally distressed? What does it really mean, in the brain, to have experiences of pleasure and distress?

Close to such human experiences, in their ways of understanding are the artists, and the fruitful study of emotions would be benefitted by a rapproachment between 'the two cultures'. And, of course, the study of the nature of emotions takes us to the heart of philosophy - to a sense of personal meaning, a sense of values, a sense of worth. Take one example: A musician often forgoes rewards of material nature and their pleasures, to pursue music single-mindedly. As one becomes more devoted to music, one becomes addicted to music. How are the satisfactions one gets from music different from those one might be able to get through stimulation of the right neurochemical receptors through appropriately combined chemical transmitters? Let us think that we are able to have a subtle and well distributed chemical delivery system that can mimic the configurations of various emotions and even sequence them. What happens to the cognitive aspects in each case? Would there really be an equivalence, or would there be an 'understanding' in one case that is absent in the other?

Here we come to one of natures own answers to such a question - always surprising - sleep and dreams. The play of our dreams unfolds without knowing that we play; entire scenarios may be created from neurochemical stimuli. In sleep there seems to be a different cohesion of the circle of interaction of the chemical and the mental than is apparent in waking. We may be very tired, but as soon as we fall asleep we may, in a dream, be not tired at all. Strangely, modern research on emotions has yet to come to grips with dreaming - the play of sleep. The initial efforts of Freud have had little further development. Neuroscience has yet to even consider the nature of dream content. That is an important field for the future to tackle. The time sense too, is quite transformed in dreaming: we experience people alive, whom we know to be dead in the waking state - and we react emotionally to them in our dreams. We create the scenery, the dialogue, the costumes, the story and all the characters in our dream - effortlessly, never wondering what to make happen next. All this creation is guided emotionally, but we do not know how such links between emotion and thought become manifest.

As the neuronal circuits for specific emotions become better known, together with the neuro-hormonal peptides that activate and inhibit them, and as we learn to understand the innate relations between emotions and cognitions better, exciting new avenues of therapy open up and will continue to develop. The conjoint application of psycho - and pharmacotherapies will become common practice. Such approaches will no longer depend just on substances that act generally as depressants or stimulants, but will be able to influence emotional experience as directly as music. One hopes such developments will progress hand in hand with an improved appreciation of the role of emotions in the lives of individuals and the social body. This is a very big task, and we are only at the beginning. Significant progress may be expected over the next few generations of research, much greater than can presently be guessed. An aim of this book however, is to project us into the future of this key area of inquiry - toward the comprehensive and vigorous study and analysis of the underlying emotional scales of human nature.

We thank all who participated in the project. We would dedicate this volume to the memory of Helen Block Lewis who, after a rich and productive life, passed on before the project was completed.

Manfred Clynes
Jaak Panksepp   June 1987

CONTENTS

The Nature of Emotions: Clinical Implications

Robert Plutchik

Albert Einstein College of Medicine,
Bronx, New York

Psychoevolutionary Theory of Emotions

Regardless of how much or how little education we have on various subjects, there is one topic on which each of us is the world's leading expert, and that subject is ourselves. And just as we know a great deal about the public and private sides of ourselves, we know a great deal about that part of ourselves called emotions. We all believe that we know our own emotions and can recognize emotions in other people. Yet, despite this belief, experts in this field seem to have a great deal of difficulty coming to any agreement about what emotions really are. But one thing that everyone does agree on is that emotions are the source of our greatest pleasures and our greatest pains. And when we have problems in life we often refer to them as emotional problems.

For the past twenty years or more I have been studying emotions and trying to make sense of their bewildering manifestations. I have written about emotions in animals, infants, mental patients, and normal individuals and have described connections between emotions and motivations, cognitions, imagery, empathy, personality, diagnoses and coping styles. Several new tests for measuring the derivatives of emotion have resulted from this work as well as a general psychoevolutionary theory (Plutchik, 1980). In the past three or four years, I have been examining the usefulness of the theory as a guide to psychotherapy. An examination of this issue is the purpose of the present chapter.

The psychoevolutionary theory is based upon seven fundamental postulates. I will briefly describe all of them but will focus my attention on the two that I believe to be most relevant to clinical issues.

Postulate 1.　　　*Emotions are communication and survival mechanisms based on evolutionary adaptations.*

The first postulate, that emotions are communication and survival mechanisms, is a direct reflection of the Darwinian, ethological tradition. Darwin (1872/

1965) pointed out that emotions have two functions for all animals. First they increase the chances of individual survival through appropriate reactions to emergency events in the environment (by fight or flight, for example). Second they act as signals of intentions of future action through display behaviors of various kinds.

Postulate 2.   Emotions have a genetic basis.

The second postulate, that emotions have a genetic basis stems directly from the evolutionary context. Darwin pointed out that emotional expressions appear in similar form in many lower animals, that they appear in infants in the same form as in adults (e.g. smiling), that people born blind show the same emotions as normally sighted ones, and that some emotional expressions appear in similar form in widely separated groups of humans.

Recent genetic studies comparing monozygotic and dizygotic twins, cross-adoption studies and other methods have revealed hereditary contributions to such temperamental (emotional) qualities as aggressiveness (Fuller, 1986; Wimer and Wimer, 1985) timidity or fearfulness (Goddard & Beilharz, 1985), assertiveness (Loehlin, Horn and Willerman, 1981) and shyness (Stevenson-Hinde, and Simpson, 1982) as well as many others.

Postulate 3.   Emotions are hypothetical constructs based on various classes of evidence.

The third basic postulate of the psychoevolutionary theory of emotion is that emotions are hypothetical constructs or inferences based on various classes of evidence. We are never certain of exactly what emotion someone else has because of the complex nature of emotion and because more than one emotion may occur at the same time. Any given display of emotion may reflect such complex states as approach and avoidance, attack and flight, sex and agression, or fear and pleasure (Hinde, 1965). We are often not even certain of our own emotions.

Postulate 4.   Emotions are complex chains of events with stabilizing feedback loops that produce some kind of behavioral homeostasis.

The fourth basic postulate of the theory is illustrated in Figure 1. Emotions are triggered by various events. These events must be cognitively evaluated as being of significance to the well-being or integrity of the individual. If such a determination is made, various feelings will result as well as a pattern of physiological changes. These physiological changes have the character of anticipatory reactions associated with various types of exertions or impulses; such impulses, for example, as the urge to explore, to attack, to retreat or to mate, among others. Depending on the relative strengths of these various impulses, a final vectorial resultant will occur in the form of overt action which is designed to have an effect on the stimulus that triggered this chain of events in the first place. For example, distress signals by a puppy or the crying of an infant will increase the probability that the mother or a mother substitute will arrive on the scene. The overall effect of this complex feedback system is to reduce the threat or change the emergency situation in such a way as to achieve a temporary behavioral homeostatic balance.

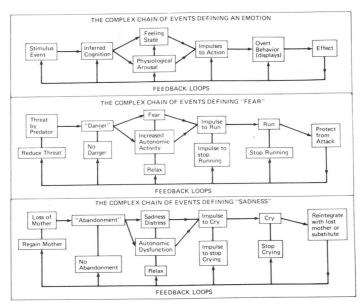

Figure 1. The complex chains of events defining emotions.

Postulate 5. *The relations among emotions can be represented by a three-dimensional structural model.*

In this model, the vertical dimension represents the intensity of emotions, the circle defines degree of similarity of emotions, and polarity may be represented by the opposite emotions on the circle. A number of studies have been published, summarized in Plutchik (1980), showing that the similarity structure of emotions can be clearly represented by means of a circle or circumplex. See also Russell (1987, in press).

Postulate 6. *There is a small number of basic, primary, or prototype emotions.*

This postulate implies that some emotions are primary in some fundamental sense, and that others are derived mixtures, compounds or blends. The concept of primary and secondary emotions has a long history in the literature of philosophy and psychology. It is entirely consistent with the results of factor-analytic studies such as those of Cattell (1957) and Nowlis (1965) that identify factors labeled as basic emotions. Ethological studies have also focused on a small number of basic emotional states (Van Hooff, 1973).

Postulate 7. *Emotions are related to a number of derivative conceptual domains.*

The concept of primary and derived emotions leads to the seventh basic postulate of the theory which states that emotions are related to a number of derivative conceptual domains. This idea has been explored in a number of different ways. For example, it has been shown that the nomenclature of mixed emotions is identical to the nomenclature of personality traits. Hostility has been judged to be composed of anger and disgust, sociability as a blend of joy and acceptance, and guilt as a combination of joy plus fear. Emotional components have been identified for hundreds of personality traits. In addition, there is now clearcut evidence that personality traits also exhibit a circumplex structure just as do emotions (Conte and Plutchik, 1980); (Wiggins and Broughton, 1985).

The idea of derivatives can be extended further. Diagnostic terms such as "depressed," "manic," and "paranoid" can be conceived as extreme expressions of such basic emotions as sadness, joy and disgust. Several studies have also revealed that the language of diagnoses also share a circumplex structure with emotions (Plutchik and Platman, 1977; Schaefer and Plutchik, 1966).

Carrying the notion of derivatives still another step, research has shown that the language of ego defenses can also be conceptualized as being related to emotions. For example, displacement can be conceptualized as an unconscious way to deal with anger that cannot be directly expressed without punishment. Similarly, projection can be conceptualized as an unconscious way to deal with feelings of disgust (or rejection) of onself by expressing this feeling to outsiders. Parallels of this sort have been made for each of the primary emotions and is described in detail in Kellerman (1979) and Plutchik, Kellerman and Conte (1979). Another derivative is the domain of coping styles which I consider to be the conscious derivatives of the unconscious ego-defenses. Thus, "minimization" corresponds to denial, "substitution" to *displacement*, and "mapping" to *intellectualization*. Other derivative domains have also been proposed (Plutchik, 1984).

Let me simply summarize the points that I have made so far. First, **emotions are universal.** They are seen as some form in all humans and in all animals. Second, **emotions are useful.** They communicate possibilities of danger, threat, retaliation, or pleasure, and, as a result influence the behavior of other people. Third, **emotions are usually mixed** because lots of things are going on at the same time, for example, being in love, and fearing that your love will not be reciprocated. Or feeling grief at a loss, and anger at the person who died for leaving you. Fourth, **certain emotions are primary or basic,** just as there are primary colors, and other emotions are secondary, or derived. Fifth, **emotions are expressed in many indirect ways,** or example, through sports, chess, parachute jumping, music, dance, poetry, migraine headaches, and ulcers, to name a few. Sixth, **emotions act as amplifiers or energizers of behavior.** A person may smoke cigarettes knowing the risk of cancer, but may stop only after he or someone close to him gets sick and he is frightened of the possibility of dying. Emotions are thus central aspects of our lives and affect all our social relations with other people. Emotions are universal, and are seen in children and in infants and in lower animals. Emotions are also helpful to us in accomplishing our goals; they communicate our intentions and expectations to other people and can express desires to become attached, desires to injure or intimidate, desires for consolation and comforting, and desires to dominate or be submissive, among many others. Emotions are complex with many aspects. This results in emotions being hard to define or pin down, and people therefore have trouble accurately describing their feelings. Nevertheless, we constantly express our emotions directly or indirectly, and through them involve ourselves in the lives of other people.

Clinical Implications of the Theory

In my judgment, psychotherapy deals with four fundamental questions. These are:

1. Who am I?
2. How did I get to be me?
3. Where do I want to go?
4. How can I get there?

These questions imply certain therapeutic activities. The question Who am I? implies a need for **assessment.** How did I get to be me? implies **historical reconstruction.** Where do I want to go? implies **goal setting,** and How can I get there? implies **skill acquisition.**

If someone asked you how to get to 42nd Street and Broadway in New York City, what you say clearly depends on where you are. You would give different directions if you are at Hollywood and Vine in Los Angeles, than if you are in Bowling Green, Ohio. Similarly, if your goal is to change someone through psycho-therapeutic means, you need to know where he (or she) is now. This means assessing various aspects of the individual.

In traditional hospital psychiatry, assessment means making a diagnosis, doing a mental status, determining family background, medical history and dynamic conflicts. In psychoanalytic outpatient practice, assessment is more likely to mean a set of judgments about personality styles, ego functions, ego defenses, and probable fixations in childhood. Sometimes projective test measures are added to the evaluations.

In contrast, Lazarus (1976) has proposed his BASIC I.D. acronym as a guide to assessment. This means measuring or evaluating the clients behavior, affects, sensations, imagery, cognitions, interpersonal relations, and need for drugs. Other important areas of assessment include an individual's social supports, his interpersonal conflicts, his sense of personal control, his willingness to take risks, his skills or competencies, and his close and loving attachments.

To facilitate assessment, my colleagues and I have developed a series of psychometric instruments designed to measure certain derivative concepts based on the theory. We now have available and in use, tests for measuring personality (The Emotions Profile Index (Plutchik and Kellerman, 1974) and the Personality Profile (Conte & Plutchik, 1986)), ego defenses (The Life Style Index (Plutchik, Kellerman, and Conte, 1979)), and coping styles (The AECOM Coping Styles Test (Buckley, Conte, Plutchik, et al., 1984)). I have also developed a series of brief self-report scales designed to provide insights into rather specific aspects of self-awareness or self-functioning. These include measures of: assertiveness, risk-taking, ability to size people up, current worries, neurotic tendencies, obsessive-compulsive behaviors, goals, and many others.

Let me illustrate the use of some of these measures. Table 1 lists the dimensions of the Personality Profile, Table 2 those of the ego defense scales, and Table 3 those of the coping scales. In a recent study these tests were administered to a group of managers at a large nationwide company. Many other measures were also obtained in a six hour interview session including a symptom checklist, (the SCL-90), the

Rorschach, The Eysenck Extroversion-Introversion Scale, the 16 PF, the Myer-Briggs Type Indicator, various stress measures, and others. Supervisory ratings and spouse's ratings were also obtained. Some high correlations were found among the various scales of the total battery. For example, managers high on Depression, Passivity, and Aggression of the Personality Profile were high on Eysenck's Neuroticism Scale and high on overall psychiatric symptoms. Managers high on Regression, Reaction Formation, and Projection as measured by the Life Style Index were high on life stress measures. And those managers who were high on the coping style of Blame were high on stress and low on adjustment.

Table 1

Scales of the Personality Profile *

Sociable
> "I SHOW THAT I LIKE OTHER PEOPLE."

Accepting
> "I DON'T MIND IT WHEN PEOPLE HAVE OPINIONS
>   DIFFERENT FROM MINE."

Submissive
> "I DO WHAT I AM TOLD."

Passive
> "I HAVE LITTLE INTEREST IN THINGS."

Depressed
> "I FEEL BLUE."

Rejecting
> "I DON'T ACCEPT NEW IDEAS OR PEOPLE EASILY."

Aggressive
> "I GET ANGRY VERY EASILY."

Assertive
> "I SAY WHAT I THINK."

*The statements in quotes are illustrations of the types of items used.

Table 2

Scales Designed to Measure Ego Defenses *

Compensation
> "I DREAM A LOT."

Denial
> "I'M NOT PREJUDICED AGAINST ANYONE."

Displacement
> "IF SOMEONE BOTHERS ME, I DON'T TELL IT TO HIM,
> BUT I TEND TO COMPLAIN TO SOMEONE ELSE."

Intellectualization
> "I'M NOT AFRAID OF GETTING OLD BECAUSE
> IT HAPPENS TO EVERYBODY."

Projection
> "IF I'M NOT CAREFUL, PEOPLE WILL TAKE ADVANTAGE
> OF ME."

Reaction Formation
> "PORNOGRAPHY IS DISGUSTING."

Regression
> "I GET IRRITABLE WHEN I DON'T GET ATTENTION."

Repression
> "I NEVER REMEMBER MY DREAMS."

The statements in quotes are illustrations of the types of items used.

Table 3

Scales of the Coping Styles Test

Mapping:
GETTING AS MUCH INFORMATION AS POSSIBLE
ABOUT THE PROBLEM BEFORE ACTING.

Minimizing:
ASSUMING THE PROBLEM IS NOT AS IMPORTANT
AS OTHER PEOPLE THINK IT IS.

Suppression:
AVOIDING THE PERSON OR SITUATION THAT YOU
BELIEVE CREATED THE PROBLEM.

Help-Seeking:
ASKING ASSISTANCE FROM OTHERS TO HELP YOU
SOLVE THE PROBLEM.

Reversal:
ACTING OPPOSITE TO THE WAY YOU FEEL; FOR EXAMPLE
SMILING WHEN YOU FEEL ANGRY.

Blame:
BLAMING OTHER PEOPLE, OR THE "SYSTEM" FOR
THE PROBLEM.

Substitution:
REDUCING TENSIONS BY MEANS UNRELATED TO THE
PROBLEM, SUCH AS MEDITATION, JOGGING,
ALCOHOL.

Replacement:
IMPROVING WEAKNESSES OR LIMITATIONS THAT
EXIST EITHER IN YOURSELF OR IN THE SITUATION.

Of particular clinical interest is the fact that blind ratings were made of the profiles for each manager separately which were then compared with the results obtrained from the six hour battery. The results of this blind analysis turned out to be quite consistent with those obtained from the rest of the battery.

Existential Problems

There is another way to look at the issue of assessing where someone is. This alternative requires evaluation of the major existential crises that that person faces or is particularly concerned with. In my view, there are four basic life crises that everyone has to deal with in some way, that have implications for individual or genetic survival. I have called these four problem areas: the problems of hierarchy, territoriality, identity, and temporality (Plutchik, 1980, 1983), and I will briefly describe them.

Hierarchy
The concept of hierarchy refers to the vertical dimension of social life. This is seen almost universally as dominance hierarchies in both lower animals and in humans. In general, the major expressions of high hierarchical positions are first access to food, to shelter, to comforts, and to sex, that is, the resources needed for both personal and genetic survival.

The vertical organization of social life is reflected in the age relations among people, in male-oriented relations between the sexes, in economic and military organizations, and in social classes. Generally speaking, hierarchical organizations reflect the fact that some people know more than other people, some people are stronger or more skillful than others, and that all people vary in affective dispositions. All individuals must face these realities and come to terms with them whether they want to or not, and whether or not they are aware of them.

Of great importance is the fact that an individual's attempt to cope with hierarchical issues implies competition, status conflict, and power struggles. People near the top of a hierarchy tend to feel dominant, self-confident, bossy and assertive, while those near the bottom feel submissive and anxious (Burski, Kellerman, et al., 1973).

Territoriality
The second universal problem area for all individuals concerns the issue of territoriality. In every species, each organism must learn what aspects of the environment and of itself "belongs" to it.

From an evolutionary point of view territories define an area or space of potential nourishment necessary for survival, or an area that is safe from attack or predation. Territories may be defined explicitly by scent markings, tree scratches, or boundary lines, or implicitly by the distance one organism allows another to approach before aggression is initiated. Crowding usually generates territorial crises.

Individuals attempting to cope with territorial issues are concerned with feelings of possessiveness, jealousy and envy. Those who are in possession of important aspects of the environment (including other people) feel in control. In contrast, individuals whose boundaries have been penetrated (or whose possessions have been taken) feel despair and lack of control. From the point of view of my model of the emotions, I assume that the feelings of control-dyscontrol are basic to the territorial issues.

Identity

The third major problem that all organisms encounter is the problem of identity. In simplest terms, this refers to the basic question of who we are, or alternately, what group or groups we belong to. The issue of identity is a fundamental existential crises for all organisms because isolated individuals neither propagate nor survive. In lower organisms, genetic coding mechanisms enable an individual to recognize other individuals of the same species. In humans, however, group memberships are very complex because of the variety of categories one can use to define an identity. The most important criteria of group membership are undoubtedly sex, race, age, religion, occupation and geography. The fact that these are often in conflict is one of the reasons for the identity crisis. Adolescents are particularly prone to a crisis of sexual identity, while older people are more likely to have to confront religious or occupational crises of identity. Certain emotions are closely tied to the sense of identity. For those who are part of our group, who share our identity, we feel a sense of belonging, of acceptance. We share language, customs, rituals, jokes and plays. We allow hugging, kissing and under certain conditions, sexual behavior. The emotion associated with a lack of identity is rejection or disgust. Prejudice against strangers is universal and reflects the sense of danger to survival connected with individuals who are not members of our group. In order to feel comfortable about rejecting someone we often try to disconnect that person from our group - to dehumanize by certain verbal labels, by calling them "pigs," or "dogs," or "gooks," for example. Acceptance and liking versus rejection and hate are the emotional poles connected with the struggle for identity.

Temporality

The fourth universal problem encountered by all organisms is the problem of temporality. This word refers to the fact of the limited duration of an individual's life. All organisms have a limited span of life, part of which is spent in infancy, childhood, and adolescence learning fundamental skills about social living. From an evolutionary point of view, the purpose of the acquisition of skills is to enable the individual to survive as long as possible and to become a successful reproducing adult member of a group. The reality of death creates the inevitability of loss and separtion for those who are living. There is a need for social solutions to the problem of loss, since individuals without support from other members of their social group do not survive well or long. During the course of evolution several solutions have evolved for the problem of loss or separation. One solution is the development of distress signals which serve as the functional equivalent of cries for help. The second evolutionary solution for the problem of loss is the evolution of sympathetic or nurturing responses in other members of the social group. It might even be argued that altruism is an extreme form of the nurturing response.

In humans, the problem of the limited span of existence has affected the evolution of a series of social institutions that deal with death and loss. These include: mourning rituals, birth, death, and reunion myths, preparation for an afterlife, and certain aspects of religion. Sadness is a cry for help that functions to attempt to reintegrate the individual with a lost person or his (or her) substitute. If the signal of a need for help and nurturance works only partly, it may produce a persistent, long-term distress signal that we call depression. If the cry for help actually works and brings help, it produces an opposite emotion, the emotion of joy. Joy may thus be thought of as the experience of rejoining or of possession.

From the point of view of existential crises, it becomes possible to make inferences from emotions to the existential issues with which an individual is most concerned. For example, someone who is proud and self conscious is probably very much concerned with his (or her) place in the ladder of life, i.e. with hierarchical issues. Someone who is an obsessive collector and envious of other people's possession is probably concerned with territorial issues. Someone who is preoccupied with issues of family closeness and loyalty is probably concerned with identity conflicts. And someone who is an avid and anxious reader of obituary columns is probably concerned with issues of temporality. Obviously, any single concern can be interpreted in more than one way. Psychotherapy has to deal with these issues and help the individual to transcend them.

Derivatives of the Exsistential Crises

If we go down a step in the level of abstraction, we recognize that there are many experiences in life that relate directly or indirectly to the existential issues. For example, if we take the problem of hierarchy we can see that such issues as being assertive, being dominant or in control, being submissive, or being controlled, seeking fame and wealth are all related to one another, and all tied to the question of finding one's place in the ladder of life. Similarly, issues concerned with keeping a job, buying a car or a house, meeting responsibilities, and establishing a personal sense of space or boundaries, are all connected with territorial problems. Issues of friendship, courtship, love and family are related to identity problems while attitudes toward illness, death, and altruism are related to temporality concerns. Clearly some overlap exists, but the conception provides an alternative schema for assessment.

The Other Basic Questions

As I indicated earlier there are four basic questions with which psychotherapists are concerned, and I have discussed only the first. The second, "How did I become me?", is one that provides the basis for much of psychoanalytic practice, which is largely concerned with historical reconstructions.

A recent study I did looked at the issue of differences among psychotherapies in their focus of concerns. My colleagues and I were interested in the actual degree of overlap of methods and concepts of two very different types of therapy: behavioral and psychoanalytic (Plutchik, Conte, & Karasu, 1984).

For this study a questionnaire was constructed which asked the clinicians the extent to which they believed in or carried out various ideas or practices. The questionnaires were sent to two diverse groups of practicing clinicians, a group of psychoanalytically-oriented psychotherapists at the Albert Einstein College of Medicine, and a random sample of members of the American Association for the Advancement of Behavior Therapy.

The results revealed that there were some striking differences between the two groups on certain items, and no differences on other items. Table 4 shows some of the major differences between the two groups of therapists.

Table 4

Some Significant Differences Between Psychodynamic and Behaviour Therapists

	Behaviour Therapists	Psychodynamic Therapists
1. Pathology involves unconscious sexual drives.	NO	YES
2. An overall goal of therapy is to resolve underlying conflicts.	NO	YES
3. The basis of therapeutic change is understanding the effects of childhood experiences on current life situations.	NO	YES
4. Therapy deals primarily with a patient's subjective historical past.	NO	YES
5. The major task of the therapist is to reward, inhibit or shape specific behavior and to provide information about how to cope with problems.	YES	NO

The psychodynamic therapists assumed that pathology involves unconscious sexual drives while the behavior therapists did not. They also assumed that the goal of therapy is to resolve underlying conflicts, and to understand the effects of childhood experiences on current life situations. The way to do this is to deal primarily with a patient's subjective historical past. In contrast, the behavior therapist interprets his task as the shaping of client behavior through information and rewards.

Table 5

Items where no significant differences were found between Psychodynamic and Behaviour Therapists

1. The prime concerns of psychotherapy are with maladaptive behavior, cognitive distortions and anxiety.

2. Pathology involves misinterpretation of self and others.

3. The overall goals of therapy are removal of symptoms and reduction of anxiety.

4. The basis of therapeutic change is the reassessment of faulty attitudes.

5. Psychotherapy deals with the patient's objective present as well as current perceptions.

6. The primary tool of treatment is shared dialogue.

Of special interest is the fact that there were some important points agreement (Table 5). Both types of therapists believe that the prime concerns of psychotherapy are to deal with maladaptive behavior, cognitive distortions and anxiety, and that the overall goal of therapy is to remove symptoms and reduce anxiety. Both believe that the basis of change is the reassessment of faulty attitudes and that the mode of operation involves dealing with the objective present as well as current perceptions through shared dialogue.

Thus it appears that two of the most diverse therapies in existence today share many goals, and tend to differ primarily in their methods and in their theories. This overlap may help us understand why the various meta-analyses of controlled psychotherapy studies have revealed that all are effective as compared to doing nothing, and to roughly the same degree (Smith, Glass and Miller, 1980). This also suggests that one should not be too timid about proposing modifications or additions to therapeutic theory and technique; they are not likely to make things worse, and may even make things better.

Let me briefly consider the last two questions that psychotherapy is concerned with: "Where do I want to go?" and "How can I get there?" Many psychotherapists tend to be more concerned with the past than the future. There seems to be an assumption that if a client can discover the supposed historical roots of a problem, then the problem is likely to disappear. Unfortunately in many such situations there is a tendency on the part of clients to become preoccupied with childhood events, and to blame others for real or imagined injuries. By focusing on old problems they tend to miss new solutions. It is doubtful that in a complex open system, as is true in human interactions, any but the most limited of causal connections are possible between events of childhood and adult behavior. For these and other reasons I have tended to place less emphasis on the search for historical "causes" of current problems.

The fourth question: "How do I get there?" is obviously concerned with issues of skills and competencies. In recent years, a considerable literature has developed that suggests that social skills training is very efficacious in producing therapeutic changes, particularly with severly troubled individuals (Liberman, 1985). Social skills training is concerned with such fundamental skills as: having a conversation, making friends, sizing people up, courtship, sex, negotiating and parenting. Although such skills training is not often thought of as part of psychotherapy, it seems to me that it should be considered to be an integral aspect.

I should like to conclude by discussing some principles of change that are useful in the psychotherapeutic interaction. There are nine strategies of interaction that may be identified as helpful in doing individual or group psychotherapy. These strategies are either based upon or consistent with the postulates of a psychoevolutionary approach to emotions.

Strategies of Interaction

Ethological research suggests that certain types of stimuli or events are very likely to trigger emotional reactions. For example, Blanchard (1983) states that aggressive behavior in humans tends to be triggered by threats, insults, challenges, and loss of control. In primates, staring behavior and certain sound patterns tend to elicit agonistic encounters while diminution in apparent body size and lack of direct eye contact act as stimuli that reduce aggression. Van Hooff (1967) has demonstrated that lip-smacking in chimpanzees and "silent grin" facial displays also act to inhibit aggression.

These observations are consistent with the postulate of my theory that says that emotions are complex chains of events that are triggered by certain classes of stimuli.

1. We can assume that in the therapeutic context, the client is not always conscious of the triggering stimuli nor able to verbalize what they may be. Therefore one therapeutic task is to identify precisely *the stimuli that trigger emotions*.

Example: One overweight client said that she ate for many reasons: to avoid boredom, to be sociable, to eliminate hunger, to soothe nervousness, when angry, after hard work, and to remind her of pleasant times in the past. She gradually discovered that the most common trigger for eating was her anger at something or someone. As she began to learn to cope appropriately with her anger, her need to eat decreased and her weight stabilized at a considerably lower value.

2. The theory emphasizes that stimuli per se are not the crucial determinants of an emotional reaction, but rather the interpretations (or evaluations) one makes of events. This idea is identical to what Lazarus (1966), Ellis (1962) and Anderson (1987, In press) have said. We don't automatically become angry at what someone says to us; we first need to interpret the comment as an insult or a threat before the affect of anger appears. This leads to the idea that *one way of dealing with stressful life events is by consciously redefining (i.e. reconceptualizing) the stimulus, or by putting it in a new context.*

Example. A woman felt angry, resentful and depressed because of an abusive alcoholic husband. When she began to think of him as "sick" rather than as "cruel," she felt less angry and sad, but more compassionate. Other examples of reinterpreting the stimulus would be to consider a difficult child as "only going through a stage," or difficult older parents as "senile, and unable to help themselves," rather than "thoughtless" or "selfish."

3. The theory proposes that all emotions are either one of the eight basic ones, or mixed states. It further assumes that the basic emotions seldom, if ever, occur in pure form, and if they do, only transiently. Most emotions, therefore, are mixed emotions or blends. A further assumption is that the blending of emotions always produces some level of conflict. Several personality tests based on these assumptions have been developed and empirical research supports the idea that different personality traits indirectly express different levels of conflict (Plutchik and Kellerman, 1974; Conte and Plutchik, 1986). The therapeutic principle this leads to is this: *Most emotional states are mixtures implying conflicts. To understand the nature of the conflict we need to identify the components.*

Example: A client said she felt guilty about leaving her husband and getting her own apartment. Previous research suggests that guilt is a mixture of fear and pleasure. It was possible to explore these components of her guilt. She was in conflict over her fear of not being able to make it on her own (i.e. continued dependence), and her pleasure at the thought of making it (i.e. being independent). She was in conflict over the fear of breaking up her family versus the joy of consolidating or remaking her family. She was in conflict over the fear that her husband would interfere and stop her from leaving and her pleasure at the thought of saying "No" to him. Examining these components separately enabled her to evaluate the relative importance of each one and to then make a reasoned decision for her life.

4. The concept that an emotion is a complex chain of events containing both feeling states and impulses to action does not necessarily mean that each component of the chain is equally distinct or accessible to consciousness. Studies by Davitz (1970), for example, have shown that the feelings of an emotion are often vague, confused and obscure and that the same emotion can be described by a large number

of different words and phrases. For example, depression has been described by college students as feeling "empty, drained, hollow, undercharged, heavy, tired, sleepy, unmotivated, helpless, insignificant, incompetent, self-pitying, sorry, and suffocating."

In contrast, the impulse to action in any given emotion is somewhat clearer, probably because there are fewer relevant actions possible. The principle implied here is: *The subjective feeling states of emotion (that is, the labels we give them) are usually more ambiguous and obscure than the impulses to action. Therefore, always examine impulses to action.*

Example: A client was talking about a brother who had committed suicide. To the question "How did you feel about it?" her answer was that she didn't know, but when she was asked what she felt like doing, she immediately replied "I felt like crying, but couldn't because I really felt like killing him myself for what he did to our mother."

5. The fact that most emotions that people experience are mixed emotions, implies that diverse impulses to action exist. This means that life is filled with feelings of ambivalence. When a client describes an emotional situation, the therapist should assume that only part of the story has been told. No one is ever certain what the "real truth" is. Ambivalences are particularly evident if a person reports that he is doing something that he does not want to do. Therefore the basic principle is: *Always look for ambivalences.*

Example: A relatively young man inherited his father's business after the father died suddenly of a heart attack. The son knew nothing about the business having been trained to go into one of the professions. He developed anxiety about making decisions and began to rely increasingly on the foreman who in turn treated him like a "kid." The young man began to hate the foreman, but in therapy gradually revealed his ambivalence based upon the foreman's undoubted skill and decisiveness. Once the ambivalence was clarified, the new owner of the business could set up a reasonable relation to his foreman.

6. Clients often report that they are reluctant or unable to do something that they want to do (for example, eat alone in a fancy restaurant, visit a nudist colony for a day, or learn parachute jumping). Conversely, they often say that they do things they really don't want to do (for example, visit people they don't like, allow themselves to be taken advantage of, or buy something they don't need or want). Close examination of such situations invariably reveals that some kind of fear is always present: fear of rejection, fear of humiliation, fear of criticism, or fear of looking foolish. Fear is the great inhibitor of action. The therapeutic principle is:
When a client appears stuck on one theme, or is reluctant to examine alternative ideas or actions, look for the fear.

Example. An older woman had recently moved into a new house. After a few weeks she called her son and asked him to come over and move some furniture for her. The son refused saying he was busy and that he would help her some other time. The woman hung up the phone and shortly thereafter developed a painful constriction in her throat and began to cry. As she explored this incident in therapy she realized that she expected help from her son, but was afraid to demand his help. The impulse to criticize her son was inhibited by fear of rejection, apparently resulting in a constriction of her throat.

7. We take it for granted that everyone is unique; talents differ, educations differ, goals differ. What we don't appreciate as clearly is that the very words we commonly use have different connotations and meanings for different people. One client described himself as "sick." When he was asked what the opposite of "sick" was, he said "free" (rather than the more obvious word "well"). It turned out that his sickness was his inability to free himself from an unhappy marriage. Another client came into the group bristling with anger. She had been brooding for a week that someone in the group had described her as "stubborn." It appeared that "stubborn" meant to her, "bad" and "mean," and the opposite of stubborn was "nice and friendly." The therapeutic principle that is implied is that the *labels people give to their feelings and emotions may have idiosyncratic meanings which need to be explored*.

8. One of the things we mean by the term emotional maladjustment is that there is a kind of emotional skewness in an individual; that is, that one or two emotions are strong, or troublesome, or at the center of his (or her) existence. Depression, for example, implies that feelings of sadness are the dominant theme and the major way of relating to other people. Someone who is hostile uses anger as the major emotion that becomes expressed in a larger number of different situations.

The theory of emotion that I have proposed implies that all emotions have survival value for the individual. Joy is an expression of pleasurable contact that may be associated with the propagation of one's genes. But fear is just as adaptive as is joy in that it mobilizes the individual to avoid threat or conflict. Similarly, anger is an adaptive emotion in the sense that it mobilizes the individual to cope with a barrier to the satisfaction of one's needs. The same general argument can be made for each basic emotion; they all are adaptive and serve survival needs.

From this point of view, an individual who appears to experience primarily only one emotion is maladjusted. Ideally, the *capacity to experience and express a wide range of emotion is a sign of successful adaptation, or good mental health*.

Example: A client described himself as coping with most problems by seeking help. This coping style was an expression of his feeling small, helpless, needy, and sad. Exploration of this imbalance in his affect states led to his awareness of his limited range of feeling, and a gradual expansion of that range.

9. When something goes wrong many people have a strong urge to find an explanation, a scapegoat, or a person to blame. They try to account for their unhappiness, depression, anxiety, or anger by relating it to a dull job, a demanding boss, or an unfaithful wife. Sometimes they may blame their neighborhood, their parents or their siblings.

Such attitudes, to the extent that they exist, are expressions of the feeling that the individual has lost some degree of control over his (her) life and that evil forces are manipulating him. Such attitudes are also expressions of the belief that events directly determine our emotions, when in fact, it is our *interpretation of events* that determine our emotions. Cognitive evaluations of life events determine what we feel, and to that extent, our world of emotions is created by our cognitions.

This is true also of our past. Everyone's past is complex, ambiguous, and impossible to define precisely. Recognizing that our cognitions determine our emotional world also implies that our cognitions also determine our conception of our own past. So-called "bad" pasts can be reinterpreted in more benign ways just as our conceptions of an unsatisfactory job can be reinterpreted to make it less stressful or boring. These changes can be brought about by the use of the various coping styles that I have described earlier. The therapeutic principle is: *Reduce the influence of the environment and disconnect from the past by using appropriate coping styles.*

Example: One member of a therapy group is 70 years old. She is married to a former alcoholic who is insensitive, withdrawn, and sometimes demanding. After several years in group therapy she changed her coping styles so that she handles problems differently. She accepts things she can't change; she is not angry all the time, she doesn't ruminate about her unhappy childhood or past; and she does more things that please her (like travel). She used the coping styles of "minimization," "suppression," and "substitution" a lot more than she did. She feels that she is largely responsible for her life now, and is not controlled by her past, nor her external environment. She reports being happier at this time than she has been most of her life.

Conclusion

Psychotherpay helps an individual achieve the goal of symptom reduction and self-growth by engaging in a complex interpersonal exchange of ideas and emotions. Three types of skills need to be acquired by the client if therapy is to be maximally successful. The first is to learn the coping skills described earlier and to use them appropriately. The second is to learn communication skills designed to decrease interpersonal conflicts. And the third is to learn how to assess the balance of motives or emotion associated with one's conflicts. These skills can be learned during the therapeutic exchanges. Other life skills connected with work, courtship, love and parenting also need to be learned, but they are generally acquired by trail and error in the outside world, rather than through the therapeutic encounter. Conceptualizing psychotherapy as problem solving, as skill acquisition and as reframing, is consistent with a broad evolutionary approach to psychology.

References

Anderson, N.H: 1987, Information integration approach to emotions and their measurement. In Plutchik, R. and Kellerman, H. (Eds.) "The measurement of emotions." Vol. 4. New York: Academic Press, In Press.
Blanchard, D.C: 1984, Applicability of animal models to human aggression. In: "Biological perspectives on aggression". New York: Alan R. Liss.
Buckley P., Conte, H.R., Plutchik, R., Wild, K.V., and Karasu, T.B: 1984,

Psychodynamic variables as predictors of psychotherapy outcome. *American Journal of Psychiatry*, 141, 742-748.

Buirski, P., Kellerman, H., Plutchik, R., Weininger, R., and Buirski, N: 1973, A field study of emotions, dominance and social behavior in a group of baboons (Papio anubis). *Primates*, 14.67-78.

Cattell, R.B: 1957, "Personality and motivation: Structure and measurement" New York: Harcourt Brace Jovanovich.

Conte, H.R. and Plutchik, R: 1981, A circumplex model for interpersonal personality traits. *Journal of Personality and Social Psychology*, 40, 701-711.

Conte, H.R. and Plutchik, R: 1986, "The Personality Profile: Development of a new circumplex measure of personality". Unpublished manuscript.

Darwin, C. (1872/1965). "The expression of the emotions in man and animals". Chicago: University of Chicago Press.

Davitz, J.R: 1970, A dictionary and grammar of emotion. In M. Arnold (Ed.). "Feelings and emotions: The Loyola Symposium". N.Y., Academic Press.

Ellis, A: 1962, " Reason and emotion in psychotherapy." New York: Lyle Stuart.

Fuller, J.L: 1986, Genetics and emotions. In: R. Plutchik and H. Kellerman (Eds.). "Biological foundations of emotion". New York: Academic Press.

Goddard, M.E. and Bailharz, R.G: 1985, A multivariate analysis of the genetics of fearfulness in potential guide dogs. *Behavior Genetics*, 15, 69-89.

Hinde, R.A: 1966, "Animal behavior: A synthesis of ethology and comparative psychology". New York: McGraw-Hill.

Kellerman, H: 1979, "Group therapy and personality: intersecting structures". New York: Grune & Stratton.

Lazarus, A.A: 1976, "Multimodel behavior therapy". New York: Springer

Liberman, R.P: 1985, Psychosocial therapies for schizophrenia. In: H.I. Kaplan andB.J. Sadock (Eds.) "Comprehensive textbook of psychiatry", IVth edition. Baltimore: Williams & Williams, 724-734.

Loehlin, J.C., Horn, J.M., and Williams, L: 1981, Personality resemblance in adoptive families. *Behavior Genetics*, 11, 309-330.

Nowlis, V: 1965, "Research with the Mood Adjective Checklist". In: S.S. Tomkins A. and C.E. Izard (Eds.) "Affect, cognition, personality". New York: Springer.

Plutchik, R: 1980, "Emotions: A psychoevolutionary synthesis" New York: Harper & Row.

Plutchik, R: 1983 Universal problems of adaptation: hierarchy, territoriality, identity and temporality. In: J.B. Calhoun (Ed.) "Environment and population: problems of adaptation". New York: Praeger.

Plutchik, R: 1984, Emotions: A general psychoevolutionary theory. In: K.R. Scherer and P. Keman (Eds.) "Approaches to emotion". Hillsdale, New Jersey, Lawrence Erlbaum Assoc.

Plutchik, R., Conte, H.R. and Karasu, T. B: August, 1984, "Survey of thematic dimensions of psychotherapy". Paper presented at the meeting of the American Psychological Association, Toronto, Canada.

Plutchik, R., and Kellerman, H: 1974, "Manual of the Emotions Profile Index". Los Angeles, California. Western Psychological Services.

Plutchik, R., Kellerman, H. and Conte, H.R: 1979). A structural theory of ego defenses. In: C.E. Izard (Ed.) "Emotions, personality and psychopathology". New York: Plenum.

Plutchik, R. and Platman, S.R: 1977, Personality connotations of psychiatric diagnoses. *Journal of Nervous and Mental Disease,* 165, 418-422.

Russell, J.A: 1987, Measures of emotion. In: R. Plutchik & H. Kellerman (Eds.) "The measurement of emotion" . Vol. 4 New York: Academic Press, In Press.

Schaefer, E.S. and Plutchik, R: 1966, Interrelationships of emotions, traits, and diagnostic constructs. *Psychological Reports,* 18, 399-410.

Smith, M.L., Glass, G.V., and Miller, T. I: 1980, "The benefits of psychotherapy" Baltimore: The John Hopkins University Press.

Stevenson-Hinde, J. and Simpson, A.E: 1982, Temperament and relationships. In: R. Porter and G.M. Collins (Eds.) "Temperamental differences in infants and young children". London & Pitman.

Van Hooff, J.A.R.A.M: 1967, Facial displays of catarrihine monkeys and apes. In: D.Morris (Ed.) "Primate ethology". Chicago: Aldine.

Van Hooff, J.A.R.A.M: 1973, A structural analysis of the social behavior of a semicaptive group of chimpanzees. In: M. von Cranach and I. Vine (Eds.) "Social communication and movement". New York: Academic Press.

Wiggins, J.S. and Broughton, R: 1985, Ther interpersonal circle: A structural model for the integration of personality research.
Perspectives in Personality, 1, 1-47.

Wimer, R.E. and Wimer, C.C: 1985, Animal behavior genetics: A search for the biological foundations of behavior. *Annual Review of Psychology,* 36, 171-218.

Genetics, Emotions and Psychopathology

J.P. Scott

Department of Psychology
Bowling Green State University
Bowling Green, Ohio 43403

Theoretical Perspectives

This theory is concerned with maladaptive behaviour that occurs as a result of living and life events, and does not include cases that are produced by various sorts of brain injury. It has been developed by analyzing the numerous cases of observed and experimentally induced maladaptive behavior in non-human animals. Perhaps the most thoroughly researched of all these is that of the audiogenic seizure in mice.

As Hall (1947) discovered, if one takes a 30-day old mouse from the DBA/2 inbred strain and places it in an old-fashioned metal wash tub to which an electric door bell has been attached, and then starts ringing the door bell, the following behavior will be observed in almost 100% of the animals. The mouse first shows an initial startle reaction, then begins to run, eventually showing a wild running pattern at top speed and then, after a few seconds, falls over on its side, goes into convulsive seizure, and dies. Death is caused by a lack of oxygen resulting from the convulsing animal not being able to breathe, as such mice can be resuscitated by artificial respiration. There can be no more dramatic example of maladaptive behaviour than this. On the other hand, if one takes mice of similar age from the C57BL/6 inbred strain and puts them into the same situation, they will show little more than the initial startle reaction and none of them go into seizures nor die (Fuller & Williams, 1951). Obviously, there are differences in genetic susceptibility to this situation.

When I first observed this behavior, I thought of it as an unusual but bizarre phenomenon that has no general application since nothing of the sort occurs in humans that are exposed to loud noises. It was only after I had compared it with other instances of induced maladaptive behavior in animals that I began to see that all of these examples had a similar theoretical basis, and that the mouse audiogenic seizure was potentially a general model for them.

The situation that produces the maladaptive behaviour in mice is composed of a combination of three essential conditions.

1) Strong motivation, of some sort, often continued over a long period of time. This motivation can be produced in a variety of ways. In the case of the mouse, it is produced by intense auditory stimulation. In the case of Pavlov's (1927) experiments with conditioned neuroses, the intense motivation was produced by repeated reinforcement of a particular act or behavior over long periods of time. In both cases, we can assume that the animal was experiencing strong emotions.

2) A second condition is that there is blocking of an opportunity for adaptive behavior (which among humans is commonly called coping behaviour). A human in a similar situation to that of the mouse would probably put his hands over his ears or plug them in some way or other. Such a solution is not within the behavioural repertoire of the mouse. All that the mouse can do is to try to escape, which is the function of the running behavior.

3) The third essential condition is thus a lack of opportunity to escape from the situation that produces the stimulation or emotions involved in intense motivation.

All three of these conditions must occur in combination in order for maladaptive behavior to follow. If there is no noise, the mouse behaves normally and can live out its life in a wash tub provided it is given food, bedding and water. If the mouse could deaden the sound in some way such as by plugging up its ears, the reaction would not occur, as can be demonstrated experimentally. Or, if the mouse is allowed to escape from the sound in the wash tub, no seizure take place.

Modifying Factors

There is obviously a great deal of individual variation, both in susceptibility to the conditions that produce maladaptive behavior, and in the kinds of symptoms that result. Such variation has three general causes.

1. Genetic Variation

Experience with the results of genetic experimentation on anatomy, physiology, and behavior leads to the conclusion that any characteristic of a living organism is subject to genetic variability. We can therefore postulate that genetic variation should occur in maladaptive behavior, both in susceptibility to the conditions that induce it, and in the form of the behavior that results. That such variation can be important is indicated by the case of audiogenic seizures, where genetic variation can make the difference between seizure susceptibility and resulting death on the one hand, and non-occurrence and continued life on the other (Fuller & Sjursen, 1967).

2. Variation in Previous Experience

Again this can result in either enhanced susceptibility or enhanced protection. Presumably this results from sensitization or desensitization of emotional arousal in certain situations. Most persons find that certain sorts of situations are unbearable because of the intensely unpleasant emotions that they arouse. Such symptoms often can be traced back to childhood experiences, the memory of which sometimes may be repressed, or the connection unrealized. On the other hand successful coping with such experiences may lead to desensitization of the response and more successful coping in later life. The sensitization effects can be demonstrated with audiogenic seizures in mice (Henry, 1967, Fuller & Collins, 1968).

Early experiences seem to be more important than later ones, for a variety of reasons. Among these, coping responses may not yet be developed. Because emotional responses have not yet been modified by learning and conditioning, they may be more intense and frightening. A child has much less control over its surroundings than does an adult.

3. Degree of Development of Behavioral Organization

As with all organizational processes, development leads to increasing stability. This could have two effects. It could lead to protection against breakdown of organization, or, if behavior becomes organized in a maladaptive fashion, it could lead to limitation of coping capacities. Increasing stability of organization is generally correlated with age, although organizational processes usually proceed more rapidly in early life. Returning to the mouse model, the same DBA mice that are susceptible to seizures at 30 days of age are non-susceptible at 50 days.

Special Human Factors

As I have implied above, the general theory of maladaptive behavior can be extended to humans, but with certain qualifications. Like any other species, humans are genetically unique. Consequently, both the situations that trigger maladaptive behavior and the symptoms exhibited may differ from other species. For example, humans do not exhibit convulsive seizures in response to loud noises, nor are they likely to die of anoxia while in convulsions, simply because their much larger body size permits storage of greater amounts of oxygen.

The most unique and pervasive difference between humans and other animals is the capacity for communication through language. Communication makes possible group problem solving (Lieberman, 1984) and thus increases alternatives for coping. On the other hand, teaching through language can reduce or limit the alternatives for coping, as can errors in logical thought. Furthermore, the possession of language makes possible a unique phenomenon affecting maladaptive behavior, that of a conflict between verbal and nonverbal thinking.

Therapy

Since a combination of all three conditions is necessary to produce maladaptive behavior, the therapeutic strategy should be to alter one of these, whichever is most easily accessible. For example, motivation, especially that arising from emotions, can be reduced by chemotherapy; the limitation is that the effect usually lasts only as long as the medication is continued. Psychotherapy, on the other hand, usually operates by helping an individual to develop alternative coping strategies, as well to alter behavior in such a way that motivation is reduced. Finally, an individual may be helped out of maladaptive behavior by the simple method of taking him out of the situation that induces the intense emotional stimulation. This is usually easiest with children, whose lives can be controlled by adults, but adults also may employ this strategy. In the last century adults frequently moved to different parts of the country. A person could always escape from an unbearable situation by going west or even, in the case of many European cultures, by emigrating to a different part of the world and so escaping from a culture that might be producing a situation conducive to the genesis of maladaptive behavior. Or they might seek asylum in some way, such as by joining a religious order.

As seen from the above discussion, escape is essentially a coping strategy. Considered in this way there are only two basic factors to maladaptive behavior: prolonged intense emotional stimulation and lack of available coping strategies. But escape is such a basic and general strategy that it needs emphasis. It is so pervasive that, like the force of gravitation, that continually affects behavior, it is easily possible to forget it. It is therefore reasonable to retain the lack of the possibility for escape as one of the essential conditions for the genesis of maladaptive behavior.

The major schools of psychotherapy employ methods based on different theoretical bases, but all may be subsumed under the above model. For example, the classic method of psychoanalysis assumes that the behavior of the patient has been organized by developmental processes in maladaptive ways; the therapy therefore consists of recalling previous experiences and assisting the patient to reorganize his or her behavior in a more adaptive fashion, thus making coping possible. On the other hand, behavior modification assumes that if the maladaptive behavior can be altered into successful coping strategies, reorganization of behavior on a deeper level is unnecessary. Other therapies assume that if a patient understands the causes of his difficulties, he or she will modify the behavior accordingly. A relatively new form of therapy, that applied to families considered as systems, has the result, if successful, of altering the social environment of the individual exhibiting the maladaptive behavior. That is, there may be nothing inherently wrong with the individual; it is the environment that he has to deal with that is defective.

No therapeutic method will work unless the person wants help and believes in the method. Therapists are therefore almost totally helpless with respect to disturbed individuals who refuse or will not seek out treatment. And in some disorders, psychotherapy cannot be employed unless the strong emotional state is reduced. Current therapy therefore includes chronic medication.

As with any sort of disorder, prevention is always better than cure. The above model leads to certain general rules for maintaining and promoting mental health.

1)   Avoid situations that lead to prolonged stimulation of unpleasant emotions. This involves dealing with such situations as quickly as possible, either to reduce the emotional response or to escape it.

2)   Always maintain many alternative modes of behavior. For thinking persons, and few of us are incapable of thinking, there are always more than two ways of dealing with a situation.

3)   Always leave a way out, so that if all other coping strategies fail, one can escape.

The Role of Emotions in Psychopathology

Any general theory of maladaptive behavior must include the role of emotions. The first of the general conditions necessary for maladaptive behavior was defined as prolonged, intense stimulation or motivation, terms which do not allude to emotion because in most cases of animal experimentation we can only infer the existence of emotions, since the animals cannot tell us how they feel. For example, the mouse in the wash tub is probably suffering from an intense fear or panic reaction, but we cannot prove it. Judging from human reports and experience, emotion is a major phenomenon, perhaps even a necessary one, for the genesis of maladaptive behavior.

Definitions of Emotions

Emotion can be defined in at least three different ways depending upon the level of organization studied (Scott, 1980). On the individual or organismic level, an emotion is a feeling, usually internal and unlocalized, but grading into sensations that follow external stimulation. On the social level, an emotion is a form of communication, information that can be transmitted and received. If one considers only one individual, as Darwin did, one can talk of the "expression" of emotions. But the intercommunication of emotions obviously plays a very important role in the interactions involved in the development of social relationships, thus leading to the integration and organization of groups. Finally, on the physiological level, emotions are accompanied by physiological changes, some of which are quite easily detectable, as in fear, anger and pain, and others of which involve more subtle changes in the nervous system. The physiological changes described do not produce emotions but usually serve to facilitate the behavior resulting from the emotions, as when the high blood pressure resulting from anger results in facilitation of motor activity.

You will note that I do not include a definition of emotions on the genetic level. Emotions do not exist in genetic systems but are created as a result of the organizing activity of genetic systems interacting with other systems in the processes of development. There is no "gene for" an emotion or emotionality; these are phenomena that exist only on higher levels of organization.

Normal Functions of Emotions

The most general function of an emotion is to prolong the effects of stimulation. An immediate motor reaction to stimulation may last as little as a fraction of a second, but an emotional response may endure for hours, days, or even longer, and thus prolong the stimulation that leads to behavior. There are many adaptive responses that cannot be achieved through simple reflexes. That is, emotions make complex adaptive behavior possible.

Certainly in the case of humans, and probably in many other social vertebrates, the communication of emotions and responses to them play a major role in the development of social relationships and in the integration of groups. Moreover, the communication of inappropriate emotions by a disturbed individual may disrupt the organization of a group.

As stated above, gross physiological changes accompanying emotions are not the emotions themselves. Therefore, while emotions may upset physiological functions, they themselves do not have such functions.

Functional Classification of Emotions

If the general function of emotion is to maintain behavior, then emotions should vary according to the kind of behavior that is maintained. Table I is a classification of behavior according to its adaptive functions, based on a survey of behavior in the animal kingdom. The precise behavior patterns through which these functions are carried out vary from species to species, and behavioral functions in some species do not include the total list. In general, the first five of these functions are widely distributed, while the last five have been evolved only in the more complex groups of animals.

Table 1

**Classification of Emotions
in Relation to Behavioral Function**

Behaviour	Associated Function
Investigative	Curiosity
Ingestive	Hunger, Thirst
Comfort Seeking	Discomfort, Comfort
Defensive Behavior	Pain, Fear
Sexual	Sexual Love, Pleasure
Care-giving	Love
Agonistic	Anger, Fear, Pain
Allelomimetic	Separation Distress
Eliminative Behavior	Discomfort, Relief
Care-soliciting	Variety of Above

Such a list leads to certain conclusions. One is that there is a relatively small number of emotions that have the function of facilitation of adaptive behavior: these should be the ones that are involved in maladaptive behavior. Second, some of these emotions, notably pain, provide motivation for more than one behavioral function. Finally, in comparison to similar lists by other authors (e.g., Plutchik, this volume), the principle difference is the lack of emphasis of the more joyful emotions. I suggest that the emotion of enjoyment of living, at least among humans, is an emotion not associated with any one activity, but a general one that will maintain and reinforce any sort of ongoing activity. Also, the list does not include those emotions that may arise out of human culturally dictated activities.

Emotions and Maladaptive Behavior

As a general theory, we can postulate that any emotion could contribute to the high degree of motivation that is essential for maladaptive behavior, either singly or in combination with other emotions. This implies that the problem of compatibility of emotions is an important theoretical question. We can also postulate that unpleasant rather than pleasant emotions are more likely to lead to maladaptive behavior, and that those emotions that are strongest in a sensory fashion, should be more likely to produce maladaptive behavior. Finally, the frequency of maladaptive behavior associated with certain emotions will depend on the likelihood of the associated behavior being blocked.

Thus, in our culture, the most highly regulated behavioral functions are those having to do with eating, sexual behaviour, and fighting. One that is frequently overlooked is that of associations with people and places which are regulated by the economic system. Eating disorders include bulimia and anorexia; sexual disorders include a variety of neurotic behaviors as well as violent manifestations such as rape and homicide; regulation of agonistic behavior may lead to a variety of psychosomatic symptoms including the circulatory and alimentary systems, and separation distress is associated with depression.

In the remainder of this paper I shall emphasize the effects of genetic variation on emotions and associated maladaptive behavior.

Emotions and Maladaptive Behaviour in Dogs

I have listed three aspects of emotions that are accessible to study. *1) Internal feelings; 2) Communication or expression; and 3) Physiological activities underlying the above two.* Of these, the last two are the most appropriate to study in dogs, as whatever the dog may be feeling can only be inferred through communication and physiological changes.

Of the various emotions listed in the table those associated with agonistic behavior - anger or rage, fear and pain - are easily recognizable in dogs, as are hunger or thirst. Curiosity is a strongly developed emotion in dogs, as can be inferred from their investigatory behavior. Love expressed as affection is easily apparent, as is separation distress.

Variation in Normal Emotional Responses

Fuller and I (1965) conducted one of the most extensive and intensive studies of behavior genetics that has ever been attempted. In it we took puppies of five different breeds and subjected them to observations and tests from birth until one year of age, then crossed two of the breeds that appeared most unlike, and tested the hybrids resulting from the reciprocal F1 crosses, F2's, and backcrosses.

The tests included as many different sorts of responses and performances as possible, including learning, problem solving, physiological responses, and, importantly for the topic at hand, various tests of emotional reactions, including some of great importance to the problems of psychopathology - fearfulness, aggressiveness, and separation distress.

One of the most important findings of the overall study was that breed differences in performance involved only one identifiable trait that could be called purely cognitive; rather, differences in performance chiefly resulted from variation in emotional responsiveness and, closely related to these, differences in motivation.

A second important finding was that there is no general trait of emotionality. Dogs vary in their emotional responses according to the kind of emotion involved and the situations that provoke it. For example, our basenjis were fearful and cautious with respect to strange apparatus, but were not at all fearful with strange dogs. In most cases we were not able to determine the physiological bases of such differences, but Fuller found that a situation involving stimulation that should have produced fear produced an accelerated heart rate in some dogs and a slowed response in others, such differences being characteristic of two contrasting breeds. Fuller's main research on the physiological basis of emotions consisted of a series of test situations chiefly involving reactions to a human experimenter - separation, response to threats and loud noises, etc. Unfortunately he did not score the test situations separately, but combined specific physiological response such as heart rates from all test situations and then combined all of these in a total measure of "emotional reactivity," essentially a hypothetical construct of the type that he later classified as "psychophenes" (Fuller, 1986). The subscores almost universally gave highly significant breed differences, indicating an important effect of genetic variation on physiological measures of emotions, but the scoring method was such that it gave little information on how heredity produced this effect.

The Dog + Human Social Relationship

Domestic dogs have been adopted into human society, and as a result have developed a special social relationship with humans in addition to their basic dog+dog relationships. This new relationship is not identical with either human + human, or dog + dog relationships (although it has some resemblances to both) but is something new, created out of an interaction between species. Also, it is within the dog + human relationship that most of the observed emotional responses of dogs have been observed.

Emotional Variation and Maladaptive Behaviour

Although the main experiment on behavior genetics was intended to keep the dogs as normal as possible, we nevertheless encountered two phenomena that led to extensive experiments on psychopathology. One of these was the discovery of the critical period for a primary socialization and attachment, and the development of the attendant emotional responses. The other was the separation syndrome, a variety of maladaptive behaviors arising after prolonged or permanent separation from the objects of attachment.

The easiest emotional response to measure in a young puppy is distress vocalization. This can arise for a variety of reasons but is a major symptom of separation. The emotion of separation distress has major importance in dogs. Their wild ancestors, the wolves, are pack animals for which such an emotion has great adaptive importance, and domestic dogs have retained it. If one wishes to understand dogs, the most important point is that a dog must have companionship, whether human or canine, and can be motivated to do almost anything to achieve a social contact.

Separation Distress and the Separation Syndrome

The strong and pervasive emotion of separation distress has been relatively little studied until recently, whether in dogs or humans or in nonhuman primates. Among young puppies it is the primary index of the attachment process, a process which first appears at about two weeks of age but is not strongly developed until four weeks. It reaches a peak at about eight weeks and then slowly tapers off, reaching a relatively low level by twelve weeks (Gurski, Davis & Scott, 1980). During this time, separating a puppy from familiar individuals and places will cause it to emit high rates of vocalizations, often as many as one hundred per minute, thus permitting an objective measure of separation distress. Recovery is almost immediate when the puppy is restored to familiar places and companions.

A critical period for the process of social attachment thus extends from approximately four to twelve weeks of age. If a puppy is exposed to both dogs and humans during this time, or, as usually happens, a puppy is removed from its kennel and litter mates during the peak of the process around eight weeks of age plus or minus two weeks, and adopted into a human family, it will become what we consider a normal dog, with well developed relationships with both species. If removed at four weeks or earlier and has contact only with humans it becomes well adjusted toward humans but maladjusted toward other dogs, usually responding antagonistically. I have observed a male raised in this fashion attacking a female in heat instead of exhibiting the appropriate behavior. A more serious effect occurs if the puppy is allowed contact only with dogs and then is adopted by humans. In this case, the puppy behaves like a wild animal, and can be tamed only with considerable difficulty, and never develops such close attachments to humans (Freedman, King, & Elliot, 1961).

Clinically, the most commonly observed maladaptive behavior resulting from disruption of the attachment process is the *separation syndrome*. A puppy is often kept in a kennel with minimal contact with human caretakers and no experience outside the kennel. Serious results begin to show up after twelve weeks if the puppy has been removed after that time. If kept in as long as six months, the result is a full blown separation syndrome which may take forms ranging from acute depression through chronic fearfulness to fear biting. If left in the kennel, the dog's behavior appears to be normal.

Genetic Variation

Puppies of different breeds and hybrids will vocalize at lower or higher average rates when separated (Gurski, Davis & Scott, 1980), but I have never encountered a puppy that would not vocalize in this situation. The process of attachment and the associated emotions appear to be vitally necessary for survival and hence are strongly integrated into the developmental processes.

On the other hand there may be wide variation in the behavioral symptoms exhibited by adults at separation, and these appear to be associated with breed differences. My own experiments with the separation syndrome mainly involved two breeds, Shetland sheepdogs and Telomians. The number of cases was small, but maladaptive symptoms appeared in every animal. Some of these exhibited depression and persistent fearfulness toward strange places and people. In one case, a Sheltie did not move, eat, drink, urinate or defecate for five days, and was returned to the kennel where its behavior came back to normal within a half hour or so. Another Sheltie was consistently fearful of strange people and places for six months. When the owners brought it back they reported that it never wagged its tail in the whole time and communicated such a feeling of sadness to them that they gave up.

Telomian dogs are a new breed from Malaysia and are ordinarily very active, alert, people oriented, and mildly aggressive. Kept in a kennel for six months and then adopted, they appeared only mildly depressed, but in several cases caused trouble by biting people, sometimes seriously, and involving the caretakers as well as strangers. Dog handlers and veterinarians classified them as fear biters, and if their history had not been known they probably would have been "put to sleep."

I was also able to observe a few beagles that had been transferred from one kennel to another while adults. They did not appear to be seriously depressed, but were consistently fearful of new individuals and anything outside the kennel itself. Although the new kennel should have been similar to the old one in which they grew up, they nevertheless exhibited symptoms of this sort year after year.

Earlier we had done an experiment dealing with the effects of acute separation distress during the first part of the critical period, designed to find out whether or not such experiences would produce permanent alterations of adaptive behavior. Puppies of two breeds, Shelties and basenjis, were isolated overnight in boxes within their home nursery rooms during 5 consecutive days, then restored to their mother and littermates for 48 hours, then isolated overnight for another 5 days, all between the ages of 5 and 7 weeks. All puppies were then run through a regular regime of testing and training, until 30 weeks of age. The experiment was designed to test the hypothesis that a traumatic emotional experience might disrupt later behavior but, as I now realize, we should have tested the sensitization/desensitization hypothesis by exposing the puppies as adults to acute separation experience such as removal from the kennel and adoption by a human family.

While there were definite differences between experimentals and controls on a variety of tests during the 5-7 week period, most of these disappeared in the weeks following. There were two interesting exceptions. One was that the experimental Shelties continued to respond more poorly to a sit test requiring the animal to sit still on command. They also showed more balks on a leash control test that required the puppies to go into a strange situation. This was the closest duplication of the acute separation that the puppies had experienced earlier.

A second interesting finding was a modification of the attachment process to humans as measured by the handling test. During the 5-7 week period, separation produced a more rapid attachment in both breeds, but as the weeks went on, these differences disappeared as the controls caught up. The basenjis were an exception; at the end of the experiment the experimentals remained more strongly attached. Thus the experiment indicates that the process of attachment is speeded up by strong emotional stimulation (in this case of an unpleasant sort), and that the degree of final attachment can be increased in animals that develop relatively weak attachment under usual conditions.

With respect to genetic variation, there appeared to be no differences between males and females. In every breed there was variation between individuals, but no attempt was made to measure this other than to equate variant individuals between experimental and control groups. This leaves breed differences.

The two breeds were originally chosen because they had exhibited large differences in other experiments that indicated that Shelties were emotionally more sensitive and hence might show more prolonged effects. While significant breed differences showed up on a variety of tests, puppies of both breeds showed considerable powers of recovery. The breed differences that could be related to the experimental treatment manifested themselves in the kinds of long-term effects that were produced; there was no indication that one breed was more seriously upset than the other.

In contrast to puppies separated at five weeks or afterwards, puppies separated at 21 days or earlier show very little distress vocalization provided they are kept warm and comfortable (Gurski, Davis, and Scott, 1980). Fuller (1967, 1979) separated puppies at 21 days and placed them in special air conditioned kennel boxes that kept the puppies warm and comfortable, clean and well fed, through 105 days (18 weeks). As observed through one way glass they appeared completely normal except that they seldom vocalized.

When removed from their kennel boxes at 19 weeks and so became separated from their familiar environment they exhibited massive emotional reactions that Fuller termed "emergence stress." These dogs had developed their full emotional capacities, but had never before experienced any sort of separation and therefore had no opportunity for desensitization and amelioration of the emotions. If the initial emotional reaction was reduced by either special handling or chlorpromazine their maladaptive behavior could be reduced. If not restrained, such puppies tended to retreat into the furthest corner of any room in which they might be placed, and showed other more bizarre behavioral reactions.

Fuller also introduced a genetic variable into the experiment by running it with populations of beagles and wire haired fox terriers. He found that puppies of the two breeds were equally affected but showed opposite symptoms; the isolated beagles tended to be less active than normal and the fox terriers hyperactive. He concluded that these breeds were equally susceptible to the treatment, but responded in different ways.

Returning to the general theory of maladaptive behaviour: long separation from an environment to which a dog has become strongly attached produces what appears to be maladaptive behavior: depression, fear of anything strange and, in the more aggressive breeds, attacks on friendly caretakers. If the dog were not confined, such reactions would probably take it away from the new environment and cause it to wander around until it found its familiar one. From a dog's viewpoint this behavior would be the most adaptive response to the situation. Thus the three major conditions are apparent: 1) prolonged, intense motivation that arises from the fact that separation distress, unlike some emotions that disappear or dissipate within 24 hours or so, may persist for weeks, months, and even years, 2) lack of opportunity to escape, and because of this 3) lack of opportunity to exhibit an adaptive or coping response. Genetic variation occurs primarily in the symptoms observed, although there also may be some variation in the intensity of the aroused emotion.

Genetic Variation in Emotions among Humans

There have been only a few serious attempts to study the genetics of emotional variation among humans and most of these involve fearfulness, this being an emotion which is easy to elicit in a child without harmful effects and is also easy to recall in an adult.

As a basis for such studies, Fuller (1986) has proposed a classification of phenotypes whose variation is available for genetic analysis. These include 1) **chemophenes** (variation in molecular synthesis directly regulated by genes), 2) **somatophenes** (variation in internal and external form), and 3) **physiophenes** (variations in physiological reactions). These are the phenotypes commonly studied by geneticists in the past. In addition he lists two classes of behavioral phenotypes: 1) **ethophenes** (variation in patterns of behavior), and 2) **psychophenes** (variation in psychological constructs such as intelligence, personality, and emotionality). The behavioral classification has the advantage of distinguishing between naturally observed phenomena and secondary characteristics that are derived from human thought processes. We would expect that psychophenes would be less directly related to genetic variation and hence be difficult to analyze, and such has been the case in the history of behavior genetics. Also, the psychophene class can be combined with physiophenes, as in Fuller's own work on emotional reactivity (Scott & Fuller, 1965).

In Fuller's classification of phenotypes, it is obvious that physiophenes, ethophenes, and psychophenes are the most closely related to emotions. While there is much work on the physiology of human emotional responses I have been unable to locate any research which deals with its genetic variation. This is somewhat surprising in view of the commonly held belief that males and females differ in their emotional reactions.

Ethophenes

Scarr and Salapatek (1970) did an extensive study of infant fear responses as indicated by crying and avoidance, both ethophenes, in infants between 2 and 23 months of age including both blacks and whites. They elicited fears by specific stimuli of six kinds: a human stranger, the visual cliff, jack in the box, mechanical dog, masks on an experimenter and loud noises. Except for the response to the masks, which went along with the fear of a stranger, all of the above developed independently, indicating that, as with dogs, tendencies to become fearful are influenced by variation in different genes. Also, they observed considerable inter-individual variation which points to the possibility of genetic variation.

Of the above, only the fear of strangers is directly related to the separation response studied in dogs.

Freedman (1974) studied the emotional responses of newborn Caucasian and Oriental infants to such tests as physical restraint and found clear population differences, with the Oriental infants tending to react passively rather than struggling. He also observed individual differences and considerable overlap between the groups but made no effort to analyze these genetically. Nor did he make studies of hybrids between the various ethnic groups.

Another ethophene studied by Freedman (1974, 1979) was the behavior pattern of smiling, one that is almost as uniquely human as language. The smile in response to a new face appears early in development, persists throughout life, and communicates friendliness or an attempt at affiliation (another term for attachment). It must also be accompanied by an emotional feeling, since it eventually appears in blind infants.

Subjectively, the emotion is a relatively mild one and is described in various terms such as friendliness, happiness, etc.

Freedman found that females smile more often than males in any culture (although there seem to be wide cultural differences that may be partly based on genetic population differences) and that babies that smile frequently as young infants continue to so so at later ages, indicating that there is probably considerable genetic variation among individuals of the same sex.

The canine equivalent of the human smile is the rapid, horizontal tail-wag (Scott and Fuller, 1965). It, too, appears early in development and communicates friendly and nonantagonistic emotions. We found strong and persistent breed differences in the frequency of tail wagging, again indicating genetically based variation.

Neither smiling nor tail wagging appear to be involved in the genesis of maladaptive behaviour, except that the absence of either one may indicate emotional disturbance. I should point out that the emotions involved and associated with these two kinds of behavior are a mild and pleasant sort.

Psychophenes

Torgerson (1979) studied common phobias in a sample of 50 monozygotic and 49 dizygotic same sexed Norwegian twin pairs aged 20-70 years. Eleven pairs were included because of hospitalization for neurotic disorder, but the others were not selected. Each twin was asked to rate his or her degree of fears of specific objects or situations. The answers were factor analyzed and produce five groups of fears. One of these Torgerson called separation fears and as those of going on a journey, or being alone. This may have been related to separation distress. In every group of fears, the correlation between MZ twins was greater than that between DZ pairs. This is an indication of hereditary effects, but, as Torgerson pointed out, there are other things than common heredity that could produce such resemblances.

A more extensive study of the same sort was that of Rose and Ditto (1983), who asked a large number of adolescents and young adults in United States culture to rate their fearfulness with respect to each item in a list of situations and stimuli that have been reported to cause fear. They, also, did a factor analysis, but obtained seven instead of five factors, accounting for 45% of the variance. Three of the factors were similar to those of Torgerson: fear of small animals, fear of criticism in social situations, and fear of dangerous places such as heights.

Included in this sample were 222 pairs of MZ and 132 pairs of DZ twins. Thus the twin sample was more than three times as large as that studied by Torgerson. As with Torgerson's data, in every factor, the correlations between MZ twins were higher than those between DZ twins. In the Rose and Ditto data, the highest correlation was that of MZ twins for the factor of social responsibility (such things as fear of public speaking, etc.). In both MZ and DZ twins the lowest inter-twin correlations involved dangerous places such as heights, closed or open spaces, etc. The authors also calaculated heritability figures based on intraclass correlations and got results ranging from .72 to .28, the highest figure being that for fear of personal death and the lowest for fear of loved ones' misfortunes.

They also found that females gave scores higher than males except for fear of death at ages over 40, when the two sexes became essentially alike in this respect. This again suggests a genetic difference, although the male/female difference could easily be confounded by cultural factors. The greatest weaknesses of both these studies are the self report measure, and the grouping of fears which may be an artificial result of verbal generalization. Nevertheless, the studies indicate that important amounts of variation in emotional responses are due to genetic differences in human populations.

Discussion and Conclusions

Based on a wide variety of nonhuman animal research on the genesis of maladaptive behavior, the 3-factor theory provides a relatively simple and easily understandable general model that should be useful in applying both preventive and therapeutic treatment of maladaptive symptoms arising out of behavioral function in a wide variety of species including the human. One of the essential factors is that of intense and prolonged stimulation of emotions, usually but not necessarily of an unpleasant sort. Consequently there are only a limited number of major emotions that may be involved, either singly or in combination. In my own experience, I have observed that people who have serious behavioral disorders usually have more than one source of difficulty. The possibility of a combination of emotional disturbances should always be considered.

Among humans, culture may define the other two contributing factors, either by blocking coping behavior or preventing escape. Our own culture in the United States strongly regulates certain kinds of behavior: eating, sexual function, aggressive behavior, and association with particular people and places. Therefore it is the emotions underlying these behaviors that are most likely to be involved in maladaptive behavior.

The modifying factors that either augment or reduce the probability that a given individual will exhibit maladaptive symptoms are: early experience which may either sensitize or desensitize an individual to the emotions aroused by a given situation, and genetic variation that can affect all aspects of behavior, including the ability to cope and emotional sensitivity.

One would expect that any individual exposed to the unbearable situation produced by the conjunction of the 3 factors would eventually break down and begin to exhibit some form of maladaptive behavior. One would also expect that individuals, as a result of the combined effects of early experience and genetic variation, would differ with respect both to susceptibility and the kind of symptoms produced. That is, there should be no 1:1 correspondence between the symptoms produced and the situation that produced them. At the same time, as many clinicians have observed, there is very little behavior that is completely non-adaptive. Rather, as in the case of the dogs exhibiting the separation syndrome, it may represent an attempt at coping that would work in other circumstances.

There is ample evidence that genetic variation in animals can affect emotional responses, and one would expect that the same would be true of humans. Unfortunately, only a limited amount of research has been done with the genetics of human emotions, probably because genetic research involves measurement, and emotions are hard to measure. But this is an important enterprise that should be undertaken. Certain guide lines can be abstracted from the animal research. Genetic variation affects different emotions in different ways; therefore the most effective research will involve specific emotions studied in specific situations. The concept of a general trait such as "emotionality" is a trap that the human behavior geneticist should avoid.

Further, we should extend research on emotions to other cases than those that I have outlined above. For example, it is possible that the maladaptive behavior associated with brain injury and brain tumors may in part be caused by neurological alteration of emotional responses. Schizophrenia, which has long been known to have a strong genetic component should be studied from the viewpoint of emotional sensitivity as well as a thought disorder.

Finally, we should extend research on nonhuman animals, not only because experimental study on humans is virtually impossible for a variety of ethical reasons, but because animals, too, suffer from maladaptive behavior that needs to be understood before it can be effectively treated. As an example, dogs show serious problems from the effects of social separation. What we have learned about them not only helps owners to deal with dog problems but strongly suggests that important problems of human maladaptive behavior result from separation and should be treated appropriately. As Fuller found with his puppies, the one thing that most effectively relieves separation distress is active social interaction.

References

Freedman, D.G.: 1974, "Human Infancy: An Evolutionary Perspective". New York, Wiley.

Freedman, D.G.: 1979, "Human Sociobiology: A Holistic Approach", New York, Free Press-Macmillan.

Freedman, D.G., King, J.A. & Elliot, O . : 1961, Critical period in the social development of dogs. *Science,* 133, 1016-1017.

Fuller, J.L.: 1967, Experiential deprivation and later behavior. *Science,* 156, 1645-1652.

Fuller, J.L.: 1979, Genetic analysis of deviant behavior. In "Psychopathology in Animals", New York, Academic press, pp. 61-79.

Fuller, J.L.: 1986, Genetics and emotions. In R. Plutchik & H. Kellerman (Eds.) Emotions: "Theory, Research and Experience, Vol. 3, Biological Foundations of Emotions". New York, Academic Press, pp. 199-216.

Fuller, J.L. & Collins, R.L.: 1968, Temporal parameters for audiogenic seizures in SJL/J mice. *Developmental Psychobiology,* 1, 185-188.

Fuller, J.L. & Sjursen, F.H.: 1967, Audiogenic seizures in eleven mouse strains. *Journal of Heredity,* 58, 135-140.

Fuller, J.L. & Williams, E.: 1951, Gene controlled time constants in convulsive behavior. *Proceedings of the National Academy of Science,* 37, 349-346.

Gurski, J.C., Davis, K. & Scott, J.P.: 1980, Interaction of separation discomfort with contact comfort and discomfort in the dog. *Developmental Psychobiology,* 13, 463-467.

Hall, C.S.: 1947, Genetic differences in fatal audiogenic seizures between two inbred strains of house mice. *Journal of Heredity,* 38, 2-6.

Henry, K.R.:1967, Audiogenic seizure susceptibility induced in C57BL/6 mice by prior auditory exposure. *Science,* 158, 938-940.

Lieberman, P.: 1984, "The Biology and Evolution of language".
Cambridge MA, Harvard University Press.

Pavlov, I.P.: 1927 "Conditioned Reflexes". Oxford, Oxford University Press.

Rose, R.J. & Ditto, W.B.: 1983, A developmental-genetic analysis of
common fears from early adolescence to early adulthood.
Child Development, 54, 361-368.

Scott, J.P.: 1980, The function of emotions in behavioral systems:
A systems theory analysis. In R. Plutchik & H. Kellerman (Eds.)
"Emotion: Theory,Research and Experience Vol. 1
Theories of Emotion", New York, Academic Press pp. 35-56.

Scott, J.P. & Fuller, J.L.: 1965, "Genetics and the Social Behavior of the
Dog." Chicago University of Chicago Press.

Torgerson, S.: 1979, The nature and origin of common phobic fears.
British Journal of Psychiatry, 134, 343-351.

Brain Emotional Circuits and Psychopathologies

Jaak Panksepp

Department of Psychology
Bowling Green State University
Bowling Green, Ohio 43403

Introduction

In this paper, I will advocate the position that psychology must begin to study emotions more earnestly at a neurological level in order to make major progress in the field. Although my style will be contentious, my hope is not to stir more sterile controversy in this troubled area, but to evoke greater enthusiasm for the psychobiological approach to understanding emotionality. I am convinced the psychobiological approach has a better chance of generating a deep understanding of the basic nature and causes of human emotionality than any other experimental approach presently available (although it has no chance of capturing the vast variety of individual emotional *experiences* in the butterfly net of its empirical measurements). I believe the neurological approach will provide the ultimate foundation for understanding the nature of the *affective/emotional* imbalances which constitute the major psychiatric disorders, even though it may add little to our understanding *the correlated non-affective content* of each individuals specific emotional experiences. It is long past time to try, once again, to blend the neurological and psychological approaches to understanding emotions into a coherent whole, as was attempted by Gellhorn and Loofbourrow ((1963). Another major example of such an attempt in the past was one developed by Magda Arnold (1960). Her perspective was both creative and broad in scope, but it was not especially well restrained by empirical data or sculpted in such a way that it could generate clear predictions in the brain-research laboratory. At the present time, existing data can sustain a more modest synthesis which can effectively guide cross-species brain research and which has the potential to promote basic understanding of the psychopathologies.

In any event, the study of emotions has finally emerged from the shadow of behaviorism, and many disciplines will provide important partial solutions to the overall puzzle. It is my contention that all of the sub-disciplines of psychology are in fact seeking to understand brain processes - some directly, most indirectly - which leads me to believe that our conceptions of emotionality will be well served if each level of analysis is constrained and guided, if at all possible, by the available knowledge of the discipline below it. At the present time the most molecular level of understanding is neurological (mostly from animal brain research), and the lessons at this level can *finally* help guide the search for solid understanding at the psychological level. For long, the flow of influence has been in the other direction: Psychological knowledge has guided our conceptions of how emotionality might be organized in the brain. This direction of influence is still substantial (though typically underused, especially in animal brain research), but now the two approaches can reciprocate to yield a much tighter and systematic analysis of the underlying issues. While psychological conceptions can guide our functional analysis, biology can restrain our conception of the fundamental nature of things.

Because the psychobiological view which I am advocating is not well represented or appreciated in the renaissance that the study of emotions is presently enjoying, I will dwell at length on the underlying strategic and conceptual issues that must be addressed if we are to fully fathom the underlying biological nature of emotionality. Since there seems to be considerable disagreement as well as confusion on such issues, I will emphasize what the psychobiological approach can seek to accomplish and how its findings can be interfaced with the many disciplines which must offer solid perspectives at phenomenological levels, especially the clinical and cognitive areas. In sum, this is a position paper. Literature citations will be used sparingly, but most of the pertinent evidence can be accessed through the reviews that are mentioned.

On the Need for Forthrightness in the Study of Emotions

The central role of emotions in the genesis of psychopathologies is generally accepted, generally dealt with in psychotherapy, and generally ignored in formal discussions of the etiology of pathological distress. Until recently, this disregard was probably based on the fact that substantive knowledge in the area was so sparse that to speak of emotional underpinnings for psychopathologies was to remain forever at a theoretical/speculative level, and an impractical one at that. It seemed both more efficient, more effective, and certainly more proper to focus on the client's behaviors, individual experiences and cognitive as well as symbolic/metaphoric processes in attempts to help them understand and occassionally to free them of their underlying emotional turmoil. In addition to such traditional approaches, however, a client's primary-process emotionality may need to be evaluated and treated as well. Hopefully direct treatment of emotional imbalances will eventually be promoted by neurological evidence concerning the underlying fabric of the primal emotive systems. Such knowledge, albeit meager at present, is finally beginning to be gathered.

Now that primary emotions can be studied as biological processes, there will be many new interfaces between the basic science of underlying brain functions and clinical applications. Also, through such knowledge we should gain a clearer understanding of archetypal subconscious processes which guide the dynamics of normal and abnormal thought. Clearly a revolution in the study of emotions is upon us, and its success will depend on the creative synthesis of perspectives as opposed to the traditional polarization between various levels of analysis.

This "revolution" is partially a consequence of the failure of mainstream neuro-science, psychobiology, clinical psychology and human experimental psychology (now flourishing under the banner of cognitive psychology) to deal forthrightly or effectively with this topic in the past. Neuroscience and psychobiology have ignored emotional concepts on the basis of logically sound but rationally shortsighted "first principles": We cannot and probably never will be able to see into the minds of other species; indeed, we have trouble enough seeing into our own, so why bother strug-gling with affective concepts! Obviously, to make headway in understanding why people do what they do, we have to continue to struggle with such issues, especially in the animal brain research laboratory. Similarly, clinical psychology deals with emotional issues routinely in practice, but in academic settings, emotions, as primary affective processes, are rarely discussed in either frank or systematic ways. Thus, the discipline behaves, at times, as if such brain functions do not exist, or are of no major consequence for understanding psychopathologies. Likewise, human experimental psychology has generally found emotionality to be a troublesomely vague area, especially as far as internal affective experiences are concerned. Thus the topic has long been avoided. Now there is a massive void to be filled, which, at present, is being filled more vigorously by human than animal research. I suspect, however, that the animal brain research, especially as guided by human introspective/cognitive data, will be decisive in generating a lasting foundation upon which our understanding of emotionality must be built. In a deep sense, the question of emotionality is a biological question; although, because of their nature, the underlying systems sustain constant reciprocal discourse with psychological, brain-software levels of individual experi-ence.

Emotions and the New Cognitive Sciences

Cognitive psychology voluntarily chose to discourage the study of emotions as part of its starting "dogma". This was to be a strategic simplifying maneuver, since emotions were deemed too complex or subtle for rigorous empirical scrutiny. As Gardner (1985) states in his history of the discipline, cognitive science made a "deliberate decision to de-emphasize certain factors" including "the influence of affective factors or emotions" (p. 6).

Although it may be wisest to (re)search where the light is brightest, it is perplexing that any area of science would intentionally discourage the attentions of its practitioners from critical parts of nature, especially parts which may be essential for unified understanding in their field. Behaviorism made just such a mistake. It not only failed to encourage experimental attention on the spontaneous behaviors of organ-isms, but it also advocated a philosophical "black-box" position toward the nervous system, which effectively dissuaded its talented adherents from the study of instinc-tual behaviors as well as the organ of those behaviors. Although it is historically understandable that the behaviorist dogma was a reaction to the circular mentalistic excesses of the time which masqueraded as explanations, the conceptual polarization advocated by behaviorism contained the seeds of its own destruction. Obviously the understanding of intrinsic organismic functions and behavioral tendencies is as important as the understanding of the environmental restrictions in which organisms must operate. The interaction between an animal and its environment is a two-way concourse, and not a one-way street as radical behaviorism sought to entertain.

One lesson from the protracted epistemological anguish of behaviorism should have been that no group of scientists should attempt to exclude relevant parts of nature by fiat, without suffering the type of intellectual treatment reserved for cults. By failing to be catholic, behaviorism promised more than it could deliver. It polarized itself over minor paradigmatic issues (e.g., that the environmental control of behavior could be studied in its own right), became defensive, and in trying to establish artificial boundaries around its legitimate "turf", could not be taken seriously as a credible *general* approach to understanding either brain or the psychological processes which generate behavior. Although it generated many findings and techniques of lasting value (which hopefully will not be tossed out with the bathwater), it did not provide a solid foundation for the construction of a lasting science of psychology. In any legitimate science, the first premise should be that one must take nature on her own terms. One might sardonically note that the cognitive "slayer of behaviorism" failed to slay this conceptual flaw of behaviorism; rather, it re-enshrined the anti-scientific concept of limiting its inquiries arbitrarily and inappropriately in the vast arena of mental faculties. Like behaviorists, some practitioners of cognitive science, hopefully a diminishing breed, also view brain science, and the constraints imposed by that knowledge, as irrelevant to their field of study. However, there are also signs in cognitive psychology of new and virulent strains of Cartesian dualism. "Information is just information and nothing else," is their motto. This is as disastrous a mistake in psychology as the slogan of the extremist opposition that all of psychology can be reduced to *intrinsic* brain functions. Obviously, the brain sustains a dynamic two-way exchange with the outside world—a dialogue between the evolutionary potentials of the brain and the here-and-now environment. A multitude of intrinsic but experientially refined sensory, attentional, perceptual, emotional and motor systems reach out into the world to construct "realities" as well as "myths" and "beliefs" from their experiences with the world. Without the ability of pre-wired brain systems to initiate and sustain such interactions, the vast memory fields of "mind" would remain empty and still. It is hard to imagine that organisms could survive without emotional circuits, and it is hard to understand why psychology took so long to focus on them.

Fortunately, such mistakes are slowly being rectified. Statements acknowledge that the study of emotions is among the important remaining issues to be tackled by cognitive science (e.g., Norman, 1980), and neural principles will soon provide major insights into recalcitrant cognitive issues (e.g., via the study of neural net computers designed on brain organizational priniciples). In light of such relaxation of artificial constraints, I would still raise a warning: The cognitive disciplines are bound to make serious future errors, especially in the area of emotions, unless they carefully hone their conceptual structures, whenever possible, within the available empirical constraints of brain-science. Without such restraint, cognitive disciplines may weave layers of theoretical fantasy which could retard understanding of the foundation issues upon which lasting knowledge of emotionality and various other fundamental psychological/brain processes must be built. I also offer such a warning because I fear that our human ability to linguistically conceptualize (via our most recent evolutionary brain skill) can as readily deceive as enlighten. Our conceptions of nature will remain more realistic if we vigorously sift fundamental from derivative processes—and for emotions the best sieve is functional neuroscience (conceptually impoverished as the area may often seem to outsiders).

For reasons such as these, I believe animal brain research presently provides a most important and credible empirical constraint for conceptualizing primary emotional issues at the human level. Unfortunately, cognitive scientists often look askance at such a position, for the cognitive agenda, in its extreme, is to create an irreducible information-based science of the mind - an agenda which obviously can only be actualized if one maintains a clear focus on human cognitive/introspective abilities. However, from my vantage, I fear a lasting understanding of the true nature of mind cannot be achieved unless cognitive science cultivates strong ties to animal psychobiology: There are simply too many special purpose mechanisms in the brain (shared in a homologous fashion in all mammals) which constrain information flow in human cortical analogs of random access memory (RAM). Also, we must remember that there is probably no true *tabula rasa - like* RAM space in the brain of any evolved creature. Perhaps language cortex comes closest, but even that circuitry is highly specialized for linguistic types of multi-modal information processing. Thus, it is coming to be widely recognized that the digital computer model, an acknowledged pillar of cognitive science, is as flawed an analogy for the brain as were the telephone switchboard and hydraulic lever/pulley models of the past. The brain bio-computer is full of intrinsic "semantic" processes (i.e., pre-wire analog circuit functions which implicitly extract and convey *values and meaning*). Digital computer programs typically do not contain such functions within their syntactic richness, and no one yet quite knows how to properly program them.

By its inability to deal directly with evolutionarily derived primary processes which are psychologically irreducible (and I believe the evidence strongly indicates that certain basic emotions are primary brain processes), cognitive science is largely limited to dealing with secondary reflections of those processes, or as is more common, ignoring them. It is thus in an ideal position to mistakenly enshrine secondary processes as primary ones, and there are signs that such a mistake is propagating at an alarming pace in the cognitive analysis of emotions. A major and pervasive mistake among some cognitivists is the assumption that emotions are in some *fundamental* sense *social constructions* . Such a mistake (and I think a broad and fair reading of the pertinent literature indicates it is entirely wrong in essence, though half-correct in human cultural practice), especially when enshrined in the literature with great intelligence, great writing skill, and great conviction (as it often has), will delay a cohesive and credible interdisciplinary understanding of emotionality. I find it poignant that such a dilemma is still with us, as big as ever, 130 some years after the renowned early associationist, Herbert Spencer (1855), sought to put it to rest on page 606 of his *Principles of Psychology* : "That the experience-hypothesis, as ordinarily understood, is inadequate to account for emotional phenomena, will be sufficiently manifest. If possible, it is even more at fault in respect to the emotions than in respect to the cognitions. The doctrine maintained by some philosphers, that all the desires, all the sentiments, are generated by the experiences of the individual, is so glaringly at variance with hosts of facts, that I cannot but wonder how any one should ever have entertained it." A century later, this same error remains *a* (perhaps, *the*) forefront cognitive conception of emotionality, and may remain so until psychologists, as a group, come to better grips with the nature of the brain.

What I mean to say by the above is summarized in Fig. 1. The main trend in cognitive thinking about emotions is that they are social constructions arising from our cognitive integration of powerful events which stir up autonomic arousal. In its extreme form, the suggestion is that there are no innate emotional systems in the brain; with emotive realities arising from undifferentiated perceptual and autonomic substrates. This is an opinion which flies against such a mass of basic biological data that for anyone to take it seriously in the present day means that 1) they simply are not conversant with the neurological facts, or 2) they subscribe to a dualistic view of animal life which places human "mind/reason" in a reified cateogory *above* other brain capacities, or 3) they are so dazzled by the obvious fact that emotional systems in the brain are designed to respond to environmental events that they forget that this in no way implies that brain emotional systems must be constructed out of environmental events (even though emotional experiences are so constructed), or 4) their implicit "scientific/artistic/political" aim is to construct nature rather than to reveal it. The evidence indicates that emotions are elaborated by brain systems, designed and molded by eons of adaptive evolutionary selection, and refined by each individual's experiences, to interact with key environmental events.

On the Cortex, Perceptions and Emotions

One basic set of data which all cognitive conceptions of emotionality should consider is the behavior of a neo-decorticate animal - creatures mutilated in this way are more emotional than neurologically intact ones. Take one example from my recent personal experience - for one of my 1985 undergraduate psychobiology class projects, I brought in a group of normal adult rats and an equal number of littermates which had been decorticated several days after birth. It was the job of students to identifiy which animal of each pair was intact and which was missing a quarter of its brain (presumably the most recently evolved "thinking" part). In 13 of 16 pairs, the decorticate animal was judged to be intact, and the faulty judgements were made largely because the decorticates were deemed more active, more inquisitive - in a phrase, *more emotionally "vital"* - than controls. This suggests, as has long been known, that one of the major functions of the neocortex is to inhibit subcortical affective processes, which is, of course, essential for focussed, "clear headed" thinking about cognitive issues. If we accept 1) the assumption that the highest reaches of human cognition are organized by massively expanded neocortical potentials (an assumption which must be made if one considers the human mind unique in any major way since that is our major, perhaps only, cerebral advantage over most of the other mammals) and 2) the fact that animals without neocortex do in fact exhibit (and probably experience) heightened emotionality, then it follows that any conception of primary emotionality which relies on *cognitive perceptual* triggering as the essential ingredient of emotional affect is *fatally* flawed. One could logically argue that behavioral expressions of emotionality do not imply the experience of emotionality, but considering that decorticate animals can learn to work for food, to self-stimulate their lateral hypothalamic "reward/foraging" circuits, to avoid shock, and to seek and escape many other incentives, such a rejoinder appears hollow. Of course, it needs to be emphasized that the experience and expressions of emotion can be dissociated at times, for instance, as a result of certain types of demyelinating brain damage in humans (Poeck, 1969) and as a result of electrical stimulation of lower brainstem fixed-action patterning circuits in animals (Delgado, 1969). However, I suspect such dissociations are generally exceptions rather than the rule, especially in lower animals in which the potential for deception is not as well developed as in humans.

I do not wish to imply that the cortex has no function in emotions. It may serve many roles: *First*, there is the possibility that the massive expansion of neocortex in humans truly provides some new and powerful emotive possibilities through the evolution of special purpose perceptual abilities. For instance, the selective elimination of facial recognition (prosopagnosia) following damage to ventral surface of temporal/occipital lobe is a case in point (Damasio, 1985). *Second*, it is possible that the cortex allows the human brain to generate new combinatorial psychic possibilities from pre-existing "old parts." For instance, perhaps the affective resonance of human music, art, dance, poetry and theatre reflect permutations whereby the power of old affective substrates are exploited in new and voluntary ways. Likewise, the deceptive use of emotions may be a pervasive new primate skill, whose psychic roots hark back to the emotionally insubstantial threat displays of certain lower animals. *Third*, it is possible that the massive cortical inhibitory functions on subcortical emotive processes (which may be essential for flexible and creative human thought and problem solving) dampen (and prolong) primary emotive tendencies to such an extent that every-day emotionality can assume new levels of subtlety, even though the ability to elaborate emotional affect still remains critically linked to the underlying primary emotive systems of the brain. For instance, as suggested by Helen Block Lewis at this meeting, shame and guilt may be integrally linked to the activity of separation-distress circuitry. There are other ways the neocortical interface with primary emotionality could filter, amplify, dampen and enrich human feelings with uniquely human cortical potentials and complexities. For instance, the symbolic abilities of the human brain surely create new measures of richness in the texture of human emotional experiences. The basic emotional systems may spontaneously mold universal human archetypal "Jungian" images via their refractions through the higher reaches of our brains. Conversely, our symbolic and motor abilities (e.g., via the sentic cycles of Clynes and various forms of artistic expression (also allow us to voluntarily control our own moods and to influence those of others to an extent not apparent in other species.

I have no doubt that all such processes actually transpire in the human brain, but my conclusion remains the same - the basic nature of the affective life has to be resolved through a deep biological understanding of subcortical areas which mediate primary-process emotionality. Any cognitive conception of emotionality which does not acknowledge the critical nature of such issues, may well be seeking artistic truths rather than scientific ones (i.e., it may be highlighting specifics as opposed to general principles). The existential manifestations of basic phenomena are always more diverse than the lawful basic scientific principles which underlie the phenomena (in all areas of nature!). Unless we keep a clear focus on the type of analysis we are pursuing, needless controversies will continue to arise.

I believe practically everyone in the emotion "business", whether of cognitive of psychobiological bent, recognizes that perceptions are an essential ingredient in the triggering of normal every-day emotional states, but the biological data suggest that this is achieved by the ability of perceptual functions of the nervous system to interact with the primary-process circuits of emotionality (Fig. 1). Such a scheme also allows for the possibility that the primary processes can reprogram other parts of the brain for derivative emotional functions (yielding potentially vast secondary layers of learned emotive processing). From such a perspective, a most important goal for the scientific analysis of emotions is the elucidation of the nature of the primal, pre-*linguistic* emotive processes of the brain from which the higher levels of complexity emerge. The primal emotive systems of the brain have operated efficiently on *physiological, behavioral and affective levels* for uncounted "evolutionary eons," and only recently have they come to interact with human cognitive, linquistic and cultural processes. Those higher interactions will remain only vaguely understood until we understand the foundation processes. Of course, the sundry learned manifestations of the systems also need to be catalogued, analyzed, and admired, but such work cannot yield a causal understanding of the basic issues. Whether there is anything truly and fundamentally new in the emotional realm since the mushrooming of the human and cetacian neocortices remains an open issue, but one that is unlikely to be addressed in a definitive fashion until the ancient primary process mechanisms are unravelled.

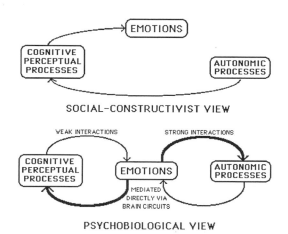

Figure 1. Two current views of of how emotions are organized in brain.

Surely there will be new constructions of a cultural sort in human expressions of emotionality (that is a historical/anthropological given), and perhaps there are even new developments at the neuro-perceptual level in humans, especially in the ability of language to instigate feelings. However, on the basis of simple evolutionary considerations, there is no reason to suspect that much has changed in the underlying affective/feeling processes which encourage animals to behave and feel in certain ways, only in the higher permutations and elaborations of those processes. The assumption of some cognitivists that the potential for feeling states may be an emergent consequence of our vast cortical complexities is wishful thinking. Such a view is without empirical support, and not simply from lack of pertinent data: Clear and replicable affective experiences can not be produced by electrically stimulating the neocortex of humans. On the other hand, affective states are consistently evoked in humans by stimulating those subcortical areas from which emotive behaviors are evoked in "lower" animals (for review see Panksepp, 1985). This simple finding highlights the substructures of emotionality, and there is presently no robust scientific alternative but to try to unravel the nature of these primal emotive systems of the human brain by studying the animal brain. At the charter meeting of the International Society for Research on Emotions (ISRE) in 1985, I suggested that it might be profitable for those who are interested in human emotions to return to the animal brain-research laboratory, but I think the proposal was not well received. The present chapter is largely a furtherance of that point of view. Indeed, I do not hesitate to admit that my research agenda during the past twenty years has been just that, to understand basic human emotions and motivations by studying the animal brain.

The vast conservation of physiological functions among the mammalian species, as is affirmed by our massively shared genetic heritage (nicely summarized by Charfas and Gribbin, 1982), suggests the data we derive from the analysis of the animal brain should translate remarkably well to the human condition, at least at subcortical levels where primary process emotionality finds it source. Skimming the psychological/phenomenological surface of such neurobiological phenomena can not take us to the heart of knowledge concerning the organization of emotions in the brain; but the cognitive/introspective approach can and must guide the search. Conversely, it is clear that the subtle and pervasive interactions of emotions and cognitions cannot yet be readily addressed in psychobiological/animal studies. Only the systematic study of the human mind, can directly confront those issues. Thus, it is long past time to join the best aspects of the two disciplines into a synthesis which I would call "Comparative Neuro-psycho-phenomenology." It will have to be a *conservative, data-constrained interface* very unlike the one that George Romanes, W. Lauder Lindsay, and others tried to create at the end of the last century. The more modern attempt of Magda Arnold was a step in the right direction, but still it was conceptually much richer (i.e., untestable with available techniques) than needed for guidance of laboratory work. In neuroscience/psychobiology, we have to start with animal basics and work up, rather than begin with human complexities and work down. Without a modest, data-constrained interface, fundamental, neurobiological knowledge in the area of emotions will remain meagre.

Emotions and Psychotherapy

The need to make clear distinctions between primary and secondary emotional processes is as essential in psychotherapy as in research. Primary emotional systems seem to be designed in such a way as to permit the creation of massive overlays of derivative, learned processes - of rationalizations, deceptions, manipulations, and a vast array of instrumental strategies to optimize personal advantage in one's social world. Indeed, the cognitive substrates of emotionality may be created entirely via the gradual developmental activities of the basic emotive circuits, perhaps via some variant of reinforcement principles, as traditionally conceptualized (Panksepp, 1986). In short, emotional learning may be constructed by the fluctuation of activities in emotive circuits as an animal or human behaves. Perhaps sudden onsets and reductions of activity in emotive circuit are the key ingredients via which reinforcement for adaptive as well as maladaptive learning are elaborated. The final symptoms of emotional distress are revealed in the clinic more often through derivative learned processes than through direct primary-process expressions of the underlying affect. Hence, the therapist typically has few options but to deal with secondary rather than primary emotional issues, but it would be a mistake to assume that the secondary processes lie at the very heart of the affective turmoil which assails the client. If affect could be changed directly, cognitive change would often follow automatically (see Clynes's and Liebowitz's chapters). The main tenet of this paper is that the underlying substructure of serious psychiatric disorders resides largely within the nature and dynamics of the primary process circuits. Modulation of secondary processes (e.g., through cognitive re-appraisal and specific, goal-oriented coping maneuvers) can, with good fortune, help control and change the underlying emotional distress, but neurophysiologically, those affective changes are presumably indirect.

Pharmacological treatments, on the other hand, will be able to modulate primary affective substrates directly (albeit typically in symptomatic rather than curative ways), while having no effect on the secondary processes which consitute the essential details of an individual's life. By alleviating the underlying primary emotive distress, however, a patient may become more capable of re-evaluating their perceptions and life circumstances, in ways which lead to effective and adaptive behavioral changes (see Liebowitz's chapter). Such a view highlights the converse, and often ignored, side of the proposition that perceptions can trigger emotions: The intensity of primary emotions governs the vigor and quality of perceptions, cognitions and intentions. In sum, the failure to distinguish primary and secondary emotive processes in clinical psychology could hinder and delay the psychotherapeutic enterprise by inextricably mixing up the causes and symptoms of distress. Why so many clinical psychologists still view the revolution in psychopharmacology with suspicion, as opposed to regarding it as a potentially powerful ally, baffles me. Most patients in serious emotional distress may be helped much more by skillful conjoint application of drug and talk therapies than either alone.

The "Neuroscience Revolution" and Emotions

The cognitive revolution is finally responding to the necessity of studying emotionality in order to understand the mind (e.g., Lang, 1984; Izard, Kagan & Zajonc, 1984; Mandler, 1984; Scherer & Ekman, 1984). Despite all I have said concerning the need for a neural view, neuroscience and psychobiology generally have a lackluster record in that regard. Granted, the basic brain disciplines never enshrined their biases as brazenly as did behaviorism and cognitive science; they simply chose to ignore the whole field. (Note the absence of any session devoted exclusively to emotions at a Neuroscience Meeting since the inaugural meeting of The Society in 1971.) By restricting their analysis to visually observable events, the basic brain disciplines decided to forego the use of intevening functional concepts such as emotions decades ago. By their unwillingness to pursue troublesome primary brain processes at a neuro-theoretical level (which is truly an essential ingredient of functional brain research, since our understanding of behavior has to be constituted by more than the study of behavior - i.e., by more than the indirect study of the patterned release of acetylcholine onto nicotininc cholinergic receptors), psychobiology and neuroscience became conceptually impoverished, at the functional behavioral level, and have thus routinely failed to focus their powerful tools on some of the most important and evident behaviors that organisms exhibit. The poverty of basic neurological work on fear, play, exploration/expectancy and separation-distress are just *a few* cases in point.

My personal research strategy of the past decade has been to proceed with a frontal assault on the nature of mammalian emotionality, unpopular as the topic seems to be among my neuroscience colleagues. The underlying rationale is that this work is the basic science side of clinical psychology and biological psychiatry. I believe that if this theoretically-guided empirical battle is waged successfully, then it will have important ramifications for understanding the genesis and treatment of psychopathologies. Accordingly, the aim of this chapter is to summarize some potential interfaces between basic brain research on emotive circuits and how it relates to the deep nature of psychopathologies.

I believe the collective evidence from several scattered research programs during this century provides an empirically based, albeit vague, road-map of how emotions are organized in subcortical areas of the brain (for summaries see, Panksepp, 1981; 1982; 1985; 1986; 1987; 1988). We are presently using this road-map to characterize the basic "hardwired/prewired" systems for emotionality. I believe we have reached a time in the development of the neurosciences, where Freud's dream to understand emotional ailments as imbalances in the biological substructure of the psyche (as enunciated in his *Project for a Scientific Psychology*) can finally be approached with robust empirical tools.

On the Basic Nature of Emotions

At this stage in the historical development of emotional concepts, no one has yet generated a verbal definition of emotions that is generally accepted. It is unlikely that such a definition can ever be constructed without resort to neurobiological principles.

Although emotional and rational processes eventually get inextricably blended in higher neural networks, I think basic emotions are concrete "agents" in the brain, to borrow Minksy's terminology (see this volume). Along with Minksy, I believe emotive networks are as simple (to understate the matter) and fundamentally alike in the brains of lower mammals and human infants (Minksy, 1987), but in animals we can pursue their rigorous study. Thus, basic emotions may be best defined with a substantial focus on neural circuit criteria. For instance, brain networks which mediate the primary emotions may share many common attributes (e.g., they may be constituted of long-axoned, trans-diencephalic, sensory-motor command system which bring behavior, autonomic/hormonal processes and dynamic psychological feeling states into rapid coherence). Obviously, it is a hazardous task to attach subjective tags to objective brain circuits, especially in animals. However, the affective consequences of various forms of brain damage and localized electrical stimulation in humans may facilitate such labelling (e.g., for a selected review of such work, see Panksepp, 1985). The weak tool that permits us to do likewise in other animals is anthropomorphism - a tool that can only help do the job when it is coupled with cross-species behavioral brain research, so the consequent ideas and findings can potentially be validated via human introspective experience.

Our present research strategy is that under certain circumstances, experimental animals are behaving "as if" propelled by real emotional feelings. From the perspectives of *monism*, I think that it is more reasonable to assume that lower animals do feel emotions than that they do not, even though we surely should not wish to use such unmeasurable feelings as explanatory principles for behavior. The "we can't ever know" premise is, I believe, short-sighted and counterproductive at the present time. If physicists had decided not to study electrons because they could never see them, our physics might still be comfortably agrarian. It is also reasonable to assume that the unmeasurable feelings of other animals emerge, as they do in humans, from the intrinsic activities of the ancient primary emotive circuits which all mammals, indeed most vertebrates, share. If this is so (and the mass of available evidence is consistent with these assumptions), then we should also assume that a careful empirical analysis of pertinent behavioral indicators in animals (e.g., sniffing, exploration, flight, attack, separation distress vocalizations, and rough-and-tumble play) in conjunction with direct manipulation of the underlying brain systems (neurochemical, electrophysiological and structural), can provide critical evidence concerning the biological characteristics of brain emotive systems in humans. Conversely, a careful study of human affect may help guide the dynamic analysis of the underlying brain systems in animals. To what extent the experience of affect actually modulates the behavioral output can remain a shelved issue until we have much more data on the basic nature of the underlying circuitry.

However, the list of possible human feelings is vast, and even the shorter lists of basic human emotions (e.g. those of Izard, 1977; Plutchik, 1980; Tomkins and McCarter, 1964) are longer than present analysis of the animal brain can sustain. The longer, open-ended lists generated by social constructivists (e.g., Mandler, 1984) may never be capable of being interfaced with careful brain research - animal or human. Still, simple questionaire studies of human feelings indicate that people only agree on a very short four item list of basic emotions, which include anger, fear, sorrow and joy (Panksepp, 1986). To what extent the additional human complexities arise from the intrinsic characteristics of the underlying neural circuits, as opposed to the derived subtlety of our human languages and cultures, remains uncertain, but I suspect that our linguistic skills are often more hindrance than assistance for a clear-headed analysis of emotions

Languages, by their societal as well as biological nature, seem designed not only to communicate (especially about external events) but also, as argued before, to deceive and manipulate others (often with regard to internal events). In addition, many affectively loaded terms, because of each individual's personal history, may have idiosyncratic meanings. Attempts to distinguish between feelings of "sympathy and empathy" and "anger and hate" come to mind. I do not think these concepts make major distinctions at the primary process level. For instance, I think hate is largely a cognitively sustained, modest level of prolonged activity in primary anger/rage circuits (or of their secondary cortical representation). I think both sympathy and empathy are motivationally guided by one's ability to resonate with the distress circuits of others - *sympathy* in a slightly cooler and aloof (i.e., cognitive) way than *empathy* (which is more deeply felt at the primary-process level).

Human words can surely create cathedrals of cultural meaning that have few clear relations with the primary-process biological world. This seems to be a problem of insurmountable proportions in the study of human emotions (where objective neural anchor points are routinely missing for concepts). Consequently, cross-species, psychobiological analysis of emotionality is one of the most effective ways for us to learn what is truly there - to distinguish the universals of the brain from the particulars of the individual, to sift the biologically permanent from the culturally changeable facets of emotionality. For such reasons, I would once again emphasize that, at present, the neurology of animal emotionality can shed more penetrating scientific light on the *basic* nature of human emotions than any other experimental approach.

One of the most troublesome aspects of studying emotions is the vast variety of distinguishable subjective feelings that humans can have. Although a cardinal attribute of emotions are feeling states, I do not think that it is especially useful to mix the reasonably rigorous neurobiological conception of emotive command systems (vide infra) with the notion of distinct affective categories. Affective feelings are really a much larger category than primary emotive states, and I would share a few ideas on how affects and the basic emotions might best be distinguished. Many needless controversies could be short-circuited if we recognize that the question of emotionality is not totally isomorphic with the question of affective states. I would reserve the concept of bona fide *emotions* for those affect laden brain systems which, by their command circuit design, bring a variety of brain functions into rapid coherence to generate coordinated behavioral, physiological, and hormonal states. On the other hand, the *affects* constitute a much broader set of brain states which may be generated by 1) all sensory systems which detect major homeostatic imbalances (yielding a large array of negative affective states such as hunger, thirst, cold, pain, tiredness etc.), as well as by 2) reafferent sensory systems which are activated by effective consummatory behaviors which alleviate the homeostatic imbalances (leading to pleasurable sensations such as taste, sexual eroticism, warmth, etc.), as well as, of course, by 3) activity in emotive command systems of the brain. Although bona fide emotive systems do generate distinct feeling states (which surely need to be studied more fully, especially at the introspective/cognitive level), the conceptual segregation of *affective* and *emotive* processes is essential to make sense of the field. If emotionality is too closely linked to the mere presence of affective "feelings", progress toward an understanding of key neurobiological issues will continue to be hampered.

At present, the study of emotive processes in the animal brain is much easier than the study of affective states, because the behavioral reflections are more clear-cut. However, it is possible that the generation of affect in the brain is also more straightforward than it appears. Certainly at the broad functional level, pleasure is a property of external stimuli which help sustain life, while feelings of aversion arise from stimuli which tend to be incompatible with survival. In the simplest brain scenario, it may turn out that the affective properties of various stimuli funnel into a few, perhaps just two, primary affective processes - generalized pleasure (such as might be mediated by brain opioids and/or dopamine) and generalized aversion (perhaps by anti-opioids and anti-dopaminergics) - with the multitude of apparent distinctions being the result of non-affective sensory details. Unfortunately, it is too early to tell whether the nervous system is really organized on that simple an affective plan. If it is, we might continue to anticipate, as has traditionally been done in the past, that some major psychiatric disorders are integrally linked to deficits in such primary processes (e.g., depression and the anhedonia of schizophrenia). At present, there is simply not enough clear and indisputable evidence to resolve the matter. In any event, if it does turn out that there are only two primary affective processes in the brain upon which all hedonic experiences rely, then it still remains likely that a large number of different transmitters feed into those systems conveying distinct types of information from various discrete homeostatic and sensory feedbacks.

Executive Emotive Circuits of the Brain

Reasonable psychobiological evidence exists for the existence of four or five primary emotive command circuits in the brain. Since the semantic labeling of such circuits with affective terms is surely problematic, I typically refer to them with multiple labels: 1) the foraging-expectancy-curiosity-investigatory system, 2) the anger-rage circuit, 3) the anxiety-fear circuit, 4) the separation distress-sorrow-anguish-panic circuit, and presently I would also include as a primal emotive system 5) social-play circuitry (Panksepp, Normansell & Siviy, 1984) which may not only be a major source of *joy* but also a primal force in the development of courage, social dominance and sociosexual competence (in other words, the executive circuit which may have evolved to help fit a social organism into the social structure in which it must live). I do not include other common human feelings which appear in modern "human" taxonomies - such as acceptance, disgust, contempt, shame and surprise - in the primal list for two main reasons: 1) There is yet no evidence that these processes are mediated by the distinct types of executive systems envisaged herein. Most of them (acceptance, contempt and shame) are probably secondary emotional processes which emerge, at least in part, as learned reflections of the primary systems (e.g., see Helen Block Lewis chapter). For instance, "acceptance" may be a cognitive reflection of social bonding which at the primary level is mediated by separation distress/panic and play mechanisms. 2) If the above affects are included as basic emotions, it is not clear on what basis a vast array of other human feelings (e.g., shyness, guilt, envy, jealousy, lust, hunger, thirst, cold, pain, boredom, frustration, distain, etc.) are to be excluded. Thus, the issue is not whether surprise, disgust and the other processes which have been deemed to be primary emotions have distinct feelings, but whether they are constructed on the same general *design principles* in the nervous system as the bona fide primary emotions. In short, the position taken is that the concept of basic emotion is best restricted to those primary emotive processes which appear to be constructed on a command system design, and those systems, it is assumed, are the basic psychoneural substrates from which the major emotional disorders arise.

There may be additional primary emotive systems than I have not listed, but in order to accept others as primary, they must be supported by hard evidence concerning distinct *neural* as opposed to just psychobehavioral markers. From such a perspective one could argue that "disgust" and "surprise" should be deemed to be primary emotions. If one accepts assumptions concerning the continuity of startle and surprise, one could utilize the rigorous neural data on the startle reflex (Davis, 1980) as a basis for adding "surprise" to the list of basic emotions. As outlined before, I believe there are cogent reasons to not include startle-surprise, nor disgust, as primary emotions (Panksepp, 1982, 1986). Of course, that in no way diminishes the importance of studying the neural underpinnings of these brain functions, and exploiting the properties of those systems to understand bona fide emotions (e.g., such as fear through the potentiated-startle response, as is being pursued by Davis and colleagues). Although there appear to be no major psychiatric disorders in western

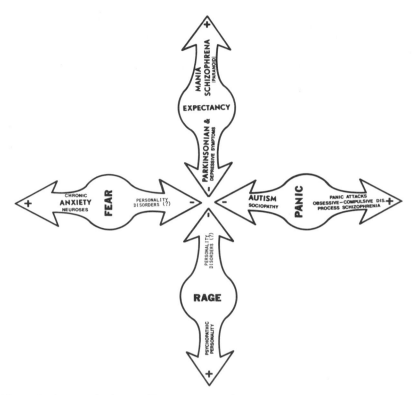

Figure 2: A general scheme of how major psychopathologies may be related to brain
emotional systems (Adapted from Panksepp, 1982).

diagnostic practice which reflect overresponsivity of startle and disgust circuits, it is
noteworthy that some societies do regard excessive startle, such as the *Latha* syndrome, to be a distinct psychic disorder (Friedmann, 1982). However, considering the
fact that the startle reflex is most commonly followed by fear, the Latha-type disorders
may in fact be special cases of anxiety neurosis.

     Sexual feelings raise other critical issues for any taxonomy of basic emotive
systems. Although it needs no emphasis that sexuality is accompanied by powerful
affective states and may be a main factor in the genesis of psychopathologies (as Freud
chose to emphasize), there is no clear neural evidence that the emotive impulse for
sexuality - the solicitive behaviors and the seeking of sexual interaction, namely the
appetitive phase of sexuality - is organized by a brain system uniquely devoted to
sexuality. These functions seem to be elaborated by several generalized emotive
systems in the brain (which I have called the "expectancy/foraging" and "social play"
systems). On the other hand, the consummatory/pleasure phase of sexual activity obviously has distinct and specific behavioral mechanisms for achieving union which
are hormonally primed. Thus, it is my contention that the emotive aspect of sexuality
is mediated by a nonspecific brain system which is utilized for all positively motivated
appetitive behaviors, and that the distinct affective states of sexuality emerge not from
the direct activity of a primary emotive system, but rather *from sensory systems which*

instigate the appetitive behavior as well as *from the reafferent processes linked to the consummatory phase of the behavior*. Of course, the absence of a primary executive system for the emotive impulse of sexuality does not mean that psychiatric disorders cannot be strongly related to issues of sexual adjustment. Some surely are, if for no other reason than cultural strictures which seek to control the "economics" of reproduction and the "ethics" of idle pleasure.

My point is that many distinct motivations may operate through a single emotive system. Thus, all of the specific positively motivated behaviors exhibited by animals (e.g., thermoregulation, feeding, drinking, salt-appetite, hoarding, predation, sexuality, maternal behavior, shelter-seeking - each accompanied by distinct affective states), are actualized to a substantial extent by a powerful shared brain mechanism - a foraging-expectancy command system which provides the primal impulse for an animal to move from where it is to where it must be to acquire materials or interactions needed for survival. In its general role of governing goal-directed activities related to positive incentives and the consequent expectancies, I would imagine that this system is especially influential in extracting positive meaning from the environment and generating hypotheses and connections about the world (which suggests how deranged processing in this system may lead to symptoms subsumed by the concept of schizophrenia).

The vast animal literature on which these ideas are based has been summarized before (Panksepp, 1971, 1981, 1982, 1985, 1986), and the aim of this chapter is to explore how our knowledge of such emotive brain systems may be related to major psychopathologies. A general conceptual scheme was presented several years ago (Fig. 2) and at the end of this chapter I plan to expand on that idea. Before proceeding to those clinical issues, however, I would cover several additional general issues concerning the neural basis of emotionality, from a slightly different vantage. To help embed the present thinking in a broad context, I would 1) briefly trace some *very general* historical threads in the study of how the brain elaborates emotions; 2) provide a general overview of how emotive systems may be best conceptualized at a general brain biocomputer level, and finally, to 3) provide a perspective on how recent developments concerning the neurochemical etiologies of psychopathologies may relate to our understanding of primary emotive systems of the brain.

A Modest Historical Perspective

The perspective of ancient scholars was that emotions emerge from the body while reason emanated from the brain. This has turned out to be fundamentally incorrect, but not without heuristic value. Indeed, the reason we feel emotions in our viscera may be as much through intrinsic generation of activities within the visceral homunculi of our limbic brains than directly via sensory impressions arising from the gut. But modern neuroscience has also revealed a complex peripheral enteric nervous system (Gershon, 1981) that guides the intrinsic movement of the viscera, which may secrete chemistries which feed back onto the brain. In addition, the immune system can interact with the CNS (Rossi, 1986; and also see chapter by Melnechuk in this volume). To what extent these systems provide reafferent control over the tone of emotive circuits in the brain remains to be seen, but it can be anticipated that the influence of the body on the experience of emotionality may be substantial.

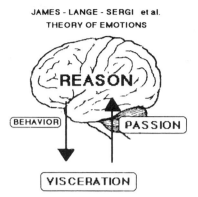

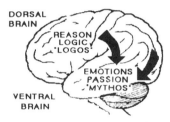

Figure 3. An overview of the James-Lange theory which is the historical precursor of the cognitive-constructivist theories of today (top) and the psychobiological conception of how emotions are organized in brain (bottom)

The next major historical landmark - the James-Lange-Sergi theory (Fig. 3, top) - suggested that the reasoning brain perceives emotions by viewing the peripheral visceral commotion caused by excited/emergency behavior patterns. Indeed, there are peripheral feedbacks, both somatic and visceral, that can modulate tone in emotional circuits (e.g., see Mancia and Zanchetti, 1981; Parkinson, 1985) and the intensity of certain emotional feelings can be reduced by spinal cord injuries (Hohmann, 1966), but there is still no clear and credible evidence that the James-Lange perspective encapsulated the key truth regarding the organization of emotive processes in the brain. It is remarkable how long the theory has survived in the absence of a substantial data base, and how lively it remains (especially in cognitive circles) even in the face of emerging knowledge about the visceral brain (an entity unknown at the turn of the century).

Functional neuroscience has convincingly revealed that the neurological substrates of emotionality reside in primitive ventromedial areas of the brain (Fig. 3, bottom). At the most general level, neural understanding of emotionality requires a distinction between functions of the ventral and dorsal brain. Emotionality is largely an intrinsic function of the ventral brain, as encapsulated in the the broad concept of the limbic system (MacLean, 1973; 1985). The dichotomy between the visceral brain, which elaborates self-preservative internal processes (including emotions), and the somatic brain, which handles information from the external world, is a simplification, but no mere metaphor. It is a biological reality supportable in terms of neurophysiological, neurochemical and functional data. Both the somatic and visceral brain funnel and blend their information through the third layer of MacLean's triune brain - the "reptilian" basal ganglia - which coordinates the patterned motor outflow. Had such knowledge been available to investigators at the turn of the century, it seems the James-Lange theory may have been recast in terms of higher brain processes influencing subcortical emotive circuits, readily explaining how cognitions come to trigger emotions (Figure 1). Since the visceral-limbic brain evolved earlier than the cortex, the higher perceptions should clearly be viewed as permissive and provocative, rather than essential, agents in the genesis of emotions.

Of course, emotions are multidimensional, and all approaches described above contribute to our understanding of emotionality. The assertion here is simply that emotional command circuits of the visceral brain appear to be the "centers of gravity" around which the other emotive processes revolve. There is abundant evidence indicating that primary emotional affects emerge from these visceral neural substrates, and I would briefly summarize the historical roots for the cognitive neodualism which presently characterizes psychology, and which, as I have already argued, continues to retard our understanding of the basic nature of emotionality.

On the General Organization of Emotions

Psychology has been haunted by mind/body dualism since its inception. And many controversies in the field emerge from the different perspectives of the various historical foundations of the field. Psychology's roots go back to both philosophic and biomedical traditions (Fig. 4), a schizm that was initiated by Descartes' dichotomy between the many functions of the brain which could be given mechanistic explanations (including *imagination, memory and the passions*) from that which could not (namely *reason*). The ensuing philosophic tradition, which focussed on reason, led nonbiologically oriented cognitivists to view brain function in terms of information flow through unarticulated computational networks (a *tabula rasa*), while those from the biomedical tradition sought to localize primal processes within the landscape of the brain - ultimately in neurochemically defined circuits. In computer terminology, the former viewpoint leads one to think of the brain as a massive random access memory (RAM), while the other leads one to view it as an ensemble of read only memories (ROMs) - the two key components of the modern digital computer. This computer analogy for the brain, though not precise, highlights a key controversy: While the cognitive perspective views emotions as RAM mediated mechanisms derived through sociocultural learning, the biological view is that emotions arise from genetically-ordained ROM processes. On the basis of available evidence, I have already argued that some variant of the biologic view must prevail, but I would again emphasize how readily it can interface with a cognitive view (Fig. 1).

To stretch the analogy a bit further, basic emotions, viewed as genetically ordained ROM-based operating systems (shared in basically homologous forms in all mammals), may set limits to the types of software programming that can be elaborated in RAM-like neural space. It must be re-emphasized, however, that to the best

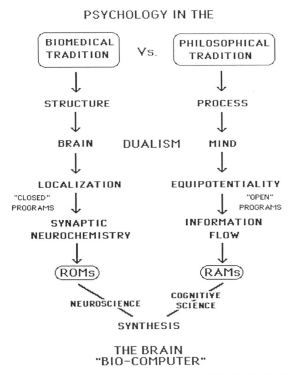

Figure 4. A historical synopsis of the causes and solutions of dualistic thinking in psychology during the past century.

of our knowledge, no part of the brain is truly analogous to the type of RAM space that one finds in digital computers. Although the construction of cortical columns does have some resemblance to generalized memory chips, all multimodal association cortices of the brain do have biological restrictions to the types of information they can organize (perhaps largely because of afferent connectivities, but also perhaps because of other intrinsic circuit restraints). For instance, the most highly evolved association cortex - that which subserves language functions in the human brain - is not just a tabula rasa but functionally specialized for elaboration of linguistic skills. Indeed, many cortical areas may have intrinsic ROM-like perceptual capacities for the initiation of activity in subcortical emotional circuits, such as the ability of the temporal lobe to instigate anger and fear, the cingulate cortex to generate panic, and the frontal cortex to elaborate plans and expectancies (Panksepp, 1985; 1986).

Figure 5. The Classical View of Major Personality Variables
(From Zentralbibliothek Zurich)

Conversely, emotive ROMs are surely not immutable, but capable of being molded and dynamically constrained by the life experiences of an organism - to yield environmentally facilitated changes in neural circuits which control temperament, personality and emotional health. With such restrictions in mind, it seems that emotional ROMs are constituted of long-axoned circuits in which the perikarya are situated subcortically. Through their wide axonal ramifications as well as via indirect multi-synaptic effects (and perhaps via vascular, ventricular, and paracrine channels), emotive command circuits are envisioned to influence many functional sub-routines in the brain, and to provide substantial control and coordination over what happens in RAM space. Conversely, with maturation, some of the software programs of RAM space may eventually exert modulatory control over ROM processes, but when this happens, there is no reason to believe that the fundamental force and source of emotionality has been shifted away from the activity of the primary emotive circuits.

In sum, if basic emotions can be adequately conceptualized as subcortical ROM processes, then their scientific understanding (i.e., at least at the proximal level) requires substantial direct analysis of the underlying brain systems. The conception that emotionality emerges from pre-wired but experientially-honed circuits of the mammalian brain, is a view consistent with major non-neural theories of emotions as proposed by Buck (1985), Izard (1977), and Plutchik (1980). My aim for the rest of this chapter is to summarize how the present conception of primary emotionality, as the activity of specific subcortical emotive circuits, might relate to traditional psychopathological categories. It would be attractive if we could relate modern conceptions of psychopathology and personality with classical thinking on the topic (e.g., Figure 5).

The Major Psychopathologies and Brain Emotive Systems

I find it gratifying that modern brain research is revealing basic emotional circuits which correspond at least in a general way with the classic temperaments: the *melancholic* personality reflecting excessive saddness emerging perhaps from chronic overactivity of the separation-distress/panic system; the *sanguine* personality exhibiting extreme joy for life emanating from activities of self-stimulation/expectancy and play circuits; the *choleric* personality may be unduly swayed by the responsivity of their anger-rage circuits; and the coldness of the *phlegmatic* may reflect the general lack of positive emotionality emerging from excessive anxiety and fear. Such a match-up between twentieth century brain research and the intuitive insights of ancient scholars, imperfect as it may be, lends credence to the conclusion that a limited number of emotive systems may guide the development of personality.

My aim for this section is to discuss how our knowledge of the emotive circuits in the brain may relate to modern diagnostic categories for the major psychopathologies. These ideas are theoretical and provisional, but I believe that the primary emotive processes of the brain, once adequately understood, will provide a natural scheme by which taxonomies of psychiatric disorders could be arranged. I will discuss the basic emotive systems in an order which may reflect their sequence of importance in clinical practice--fear, panic, expectancy, rage and play. First, however, I will focus on depression, the syndrome which appears to be caused, in part, by the brain's inability to elaborate pleasurable affect.

A)   Disorders of Affect: Pleasure Deficits and Depression

Since several fine monographs have recently summarized the impressive literature on the psychobiology of depression (Whybrow, Akiskal & McKinnery, 1985;
Willner, 1985), I will not devote much time to affective disorders here. Also, there is
no evidence that depression or mania emerge from an imbalance of distinct emotive
systems, as conceptualized here. These disorders appear to be linked more to systems
which control overall levels of mood and brain functioning. Imbalanced biogenic
amine activity appears to be at the root of affective disorders, and those systems
(especially norepinephrine and serotonin) appear to provide very generalized affec-
tive/arousal control over all major emotional ROMs in the brain (Panksepp, 1986).
While the biogenic amine deficit theories of depression remain a major force in the
field, recent approaches show promise in dealing with the remaining empirical gaps.
For instance, the slow time-course of antidepressant therapies may be due to gradual
changes in the sensitivities of post-synaptic membranes (Stone, 1983).

Although everyone agrees that the underlying causes of depression remain to be
identified, it is gratifying that a core brain system has been discovered, the corticotropin release factor (CRF) circuits, which could be a key ingredient in mediating the
stressful events which eventually snowball into depression. The activity of the CRF
system can be restrained by brain norepinephrine (NE) activity (Feldman, 1985), and
it is clear that brain NE systems can be drained by stress. (Anisman, 1978; Stone, 1983).
Part of this depletion may be due to CRF innervation of amine cell groups such as the
locus-coeruleus (Swanson, et al., 1983). One can envision this reciprocal relationship
gradually falling out of balance during prolonged stress. As norepinephrine is
depleted, and no longer exerts a homeostatic restraining influence over the stress
facilitating CRF systems, a vicious cycle could be established whereby the pro-stress
effects of CRF prevail. This raises the possibility that new drugs which would block
CRF receptors could be powerful therapeutic tools in treating "burn-out" and potentially preventing the neural instabilities which lead to certain forms of endogenous
depression and to post-traumatic stress syndromes. If the system is organized in this
way, timely biochemical intervention within the CRF-NE cylce might increase the
success of concurrent psychotherapies.

Especially important from the emotional command system perspective is the
possiblity that certain emotions, such as separation distress/panic, operate directly
via CRF transmission (vide infra). If so, that would establish a mechanistic link to the
established relationship between prolonged separation distress and the development
of depression.

B)   Disorder of the Fear/Anxiety System

Disorders of trepidation may arise from several distinct brain systems, and one,
the fear system, appears to be uniquely designed to respond to emergency situations
which threaten the life of an organism. At primitive levels of organization, it is
probably driven by pain and at higher levels, by the perceived threat of pain and
destruction. The unconditional manifestations of the system yield terrified flight,
while in its conditional/cognitive mode, it probably promotes the opponent process
of flight, namely immobility and freezing. Fear/flight behaviors can be evoked from

widespread areas of upper brain stem and related limbic areas, and it is reasonable to hypothesize that the underlying circuit is the primal, core system which mediates specific phobic anxieties as well as diffuse chronic anxiety neuroses. The higher perceptual mechanisms which may feed into this circuit probably emanate, to some extent, from lateral temporal lobes and amygdala. An alternative neural viewpoint, focussing on the septal-hippocampal system, has been discussed by Gray (1982).

Stated quite simply, the present theoretical perspective is that the genesis of phobias and and anxiety neuroses is largely the consequence of excessive activity of trans-diencephalic brain fear circuits. Free floating anxiety occurs, presumably, when these circuits become endogenously overactive. Specific phobias and neuroses may reflect associative processes whereby neutral stimuli develop strong interactions with these unconditional fear substrates. If we knew the neurochemcal linkages by which such associations are established, we should be able to devise pharmacological strategies to reduce the incidence of maladaptive linkages, or to facilitate their dissolution once formed.

Although there are practically no pertinent clinical or psychobiological data which bear upon the above scenarios, it is clear that the various drugs which alleviate anxiety, including benzodiazepines and alcohol, have direct effects on the transhypothalamic fear/flight circuitry (Bovier, Broekkamp and Lloyd, 1982; Brandao, de Aguiar and Graeff, 1982; Moriyama, Ichimaru and Gomita, 1984; Panksepp, Gandelman & Trowill, 1971). Furthermore, direct facilitation of GABA activity reduces such fear behaviors (Brandao, DiScala, Bouchet and Schmitt, 1986), and it presently seems evident that antianxiety agents work indirectly by facilitation of GABA transmission (Tallman and Gallager, 1985). The brain also contains peptides such as Diazepam Binding Inhibitor, which promote activity in the system (Ferrero, Guidotti, Conti-Tronconi & Costa, 1984). The throughput transmitter for fear is not conclusively known, but several peptides could be considered reasonable candidates, including vassopressin, alpha-MSH, and CRF. Further, the ability of cholinergics to promote fear/flight like states implicate acetylcholine as a possible command transmitter (for more complete review of the brain-fear literature see Panksepp, 1988,1989).

Considering the likelihood that this system is an essential ingredient in human phobic and anxiety disorders, it is remarkable how little basic work has been done on the fear/flight system. This probably reflects the assumption that this circuit may simply control motor output, since available evidence suggests that animals do not readily learn to avoid brain stimulation which yields fear/flight. I suspect the failure in avoidance reflects other factors than the presumed absence of affect, such as the difficulty of relating internal fear states to external cues when there are no major environmental changes to which the fear might be attributed. In any event, we feel confident that such stimulation does actually produce a real feeling state, for in recent work we have found that the basic reflection of fear conditioning, namely freezing behavior, readily elaborates to environmental cues in which rats received brain stimulation which elicits flight (Sacks & Panksepp, 1987). I would suggest that the careful study of the underlying neural circuits should elucidate basic facts which may be useful for development of new therapeutic approaches. I find it perplexing that so little basic work is being conducted to understand the anatomical, biochemical and functional properties of this system, for the implications of such knowledge for fundamental understanding of anxiety states should be far-reaching. For instance, considering the fact that the final major step in quelling activity in fear/anxiety circuits is GABA, one might envision the development of amino acid precursor strategies for combatting anxiety, such as dietary administration of glutamine or perhaps even GABA itself (if enough can be coaxed to enter the areas of the brain where fear circuits course).

C)   Disorders of the Separation-Distress/Panic System

Even less work has been done on brain systems which mediate separation distress than fear, but I am especially willing to speculate about the clinical implications of such circuits since much of existing work has come from our own laboratory and because derangements in social emotions seem to be at the root of so many psychiatric disturbances. The basic-science aspects of our work has been reviewed several times (Panksepp, Herman, Vilberg, Bishop & DeEskinazi, 1980; Panksepp, 1981; Panksepp, Siviy & Normansell, 1985; Panksepp, 1986; Panksepp, Normansell, Herman, Bishop & Crepeau, 1988), and I will not repeat that material here, except to indicate that our guiding idea has been that there are basic neurophysiological similarities between separation distress and opiate-withdrawal processes. We now know that that idea is more than a research-guiding analogy. Our data strongly affirm that endogenous brain opioids are a key system for the elaboration of social comfort (i.e., the system which alleviates separation distress). In addition to the obvious psychiatric implications, this suggests that a key psychodynamic reason for narcotic addiction may be the desire of people to increase social emotional homeostasis.

Although the neurochemical character of the throughput system for separation distress has not been definitively identified, our best estimate at the present time is that the core executive structure of the separation-distress response is confluent with the Corticotropin Release Factor (CRF) system of the brain. The anatomy of this circuit, as detailed in rats (Swanson, et al., 1983), matches our knowledge of the anatomy of the separation distress circuit remarkably well (for summary, see Panksepp, et al., 1988), and when CRF is applied intraventricularly to the brain of young chicks, they begin to distress vocalize for prolonged periods (up to 6 hrs following 1 ug) in the presence of social stimuli which normally inhibit DVs (Distress Vocalizations), (Panksepp, Crepeau & Clynes, 1987). Of course, the CRF system is also presently a prime candidate for a much more generalized stress system in the brain, and only future research can reveal which parts, if any, are uniquely devoted to elaborating the separation response. Also, other neurochemistries are important. For instance we can also turn on DVs by administering curare and glutamate receptor agonists into the brain (Panksepp et al., 1988). Accordingly, for present purposes we will simply talk about the separation-distress/panic system in a generic way without trying to specify possible neurochemical functions any further. Also it should be remembered that the emotional system which mediates crying does not react just to social cues, but also others such as hunger, cold and pain. With modern techniques, it should be possible to work out the various interactions in detail.

We believe the psychic force for the development of a variety of psychiatric disorders emanates from imbalances of this panic circuit. We believe, as does Klein (1981), that activity in the separation-distress circuit may be the trigger for agoraphobic panic-attacks, and as suggested by van der Kolk (1987) this system may also participates in the genesis of the post-traumatic stress syndrome. Furthermore, I would suggest that less precipitous chronic activity in this system (as well as perhaps synergistic input from fear systems) establishes the emotional motivation which can lead to the genesis of obsessive-compulsive symptoms as an instrumental maneuver to alleviate affect generating activity in the separation distress circuit. By the intrinsic ability of repetitive "consummatory" acts to reduce arousal of the system, a vicious cycle of undesiarable compulsive behaviors may be established.

There is now abundant literature indicating that people who experience these types of emotional disorders have had more frequent and more intense forms of childhood separation experiences than the general population (Faravelli, et al. 1985; Gittelman & Klein, 1985; Torgersen, 1986). This suggests that intense early activation of separation-distress circuitry may sensitize the system for heightened activity of the system during adulthood. It is clear that the sensitivity of this circuit diminishes markedly with maturation, as evidenced by the developmental decline in the frequency of separation DVs as all mammals grow older. Whether early experience retards this decline, or leaves stronger perceptual access routes to the circuit intact, is unknown, but could be evaluated in animal models. Likewise, it is possible that excessive separation distress during development may actually promote biochemical strengthening and neuronal proliferation of the circuit. If this system does, in fact, underlie such psychiatric disorders, then the neurobiological analysis of the circuit characteristics should be a top item in the scientific agenda of biological psychiatry.

Underactivity of the separation-distress system may also lead to psychiatric ailments characterized by diminished social affect and intent such as early childhood autism. Such underactivity could be caused by excessive activity of systems which normally inhibit panic circuitry, such as endogenous opioids - an idea which we have discussed previously (Panksepp, 1979, 1981; Panksepp & Sahley, 1987). Indeed, recent work from several laboratories suggests that opioid receptor blockade with naltrexone is effective in alleviating a variety of autistic symptoms (Campbell, et al., 1985; Herman, et al., 1986).

D)   Schizophrenia and the "Expectancy" System of the Brain

Although the surface symptoms of schizophrenia have been extensively described, there is no agreement on the deep psychological structure of the disorder(s). In its acute adult-onset form, it appears to be a disease of a primary reality-creating mechanism of the brain—a major imbalance of brain functions which normally coordinate and join cognitions and emotions into a harmonious whole. Unconscious powers gain ascendancy, and previously restrained mental "energies" become insistent. Although the cause of the disorder remains unknown (but some forms clearly have structural derangements (see Tyrer & Mackay, 1986)), there is a growing consensus that a final *common pathway* for at least one functional variant of the disorder is *excessive or aberrant information flow in one of the three major dopamine pathways of the brain*, the mesolimbic one which emanates largely from the ventral tegmental area of the midbrain and ascends to influence the ventral basal ganglia such as the nucleus accumbens, the amygdala, as well as the frontal cortex. The biochemical changes of this and other brain systems have been documented (Ferrier, et al., 1984). Schizophrenics typically have hightened levels of dopamine in the left temporal lobe (Reynolds, 1983) as well as proliferation of D-2 dopamine receptors in some areas of the brain (Wong, et al., 1986).

Perhaps the best available model of schizophrenia is the *crazed* self-stimulation behavior that animals exhibit for electrical current along the trajectory of ascending dopamine systems. Another potential feature of the animal work is that it can begin to address the deep psychobehavioral functions of these systems. Although psychobiology has demonstrated conclusively that this system mediates the initiation of various responses—curious exploratory behaviors, and the seeking of environmental incentives—the full subtlety of the functions of this system remain to be vigorously pursued. There is no unanimous aggreement about the major adaptive functions of the system (see Wise, 1982), but it presently seems that *brain dopamine activity provides a fundamental brain substrate for anticipatory eagerness* (both motoric and sensory-perceptual) which facilitates vigorous and effective goal-directed behaviors and which generates the mental invigoration to create new solutions to major adaptive challenges. When this system is normally active, the animal or person operates efficiently and with ease upon the problems it must solve in its search for optimal survival. When the system is underactive, as might occur in certain forms of Parkinson's disease and depression, the vigor of the foundation processes for spontaneous, "energetic" coping are compromised. When the system is excessively active, as occurs in certain functional schizophrenias, the system encourages the rest of the brain to reach for possibilities which do not exist in the real world, yielding the creative, suspicion-ridden turmoil of delusional crises. Cortical innervation by dopamine systems ascending from the mesencephalon is now known to be much more extensive than was originally thought (Lewis, Campbell, Foote, Goldstein and Morrison, 1987). From the perspective of psychogenic vectors which promote schizoid breaks, it is noteworthy that of the various dopamine systems, the meso-cortical limb of the meso-limbic system is especially sensitive to the effects of stress (Blanc, et al., 1980).

E)   The Rage System and the Sources of the Other Personality Disorders

A premise of the present paper is that the activities of the basic emotive systems of the brain are a major source of personality dimensions. The emotional imbalances which cause modest personal problems but which do not prevent an individual from operating in society are called personality disorders. Every emotive system probably contributes instances to this wastebasket category, but the anger/rage system stands out as a major contributor since it appears to have no unique relation to any major traditional psychiatric category.

Obviously, overactivity or oversensitivity of anger circuitry could be disasterous for the lives of afflicted individuals and the people around them. Although many features of aggression are learned, the core problem is the ability of the brain to feel anger and hence to become excessively defensive, paranoid, sensitive to insult, and trigger-happy. Such problems are often seen to be matters of character rather than matters of unstable neural circuitries, since people should be able to control their emotive impulses. However, we know little of how primary emotive circuit instabilities may emerge, and how persuasive their activities can be to the rest of the nervous system. *If one takes the abundant animal and sparse human brain-stimulation data, the psychic insistence of these circuits appears to be overwhelming.* Surely life events and frustrations can precipitate activity in the system, but there are also more insidiuous biological causes. There are genetic and hormonal dispositions, on top of which there may be physical irritations to the circuitry (e.g., tumors and epileptic foci), and possibly the effects of nutrient imbalances, as well as the overriding interplay of modulatory excitatory and inhibitory chemistries, such as of serotonin, norepinephrine and GABA. Although many drugs can alleviate aggressiveness, some merely by sedating, others by reducing impulsivity, and some apparently by specifically quelling anger (Flannelly, Muraoka, Blanchard & Blanchard, 1985; Olivier, 1981), our knowledge about basic controls and dynamics of the underlying circuits remains so poor that more intensive basic work is needed. Why such work is not being encouraged more earnestly by funding agencies is perplexing.

F) Derangements of Play Circuits

Less is known about this emotive circuit than any other. But considering that this system is as fundamental a part of brain emotive organization as any of the others (Panksepp, Siviy and Normansell, 1984), it is at least worth speculating what disorders may eventually be connected to this system. The most obvious ones are mania and other forms of impulse control. Clearly, the play system is designed to take a young organism onto the playing field of life with considerable energy and egotism - probably more than most adults can tolerate for long, especially in structured classroom situations. Maybe hyperkinesis/minimal-brain-disorder diagnoses biologically reflect, in part, the excessive activity of play circuits. This would be congruent with our animal data since stimulants which are prescribed to quiet such children are very effective in reducing rough and tumble play in animals, and parents often complain that the stimulant medications have drained the appealing childishness from their children. See Panksepp, Normansell, Cox, Crepeau, and Sacks (1987) for a review of the pharmacological literature on play.

Considering the value of play for the developing nervous systems, it is somewhat puzzling that the intrinsic reinforcements of this system have not been more efficaciously used in token-economies designed to promote behavioral change. If opportunities for recess and free play in schools were made contingent on "good" conduct, behavioral management in many situations might be vastly facilitated. Presently most systems use restriction-of-play as a punishment rather than opportunity-to-play as a reward, but perhaps any change in that traditional approach would be inconsistent with our cultural self-concept.

Another possible disorder which may have direct relations to activity in play circuits is the Gilles Tourette syndrome, which is characterized by a vast variety of bodily and verbal tics. (Abuzzahab, 1982). Many play sequences are characterized by staccato types of motor impulses, and perhaps it is not too far-fetched to suppose that some Tourette's tics may be manifestations of the underlying motor impulses of play. This might explain the urge to emit profanities in such children. After all, play seems designed to test the perimeters of one's knowledge, and surely social strictures constitute a barrier worthy of assult, especially among very playful children, whether consciously or subconsciously. Conversely, autism may be characterized, in part, by excessive neurochemical restriant over play circuitry, and our animal work suggests that autism could be caused or promoted by excessive activity of endogenous opioid systems (for summary of this work see Panksepp & Sahley, 1987 or Sahley &

Panksepp, 1987). As mentioned before, preliminary clinical trials with opiate receptor blocking agents have yielded positive results. If the therapeutic trend is confirmed, this may be the first example of how a neuro-theoretical analysis of emotional systems in the animal brain can yield effective pharmacological approaches for psychiatric practice.

I am convinced that such neuro-theoretical perspectives may take us closer to the deep functional nature of various psychiatric disorders than any other approach available at the present time. This, of course, may seem like a remarkable assertion when most of Neuroscience still holds the bias that concepts as fuzzy as emotions can not be rigorously probed by the brain sciences, and probably should be ignored in preference to a theory-free analysis of behavioral controls.

Peptide Systems and Psychopathologies

If most psychiatric disorders are ultimately the result of neurochemical imbalances of basic emotional systems, then little progress can be made in understanding the causes of such disorders without a clear knowledge of the neurochemical character of the underlying systems. At present, the rapidly developing knowledge of brain peptide systems holds considerable promise of providing the basic substrates from which emotions and affects are constructed. *It is possible the chemical coding of intrinsic psychobehavioral functions (the instinctual ROMs), including the basic emotions, may be largely constituted from such circuits.* Although we cannot yet be certain that the next round of chemo-phrenology (the search for neurochemical codes of behavior) will be any more successful than the last, the peptide systems have enough intrinsic resolution to elaborate such information. If so, many psychiatric disorders may turn out to be fundamentally neuropeptide disorders. At present, there is considerable speculation along these lines, but very little concrete information. Only one integrative idea is guiding research: The peripheral and central functions of peptides may be related, and hence the known peripheral functions can be used to guide the analysis of central functions (for a more extensive discussion of these issues see Panksepp, 1986).

The neuropsychiatric literature concerning possible dysfunctions is growing (van Ree and Matthysee, 1986), and at present the most promising lines of research appear to be related to schizophrenic disorders, largely because we have an excellent candidate substrate for a final common pathway (the mesolimbic/mesocortical dopamine system arising from the ventral tegmental area). Basic anatomical work has revealed not only the co-localization of peptides such as choleosystokin in dopamine neurons, but also a convergence of a large number of peptides which can promote activity in these dopamine cells, such as neurotensin, Substance P, and endogenous opioids (for review see Kalivas, 1985). Derangements in any of these systems could lead to schizoid disorders, and there is direct biochemical evidence for dysregulation in cholecysokinin and neurotensin systems (Nemeroff and Prange, 1982; Vanderhaeghen and Crawley, 1985). Although the literature in the peptide/psychopathology area remains preliminary and messy, it is especially important to emphasize, in the present context, that the proper analysis of these systems will require deliberate cultivation of animal brain research which invests in ethological approaches to studying behavior.

Since most neuropeptide systems cannot be studied via the use of peripheral pharamcological maneuvers, and since most peptides do not enter the brain following systemic injections, central administration studies in animals appear to be the major avenue via which the functions of the systems must be unravelled. It is unlikely that we will learn much about the functions of these systems unless we devote considerable efforts to observing the *natural* behaviors of animals in a large variety of situations. Considering the potential importance of such work to understanding psychological disorders, it would seem that such research could become a major basic-science research area for clinical psychology. Although there is great optimism in this field, whether the peptides will, in fact, prove to be the primal substrates for emotionality remains to be empirically demonstrated. The only peptide we can have considerable assurance about at the present time is CRF, as described above, although many of the others appear very promising on the basis of preliminary data.

Hemispheric Specialization and the Emotions

The functions of the dorsal (rational) and ventral (emotional) brain are not as readily addressed in human research as the functions of the hemispheres which can be directly accessed, explaining the popularity of that level of analysis. As summarized in Fig. 6, emotionality has been deemed to be one of the functional specializations of the hemispheres.

At first it seemed that the right hemisphere is generally *more* emotional and less analytical than the left hemisphere, but additional work suggested that perhaps the right hemisphere was a specialist in negative emotions while the left hemisphere focussed more on the positive affective side of life (for review see Heilman & Satz, 1983). This would explain why patients would often neglect right hemisphere strokes while having emotionally catastrophic responses to comparable left hemisphere infractions. Although it seems evident that the emotional communication, both expressive and receptive, is more impaired after right than left hemisphere damage (Ross, 1984), the positive-negative emotional dichotomy for left vs right hemispheres presently seems too simplistic. For instance, on an affective continuum, patients with left anterior cortical damage exhibit more depressive symptoms than those with comparable right frontal damage, while those with right posterior damage exhibit more despair than those with comparable damage on the left side (Robinson, et al., 1984). In general, the literature on the topic remains quite variable, weak and hard to replicate. Current evidence and thinking in the field will soon be summarized in a forthcoming supplemental edition of *Experimental Brain Research*, which summarizes work presented at the Giuseppe Moruzzi memorial symposium on "Emotions and Hemispheric Specialization" held in Rome, November 1986.

Rather than trying to do justice to the growing literature in the area, my intent for this section is to focus on the possiblity of using lateralized facial expression as an objective measure of the emotional status and responsivity of an individual. Many experiments have analysed the tendencies of the right and left halves of the human face to express emotions. As summarized elsewhere (Bryden & Ley, 1983; Overman & Doty, 1982), impressive results have been obtained with split-image techniques where full-facial composites are constructed of the right and left halves of the face. Intially this type of work suggested that the right side of the face could smile more

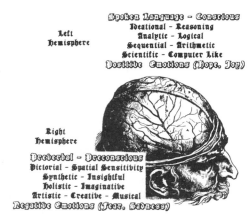

Figure 6. An overview of putative hemispheric specializations.

readily, but latter work suggested that may only be the case for social smiles and not necessarily for spontaneous "real" smiles. I have tried to replicate these phenomena several times with mixed success, as have others (for summary see Borod, Koff & Buck, 1986).

Summarzied in Fig. 7 are my personal renditions of six feelings which are widely deemed to be primary emotions (taped, digitized, computer rotated/connected and depicted via dot-matrix printer), and this type of technology will be essential to eliminate the many confoundings that can exist in this type of research (i.e., influences of lighting and face shadowing, natural head asymmetries, hair styles, choice of still poses from a dynamic movement pattern). In constructing such materials and collecting such data, I have been struck by several consistent patterns that speak to the issue of what are the primary emotions. While anger, happiness, saddness and fear do exhibit substantial variability in the specific details of expression among individuals, I am convinced that they appear to fall into homogeneous expressive categories, while requests to express surprise and disgust do not. For instance, as is clear from Fig. 7c, my voluntary surprise face had a strong component of "fear-like" affect to it, (which I believe is the ethologically correct, cross-species surprise response) but among the majority of my students, the main affect conveyed has been the type of "joyful-surprise" summarized in Fig. 8a (which I think is the more common social-construction of surprise in our society). Usually, this socially-constructed surprise also was generated in two distinct phases, with an initial quite happy surprise followed by a spurt-like intensification of the gesture.

Similarly, when my students have generated "disgust," two qualitatively distinct patterns have emerged. About half the people generate, as I did (Fig. 7g), a face that one might make if they had stepped in fresh dog droppings. Others (more frequently females) have generated a different, asymmetric face which conveys to most people the feeling of social disgust which, in a word, might be described as "scorn" (Fig. 8b). The social disgust usually takes the form of an asymmetric movement of the face while sensory disgust is more symmetrical. This dichotomous pattern suggests that there is

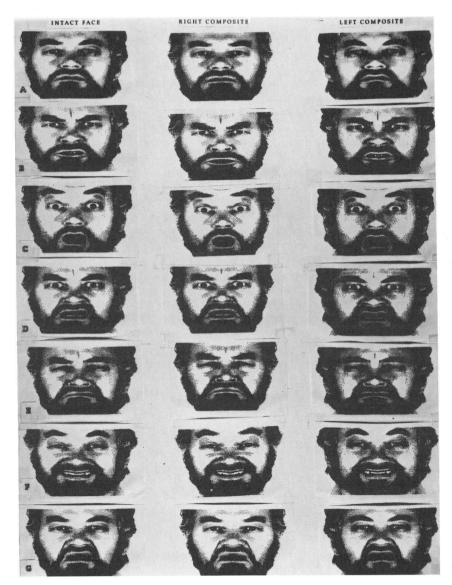

Figure 7. The author's voluntary renditions of the following emotions: A) neutral, B) angry, C) suprise, D) fear, E) sorrow, F) joy, and G) disgust.
Right and left face composites were constructed via computer.

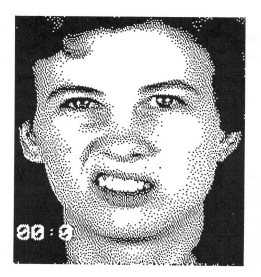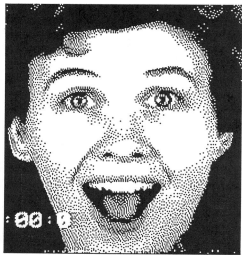

Figure 8. Expressions which I consider to be socially-constructed surprise (right) and socially-constructed disgust (left). Faces were taped from the same distance, but difference in size indicates that one pulls backward during the emission of disgust but moves foreward during emission of surprise. These faces are being shared, with consent, by Kathy Morris.

considerable intrinsic ambiguity in the concepts of surprise and disgust, and hence they may not represent primary process emotions which emerge from an intrinsic command system.

What is especially intriguing about facial analysis, however, is the possibility that if basic methodological and analytical techniques are developed further, we may be able to construct direct measures of affective "trait" responsivity of individuals. At present all we have are verbal/cognitive/affective tests (as summarized by Greenberg & Pinsof, 1986), and it would be desirable to have psychometric tests which are designed to tap activities of the primary emotive systems as directly as possible. It is noteworthy that Spielberger (1979; 1985), for his State-Trait Personality Inventory (STPI), has generated evaluative tests for three of the five affective processes which are herein deemed to be fundamental emotions - the anger (rage), anxiety (fear) and curiosity (expectancy) scales. What seems to be need now are sorrow/panic and play scales to make that system complete. I am still willing to hold out the hope that the human face (despite its exquisite ability to deceive) may be willing to reveal some of the underlying secrets of "the heart" directly. Although everyone realizes, all too well, how deceptive one's face can be, enough methodological approaches remain to be explored before we should become disillusioned with this "new physiognomy". I suspect that dynamic facial analysis, carefully employed, could yield remarkable dividends for both the diagnosis of underlying emotional turmoil as well as prognostic indicators of therapeutic outcome. Such techniques may be especially efficacious for evaluating the emotional traits of older people, in whose faces time has more permanently carved each person's emotional personality. Perhaps it is true that "you have the face you deserve by the time you reach forty." The new video and image-analysis technologies should set the area of facial analysis onto fruitful paths that may be able to capture the manifestations of both normal and abnormal activities of the deep emotive circuits of the brain. Of course, whether this new round of physiognomy will be more fruitful than the last remains to be seen.

Concluding Remarks and a Therapeutic Note

Although I have focussed on the primary emotive processes of the mammalian brain, humans surely have additional layers of intrinsic emotive organization above the primary process level. For instance, shyness, jealousy, shame, guilt, social disgust, distain, awe and many other emotive states may be special-purpose outgrowths of the more primal systems--systems which are especially sensitive to being molded by social learning. Unfortunately, except for introspective evidence from neurological patients, there is presently little chance of studying such processes at the neurobiological level. For such reasons, the animal psychobiological analysis of primary process emotionality should remain minimalist, focussing its resources on the lowest level of analysis which has the most objective behavioral referents. However, some intermediary types of emotive processes, such as "greed", may be capable of being analysed in animals through the use of concrete behavioral measures such as "possessive pivoting" (e.g., the tendency of one animal to keep a desired resource away from other animals by turning away when others approach).

On top of these higher-order intrinsic emotive processes of the brain, which may be elaborated in distinct paleocortical brain areas, there are surely many cultural emotional constructions in humans which may be almost completely learned. Such tendencies greatly amplify the diversity of experiences and expressions which characterize different cultures, but it is a mistake to assume that the vast cultural plumage reflects the basic nature of emotionality. Since it is so difficult for cognitive psychology to sift intrinsic from derivative emotive processes, I believe the neurophenomenological evidence should be used as the foundation for all other levels of analysis. Conversely, knowledge derived from human subjective experience needs to be used more insightfully to guide our functional analysis of the animal brain. To this end, it will be essential for the clinical disciplines to not only remain open to advances in neuroscience, but also to develop more forthright and subtle techniques for studying human psyche and behavior. Techniques which may be especially efficacious are ones which focus on natural behaviors and non-verbal communication as opposed to linguistic responses. The International Society for Human Ethology has now been established, and may be a major force in promoting such work. Also, it is gratifying that productive research on nonverbal communication in clinical contexts has been recently implemented (see Blanck, Buck and Rosenthal, 1986).

In this complex area of human knowledge, we need to build a cohesive structure. At present some ongoing theoretical battles resemble squabbling between members of different sects who have their own myths to uphold. Verbal battles are unlikely to take us to the "truth" about the underlying issues. Only clear and replicable results can do that. For me, the most important *major* result in the field is the ability of brain stimulation to produce emotive states and behaviors. For that reason, I continue to use such data as the major basis of my own thinking about the basic issues.

Perhaps the most serious casualty of the vacuum of research in the area has been the quality of clinical application. The psychotherapeutic enterprise needs to deal forthrightly with the basic nature of emotions; it needs to foster and to keep an eye on basic science developments in the area; it needs to maintain its therapeutic flexibility in the absence of solid knowledge. Although the prevailing ignorance is fertile ground for the sprouting of polarized "schools of thought", clinical practice needs to actively instill open attitudes and flexibility amongst its practitioners, as opposed to being guided by the fear that it will be stigmatized if it cultivates new non-verbal therapies. It is likely that many approaches, some of which are presently actively avoided, could be useful in controlling emotional distress and facilitating cognitive adjustments. When one is dealing with a neurally and psychologically hidden process such as primary-process emotionality, it seems that a multi-modal perspective (Fig. 9) should be foremost in each practitioner's mind. In addition to promoting new cognitive perspectives and living skills, psychotherapies must also seek to rebalance emotional turmoil at a primary process level. It seems to me that the approach Clynes has shown (this volume) holds such promise. So also do many others even if some of those may not be deemed "respectable". No approach should be deemed beyond the pale simply because of long standing theoretical traditions and biases.

Indeed, if an ultimate goal of psychotherapy is the readjustment of emotional balances (as opposed to just promoting changes in cognitive perspectives), then the brain areas which need to be targeted are, in fact, the primal neural circuits of the visceral brain. For such reasons, we should remain open to the diversity of maneuvers that may be able to influence and rebalance these circuits. The psychotherapist needs to see psychopharmacology as an ally rather than a protagonist (as is affirmed by the type of data summarized by Liebowitz in this volume). Clinicians should become more conversant with the effects of diet on brain chemistries, with the effects of exercise and other somatic influences on brain activities, and with the consequences of stress on basic brain functions. They should begin to understand the deep psycho-logical nature of emotionality more through formal educational experiences rather than haphazard personal and professional experiences. How this could be done within a structured educational system needs to be resolved rather than ignored. The new generations of clinicians should be fully exposed to the revolution in the brain sciences, even if it seems excessively difficult and irrelevant at times. Students will need this type of information to be able to think reasonably about the underlying issues. The failure of psychology, as a unified scholarly field, to deal effectively with emotions, and the other intrinsic potentials of the brain, is one of the major reason the discipline has failed to become a coherent field of science. If psychology were willing to go back and cultivate its physiological roots, it would find a foundation which could constitute the "core" of the discipline. If the psychotherapeutic disciplines forsake their allegiance to such basic science traditions, then they will have abandoned the substantive future of their discipline.

The intrinsic psycho-neural processes of organisms should be the foundation for our thinking about both clinical and cognitive issues. Although the higher reaches of the human brain can construct social and cultural realities of magnificent proportions (and all of that needs to be understood and catalogued in all its diversity and detail) a lasting *foundation* for understanding that vast plumage must be built from a basic analysis of the intrinsic functions of the brain. Emotions are among the most important of those functions, and we can understand them only by theoretically guided successive approximations. At this point in our knowledge, we can be sure that basic emotions are not just social-constructions, but basic brain plans for action. Indeed, the underlying emotive systems probably guide the construction of individual personalities as well as cultures. The complexity which results from these systems is vast, even though the underlying biological principles may be relatively simple. The third of Descartes' *four rules* can guide our analysis of these system: "to think in an orderly fashion when concerned with the search for truth, beginning with the things which were simplest and easiest to understand, and gradually and by degrees reaching toward more complex knowledge, even treating, as though ordered, materials which were not necessarily so."

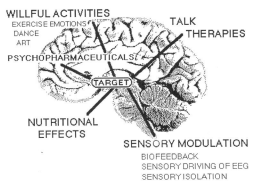

Figure 9. Many influences may converge on emotive circuits that could be used to homeostatically regulate the primal affective substrates.

References

Abuzzahab, F.S., Sr., 1982, Gilles de la Tourette syndrome or multiple tic disorder. In "Extraoridinary Disorders of Human Behavior, " C.T. H. Friedmann & R.A. Fauget (Eds.) Plenum Press, New York.

Anisman, H., 1978, Neurochemical changes elicited by stress.
    In "Psychopharmacology of Aversively Motivated Behavior", H. Anisman &
    G. Bignami (Eds.), Plenum Press, New York.
Arnold, M.B., 1960, "Emotion and Personality, Vol 1., Neurological and
    Physiological Aspects", Columbia University Press: New York.
Blanck, P.D., Buck, R., and Rosenthal, R., (Eds.), 1986, "Nonverbal Communication In
    the Clincal Context," Pennsylvania State Univ. Press., University Park.
Bovier, Ph., Broekkamp, C.L. and Lloyd, K.G. 1982, Ethyl alcohol on escape from
    electrical periaqueductal gray stimulation in rats.
    Pharmacol. Biochem. Behav., 21, 353.
Brandao, M.L., de Aguiar, J.C., and Graeff, F.G., 1982, GABA mediation of the
    anti-aversive action of minor tranquilizers. *Pharmacol. Biochem. Behav., 16*: 397-
    402.
Brandao, M.L., DiScala, G., Bouchet, M.J. and Schmitt, P., 1986, Escape behavior
    produced by the blockade of glutamic acid decarboxylase (GAD) in the
    mesencephalic central gray or medial hypothalamus.
    Pharmacol. Biochem. Behav. , 24: 497-501.
Bryden, M.P. and Ley, R.G., 1983, Right-hemisphere involvement in the perception
    and expression of emotion in normal humans. In "Neuropsychology of Human
    Emotion", K.M. Heilman & P. Satz, (Eds.) The Guilford Press, New York.
Buck, R., 1985, Prime theory: an integrated view of motivation and emotion.
    Psych. Rev., 92: 389-413.
Campbell, M., Small, A.M., Perry, R., Palij, M., Nobler, M., Polonsky, B. and Shore, H.,
    1985, "Naltrexone in autistic children" Paper presented at the 17th Annual
    Meeting and Conference of the National Society of Children and Adults with
    Autism. Autism Research Symposium, Los Angeles, CA.
Clynes, M., 1973, Sentics: Biocybernetics of emotion communication, *Annals N.Y.
    Acad. Sci.,* 220(3): 55-131
Damasio, A.R., 1985, Prosopagnosia, *Trends Neurosci.* 8: 132-135.
Davis, M., 1980, Neurochemical modulation of sensory-motor reactivity:
    Acoustic and tactile startle reflexes. *Neurosci. Biobehav. Rev.* 4: 241.
Delgado, J.M.R., 1969, "Physical Control of the Mind" Harper & Row, New York.
Ferrero, P., Guidotti, A., Conti-Tronconi, B. and Costa, E., 1984, A brain
    octadecaneuropeptide generated by tryptic digestion of DBI (diazepam binding
    inhibitor) functions as a proconflictligand of benzodiazepine recognition sites.
    Neuropharmacol., 227: 1359-1362.
Faravelli, C. et al., 1985, Prevalence of traumatic early life events in 31 agoraphobic
    patients with panic attacks. *Amer. J. Psychiat.* 142: 1493.
Ferrier, I.N., Crow, T.J., Roberts, G.W., Johnstone, E.C., Owens, D.G.C., Lee, Y.,
    Barachese-Hamilton, A., McGregor, G., O'Shaughnessy, D., Polak, J.M., and
    Bloom, S.R., 1984, Alterations in neuropeptides in the limbic lobe in
    schizophrenia. In "Psychopharmacology of the limbic system" M.R. Trimble &
    E. Zarifan (Eds.) Oxford University Press, Oxford.
Flannelly, K.J., Muraoka, M.Y., Blanchard, D.C. and Blanchard, R.J. , 1985, Specific
    anti-aggressive effects of fluprazine hydrochloride, *Psychopharmacol., 87*: 86.
Friedmann, C.T.H., 1982, The so called hystero-psychoses: Latah, windigo and
    Pibloktoq. In "Extraordinary Disorders of Human Behavior",
    C.T.H. Friedmann & R.A. Faguet (Eds.) Plenum Press, New York.
Gardner, H., 1985, "The Minds's New Science: A History of the Cognitive
    Revolution", Basic Books, Inc., New York.

Gellhorn, E. and Loofbourrow, G.N., 1983, "Emotions & Emotional Disorders," Harper & Row, New York.

Gershon, M.D., 1981, The enteric nervous system. *Ann. Rev. Neurosci.,* 4: 227.

Gittelman, R. and Klein, D.F., 1985, Childhood separation anxiety and adult agoraphobia. In: "Anxiety and the Anxiety Disorders," A.H. Tuma & J. Maser (Eds.), Erlbaum, New Jersey.

Gray, J.A., 1982, "The Neuropsychology of Anxiety: An Enquiry into the Functions of the Septo-hippocampal System," Oxford University Press, Oxford.

Greenberg, L.S. and Pinsof, W.M., (Eds.), 1986, "The Psychotherapeutic Process: A Research Handbook". The Guilford Press, New York.

Gribbin, J. and Cherfas, J., 1982, "The Monkey Puzzle," McGraw-Hill Book Co., New York.

Heilman, K.M. and Satz, P. (Eds.), 1983, "Neuropsychology of Human Emotions," The Guilford Press, New York.

Herman, B.H., Hammock, M.K., Arthur-Smith, A., Egan, J., Chattor, I., Zelnick, N., Corradine, M., Appelgate, K., Boeckx, R.L., and Sharp, S.D., 1986, Role of opioid peptides in autism: effects of acute administration of naltrexone. *Neurosci. Abst.* 12: 1172.

Hohmann, G., 1966, Some effects of spinal cord lesions on experimental emotional feelings. *Psychophysiol.* 3: 143.

Izard, C.E., 1977, "Human Emotions," Plenum Press, New York.

Izard, C.E., Kagan, J. and Zajonc, R.B. (Eds.), 1984, "Emotions, cognitions, and behavior," Cambrdige University Press, Cambridge.

Kalivas, P.W., 1985, Interactions between neuropeptides and dopamine neurons in the ventromedial mesencephalon. *Neurosci. Biobehav. Revs.* 9: 573.

Klein, D.F., 1981, Anxiety reconceptualized. In. "Anxiety: New Research and Changing Concepts" D.F. Klein and J. Rabkin, eds., Raven Press, New York.

Lang, P.J., 1984, Cognition in emotion: Concept and action. In: "Emotions, Cognition, and Behavior," C. Izard, J. Kagan, & R.B. Zajonc (Eds.), Cambridge University Press, New York.

Lewis, D.A., Campbell, M.J., Foote, S.L., Goldstein, M. and Morrison, J.H., 1987, The distribution of tyrosine hydroxylase-immunoreactive fibers in primate neocortex is widespread but regionally specific. *J. Neurosci.* 7: 279.

MacLean, P.D. (1973) "A Triune Concept of the Brain and Behavior," Toronto, University of Toronto Press.

MacLean, P.D. (1985) Brain evolution relating to family, play and the separation call. *Arch. gen. Psychiat,* 42: 405.

Mancia, G. and Zanchetti, A. (1981) Hypothalamic control of autonomic functions. In: "Handbook of the Hypothalamus: Vol. 3, Part B. Behavioral Studies of the Hypothalamus." P.J. Morgane and J. Panksepp (Eds.) Dekker, New York.

Mandler, G., 1984, "Mind and Body: Psychology of Emotiona and Stress," W.W. Norton & Co., New York.

Minsky, M., 1987, "The Society of Mind," Simon and Schuster, New York.

Moriyama, M., Ichimaru, Y. and Gomita, Y. (1984) Behavioral suppression using intracranial reward and punishment: effects of benzodiazepines. *Pharmacol. Biochem. Behav.* , 21, 773.

Nemeroff, C.B. and Prange, A.J.J. (Eds.) "Neurotensin, A Brain and Gastrointestinal
    Peptide," *Ann. N.Y. Acad. Sci.* Vol. 400.
Norman, D.A., 1980, Twelve issues for cognitive science. *Cognitive Sci.* 4: 1.
Olivier, B., 1981, Selective anti-aggressive properties of DU27725: Ethological
    analyses of intermale and territorial aggression in the male rat. *Pharmacol.
    Biochem. Behav. 14:* 61.
Panksepp, J., 1971, Aggression elicited by electrical stimulation of the hypothalamus
    in the albino rat. *Physiol. Behav.,* 6, 321-329.
Panksepp, J., 1981, Hypothalamic integration of behavior: Rewards, punishments and
    related psychological processes. In "Handbook of the Hypothalamus, Vol. 3B.
    Behavioral Studies of the Hypothalamus," P.J. Morgane & J. Panksepp (Eds.)
    New York, Marcel Dekker.
Panksepp, J., 1981, Brain opioids—a neurochemical substrate for narcotic and social
    dependence. In "Theory in Psychopharmacology, Vol. 1," S.J. Cooper (Ed.)
    London: Academic Press, pp. 149.
Panksepp, J., 1982, Toward a general psychobiological theory of emotions.
    Behav. Brain Sci., 5, 407.
Panksepp, J., 1985, Mood changes. In. "Handbook of Clinical Neurology," Revised
    series Vol. 1(45), "Clinical Neuropsychology," P.J. Vinken, G.W. Bruyn & H.L.
    Klawans (Eds.) Amsterdam: Elsevier, pp. 272-285.
Panksepp, J., 1986a, The anatomy of emotions. In: "Emotions: Theory, Research and
    Experience, Vo. 3. Biological Foundations of Emotions," R. Plutchik &
    H. Kellerman (Eds.) New York: Academic Press, pp. 91.
Panksepp, J., 1986b, The psychobiology of prosocial behaviors: separation distress,
    play and altruism. In: "Altruism and Aggression: Biological and Social Origins,"
    C. Zahn-Waxler, E.M. Cummings & R. Iannotti (Eds.) Cambridge: Cambridge
    Univ. Press. pp. 19-57.
Panksepp, J., 1986c, The neurochemistry of behavior. *Ann. Rev. Psychol. 37:* 77.
Panksepp, J., 1988, The neurobiology of emotions: The animal brain and human
    feelings. In. "Handbook of psychophysiology: Emotion and Social Behavior,"
    H. Wagner & T. Manstead (Eds.) Wiley, London.
Panksepp, J., 1989, The psychoneurology of fear: Evolutionary Perspectives and
    Animal Models. In *Handbook of Anxiety, Vol. 3,* Elsevier, Amsterdam. In Press.
Panksepp, J., Crepeau, L. and Clynes, M., 1987, Effects of CRF on separation distress
    and juvenile play *Neurosci. Abst., 13,* 1320.
Panksepp, J., Gandelman, R., and Trowill, J., 1970, Modulation of hypothalamic
    self-stimulation and escape behavior by chlordiazepoxide. *Physiol. Behav., 5:*
    965.
Panksepp, J., Herman, B.H., Vilberg, T., Bishop, P. & DeEskinazi, F.G., 1980,
    Endogenous opioids and social behavior, *Neurosci. Biobehav. Revs., 4:* 473.
Panksepp, J., Normansell, L., Cox, J.F., Crepeau, L.J. and Sacks, D.S. (1987). Psy-
    chopharmacology of social play. In: "Ethopharmacology of Social
    Behavior," J. Mos (Ed.) Holland: Duphar.
Panksepp, J., Normansell, L., Herman, B., Bishop, P. and Crepeau, L., 1988, Neural and
    neurochemical control of the separation distress call. In "The Physiological
    Control of Mammalian Vocalization" J.D. Newman (Ed.), Plenum Press, New
    York.

Panksepp, J. and Sahley, T., 1987, Possible brain opioid involvement in disrupted social intent and language development in autism. In: "Neurobiological Issues in Autism," E. Schopler & G. Mesibov (Eds.) New York: Plenum Press.

Panksepp, J., Siviy, S. and Normansell, L., 1984,The psychobiology of play: Theoretical and methodological perspectives. *Neurosci. Biobehav. Revs., 8:* 465.

Panksepp, J., Siviy, S. and Normansell, L., 1985, Brain opioids and social emotions. In: "The Psychobiology of Attachment and Separation," M. Reite & T. Fields (Eds.) New York: Academic Press.

Parkinson, B., 1985, Emotional effects of false autonomic feedback. *Psych. Bull. 98:* 471.

Plutchik, R., 1980, "Emotions: A psychoevolutionary Synthesis," Harper & Row, New York.

Poeck, K., 1969, Pathophysiology of emotional disorders associated with brain damage. In: "Handbook of Clinical Neurology, Vol. 3, Disorders of Higher Nervous Activity," P.J. Vinken & G.W. Bruyn (Eds.), North-Holland Pub. Co., Amsterdam.

Reynolds, G.P. 1983, Increased concentrations and lateral asymmetry of amygdala dopamine in schizophrenia. *Nature,* 305, 527.

Robinson, R.G., Kubos, K.L., Starr, L.B., Rao, K., and Price, T.R., 1984, Mood disorders in stroke patients: Importance of location of lesion. *Brain,* 197: 81.

Ross, E.D., 1984, Right hemisphere's role in language, affective behavior and emotion. *Trends Neurosci.,* 7: 342.

Rossi, E.L., 1986, "The Psychobiology of Mind-Body Healing" W.W. Norton & Co., New York.

Sacks, D.S. and Panksepp, J., 1987, Electrical stimulation of the lateral hypothalamic fear/flight sites in rats produces conditional freezing. *Neurosci. Abstr.,* 13.

Sahley, T.L. and Panksepp, J., 1987, Brain opioids and autism: An updated analysis of possible linkages. *J. Autism Devel. Dis.,* 14: 199.

Scherer, K.R. and Ekman, P., 1984, "Approaches to Emotion," Lawrence Erlbaum, Hillsdale, New Jersey.

Spielberger, C.D., 1979, "Preliminary manual for the State-Trait Personality Inventory (STPI) Unpublished manuscript, Unviersity of South Florida, Center for Resarch in Community Psychology, Tampa.

Spielberger, C.D., 1985, Assessment of state and trait anxiety: conceptual and methodological issues. *Southern Psychologist,* 2: 6.

Stone, E.A., 1983, Problems with curent catecholamine hypotheses of antidepressant agents. *Behav. Brain Sci.* 4: 535.

Swanson, L.W., Sawchenko, P.E., Rivier, J. and Vale, W.W., 1983, Organization of ovine corticotropin-releasing factor immunoreactive cells and fibers in the rat brain: An immunohistochemical study. *Neuroendocrinol.* 36: 165.

Tomkins, S.S. & McCarter, R., 1964, What and where are the primary affects? Some evidence for a theory. *Percept. Mot. Skills., 18:* 119.

Tallman, J.F., Gallagher, D.W., 1985, The GABA-ergic system: A locus of benzodiazepine action. *Ann. Rev. Neurosci.* 8: 21.

Torgersen, S., 1986, Childhood and family characteristics in panic and generalized anxiety disorders. *Am. J. Psychiat. 143:* 630.

Tyrer, P. and Mackay, A., 1986, Schizophrenia: No longer a functional psychosis. *Trends Neruosci., 9,* 537.

van der Kolk, B.A., 1987, The separation cry and the trauma response: Developmental issues in the psychobiology of attachment and separation. In: "Psychological Trauma," B.A. van der Kolk, ed. American Psychiatric Press, Washington, D.C.

Vanderhaeghen, J.-J. and Crawley, J.N., (Eds.), 1985, "Neuronal Cholecystokinin," *Ann. N.Y. Acad. Sci.*, Vol. 448.

van Ree, J.M., and Matthyswse, S., (Eds.) 1986, "Psychiatric Disorders: Neurotransmitters and Neuropeptides," Elsevier, Amsterdam.

Whybrow, P.C., Akiskal, H.S. and McKinney, W.T., 1985, "Mood Disorders: Towards a New Psychobiology," Plenum Press, New York.

Willner, P., 1985, "Depression: A Psychobiological Synthesis," John Wiley & Sons, New York.

Wise, R.A., 1982, Neuroleptics and operant behavior: The anhedonia hypothesis. *Behav. Brain Sci.*, 5: 39.

Wong, D.F., Wagner, H.N., Jr., Tune, L.E., et al., 1986, Positron emission tomography reveals elevated D_2 dopamine receptors in drug-naive schizophrenics. *Science* 134, 1558.

Wyatt, R.J., 1986, The dopamine hypothesis: variations on a theme (II). *Psychopharmacol. Bull.*, 22: 923.

Pharmacotherapy of Personality Disorders

Michael R. Liebowitz

Anxiety Disorders Clinic
New York Psychiatric Institute
New York, New York 10032

While the major pathogenic theory of personality disorders held by American psychiatrists is psychoanalytic (Abraham, 1949; Reich, 1949; Knight, 1953; Kernberg, 1975), the biological approach to personality disorders has an equally lengthy history. The modern era began with Kraepelin (1921), who observed affective temperaments in the premorbid history of many manic depressives and their non-ill biological relatives. Later investigators, such as Kretschmer (1936) and Schneider (1959) described constitutional factors thought to underlie both normal and deviant personality types. The major thrust of these studies was the notion that diluted versions of major schizophrenic, affective, and organic disorders could express themselves as chronic, maladaptive patterns of experiencing and functioning in the world; that is, personality disorders. With the modern tools of psychopharmacology, psychobiology, family studies, and clinical studies, these theories can be better tested.

The goals of psychopharmacotherapy are to decrease vulnerability to affective or cognitive decompensation; enhance pleasure capacity; normalize activation; and correct dysregulation. These changes enable patients to function more normally and, where indicated, to benefit more from psychotherapy. To the degree that biological therapies are helpful, it would suggest that at least some patients who are considered to have disordered personalities are chronically coping with neurochemically based pathological vulnerabilities to affective instability, cognitive instability, or both.

While the goals for somatic therapy vary according to the patients' particular problems, it is important in all cases to specify treatment targets prospectively. This may include: a) the reduction of transient psychotic episodes, or b) the relieving of agitation with a neuroleptic; c) greater affective stabilization, or d) blockade of panic attacks with a tricyclic; e) reduction of autonomous mood shifts with lithium, or f) relief from depression, social phobia, panic attacks, or hypersensitivity to rejection with an MAOI; and others. Discussion with a family member or close friend (with the patient's permission) from time to time during the course of treatment is useful for monitoring progress. For some personality disorder patients, a goal of medication is to render them more able to participate in psychotherapy. For others, effective medication helps them leave psychotherapy.

Given the current state of knowledge, drug treatment for any given patient should be thought of as a *mini-experiment in which therapist and patient participate*. A medication is tried, and the results examined over time. Therapeutic gains tend to support the hypothesis that a drug treatable condition existed, although in the absence of placebo controls, contribution of other treatment factors such as therapeutic relationship cannot be partialed out.

Contraindications to specific drug therapy include previous failures with a vigorous trial of that medication. Active drug or alcohol abuse, prominent suicidal ideation or behavior, or inability to comply with certain common-sense requirements of therapy (such as following a low tyramine diet on MAOIs) may render drug therapy inadvisable. Initial trials may be conducted on an inpatient basis, in the hope that once stabilized, the patient could safely be transferred to outpatient status. Chronic neuroleptic therapy should be undertaken with great reluctance, given the risk of tardive dyskinesia.

Treating possible personality disorder patients with drug therapy is both similar to and different form applying these same treatments to other psychiatric disorders. The similarity lies in the requirement of basic knowledge of the indications, dose range, dosage schedules, and potential adverse effect of the different drug classes. A difference is that personality disorder patients experience interpersonal difficulties in a variety of encounters, including those with psychopharmacologists. Therefore, establishing rapport and setting limits may require more attention in medicating personality disorder patients than would be required with other psychiatric disorders. In particular, histrionic types may experience an abundance of unusual side effects (or overreact to standard ones); obsessionals may experience medication as a loss of control and need extra educational efforts; while borderlines may act out with their medication or attach unrealistic expectations to it. Transference and counter-transference reactions may complicate the pharmacotherapy of many personality disorder patients, especially when drugs are being added to an ongoing psychother-apy or vice versa (Gunderson, 1984). Psychopharmacological consultants may be helpful to general psychiatrists in determining whether drug therapy is indicated, and in helping to monitor the treatment program.

One additional problem is that personality disorder diagnoses are less reliable then Axis I DSM-III-R conditions. The reasons include the following: diagnostic criteria are less operationally defined; chronic trait rather than acute state behaviors are being assessed; patients themselves are often less able to recognize or report on their maladaptive personality traits, and outside informants may be needed. Also, the various DSM-III-R Axis II conditions are not mutually exclusive, so that patients may qualify for more than one. At times criteria for the various disorders overlap.

Pharmacotherapy of the Specific DSM-III Personality Disorders
(Summarized on Table 1)

Paranoid Personality Disorder

The essential features of this personality disorder are pervasive and unwarranted suspiciousness and mistrust of people, hypersensitivity, and restricted emotionality.

Phenomenological and genetic data (Kety et al, 1968; Rosenthal et al, 1968) suggest that paranoid personality disorder lies on a spectrum with schizophrenia and may represent a diluted manifestation of schizophrenic vulnerability. If so, one would expect that neuroleptics might, at times, be helpful for these patients should they be willing to take them. Data to actually support neuroleptic efficacy for paranoid personality disorder, however, are vary sparse.

One open clinical trial examined the effects of the antipsychotic drug pimozide 1 - 8 mg per day in 120 outpatients with a variety of personality disorders, including schizoid, paranoid, obsessive - compulsive, hysterical, borderline, inadequate, and sexually deviant (Reyntjens, 1972). Patients were treated for two months, and optimal dose was found to be 3 mg per day. Global improvement was rated as excellent in 30 patients (44 percent), moderate in 27 patients (22.5 percent), and poor in 10 patients (3.5

Table 1

Personality Disorder	Possible Pharmacotherapy	
Paranoid	Neuroleptics e.g. Pimozide 1-8 mg/day	
	Thipridizine 25-300 mg/day	
Schizotypal	Neuroleptics e.g. Thiothixene 2-10 mg/day	
	Haloperidol 2-10 mg/day	
Histronic	Phenelzine	30-90 mg/day
	Tranylcypromine	20-60 mg/day
Borderline	Phenelzine	30-90 mg/day
	Imipramine	50-300 mg/day
	Thioridizine	25-300 mg/day
	Trifluperazine	2-10 mg/day
	Lithium	.6-1.2 meg/L
	Carbamezapine	8-12 ng/ml
	Methylphenidate	5-60 mg/day
Dependent	Imipramine	25-300 mg/day
	Phenelzine	30-90 mg/day
Compulsive	Chlorimipramine	50-300 mg/day

percent). A separate analysis of subgroups revealed greater improvement in schizoid and paranoid personality, but the superiority was not statistically significant. A limitation of this study was that it was an open clinical trial in which 36 psychiatrists collaborated with no apparent standardization of diagnostic criteria, outcome criteria, or dosage schedule.

A second study (Barnes, 1977) examined the effect mesoridazine (a low potency neuroleptic structurally similar to thioridiazine) in 30 adolescents, aged 13 - 18, diagnosed as having some form of personality disorder. Included in the group were patients with passive - aggressive, antisocial, schizoid, explosive, hysterical, paranoid, and inadequate personalities. The study lasted six weeks and the mean daily mesoridazine dose for the last week was 44.7 mg. There was significantly greater drop-out in the placebo group. Statistical analyses revealed superiority for mesoridazine on a variety of measures common to personality disorder patients, such as tendency to blame others, outburst of rage or verbal aggressiveness, low frustration tolerance and conflict with authority, as well as anxiety, hostility, and depression. One disadvantage of this study is that it did not elucidate whether treatment was helpful for any specific personality disorders. Also, statistical comparison included some of the drop-outs; since there were more placebo noncompleters, this made mesoridazine look better than it would have if drop-outs had been excluded. However, some of the features specifically responsive to the drug are common in paranoid personality patients, including tendency to blame others, low frustration tolerance, outbursts of rage, and difficulty accepting criticism.

Schizotypal Personality Disorder

Whereas the essence of "paranoid" is suspiciousness, the essence of "schizotypal" is eccentricity or, perhaps more accurately, eccentricity combined with shyness.

Like paranoid personality disorder, schizotypal personality disorder phenomenologically and genetically appears to lie on a schizophrenic spectrum and represent a forme fruste of schizophrenia (Kety et al, 1968, Rosenthal et al, 1968). Several studies suggesting neuroleptic efficacy for schizotypal patients support this association. In a preliminary report of one study, 14 outpatients and six inpatients satisfying DSM-III (The Diagnostic and Statistical Manual, Third Edition, of the American Psychiatric Association, 1980) criteria for schizotypal personality disorder were treated with low does of haloperidol (up to 14 mg per day) for a period of six weeks after two weeks of placebo (Hymowitz et al, 1984). Improvement in schizotypal features as a whole, and on social isolation and ideas of reference, were noted in this open trial. However, only 50 percent of the patients were able to complete the medication trial because of side effects such as akathesia and drowsiness.

Brinkley et al (1979) reported a number of borderline patients who were substantially helped by low dosages of high potency neuroleptics in an open clinical trial. The most important predictor, which makes sense clinically, was "a history of recurrent, regressive, psychotic symptoms, frequently of paranoid quality and including some looseness of association, thought-blocking, impairment of reality testing, and disturbed states of consciousness, all of which were stress related, reversible, transient, ego-alien, and unsystematized" (p. 322). In DSM-III parlance, such patients would be called schizotypal rather than borderline.

Serban (1984) recently reported a controlled, double blind comparison trail of thiothixine (mean dose 9.4 mg) and haloperidol (mean dose 3.0 mg) in 52 patients meeting criteria for borderline or schizotypal personality disorder. In addition, prior to admission, patients had to have experienced a mild transient psychotic episode. Overall, 56 percent of the patients are reported to have "improved markedly during the six to 12 weeks that patients were followed," with a trend toward more favorable results in those receiving thiothixene. However, it is impossible to document drug efficacy per se in the absence of a placebo group. In another study (Goldberg, et al, 1986) 50 outpatients meeting DSM-III criteria for schizotypal and/or borderline personality, and having at least one psychotic symptom, were randomly allocated to thiothixene or placebo and treated for 12 weeks. Mean end-of-study thiothixene dosage was 8.7 mg per day. There were *no* drug - placebo differences found for global improvement or total borderline or schizotypal scores, although interviewer rated scores on illusions and ideas of reference, and self-rated scores on psychoticism, obsessive - compulsive symptoms, and phobic anxiety showed greater improvement with the active drug. Large placebo effects were seen on self-rated anger-hostility and interpersonal sensitivity, and on observer rated suspiciousness and overall borderline and schizotypal scores, arguing for a placebo control for all drug treatment studies of borderline and schizotypal patients.

Soloff et al (1986a) are currently completing a five-week study comparing haloperidol (mean end-of-study dose 7.2 mg), amitriptyline (mean end-of-study dose 147.6 mg), and placebo in borderline and schizotypal patients. In the 64 patients studied thus far, haloperidol was found superior to placebo on the hostility, paranoia, and total scores of the inpatient multidimensional psychiatric rating scale (IMPS), and on all 10 SCL-90 factors and on the Beck Depression Inventory (BDI). Amitriptyline was superior to placebo on the BDI and IMPS excitement scores, but was associated with worsening of impulsivity on a ward behavior scale. Haloperidol was superior to amitriptyline on the hostility, paranoia, anxiety, and interpersonal sensitivity factors of the SCL-90, on a schizotypal symptom inventory, and on the ward behavior scale. Haloperidol resulted in greater decrement in overall severity than did amitriptyline or placebo (which did not differ), and benefited patients with both prominent affective and/or cognitive symptom profiles. Borderlines with major depression were no more likely to benefit from amitriptyline than those without major depression.

Taken together, these results suggest modest but distinct and diverse benefits from low does neuroleptics in schizotypal patients, although further studies are required.

Additional studies with antidepressant and antianxiety agents remain to be done with this group. Several studies have indicated antidepressant responsivity of *pseudoneurotic schizophrenia*, a nosological forerunner of schizotypal and borderline. In one trial (Klein, 1967) placebo, chlorpromazine, and imipramine were administered on a randomized double-blind fashion to 311 hospitalized patients, including 32 pseudoneurotic schizophrenics. For the pseudoneurotic groups, a significant drug-placebo effect was found for imipramine, but not for chlorpromazine, with regard to global improvement.

Similarly, Hedberg et al (1971), compared the MAOI tranylcypromine, the neuroleptic trifluoperazine, and the combination of both, in a double blind crossover trial in a schizophrenic population that included 28 pseudoneurotic patients. In contrast to the group as a whole, a significantly greater number of the pseudoneurotic patients responded to tranylcypromine than to the other drug regimens. Recently, a newer antidepressant, amoxapine, was found useful in five of seven pseudoneurotic patients in an open clinical trial (Aono et al, 1981).

As with paranoid and schizotypal personality disorders, *schizoid* personality disorder shows phenomenological and genetic evidence of belonging to a schizophrenic spectrum. Schizoid personality disorder should be differentiated from avoidant personality disorder, in which social isolation is due to hypersensitivity to rejection, but a desire to enter social relationships is manifest if there are strong guarantees of uncritical acceptance.

In terms of drug treatment, two strategies may be worth pursuing. Neuroleptic therapy is supported by the notion that schizoid personality disorder lies on a schizophrenic spectrum, and by studies that found evidence for neuroleptic efficacy in mixed personality disorder groups that included schizoid patients (Reyntjens, 1972; Barnes, 1977). Another strategy is to assume that the distinctions between schizoid personality disorder and avoidant personality disorder are quantitative rather than qualitative, and that in schizoid patients, also, hypersensitivity to rejection or criticism causes their social isolation and interpersonal aloofness. If so, then recent findings of beta-adrenergic blocker (Gorman et al, 1985) and MAOI (Liebowitz et al, 1986) efficacy for avoidant personality disorder, as detailed below, might also apply to schizoid patients.

Histrionic Personality Disorder

The DSM-III description of histrionic personality answers to a somewhat more maladaptive disorder than the usual descriptions of the "hysteric" in the earlier psychoanalytic literature (Chodoff, 1974). The narcissistic attributes (vanity, self-indulgence, shallowness) and impulsivity (suicide threats, angry outbursts) included in DSM-III suggest a decompensated hysterical type; that is, a histrionic at the borderline level. Better integrated patients, who show merely fickleness, seductiveness, stimulus-seeking, sociability, and overemotionality often respond well to an exploratory *psychotherapy* focusing on classical oedipal conflicts.

Psychopharmacotherapy may be of distinct help for some histrionic or hysterical patients. Liebowitz and Klein (1979, 1981) report MAOI responsivity for a depressive subtype that they call hysteroid dysphoria. These patients are highly sensitive to rejection, and are vulnerable to severe depressive crashes in the face of romantic or other disappointments. They also crave attention and admiration, which often leads to inappropriate choice of romantic partners, or leads to such demanding behavior that appropriate partners are driven away. When depressed they over eat, oversleep, and isolate themselves socially, but remain able to be at least transiently buoyed by pleasant events. In a preliminary drug and psychotherapy study of hysteroid dysphoria, phenelzine appeared to reduce rejection sensitivity and the need for constant attention and admiration form other, stabilizing patients' functioning (Liebowitz and Klein, 1979; Liebowitz and Klein, 1981). In a double blind trial of phenelzine, imipramine, and placebo in an atypical depressive sample, the hysteroid dysphoric subsample again showed specific responsivity to phenelzine (Liebowitz et al, 1984).

Some psychotherapy nonresponsive histrionic patients may suffer, at least in part, from affective disorders and required pharmacological stabilization alone or in addition to psychotherapy. Further, this affective instability may give rise to the interpersonal demandingness and acting out that make these patients difficult to treat in psychotherapy.

Narcissistic Personality Disorder

Narcissistic disorders, characterized by grandiosity, preoccupation with fame, beauty, wealth, shallowness, entitlement, exploitativeness, and poor empathy, occur at all levels of general adaptation.

There are no pharmacological trials that bear directly on this personality disorder. Extrapolating from existing findings, one would attempt to treat excessive affective lability either with lithium carbonate if there is some evidence of autonomous hypomanic or depressive mood swings, or an MAOI for exaggerated vulnerability to rejection or disappointment. In addition, patients with narcissistic personality disorder might be expected to go into more prolonged depressive episodes when they encounter disappointments of defeats in life. Some of these might be amenable to antidepressant therapy, in conjunction with an insight - oriented psychotherapy approach.

Antisocial Personality Disorder

The voluminous literature on antisocial personalities is a testimonial to their ubiquitousness and troublesomeness, not to their treatability. The more manipulative, ruthless, and contemptuous of others, the worse the amenability to therapy of any kind.

Antisocial personality disorder per se has not been the subject of psychopharmacological investigation. Antisocial behavior occurring in the contest of other disorders has, however, shown some drug responsivity. Stringer and Joseph (1983) reported two hospitalized patients with antisocial personality disorder and histories of childhood attention deficit disorder, who became less aggressive during trials of methylphenidate. Liebowitz et al (1976) treated a patient with evidence of psychosis whose sociopathic behavior between episodes responded to lithium in a double blind, cross-over design. Features that suggested possible lithium responsivity in this patient were family history of lithium - responsive illness; recurrent depression; and aggressiveness, impulsivity, and hyperactivity between psychotic episodes.

A number of animal and human studies have linked low CNS serotonin (as evidenced by low CSF 5 HIAA) to increased aggressive and impulsive behavior, and to violent suicidal acts in man. (Brown and Goodwin, 1986). In one study of military personnel undergoing psychiatric examination, those with personality diagnoses associated with behavioral impulsivity (anti-social, explosive, immature, hysterical) had significantly lower CSF 5HIAA than less impulsive individuals with passive aggressive, passive dependent, schizoid, obsessive-compulsive or inadequate personality profiles. Concordant with this, borderline patients not responding to chronic amitriptyline treatment, which would down-regulate 5HT receptors, showed an increase in demandingness, suicide threats and assaultive behavior, as compared to placebo-nonresponders. (Soloff, et al, 1986b).

At the opposite extreme from impulsivity, obsessive compulsive (OC) patients demonstrate upregulated serotonergic status compared to normal controls, which may account for their doubt, indecisiveness, chronic worry and uncertainty (Liebowitz et al, 1987). Successful pharmacotherapy of OC patients correlates positively with reduction in serotonergic status.

These findings suggest a serotonin spectrum. At one extreme is high 5HT status associated with obsessional doubt, worry, and overconcern about the consequences of one's behavior. At the other extreme, low 5HT status in some individuals (other low 5HT patients are normal) is associated with impulsivity, aggression, and psychopathy, all manifestations of lack of concern about the consequences of one's actions. Chronic treatment with potent 5HT reuptake blockers, which downregulates 5HT status, appears helpful for OCD. Lowering 5HT status in animals releases behaviors previously inhibited by punishment. Perhaps the reverse strategy, namely pharmacological treatment to upregulate 5HT function, might help to reduce impulsive, aggressive and psychopathic behavior.

Borderline Personality Disorder

Psychotherapy of borderline patients is usually directed at their fragile sense of identity, at their shifting and highly contradictory impressions about themselves and those close to them, and at their highly conflicted and anxiety - provoking manner of existing within a love relationship, which they tend, unwittingly, to demolish. Borderlines are people of extremes, oscillating between adoration and vilification of love partners or, in the transference situation, of the therapist. Characteristically they are, when engulfed in one extreme attitude, completely out of touch with the opposite attitude - one that may have held them in its grip the hour or the day before.

NEUROLEPTIC TRIALS. Leone (1982) reported 80 borderline patients randomly assigned to six weeks of neuroleptics, either loxapine or chlorpromazine, in a double blind outpatient study. Both groups showed significant global improvement over baseline, with a nonsignificant trend favoring loxapine. Loxapine was reported rapidly effective in controlling anxiety, hostility, suspiciousness, and depressed mood. A major problem with this study was the lack of a placebo group, rendering it impossible to determine whether any true medication effect was seen with either drug.

Serban (1984) and Soloff et al (1986a) also recently reported preliminary results from neuroleptic trials involving borderline as well as schizotypal patients. These studies, as described earlier in this Chapter, found positive results for neuroleptic therapy.

Taken together, these results suggest that modest and selective benefits are to be derived form neuroleptics in borderline patients, although further studies are required.

OTHER DRUG TRIALS IN BORDERLINE PATIENTS. Neuroendocrine (Carroll et al, 1981; Garbutt et al, 1983; Baster et al, 1984), sleep EEG (Akiskal, 1981; McNamara et al, 1984), family (Stone, 1979; Akiskal, 1981) and clinical (Klein, 1975; Liebowitz, 1979; Akiskal, 1981) data all suggest an overlap between borderline personality as defined in DSM-III and affective disorder. Further controlled trials of tricyclic antidepressants and MAOI in borderline patients are therefore particularly needed. As mentioned in the section on antisocial patients, however, drugs which down regulate serotonergic status with chronic administrations may exacerbate impulsivity, aggressiveness and suicidality.

With regard to benzodiazepines, Faltus (1984) described three extensively treated borderline cases who benefited from alprazolam. However, alprazolam has also been reported to occasionally cause dangerous emotional and behavioral disinhibition (Rosenbaum et al, 1984), and so must be given to borderline patients with caution. Cowdry and colleagues are conducting placebo controlled trials of a variety of drugs in borderline patients with prominent behavioral dyscontrol (overdoes, angry outburst, wrist cutting) and rejection sensitivity. Alprazolam (up to 6 mg per day) and the anticonvulsant carbamazepine (up to 1200 mg per day) were compared with placebo in random order cross-over trials; the phenothiazene trifluoperazine (up to 12 mg per day) and the MAOI tranylcypromine (up to 60 mg per day) were compared in the same patients in a second study. Patients found tranylcypromine the most consistently helpful. Therapists gave highest ratings to carbamazepine and next highest ratings to tranylcypromine, both of which helped dyscontrol as well as having antidepressant, antianxiety, and antianger effects. Carbamazepine helped dyscontrol most, although patients did not particularly like the drug, while tranylcypromine had primarily antidepressant effects with antidyscontrol features as a secondary benefit. In this series as well, several instances of serious behavioral disinhibition with alprazolam were noted (Gardner and Cowdry, 1985).

There are no systematic trials of other benzodiazepines in borderline patients (Schatzberg and Cole, 1981).

Pharmacological trials of hysteroid dysphoria (Liebowitz and Klein, 1979, 1981; Liebowitz et al, 1984), phobic anxiety (Klein, 1964, 1967), emotionally unstable character disorder Rifkin et al, 1972), pseudoneurotic schizophrenia (Klein 1964, 1967; Hedberg et al, 1971), adolescent and adult minimal brain dysfunction (MBD) (Wood et al, 1976; Wender et al, 1981), and episodic dyscontrol syndrome (Bach-Y-Rita et al, 1971; Andrulonis et al, 1980) also involve patients who would meet DSM-III criteria for borderline personality disorder. Pseudoneurotic schizophrenia is a nosological forerunner of borderline and schizotypal personality that has been discussed in the section on schizotypal patients. The other syndromes involve discrete symptom constellations that may be more biologically and pharmacologically homogeneous than are DSM-III personality disorders in general, and borderline personality disorder in particular. Phobic anxiety is discussed in the section under dependent personality disorder; emotionally unstable character is discussed under the affective spectrum; and MBD and episodic dyscontrol are discussed under organic spectrum disorders.

Avoidant Personality Disorder

The term "avoidant personality" was coined by Millon (1969) to describe persons who demonstrate active aversion to social relationships, as contrasted with the passive avoidance and detachment of the schizoid.

Evidence is accumulating that some aspects of extreme social anxiety may be highly drug responsive. In their studies of atypical depression, Liebowitz et al (1984) found that self-rated interpersonal sensitivity, an index of sensitivity to criticism or rejection, responded quite well to treatment with the MAOI phenelzine, but was less responsive to the tricyclic imipramine or placebo. This was also found by Nies et al (1982). A recent study involving social phobic patients with diffuse social anxiety and avoidance has shown that the MAOI phenelzine (Liebowitz et al, 1986) may be of marked benefit.

The case of a 19-year-old outpatient is revealing:

Mr. X dropped out of high school at age 17 because of marked discomfort when having to speak in class or deal with peers. Prior to coming for treatment, he would go out of the house almost exclusively at night. He found the scrutiny of salespeople while waiting on a check-out line intolerable, and felt that people in the streets could sense his discomfort. He had no history of psychotic illness, although he had a depressive episode with a suicide attempt at age 16. Three years of psychotherapy had not been of help. The patient was diagnosed as a social phobic and put on the peripherally acting cardio-selective beta-blocker atenolol. After three weeks of treatment on 100 mg per day, the patient was far more comfortable going out of the house. He was able to obtain a part-time job and return to school.

However, he was still unable to speak up in class. Furthermore, although he could interact with male peers, he felt too frightened to approach socially any of the females in his class. After eight weeks he was taken off the beta-blocker and switched over to phenelzine. During the cross-over his symptoms returned. After several weeks on phenelzine, 60 mg per day, however, he again noted substantial improvement both in work and in class. Moreover, on phenelzine he was also able to speak up in class and began asking girls out for dates. Improvement persisted for six months of drug treatment, at which time the patient was lost to follow-up.

While controlled studies are needed, this preliminary evidence suggests that at least some patients characterized as having avoidant personality disorders can benefit from pharmacotherapy. The mechanisms underlying this drug response appear to involve blockade of peripheral autonomically mediated symptoms (tachycardia, trembling, seating, blushing), and perhaps for the MAOI, central anxiolytic effects as well (Liebowitz et al, 1986).

Dependent Personality Disorder

Psychotherapy. Besides their passivity, deferentiality, and lack of self-confidence, patients with dependent personality tend to form "anaclitic" (clinging) relationship with others. They barely tolerate being physically separated from spouse or partner even indoors, let alone outdoors, the latter quality mimicking the behavior of the agoraphobic.

Dependent patients have not, per se, been subject to pharmacological trials. However, agoraphobic patients with panic attacks often become quite dependent on other people. These patients suffer from panic attacks that are sudden, unprovoked episodes of extreme anxiety accompanied by such features as palpitations, tachycardia, sweating, trembling, shortness of breath, and apprehension that they are about to die, lose control, or go crazy. Panic attacks are the core psychopathological feature of panic disorder and of almost all cases of agoraphobia. Patients with panic attacks and agoraphobia show unusual interpersonal dependency as adults, in part because they are less vulnerable to attacks when going out accompanied by a trusted figure, and hence become dependent on others to be able to get about in the world. In addition, many have histories of childhood separation anxiety, often manifesting as school phobia.

Controlled studies have demonstrated that tricyclic antidepressants and MAOIs both block panic attacks and are of marked benefit in overcoming agoraphobic avoidance patterns (Klein 1963, 1967; Sheehan et al, 1980). In open clinical trials, alprazolam also appears quite useful in blocking panic attacks (Sheehan et al, 1984; Liebowitz et al, 1985). Before there was widespread recognition of a biological basis and pharmacological treatment of agoraphobia with panic attacks, such patients were viewed as suffering marked lags in psychological development, particularly a failure to overcome separation - individuation conflicts. It now appears that intensive psychotherapy is needed for only the small fraction of panic disorder or agoraphobic patients who fail to respond fully to pharmacological therapy, behavior therapy, or a combination of the two. Once a highly dependent agoraphobic patients is helped by pharmacotherapy, marital therapy may be helpful in sorting out conflicts in the relationship with the partner.

Compulsive Personality Disorder

Psychotherapy. Just as there is a particular life-style and prescription for living adhered to by the histrionic, the compulsive has his own prescription: one that gives primacy to reason, logic, orderliness, and respect, but that customarily is accompanied by certain annoying traits; namely parsimony, stubbornness, hostility (expressed or covert), perfectionism, and an attitude of "all work and no play". Compulsives also show persistent preoccupations with power and status along with inordinate fears of losing control, going "crazy," or appearing "weak."

There are no reported pharmacological trials of compulsive personality disorder. There is, however, evidence that obsessive - compulsive disorder, characterized by true obsessions and compulsions, is responsive to the tricyclic antidepressant clomipramine (Thoren et al, 1980). Whether that has therapeutic applicability for compulsive personality disorder remains to be seen.

Passive - Agressive Personality Disorder

The salient features of this personality disorder involve procrastination, stubbornness, intentional inefficiency, and other forms of covert hostility toward and noncompliance with the demands of society, work, and family life.

It is as yet unclear whether treatment of affective concomitants has any modifying effect on the passive - aggressive behavior patterns. In addition, to the degree that the passive - aggressive pattern is due to anxiety - mediated inhibitions concerning direct expression of assertiveness, pharmacological disinhibition with benzodiazepines, stimulants, or MAOIs all merit consideration.

NonDSM-III Personality Disorders

Pharmacotherapy of the Affective Spectrum

Yerevanian and Akiskal (1979) applied neuroendocrine, sleep EEG, family, follow-up, and pharmacological challenge strategies to distinguish "characterological" depressions from chronic subsyndromal affective disorder. One study sample was characterized by depressive onset before age 25, illness duration of at least five years, prominent depressive symptoms most days of the year, and symptoms falling short of DSM-III criteria for major depression. In all cases the clinical presentation made it difficult to decide whether the patient suffered an affective or character disorder. Twenty of 65 patients showed a good response to tricyclic antidepressants, suggesting subsyndromal affective disorder. An even higher percentage might have responded had systematic trials of MAOIs and lithium also been carried out.

Recently, the clinical profile of a typical depressives specifically responsive to MAO inhibitors has become clearer. A placebo - controlled comparison of the MAOI phenelzine and the tricyclic imipramine found that patients who met Research Diagnostic Criteria (RDC) for major, minor, or intermittent depression, who could still be cheered up at least temporarily while depressed, and who showed two or more of the symptoms of overeating while depressed, oversleeping while depressed, extreme fatigue when depressed, and chronic rejection sensitivity, did better on phenelzine than on imipramine or placebo (Liebowitz et al, 1984). Patients meeting criteria for hysteroid dysphoria, however (extreme rejection sensitivity and an extreme demand for attention), in addition to features of atypical depression - or atypical depressives with any history of panic attacks - may constitute specifically MAOI - responsive subgroups within this larger atypical depressive spectrum.

These considerations lead us to the recommendation that all patients with chronic depressive symptoms should undergo rigorous trials with tricyclic antidepressants and, if unresponsive to that, should undergo trials with MAOIs before being called "characterological" depressives. (Partial responses to tricyclics can be augmented with dextroamphetamine, lithium, or thyroid, while a moderate MAOI response can be supplemented with lithium, thyroid, or, as recently shown, low dose of stimulants) (Feighner, 1985). Work is still in progress to define subgroups for whom MAOI may be given as the first treatment.

Subtle manifestations of bipolar disorder may also be the basis of some of the psychopathology labeled as personality disorder. Akiskal et al (1979) found that patients with cyclothymic disorder manifested irritable - angry - explosive outbursts that alienated loved ones; episodic promiscuity; repeated conjugal or romantic failure; frequent shifts in line of work, study, interests, or plans; frequent resorting to alcohol and drug abuse as a means for self-treatment or augmenting excitement; and occasional financial extravagances. These features, at least in cyclothymics, may be lithium - responsive.

One controlled study has demonstrated the utility of lithium in characterologically disturbed patients who also have frequent, unprovoked mood shifts. Rifkin et al (1972) found that patients with chronic maladaptive character traits such as difficulty with authority, truancy, job instability, and manipulativeness, who also have had apparently unprecipitated depressive and hypomanic mood swings that lasted from hours to days, benefited from lithium. In a placebo - controlled study, lithium was found to significantly diminish the mean daily mood range, reducing both hypomanic and depressive swings. In addition, these emotionally unstable character disorder (EUCD) patients became more responsive to nonpharmacological treatment when their mood dysregulation was diminished.

One patient seen in consultation was a 26 year old woman who had numerous short and several long psychiatric hospitalizations for repeated suicide attempts that were both attention getting and nearly fatal. What had gone unnoticed were repeated unprecipitated mood shifts into mild highs as well as devastating lows (during which the suicide attempts occurred). Placing the patient on lithium carbonate greatly reduced the mood shifts and ended the suicide attempts, making her much easier to treat in psychotherapy.

Pharmacotherapy Of The Organic Spectrum

Subtle neurological dysfunction may also underlie some syndromes thought to be personality disorders. In the emotionally unstable character disorder groups described above, Quitkin et al (1976) found a higher than expected incidence of soft neurological signs. Wood et al (1976) claim efficacy for methylphenidate for the treatment of adult minimal brain dysfunction (MBD), now called attention deficit disorder, residual type. They assembled a sample of 15 adults identified on the basis of current MBD like complaints, self-description of MBD characteristics in childhood, and parental rating of a standardized form for hyperactivity in childhood. Hypothesized adult MBD characteristics include history of long - standing impulsiveness, inattentativeness, restlessness, short temper, and emotional lability. Methylphenidate was clearly superior to placebo in a double blind, controlled cross-over trial; eight of 11 patients showed a significant response to the active drug, with no tendency to abuse it. The maximum dose of active drug varied from 20 to 60 mg per day in the four week trial (two weeks on the active drug, two weeks on placebo). Interestingly, drug improvement seemed to occur on dimensions of calm to nervous; concentrating to mind - wandering; and cool tempered to hot tempered, rather than happy to sad, suggesting that the drug was not acting as a simple euphoriant.

A second study (Wender et al, 1981) examined the efficacy of the psychostimulant pemoline for adult MBD. While a drug placebo difference was not found for the study group as a whole, patients whose parents had rated their childhood behavior as evidencing hyperactivity did show significant pemoline effect on motor hyperactivity, attentional difficulties, hot temper, impulsivity, and stress intolerance.

Turnquist et al (1983) recently reported a case of a 25 year old man with a diagnosis of attention deficit disorder and alcoholism, where treatment with pemoline substantially improved the patients's response to alcoholism treatment and after care.

Examining 91 hospitalized psychiatric patients meeting DSM-III criteria for borderline syndrome, Andrulonis et al (1981) found that 27 percent of the total sample had a positive history of childhood minimal brain dysfunction or learning disability, including 53 percent of the 32 males in the sample. In the same sample, 27 (84 percent) of the male patients and 32 (54 percent) of the 59 female patients met criteria for episodic dyscontrol syndrome, although there was substantial overlap between this group and the group with a history of minimal brain dysfunction.

While DSM-III classifies people with intermittent impulsive violence as intermittent explosive disordered, many such patients meet criteria for borderline. These patients have explosive episodes provoked by little or no stress, which are repetitive, short in duration, and result in efficient, coordinated, and even purposeful violent behavior. This loss of control is followed by partial amnesia and relief of tension (Bach-Y-Rita et al, 1971; Andrulonis et al, 1080). In addition to acts of violence, episodic dyscontrol patients are characterized by drug or alcohol abuse, traffic violation, arrest, job or school failures, suicide attempts, and resistance to conventional psychiatric interventions. There is often a history of head trauma; hyperactivity and learning disability in childhood; family history of alcoholism, sociopathy, and violence; certain characteristic EEG abnormalities; and positive findings for soft neurological signs. Andrulonis et al (1980) suggest that acts of violence in episodic dyscontrol patients are triggered by "complex partial ictal events resulting from recurrent excessive disorderly discharges from the temporal lobes to the limbic system," and present preliminary data support the efficacy of the anticonvulsant ethosuximide for these patients. Cowdry (1985) finds carbamazepine useful for behavioral dyscontrol in borderlines.

Pharmacotherapy for pathological aggression in general has received a certain amount of investigation in the past few years. Tupin et al (1973), as well as Sheard et al (1976), found lithium useful in aggressive prisoners: while propranolol (Elliot, 1977; Yudofsky et al, 1981, Ratey et al, 1983) has been found helpful in both provoked and unprovoked episodes of rage in individuals with organic brain damage.

Possible side effects of psychotropic agents:

Neuroleptics
> High potency - (trifluperazine, haloperidol, thiothixene)
> <u>acute</u> - Pseudoparkinsonism, dystonia, akithesia.
> <u>chronic</u> - Tardive dyskinesia.
>
> Low potency - (thioridizine, chlorpromazine)
> <u>acute</u> - Sedation, postural hypotension.
> <u>chronic</u> - Tardive dyskinesia, ejaculation difficulties in males.

Tricyclic Antidepressants
> Imipramine, chlorimipramine, - dry mouth, constipation, difficulty urinating, sexual difficulties, weight gain, insomnia, postural hypotension, paroxysmal hypertension if dietary precautions are not observed.

MAO Inhibitors
> Phenelzine, tranylcypromine - dry mouth, constipation, difficulty urinating, sexual difficulties, weight gain, insomnia, postural hypotension, paroxysmal hypertension if dietary precautions are not observed.

> Lithium
> > Weight gain, tremor, urinary frequency, excesive thrist, reversible hypothroidism, renal impairment.

Carbamezapine
    Drowsiness, imbalance, suppression of bone marrow, liver irritation.

Methylphenidate
    Jitteriness, insomnia

Concluding Remarks

Studies to date suggest that drug therapies may be of use to some patients who meet criteria for DSM-III personality disorder. Future studies are needed to clarify which personality disorders, which aspects of those disorders, and which subsets of patients meeting criteria for the various disorders specifically benefit from neuroleptics, tricyclics, MAOIs, lithium, benzodiazepines, psychostimulants, anticonvulsants, biogenic amine precursors, and beta adrenergic blockers. In light of the positive pharmacotherapy data currently available, the belief that personality disorders can always be clinically distinguished from chronic biological dysregulation requires reconsideration.

References

Abraham K., 1949, Selected Papers on Psychoananlysis (1921-1925), London, Hogarth Press.

Akiskal H.S., 1981, Subaffective disorders: Dysthymic, cyclothymic and bipolar II disorders in the "borderline" realm. *Psychiatr. Clin. North Am.* 4:26-46.

Akiskal H.S., 1979, Khani M.K., Scott-Straus A: Cyclothymic temperamental disorders. *Psychiatr. Clin. North Am.* 2:527-554.

Andrulonis P.A., Donnelly J., Glueck B.C. et al: 1980, Preliminary data on ethosuximide and the episodic dyscontrol syndrome. *Am. J. Psychiatry* 137:1455-1456.

Aono T., Kaneko M., Numata Y., et al: 1981, Effects of amoxapine, a new antidepressant, on psuedoneurotic schizophrenia. *Folia Psychiatr.Neurol.* Japan, 35:115-121.

Bach-Y-Rita G., Lion J.R., Climent C.E., et al: 1971, Episodic dyscontrol: A study of 130 violent patients. *Am.J .Psychiatry* 127:1473-1478.

Barnes R.J: 1977, Mesoridazine (Serenitil) in personality disorders - a controlled trial in adolescent patients. *Diseases of the Nervous System* 38:258-264.

Baxter L., Edell W., Gerner R., et al: 1984, Dexamethasone suppression test and Axis I diagnosis of in-patients with DSM-III borderline personality disorder. *J. Clin. Psychiatry* 45:150-153.

Brinkley J.R., Beitman B.D., Friedel R.O.: 1979, Low-dose neuroleptic regimensin the treatment of borderline patients.*Arch Gen Psychiatry* 36:319-326.

Brown G.L. and Goodwin F.K.: 1986, Human aggression: A biological perspective in Unmasking The Psychopath: Antisocial Personality and Related Syndromes. Edited by Reid W.M., Dorr D., Waller JI. et al. W.W. Norton, N.Y.

Carroll B.J., Greden J.F., Feinberg M., et al: 1981, Neuroendocrine evaluation of depression in borderline patients. *Psychiatr. Clin. North Am.* 4:89-98.

Chodoff P.: 1974, diagnosis of hysteria - an overview. *Am. J. Psychiatry* 131:1073-1078.

Elliot F.A.: 1977, Propranolol for the control of belligerent behavior following acute brain damage. *Ann. Neurol* 1:489-491.

Faltus F.J.: 1984, The positive effect of alprazolam in the treatment of three patients with borderline personality disorder *Am. J. Psychiatry* 141:802-803.

Feighner J.P., Herbstein J., Damlouji N.:1985, Combined MAOI, TCA, and direct stimulant therapy of treatment-resistant depression. *J .Clin .Psychiatry* 46:206-209

Garbutt J.C., Loosen P.T., Tipermas A., et al: 1983, The TRH test in patients with borderline personality disorder. *Psychiatry Res.* 9:107-113.

Gardner D.L., Cowdry R.W.: 1985, Alprazolam - induced dyscontrol in borderline personality disorder. *Am. J. Psychiatry* 142:98-100.

Goldberg S.C., Schulz S.C., Schulz P.M. et al: 1986, Borderline and schizotypal personality disorders treated with low dose thothixene vs. placebo. *Arch. Gen. Psychiatry*, 43:680-686.

Gunderson J.: 1984, Borderline Personality Disorder. Washington DC, American Psychiatric Press, Inc.

Hedberg D.L., Houck J.H., Glueck B.C.: 1971, Tranylcypromine - trifluoerazine combination in the treatment of schizophrenia. *Am. J. Psychiatry* 127:1141-1146.

Hymowitz P., Frances A.J., Hoyt R., et al: 1984, Neuroleptic Treatment of Schizotypal Personalities. Presented at the 137th Annual Meeting of the American Psychiatric Association, Los Angeles.

Kernberg O.F.: 1975, Borderline Conditions and Pathological Narcissim. New York, Jason Aronson Inc.

Kety S.S., Rosenthal D., Wender P.H., et al: 1968, The types and prevalence of mental illness in the biological and adoptive familes of adoptive schizophrenics, in The Transmission of Schizophrenia, ed. Rosenthal D., Kety S.S., Oxford Pergamon Press.

Klein D.F.:1964, Delineation of two drug-responsive anxiety syndromes. *Psychopharmacologia* 5:397-408.

Klein D.F.: 1967, Importance of psychiatric diagnosis in the prediction of clinical drug effects. *Arch. Gen. Psychiatry* 16:118-126.

Klein D.F.: 1975, Psychopharmacology and the borderline patient, in *Borderline States in Psychiatry*. Edited by Mack JE, New Yor, Grune & Stratton.

Knight R.P.: 1953, Borderline states. *Bull. Menningner Clin.* 17:1-11.

Kraepelin E.: 1921, Manic Depressive Insanity and Paranoia. Edinburgh, E & S Livingston.

Kretschmer E.: 1936, Physique and Character, 2nd edition. London, Routledge.

Leone N.F.: 1982, Response of borderline patients to loxapine and chlorpromazine. *J . Clin. Psychiatry* 43:148-150.

Liebowitz J.H., Rudy V., Gershon E.S., et al: 1976, A pharmacogenetic case report: Lithium -responsiveness postpsychotic antisocial behavior. *Compr.Psychiatry* 17:655-660.

Liebowitz M.R.: 1979, Is borderline a distinct entity? *Schizophr. Bull.* 5:23-38.
Liebowitz M.R., Klein D.F.: 1979, Hysteroid dysphoria.
    Psychiatr. Clin. North Am. 2:555-575.
Liebowitz M.R., Klein D.F.: 1981, Interrelationship of hysteroid dysphoria and
    borderline personality disorder. *Psychiatr. Clin. North Am.* 4:67-87.
Liebowitz M.R., Quitkin F.M., Stewart J.W., et al: 1984, Phenelzine vs. imipramine
    in atypical depression:A preliminary report.*Arch. Gen. Psychiatry* 41:669-677.
Liebowitz M.R., Gorman J.M., Fyer A.J., et al: Social phobia: 1985, Review of a
    neglected anxiety disorder. *Arch. Gen. Psychiatry* 42:729-736.
Liebowitz M.R., Fyer A.J., Gorman J.M., et al: 1986, Phenelzine in social phobia.
    J. Clinic. Psychopharmacol. 6:93-98.
Liebowitz M.R., et al: Obsessive compulsive disorder: Paradigmatic shift and an
    improved prognosis (submitted for publication)
McNamara E., Reynolds C.F., Soloff P.H., et al: 1984, EEG sleep evaluation of
    depression in borderline patients. *Am. J. Psychiatry* 141:182-186.
Millon T.: 1969, Modern Psychopathology: A Biosocial Approach to
    Maladaptive Learning and Functioning. Philadelphia, WB Saunders.
Nies A., Howard D., Robinson D.S.: 1982, Antianxiety effects of MAO inhibitors,
    in The Biology of Anxiety, ed. Mathew RJ. New York, Brunner/Mazel.
Quitkin F., Rifkin A., Klein D.F.: 1976, Neurologic soft signs in schizophrenia and
    character disorders: Organicity in schizophrenia with premorbid asociality
    and emotionally unstable character disorders. *Arch. Gen. Psychiatry*
    33:845-853.
Ratey J.J., Morrill R., Oxenkrug F:. 1983, Use of propranolol for provoked and
    unprovoked episodes of rage, *Am. J.Psychiatry* 140:1356-1357.
Reich W.:1949, Character Analysis, New York, Noonday Press.
Reyntjens A.M.: 1972, A series of multicentric pilot trials with pimozide in
    psychiatric practice, I: Pimozide in the treatment of personality disorders.
    Acta. Psychiatr. Belg. 72:653-661.
Rifkin A., Quitkin F., Carrillo C., et al: 1972, Lithium carbonate in emotionally
    unstable character disorder. *Arch. Gen.Psychiatry* 27:519-523.
Rosenbaum J.F.,Woods S.W., Groves J.E., et al: 1984, Emergence of hostility during
    alprazolam treatment. *Am. J. Psychiatry* 141:792-793.
Rosenthal D., Wender P.H. Kety S.S., et al: 1968, Schizophrenics' offspring reared
    in adoptive homes, in The Transmission of Schizophrenia, ed.
    Rosenthal D, Kety S, Oxford, Pergamon Press.
Schatzberg A.F., Cole J.O.: 1981, Benzodiazepines in the treatment of depressive,
    borderline personality, and schizophrenic disorders. *Br. J. Clin. Pharmacol.*
    11:175-225.
Schneider K.: 1959, *Clinical Psychopathology*. New York, Grune & Stratton.
Serban G.: 1984, Borderline and schizotypal personality disorders: Criteria for
    diagnosis and treatment. *Am. J.Psychiatry* 141:1455-1458.
Sheard M.H., Marini J.L., Bridges D.I., et al: 1976, The effect of lithium on
    impulsive aggressive behavior in man. *Am. J. Psychiatry* 133:1409-1413.
Sheehan D.V., Coleman J.H., Greenblatt D.J., et al: 1984, Some biochemical
    correlates of panic attacks with agoraphobia and their response to a new
    treatment. *Clin.Psychopharmacol.* 4:66-75.

Soloff P.H., George A., Nathan R.S,. et al:1986 a, Progress in pharmacotherapy of
    borderline disorders. *Arch. Gen. Psychiatry* 43:691-697.
Soloff P.H., George A., Nathan R.S,. et al: 1986 b, Paradoxical effect of
    amitriptyline on borderline patients. *Am. J. Psychiatry* 143:1603-1605.
Stringer AY, Joseph NC: 1983, Methylphenidate in the treatment of aggression in
    two patients with antisocial personality disorder. *Am. J. Psychiatry* 140:1365-
    1366.
Stone M.H.: 1979, Contemporary shift of the borderline concept from a
    subschizophrenic disorder to a subaffectve disorder.*Psychiatr. Clin. North
    Am* . 2:577-594.
Thoren J.P., Asberg M., Cronholm B., et al: 1973, Clomipramine treatment of
    obsessive -compulsive disorder. *Arch. Gen. Psychiatry* 37:311-317.
Tupin J.P. Smith D.B., Clanon T.l., et al: 1973, The long-term use of lithium in
    aggressive prisoners. *Compr. Psychiatry* 14:311-317.
Turnquist K., Frances R., Rosenfeld W., et al: 1983, Pemoline in attention deficit
    disorder and alcoholism: A case study. *Am. J. Psychiatry* 140:622-624.
Wender P.H., Reimherr F.W., Wood D.R.: 1981, Attention deficit disorder (mini-
    mal brain dysfunction) in adults. *Arch. Gen. Psychiatry* 38:449-456.
Wood D..R., Reimherr F.W., Wender P.H., et al:1976, Diagnosis and treatment of
    minimal brain dysfunction in adults. *Arch. Gen. Psychiatry* 33:1453-1460.
Yerevanian B.I., Akiskal H.S.: 1979, "Neurotic," characterological, and dysthymic
    depressions. *Psychiatr. Clin. North Am.* 2:595-617.
Yudofsky S., Williams D., Gorman J.M.: 1981, Propranolol in treatment of rage and
    violent behavior in patients with chronic brain syndrome.
    Am.J. Psychiatry 138:218-220.

The Role of Shame in Symptom Formation

Helen Block Lewis

Yale University
New Haven,
Connecticut, U S A

Introduction

Let me first express my delight at the chance to discuss the psychoanalysis of shame and guilt with neuro-behavioral scientists. I have been devoting the past 25 years of my life to these two grisly states - in my view human beings' principal moral emotions. And of course it does not take much thinking to realize that the reason I have had to focus on shame and guilt is that in psychoanalytic work and psychotherapeutic work of any kind these are the two prevailing emotions with which clients address us.

Let me confess first of all that I have something of a struggle to overcome my awe and my envy of the remarkable achievements of neuroscience. That is an attitude that is frequent among psychologists who deal with so-called soft data. I find it a comfort, however, to recognize that the careful and delicate description of human emotions can indeed contribute to progress in neurophysiology, as it helped me in my therapeutic work. So for example a review of functional neurochemistry suggests that the difference between schizophrenia, which involves "the stress of social interaction" and depression, which is "a stress reaction to social loss", points to the existence of very different patterns of neuro-regulators. As Manfred Clynes put it: "Now that we are finding a way to measure the biologic coherence between the forms of expression and experience... we begin to see that the sphere of qualities of emotions belongs to ordered reality as much as the genetic code" (Clynes, 1977). It is indeed an exhilarating opportunity that this conference offers.

I shall begin by plunging in where angels fear to tread. I am going to try to make three links between my work on shame and guilt and neurophysiology. These links I began to see when I began to study the works of Panksepp (1982), and I have known John Paul Scott's work since my graduate student days.

1. Separation, Distress and Shame.

The first link is separation, distress and shame. The proposition that separation

95

distress/ panic is one of the four major circuits of the mammalian brain suggests that the uniquely human state of shame may indeed be one of the primary emotions as Tomkins (1963) and Izard (1972) have argued. Shame is the state into which adults and children fall when they are faced with separation experienced as rejection or failure or as we psychoanalysts used to put it - loss of love. Guilt by contrast is the state generated by castration anxiety, a more specific threat to physical safety.

Shame is often accompanied by blushing and sweating, two powerful autonomic responses that also reflect our uniquely human morality. We are the only species that blushes, and our morality thus seems to go quite deep. People tell us that in the state of shame they feel something like panic. They want to cut and run. But they also feel paralyzed. So shame and separation distress/panic are clearly linked descriptively and both have direct physiological indicators. What is most exciting is some recent evidence for the operation of something like shame during the Ainsworth "Strange Situation Method " of evoking separation distress in human infants.

There is also a general clinical observation that shame can be *discharged* in good-humored laughter at the self and its relation to others. Shame carries the cognitive message that it is only about the self, and it seems also to evoke laughter, both at the self and at the other. You notice as soon as shame was mentioned everybody giggled, in this audience as well. The observation that shared laughter dissolves humiliation was actually first made by Freud (1905) in his neglected "Humour and the Unconscious."

A study using videotapes of the facial expression of people coping with resentment regarded as a mixture of shame and fury recently showed that triumphant laughter decreased both shame and hostility . In any case, the inverse relationship between shame and laughter suggests once again the inverse relationship between the circuits for separation distress and expectancy/foraging/play.

2. Guilt and Fear Circuits

Consider guilt and the distinction between circuits governing fear for physical safety, individual safety and social fear. Pschyoanalysts tell us that guilt, in contrast to shame, is the state generated by castration anxiety - a specific threat of physical injury. There is in fact some empirical evidence that these two forms of anxiety - castration anxiety and a loss of love anxiety - are distinguishable. In psychoanalytic jargon they are also distinguished as threats resting on the so-called anaclytic or loving identifications versus introjective or threatening identifications. These have been extensively studied, especially as related to aggression, in longitudinal studies of human development such as those by Sears (1957, 1965), and Kagan and Moss (1962).

As one might guess, women are more prone to fear the loss of love, while men are more prone to fear castration threat. Also important is the distinction that present-day psychiatry makes between so-called specific or simple phobias (which are fears of snakes, elevators, heights and the like) and so-called agoraphobias (in which the stimulus cannot be so readily defined but which clearly comprehends the dread of social isolation as experienced almost literally in open space). There is good evidence (Seif & Atkins, 1979) that agoraphobics are more likely to show the cognitive style called "field dependence" while specific phobics are more often "field independent". And there is now some evidence that field independent patients are more prone to express guilt while field dependent patients are more prone to express shame in their early therapy sessions .

So, by a very roundabout chain of connections, we might speculate that the circuits governing separation are linked to shame, while the circuits governing physical safety are linked to guilt. Thus I wonder whether the two kinds of phobias might not react differently to different drugs. (See chapter by Liebowitz in this volume.)

3. Shame and the Circuits for Sexuality and Separation Distress

Next, consider shame and the overlap between brain areas mediating sexuality and those mediating separation distress. As we all know, Freud (1905) at the beginning of his work insisted that sexuality was the key drive that had to be tamed, and that shame was one of the three inherent forces, the others being morality and disgust, that did the taming. Since Freud, we know from the work of Bowlby (1969-73) and the Harlows (1963) that sexuality and the attachment system are two separate systems, and that the latter strongly influences the former. Indeed, as ethologists have shown, so much of animal behavior seems to be embedded in a social context that even the salivary system of the sheep, for example, is governed by social stimuli.

In any case, we now know that faulty attachment results in serious disturbances in the sexual system of monkeys, along with serious disturbances in learning, curiosity and sociability. Faulty attachment injures human beings similarly as well, as Bowlby and Aisnworth and their students have shown. This seems to be congruent with Panksepp's (1982) idea that lust may not be a bona fide emotion, but that it may rely for its emotive impulse on the arousal of the foraging, expectancy and play systems. By the same token, the evocation of separation distress is aversive to foraging/expectancy and play. If we assume that a major target of foraging/expectancy and play in the infant is the mother and that the evocation of separation distress is aversive, we may help to clarify how it is that social isolation injures sexual competence. Perhaps it is because social isolation breeds something like shame.

At this point, another factor needs to be added to the complexity of things, and that is the factor of *sex differences*. Evidence on the primate level suggests that female monkeys are less injured by maternal deprivation than males. Sackett (1974) has shown that male monkeys raised in isolation are totally unable to copulate in adulthood, while female monkeys are less impaired. Moreover, females reared in isolation are less injured than males in their curiosity, social behavior and learning capacity. As Sackett puts it, summarizing the findings: "Females are the buffered sex. What they are buffered by perhaps is a slight edge in their sociability which makes them better able to withstand the injuries of isolation."

Studies of monkeys also show that mother monkeys treat the two sexes differently. Mothers punish their male infants more than their females. They pay them less attention, and carry them around less frequently than females. (This finding among primates has its forerunner among mice - female pups are retrieved more often by their mothers than male pups.) No-one yet understands the basis for this difference in mother-infant interaction among monkeys. One can speculate that male infants are innately more aggressive than females and so induce more aggression in their mothers, in turn perpetuating male aggression. One can also speculate that a greater degree of sociability in females is expressed by and in turn perpetuates females' greater sociability.

The findings among monkeys are paralleled by similar findings about sex differences in the mother-infant interaction among ourselves. I have no time to go into that literature, but a recent literature review by Haviland and Malatesta (1982) offer strong support for the greater irritability of male infants and the greater consolability of female infants.

What this evidence suggests is that there may be corresponding *sex differences in the way the circuits for expectancy and for separation distress operate.* . We do know that there is a hormonal basis for females being less disposed to anger than males and on the human level, womens' lesser disposition to anger and greater disposition to sociability have been well documented. On both these counts, as well as their second class citizenship in the world of power, women cope with shame more often than men.

Now that I have sketched these three links to brain circuitry it is time for me to come home to my own domain and to tell you something about the psychoanalysis of shame and guilt, and how the cognitive style called field dependence / field independence became linked with shame and guilt.

Over the past forty years as a practising psychoanalyst, much of this time coinciding with ongoing research and collaboration with H.A. Witkin (1954, 1965, 1968) on field dependence, I have slowly been pushed to the realization that undischarged shame (either overt but unacknowledged, or else by-passed shame) is implicated in the formation of neurotic and psychotic symptoms. These observations grew in part out of a few surprising but very troubling therapeutic failures of my own. What I can now describe, that was not apparent to me when I began analytic work in 1945, is a lightning speed sequence from an evoked state of shame almost immediately, simultaneously, into humiliated fury and thence into guilt - for what is processed by the person as forbidden anger - unjust, wrong or inappropriate anger. My observations about the role of shame thus connect with Freud's concept of unconscious, archaic or irrational guilt as the source of neurosis and psychosis. "The patient does not feel guilty," he wrote, "he feels ill." But I specifically add *undischarged shame as the emotional force fueling guilt over "unjust" anger.*

Differentiating between Shame and Guilt

Before I go further, let me ask you to bear with me about definitions. Shame and guilt often occur simultaneously, especially when one has committed a moral transgression. We say "How could I have done that?" or we say "How could I have done that?" And it's a difference. The two states, however, are quite distinguishable phenomenologically as I have shown in my book (Lewis, 1971) and as a series of recent investigations, both clinical and experimental, has clearly confirmed. There are now at least six studies differentiating between shame and guilt. I use the term *"shame"* as the cover term for a family of feeling including humiliation, mortification, shyness, painful self-consciousness, feeling ridiculous, chagrin, embarrassment - all of which differ from each other but nevertheless share in common that all these negative states focus on the *helpless self.* Guilt similarly refers to a family of feelings, including fault, blame, obligation, and responsibility, all of which although different from each other, share the common theme that the self has *done* or *not done* something that it was *able to do.*

Shame and guilt thus differ sharply in the way the self functions in the field. They also differ *in the way the self processes anger*. Shame appears to create its own feeling trap for anger. Shame forbids the unjust expression or sometimes even the feeling of retaliatory rage ("turning the tables, getting even"), at the same time that it presses toward the discharge. There seem to be two components in this inhibition of discharge. The first inheres in the experience of shame, which tends to evoke the shame of being ashamed. The second component derives more directly from our attachment to others - which evokes guilt for harming them by retaliatory shaming.

Shame Evokes further Shame

Let us look first at the way the experience of shame evokes more shame. When shame is overt, it is an acute experience, at which the self is the center of experience. Helen Lynd (1958) put it most beautifully; she says "Shame catches the self at the quick." Darwin (1872) was in fact the first scientist to describe shame. He not only observed that it is a state of acute painful self-consciousness, especially involving the face, but he observed that "under the press of shame there is a strong desire for concealment." He also told us that shame produces a confusion of mind, which puts it mildly.

The paradox of shame is thus an *acute self-consciousness occurring together with an acute momentary need for unconsciousness*. Adults who introspect on shame tell us that along with the blushing, sweating and palpitations that signal it there is the simultaneous realization that these are "excessive" or "irrational" responses and beyond self-control. This creates a sense of incongruity about their adulthood. People therefore are ashamed of being ashamed as I said before, and often automatically disclaim or deny that they are in a state of shame because of their being ashamed of their state. Their disclaimer or denial reflects their own recognition of the incongruity or "childishness", as many people put it, of the shame response.

Second, the humiliated feeling that is being evoked almost simultaneously with shame (signalled perhaps by the flushing and increased heartbeat), is in response to the experience of rejection or loss of love by a significant or symbolic attachment figure. Humiliated fury is blocked however by the person's attachment which has rendered the person vulnerable to begin with. Guilt automatically accompanies the impulse to retaliate or hurt the other in revenge. The more psychologically sophisticated among us now say "Don't get mad, get even," but this is not an easy proposition if one really cares about one's lover, one's child, one's parent, or one's therapist. Thus shame exerts its almost lethal momentary effect on the self because it is being processed as shameful while its natural push for rageful retaliation is being processed as forbidden, or guilty. I have many, many excerpts from psychotherapy sessions showing in detail the sequence from shame into humiliated fury into guilt. But it is not possible to show these here.

Freud's role in the discovery and the neglect of shame is a fascinating story in its own right. His original discovery was that neurosis and psychosis could be traced to forbidden sexual longings - forbidden obviously by shame and guilt. His first insight into the emotional basis of mental illness was mainly derived from the sufferings of hysterical women. These women were members of the second sex in middle-class Vienna and they were living within a set of patriarchal values that fostered an apparently benign degradation of their sex. Some of them somehow transformed forbidden sexual longings into incapacitating neurotic symptoms and I say "somehow" advisedly because we still don't quite understand the process, although attempts have been made to describe it.

Freud in Relation to Shame and Guilt

Freud, following Breuer's lead, traced the sequences from forbidden affects into "compromise formations" of neurotic symptoms that both concealed and expressed these longings. He invented a necessary technique of listening, that is an "analytic" attitude in which moral judgement (that is, both shame and guilt) are implicitly and explicitly to be suspended. Freud's descriptive account of his cases are full of the shame and guilt with which his patients were struggling, in spite of analytic "permission". Yet he framed his theoretical account of what was happening in terms of "excitation" and "discharge" - and in terms of Darwinian individual instincts of sex and aggression.

Evolutionary biology, on which Freud relied was quite sexist. It has been very slow to recognize that our primate heritage includes not only Tarzan, the Mighty Hunter come out of the trees with his superior cunning, upright posture, big brain and opposable thumb, but Ms. Mighty Hunter, the nurturant female primate mother carefully suckling and tending her young. Amusingly enough Lovejoy (1981) has recently suggested that human beings' advanced material culture may be the result, not the cause of their sociability since, "an already established hominid system of parenting and social relationships " preceded cultural development. Lovejoy also observes that walking on two feet may have freed our hands for provisioning, not only for carrying spears - that is, carrying food to the young and thus increasing survival chances. It is only recently that nurturance as a force governing human evolution has gained some scientific respectability. Elaine Morgan's witty "The Descent of Woman" 1973) gave this idea some of its momentum. An ethical system based on the premise that human nature is evil or aggressive will emphasise guilt as its major control, while an ethical system that includes human sociability as a given will also emphasize the shame in one's own eyes of losing the love of the other.

We have recently been reminded that many of Freud's hysterical patients were actually victims of sexual abuse by father figures. Freud found that he had eighteen cases of childhood sexual abuse in his first eighteen cases of hysteria. He naturally therefore at first formulated the hypothesis that seduction and sexual abuse were important factors in the etiology of hysteria. But he found it difficult to believe that this heinous crime could be committed by so many respectable men. When he made his discovery of infantile sexuality, he abandoned his seduction theory in favor of the idea that guilt over their illicit childhood fantasies was the source of his patients' hysteria. And it began to seem to him and to his followers as if one could not believe in actual seductions and still believe in the psychoanalytic discovery of infantile sexuality. We now know, nearly a hundred years later, that Freud was close to being right the first time. The statistics now being assembled make it very clear that child sexual abuse is widespread, and that as many as sixty percent in one study of hysterical women patients (now diagnosed as borderline), have actually been sexually abused in childhood.

In turning his attention away from actual seductions to guilt over fantasies Freud turned away from shame. This *is what children experience* when they are sexually molested by an adult. I don't know what the reason is for that. It just is. I think it is that the adult has betrayed their trust and thrown them into a state of shame on the loss of their most profound attachments. They fall speedily also into a state of guilt. It is not that Freud did not accurately describe this state of affairs. For instance, when he was treating Dora who had been molested by a father-figure for years and was disbelieved by her father when she told, Freud called her state mortification - it's a shame variant - at being betrayed. But when Dora fell into a state of guilt for her humiliated fury and blamed herself for "exaggerating her injuries", Freud agreed with her. He said: "Since no actual contract had been violated, Dora was right to feel that she was exaggerating her injuries and her father's guilt." Besides, Freud tried to show her that she did have sexual fantasies for which she might well feel guilty. No wonder she left treatment with him abruptly.

Although his descriptions of primary process transformations into symptoms when people are under the press of undischarged shame and guilt were so accurate, there was no room in Freud's theoretical system for the shame that follows personal betrayal. Women who have suffered from sexual abuse in childhood are only now struggling to break the silence - that is, to overcome the shame which their attachments still seem to require.

The Theory of Shame and Field Dependence

Ironically, it was as a researcher rather than as a psychoanalyst that I first became involved in studying the problem of the nature of human nature and, indirectly, the problem of shame. When Max Wertheimer, a founder of Gestalt psychology, came to the New School's University in Exile in as a refugee from Hitler, I had the good fortune to meet him and to encounter the possibility of studying such problems empirically. It was an eye-opener for me, straight out of Columbia graduate school.

Wertheimer (1912, 1938) argued from the premise that the human self or ego, although central in the organization of experience, is nevertheless not egotistical. Under Wertheimer's influence, I first undertook an experiment designed to show that when people are engaged in co-operative work, they will not particularly remember whether they or their co-operating partners actually completed the task. With the help of Muriel Franklin (1944) I was able to demonstrate that tasks literally completed by another person, the partner, were experienced as completed by the self. There was of course a hint in our findings that some few people were more vulnerable than others to the experience of failure if they had not actually completed the task themselves. At the time of these experiments, although I was observing "failures", I hardly realized the fact that *ideas of failure are the cognitive side of the emotion of shame.*

Also under the influence of Wertheimer two colleagues of mine, Asch and Witkin, (1948) became interested in his experiments on the way in which people orient themselves in space. Under ordinary conditions we orient ourselves in space by relying on both the visual framework offered by all the horizontals and verticals that abound in the world, and on many postural cues issuing from the pull of gravity on our bodies. Ordinarily these two sets of cues coincide and we are very accurate in the degree to which we can judge the true upright in space. Wertheimer proposed that even the perception of one's own position in space is governed by the relationship between the self and its surrounding field. What would happen, he asked, if we could separate the postural from the visual cues?

In Berlin, Wertheimer used a mirror which he tilted slowly. Objects were reflected in the mirror and he asked people what they saw. In Berlin everybody began to right the perception, and said there was nothing wrong, they just saw some things in the mirror. In Cornell, when Gibson and Mowra (1938) tried to repeat the experiment everybody was bothered by the tilt. There was a clear discrepancy of findings. It was in order to try to resolve this discrepancy that Asch and Witkin (1948) undertook their study of the percpetion of the upright, using no longer the mirror but bringing subjects into a totally darkened room in which there was a luminous frame and a luminous stick. The person is asked to make the stick "straight with the walls of the room". On average, Wertheimer's hypothesis was confirmed. The average deviation from the true upright in these conditions is about twelve degrees, so on average people are influenced by the prevailing framework.

But it was Witkin who made the observation - as he was doing these experiments in the basement of Brooklyn College where we were both connected at the time - that he thought he could tell which people would be influenced by the framework and which people would not be influenced by the framework. And he came to me, and he said "I think I can tell," and he said, "Would you like to guess?" So, sitting with Dorothy Dinnerstein then a senior at Brooklyn College, and giggling mightily because we were embarassed at our inability to specify how we were telling, how we were guessing - we guessed. And we guessed eighty percent correctly. So we were convinced that there was something about the personality of the person that allowed us to guess which way the person would go, whether be influenced by the framework or not influenced by the framework. That was our first report published in 1954 (Witkin, H.A., Lewis. H.B., Hertzman, M., et al).

Since then, there have been literally thousands of studies on field dependence. I want to say how it was that, struggling with field dependence/field independence and its clinical implications, I came to think about shame and guilt. This happened at the same time that I was worrying about therapeutic failures . There was a coalescence of stimuli to make one think.

The first observation we made about field dependence was in our hospital sample (1954), and there it became clear that extent of field dependence is not related to pathology, but is a form of it, and we would intuitively predict field dependent patients are more depressed . Field independence goes with paranoia. That was a first sort of sweeping observation that we made. There are many studies that suggest this kind of connection between form of patholology and field dependence. And thinking about guilt - archaic, irrational guilt; what we analysts were trained to think about - it began to occur to me that maybe we could show a difference between field dependent and field independent people in their proneness to shame or to guilt.

So, Edmund Weil and Witkin and myself (1968) designed a study to put our hypothesis to test, that there would be more shame in the therapy transcripts of field dependent patients and more often guilt in the transcripts of field independent patients than conversely. We studied 172 consecutive admissions to Kings County Outpatients. We found four extremely field dependent persons according to our criteria, and four extremely field independent patients, matched as a group, for age and sex. Actually we found our first four field independent patients in a year. It took us two years to get the four field dependent ones because we wanted them extreme, and apparently field dependent people are shy enough so that they don't go too near Kings County Outpatients clinic. We offered these patients twenty sessions with a therapist and put the patients as pairs, one very field dependent, one very field independent, in therapy with the same therapist. We tape recorded the twenty sessions. Gottschalk and Gleser's method of assessing verbal content (1969) was used, a very reliable and valid method. There was a very striking difference in that the transcripts of the field dependent patients were just loaded with shame more than guilt, and the transcripts of the field independent patients were loaded with guilt more than shame. There is no missing it. Samples are included in"*Shame and Guilt in Neurosis*", (Lewis, 1971), and the phenomenology of shame and guilt can be seen as one reads these transcripts. It is well documented.

There is also evidence, collected around the seventies, of the difference between agoraphobics and specific phobics - agoraphobics being more field dependent and simple phobics being more field independent. I think that shame and guilt are in there, in the appropriate ways.

Shame and guilt occur together. The stimulus to shame may be twofold, not just moral transgression, but failure. Ausubel (1955) distinguishes between what he calls moral and non-moral shame. Non-moral shame is when you have failed, you are sexually rebuffed, you have been in a contest and you have lost. Shame goes with failure. Guilt is about some things that you did or didn't do. Shame has an affinity for depression - the same way you hang your head and avert your gaze and feel very little when you're going to be depressed, whereas with guilt you start to get dizzy in your head, you start to say "Well if I had done this then that wouldn't have happened, and if he'd done that, then *that* wouldn't have happened... " You get involved in the problem of how you should make amends for the guilty act and the affect can diminish. In some instances there is affinity between guilt and obsessional thinking and a little paranoia as the obsessional thinking won't quite settle.

Shame has many autonomic accompaniments - I think guilt has fewer. Shame is a global experience. Guilt is specific. That was the basis on which Seif and Atkins (1979) did their phobia study. Shame leads to identity thoughts. Nothing like it in guilt. Shame is the vicarious experience of the other's disapproval. Guilt is a set of thoughts about what one needs to do to make things right.

Shame and Attachment

Let us consider shame and the attachment emotions. Why should shame be the response to loss of love? What role does humiliated fury play in the picture? In a way that has puzzled psychoanalysts beginning with Freud, losing someone to whom one is attached evokes humiliated fury because it feels like a loss of self esteem. Vicarious emotional experience is the foundation of attachment on both sides. It is the price we pay for it. Shame is the empathetic or vicarious experience of the other's rejection of the self. Shame is the state in which one accepts the loss of the other as if it were a loss in the self. Humiliated fury, which is an inevitable accompaniment of shame, angrily protests the loss at the same time that it demands restitution of the other's positive feeling. But being angry at, and wanting the love of the same person is inherently disorganizing. It is a useful reaction only if the other person is actually stably affectionate. In that case, the guilt that comes with humiliated fury is a useful reminder of affectional ties. When the other person is always rejecting, or unable to be stably affectionate, humiliated fury is useless. It will not effect the change in feeling that is required. It leads back to shame and chronic, "irrational" guilt.

Some observations from empirical studies using Ainsworth's technique suggest that shame or some forerunner of it may be operating in the behavior of infants. Ainsworth and Whittig (1969) describe the crying that occurs in infants on separation as "outraged" crying. In his earlier studies of older children on separation, Bowlby (1969) used the term "bitter protest". I suggest that outraged crying and bitter protest are both expressions of humiliated fury. Bowlby suggests that the bitter reproaches are designed to prevent a repetition of the mother's desertion: she cannot stand to hear that, so she is not going to do that again. I think they also function so as to communicate a very complex message: the infant feels separation as a rejection. Rejection by the other is experienced as a loss in the self. The infant is furiously demanding that mother change her feeling state (rejection) and resume affectionate attention. The infant's fury is the forerunner of humiliated fury, and the emotional loss experienced in the self is like a forerunner of shame in infancy. Both humiliated fury and shame are communications to the other as well as emotional states experienced by the self.

The complex emotional communications involved are illustrated in some recent findings of Main and Weston (1981,1982), two of Ainsworth's students. Videotapes of "secure" infants responding to their mother's return after separation show that even while they are seeking and accepting reunion there is at least brief gaze aversion or a blank expression on their faces. Gaze aversion has been shown empirically in adults to be associated with shame. Even with secure attachment, reunion after separation is apparently experienced with a mixture of pleasure and some hint of shame. When we look at what happens to insecurely attached infants we find some of them angrily resist reunion with the mother at the same time as they are obviously seeking it. This ambivalence is familiar to all of us when we are in a state of humiliated fury. Other insecure infants show an even more astonishing pattern. They do not show any anger. Rather they actively avoid the mother. "Picked up, they indicate (in an emotionless way) a desire to be put down, often pointing to a toy in order to distract the mother. They are often markedly more friendly to a stranger than to the mother, which makes their behavior even more pointed."

It seems to me that these avoidant, insecurely attached infants may be showing the forerunner of a pattern of reaction that involves what I call the bypassing the shame of being rejected. They do not directly express humiliated fury. Rather, they behave as if they were turning the tables on the rejecting mother by rejecting her. It is fascinating, moreover, that some infants who, avoidant of their mothers in the laboratory, were quite angry with them at home, often quite inexplicably so. "The baby is creeping across the floor smiling. Suddenly he veers toward his mother, strikes her leg, and creeps away. " Humiliated fury, as we older people are familiar with it, often has just this quality of being throttled in shame and then appearing at other, unpredictable times pushing to turn the tables on the humiliating person. Main & Weston tell us further that an insecure infant "when held by mother clings, then angrily pushes her away, then clings, then pushes away, then clings again. This highly distressed and disorganizing behavior is very distressing to witness." This reminds us of how distressing it is to watch humiliated fury and shame in adults. Perhaps the ablation of the self in shame helps to postpone or avoid this disorganization.

A cautionary note is needed at this point. No-one knows just what all the ingredients are that go to make up a securely attached infant. We do know some few things however, and one of them is that mothers learn to distinguish early between what they call "mad" cries which signify that the infant is just angry and can cry it out alone, and cries signifying real "distress", which means that the infant gets picked up. Infants need to learn that not every separation signifies rejection although it may feel as if it does. And they do need to manage some things on their own, in harmony with the caretaker's expectations. Thus a sequence from shame, into humiliated fury, and thence into guilt, for not doing what one is able to do, is adaptive. Infants need both shame and guilt experiences. These are clearly best developed in a stably affectionate and just world. The trouble that can breed neurosis comes when our two principal moral emotions, shame and guilt, have to function in an insecurely affectionate environment in childhood and later on in a very unjust world.

In summary, what is so exciting to me in thinking about an expectancy/foraging/play circuit and a separation distress/panic circuit is that both speak to the idea that there is a biological grounding for the intrinsically social nature of human nature. I am aware that I am treading on dangerous ground, especially since I have no wish to follow the sociobiologists into their social Darwinism. But I have entered the lion's den of neurophysiology and found there evidence for brain circuits that I can interpret as suggesting the biological basis of human nurturance, out of which human morality is born.

References

Ainsworth, M. & Wittig, M., 1969, Attachment and exploratory behavior of one-year-olds in a strange situation, in: "Determinants of Infant Behavior," vol.4, B.M.Foss, ed., Methuan, London.

Ausubel, D. 1955, Relationships between shame and guilt in the socialising process. *Psychol. Rev.*, 62:378-390.

Asch, S.E., 1956, Studies of independence and conformity (Part1): A minority of one against a unanimous majority, *Psychol. Monogr.* 70(9):1-70.

Asch, S.E., & Witkin, H.A., 1948, Studies in space orientation I and II, *J. Exp. Psychol.*, 38:325-337; 455-477.

Bowlby, J. 1969-73, in: "Attachment and Loss," vols. 1 & 2. Basic Books, London.

Clynes, M., 1977, "Sentics, The Touch of Emotion", Doubleday - Anchor, New York.

Darwin, C., 1872, "Expression of Emotion in Man and Animals".

Freud, S., 1905,   Humour and the Unconscious".

Gibson, J. & Mowrer, O.H. 1938, Determinants of the perceived vertical and horizontal. *Psychol. Rev.* 45:300-323.

Gottschalk, L. and Gleser, G. 1969, in: "The Measurement of Psychological States through the Content Analysis of Verbal Behavior," U. Calif. Press, Berkeley.

Harlow, H., Harlow, M., & Hansen, E., 1963, The maternal affection system of Rhesus monkeys, in: "Maternal Behavior in Mammals," H. Rheingold, ed., Wiley, New York.

Izard, C., 1972, in: "Patterns of Emotion: A New Analysis of Anxiety and Depression," Academic Press, New York.

Kagan, J. & Moss, H., 1962, in: "Birth to Maturity: A Study in Psychological Development," Wiley, New York.

Lewis, H. B. , 1971, in: "Shame and Guilt," Int. Univ. Press, New York.

Lewis, H.B. and Franklin, M., 1944, An experimental study of the role of the ego in work. II. The significence of task-orientation in work, *J. Exper. Psychol.* 34:195-215.

Lovejoy, O. 1981, The origin of man. *Science,* 216,341.

Lynd, H., 1958, in: "On Shame and the Search for Identity," Harcourt, Brace, New York.

Main, M. & Weston, D.R., 1981, The quality of the toddler's relationship to mother and to father: Related to conflict behavior and to readiness to establish new relationships, *Child Development,* 52, 932-940.

Main, M. & Weston, D.R., 1982, Avoidance of the attachment figure in infancy: descriptions and interpretations, in C.M. Parkes & J. Stevenson-Hinde eds., "The Place of Attachment in Human Behavior" (pp.31-59) Basic Books, New York.

Malatesta, C.F. & Haviland, J., 1982, Learning display rules: The socialization of emotion expression in infancy. *Child Development,* 53, 991-1003.

Morgan, E., 1973, in: "The Descent of Woman", Bantam Books, New York.

Panksepp, J., 1982, Toward a general psychobiological theory of emotions.*The Behavioral and Brain Sciences,* 5, 407-468.

Sackett, G.,1974, Sex differences in rhesus monkeys following varied rearing experiences, in R. Friedman, R. Reichert, & R. Vandeweile eds., "Sex differences in Behavior", Wiley, New York.

Sears, R.R., Maccoby, E. & Levin, H. 1957, in: "Patterns of Child Rearing," Row, Peterson, Evanston.

Sears, R.R., Rau, L. & Alpert, R., 1965, in: "Identification and Child Rearing", Stanford Univ. Press, Stanford.

Seif,M., & Atkins, A., 1979, Some defensive and Cognitive Aspects of Phobia, *J. Abn. Psychol.* 88:42-51.

Tomkins, S. 1963 , in: "Affect, Imagery and Consciousness", vol. 2. Springer & Co., New York.

Wertheimer, M. 1912, Experimentelle Studien uber das Sehen von Bewegung. *Zeit. f. Pscychol.* 61:161-125.

Wertheimer,M. 1938, Gestalt Theory, in "Source Book of Gestalt Psychology", W.D.Ellis, ed., Harcourt, Brace., New York.

Witkin, H.A. & Lewis, H.B. 1965 The relationship of experimentally induced pre-sleep experience to dreams. *J. Amer. Psychoanal. Assn.* 13:819-849.

Witkin, H.A. , Lewis,H.B., Hertzman, M., Machover, K., Meissner, P. & Wapner, S. 1954, in: "Personality through Perception", Harper & Bros., New York.

Witkin, H.A. & Lewis, H.B. & Weil, E. 1968, Affective reactions and patient therapist interaction among more differentiated and less differentiated patients early in therapy. *J. Nerv. & Ment. Dis.* 146:193-208.

Generalised Emotion
How it may be produced, and Sentic Cycle Therapy

No
more
Silence
Without love

Only silence
now
For me   For you
To you   To me
Now

Love with Silence
Silence with Love

Manfred Clynes

Department of Psychology
University of Melbourne
Melbourne, Australia, 3052

I. Introduction

In this chapter we are concerned with a novel, yet natural way of producing emotions using dynamic expression and touch as a mode for the precise expression of emotions, and as a special, new art form. This way is outside the life-line of an individual, i.e., does not depend on events happening to that person, is controllable, easily achieved, tells us much about the nature of emotion and its communication - and results in preventive and therapeutic applications for emotional balance.

First discovered in 1968 (Clynes, 1968, 1969, 1973a), it probably is still new to many psychologists. Indeed, it can seem novel and perplexing from a social perspective not quite unlike had music been invented for the first time. (Like music, it selectively engenders and utilises generalised emotion.)

Among the advantages of this form of producing and expressing emotion - which uses dynamic finger pressure - is that it permits emotion and its properties to be carefully studied in several aspects, and it is very easy to learn, unlike music. The therapeutic/preventive method of generating and experiencing a sequence of emotions is called Sentic Cycles. We shall describe results with over 1,000 subjects, in this regard. First, however, it will be helpful briefly to consider the nature of emotion, in order to better understand the method.

In our age of information processing and communication, the *dynamics* of the remarkable, highly ingenious and precise systems of communicating emotion which nature has evolved (including coordinated function of production and recognition, of sending and receiving) have received comparatively little attention, especially as applied to man.

In man-made information processing systems the transmitting units (consisting of zeros and ones) have no meaning related to the messages. In nature's system of communicating emotions the message units themselves have analog (spatiotemporal form) features that act like keys in locks of our nervous system; the language, sender and receiver are co-designed with vocabulary and meaning evolved by nature.

The ability for the communication of emotion to be a link between individuals, a window across individual isolation , makes these processes central to our existence, and reveals much about the nature of emotion, and thus about human nature.

Indeed, an approach to the question of what kind of entity constitutes an emotion is to consider those qualities of experience which can be communicated by means of direct *temporal* expression. If the contagion of qualities of experience is selected as a common property we obtain a class of qualities of experience nearly all members of which are commonly called emotions. Love, grief, joy, anger, hate, laughter, sexual excitement, reverence, hope and fear may be propagated through dynamic communication, by using the tone of voice (even for example through the telephone), expressive gesture, facial expressive movement. (Yawning is also contagious in this sense, but is not usually classified as an emotion.)

There seems to be a class of qualities of experience which are inherently linked with the motor system, and their expression and state may be considered as a single existential entity. Such a category includes most emotions. Other emotions, such as jealousy, or guilt are not communicable through a contagious process of expression (and thus also are not encountered in music). It turns out that this second group of emotions is largely similar to those recently termed "social emotions" (eg. Zivin 1987); as distinguished from the "biological emotions".

A number of important aspects of the nature of emotion have become clear in the course of working in this direction (Clynes 1969,1973a,1977). Foremost among these is:

- *The Coherence principle,* that there is a biologically given coherence between a basic emotion and the dynamic form of its expression; and further, that:

- For a given output mode, the closer to that 'pure' form the expression, the more effective it is.

- A key - and - lock relation programmed into the central nervous system is seen to exist between the expression and its power to generate emotion, both in the person expressing and in the perceiver.

- Production of the dynamic form, possible by means of various motor output modes, and its recognition are found to be coordinated biologically by the central nervous system, thereby permitting contagion of emotion. (For a very clear but little studied primitive example of this, consider yawning.)

Emotion as an Entity

Consider then further, what kind of entity is an emotion   - that extraordinary entity which we thrive on, battle, that we like and not like to control, that affects our energies and governs our dreams? That makes living so worthwhile, or so unbearable?

Because emotion does not connect directly to the environment through known sensory structures, as does vision and hearing for example, its distinct qualities have not been accorded the same scientific credence as universals as have color and sounds.

There was much doubt, in the first half of the twentieth century, that they are indeed entities.

Around 1800, at the time of Schiller and Goethe, the various emotions were regarded as distinct natural phenomena of considerable interest (Schiller, 1803), involving mind and body. This view, however, became side-tracked after Darwin, in spite of his own seminal contribution to the study of their expression (Darwin, 1872) - as the Zeitgeist became survival and conditioning, rather than study of inherent mind - body windows. Through recent discoveries of numerous and specific neurohormonal transmitters and receptors, and of specific 'circuits' as sensors within the brain for producing particular emotions (see Panksepp, this volume, and 1986), the qualities and the spectrum of emotions are becoming amenable to be identified and isolated as existential entities, as happened with chemical elements at the time of the elaboration of the periodic table (we may even begin to consider scientifically the evolutionary development of the quality of life). Establishing these can be expected to have vast though not immediate consequences on the social fabric - on the aims of society and of the individual. To be able to alter an individual's emotions at will with specific interventions opens up challenging and dangerous avenues for the future. But note, we already have had one way of doing just that for thousands of years: man's invention of music !

A number of distinct qualities of experience demand to be named: joy, anger, grief and love for example are found in virtually all languages. But of course to be named by language is not a guarantee of an existence as a simple entity; complex and mixed phenomena may have simple names; sometimes the naming is, to a degree, confused and confusing; other emotions remain nameless. At times a similar emotion but of different intensity is given a different name: for example anger, rage. Here language draws our attention to the fact that the entity 'emotion', as a quality of experience, has **intensity** as well as particular quality - as do sensory qualities - an aspect that our view of brain function in regard to emotion must accomodate.

An emotion requires consciousness to be felt: it is a characteristic of consciousness that emotions may be experienced. In that aspect it is not very different from sensory perception. We do not know today what brain functions permit these varied qualities to be experienced, and how a particular unique experiential quality is produced in the brain. Because we do not know this and since that is a very uncomfortable state of affairs, we tend to sweep that whole question under the carpet, i.e. repress it, and declare (eg. Minsky, 1987) that there is no problem in grasping how red looks red, and sweet is sweet and so on. This view would hold that there is no problem to understand, from a brain function point of view, how anger feels like anger, how love feels like love, joy feels like joy, and so on. I consider this question, however, to be a real question not a pseudo question and one central to understanding brain function in perhaps its most intriguing aspect: how it gives rise to consciousness. This is not to posit a "little green man" who looks at a screen inside our brain and an infinite regression of such little men. (In fact, we see a screen inside (in front of) our head - which turns when we turn our head (note this with eyes closed) but not when we turn our eyes.) Conversion of discontinuous events in the brain - nerve firings, aggregation of molecules - to continuous experience of a considerable number of distinct qualities is an unsolved, and centrally important scientific question.

We need to look at 'circuits' in the brain attributed to particular emotions (Panksepp, 1982, 1986) in that light also. We know that there are many places in the brain and the nervous system, whose stimulation produces a sensory experience of "red" when stimulated electrically (and probably also chemically) - at places on the retina, along the optic nerve, at the visual cortex - but those structures, while essential to normal vision, are not where vision is experienced. Likewise, 'circuits' in the brain which, when stimulated, give rise to the experience of a particular emotion may not be the structures with which the emotion is in fact experienced. These circuits ('pathways' may be a more appropriate term), may also be seen as input stages towards such experience, analogously to the sensory input pathways and processing structures of the nervous system as those of the ear or retina, but with the difference that they pick up stimulation **from internal sensing stations** (Clynes, 1973a), rather than interfacing with the external environment. At present we are in a position where we cannot distinguish, so to speak, between the light switch and the light - but it is nice to know where the switch is! While we know how to turn on an emotion, we have no idea with what brain structures they obtain their particular feel, or their cognitive correlates. The same is true of the experience of hunger. Seemingly, genetic elucidation shall help us towards answers more readily than neurophysiologic observations alone.

When an individual dreams of a particular emotion, he experiences it vividly, with very similar quality as in the wake state. Yet probably much of the brain "circuitry" attributed to generating that particular emotion is not active in the way it is when the emotion is experienced in the awake state - a different "switch" may be used. We should therefore be careful to avoid saying that the quality of emotional experience is due to the brain circuits that have been identified, which, when stimulated, give rise to emotional experiences. With this caveat, it is clear (at least for some emotions) that both the quality of an emotion entity and its intensity can be elicited by stimulation of appropriate brain structures, either chemically or electrically.

What Produces an Emotion?

Let us list then how emotion may be produced:

1. Electrical or chemical stimulation
Appropriate stimulation (or disinhibition, like with the visual receptors concerned in seeing black) at the right places in the brain.

2. The cognitive interpretation of events (K1)
The most common way. We may suppose that in the course of cognitive interpretation of events which give rise to an emotion, the brain functions referred to above appear to be stimulated through particular pathways. (Such cognitive interpretation is influenced by character structure, and may be in part inherent and biologically determined, and in part learned culturally and individually). **We shall call these input cognitions K1,** and distinguish them from output cognitions, i.e. cognitive effects produced by the emotion, which we shall call K2.

3. *Recalled emotion*

Emotions may be stored in memory, accessible to recall, or not readily accessible, repressed (repression may be partial, so that some of the body effects remain, though devoid of conscious emotional significance). (Little is known yet of how the emotion brain circuits link with unconscious aspects of emotion, such as processes of repression, for example.)

4. *Emotions produced in dreams*

Emotions can be experienced in dreams, but more remarkably, they can **generate dreams.** Stored emotion and spontaneously arising emotion both may function in dreams. Emotions released from memory may or may not affect specific brain circuits to which we have referred, and may affect them differently depending on whether they are experienced in dreams or in an awake state.

5. *Communication and generation of emotion through expression*

It is part of the entity of emotion, for most emotions, that there is an *urge* for expression. The entity emotion is linked in an inherent way to motor outputs and these - sounds, facial expressions, touch or gesture - are perceived and act contagiously to generate the emotion that is expressed in other individuals, a social function. But this generating action also acts on the individual who is expressing - so that we may speak of *auto - or cross-communication* of emotion. In this mode, as with electrical or chemical stimulation, the emotion may be generated without cognitive reason other than the expression itself - *there is no K1 required*.

Perceptions such as warmth, sunshine, colors, and so on, may evoke some emotional qualities directly, involving neither expression of a living organism, nor substantive input cognition.

Although in daily life emotion is frequently associated with K1, this is not always so; and is largely not so in music, dance and art. For example, joy or anguish in Mozart's music may be experienced without a cause, other than the music itself. In acting, there is partial involvement with K1.

(Current views and controversies in the field concerning the relation of cognition to emotion may be found in Leventhal and Scherer (1987), Lazarus (1984), Zajonc (1984), Oatley and Laird (1987). These reports are little concerned however with generating emotion through dynamic forms, and with cognitive aspects of this.)

Cognitive Output Function Effects of Emotion: K2

Emotions are involved with cognition not only at the input but they affect cognitive processes as an output - they are not only stimulated by cognitive evaluation of events but they affect cognitive thought and thus decisions and action. In this they resemble "instincts" (it would seem "instincts" (a no longer useful word hiding our ignorance) are in fact, most likely, particular emotion). We may thus look upon emotion as an 'invention of nature' to incorporate aspects of knowledge in a hard-wired manner for particular functions (see also Plutchik and Scott, this volume).

Among the first such inventions of nature was hunger. (The word 'nature' appears to impose itself upon the sentence: clearly, however, there is no nature, only the universe and its laws - we thus must consider 'hunger' to be a result of universal laws and biologic organisation, and as an entity partaking both of body and mind). Here we see as an example that the biochemical function of chemotaxis in primitive organisms - the automatic ability to move to where needed food is sensed to be - becomes a function of consciousness. The entity 'hunger' carries the meaning and information required - it tells the organism *when* it needs to eat, *that* it needs to eat, *what* it needs to eat and *how much*. (Note how selective that knowledge is : a hungry person who likes cake, still will not wish to eat more than say 4 or 5 pieces of cake even though still hungry, and will then want to eat something else.) This knowledge is present in the *feeling* of hunger.

Likewise, emotions appear to affect cognitive functions in specific characteristic ways. This "knowledge" carried by the emotion as an output function is part of its nature and cannot readily be separated from it. We may consider that *many aspects of this "knowledge" would be invoked regardless of the mode of stimulation of the emotion* , i.e. regardless of whether it was produced through the interpretation of an event, or through chemical or electrical stimulation of appropriate brain circuits, or indeed through dynamic expression. We shall call these output cognition effects K2.*

An emotion can at times provide its own, continuing *motivation* , regardless of how it came to exist: whether by interpretation of events by electrical of chemical stimulation, or through expressive communication, providing a (limited) degree of predictability. In that way, too, it resembles instincts. (The concept of motivation, a rather ill defined tool of trade of traditional psychology, here acquires a special meaning: see Scott, this volume.)

The cognitive output substrates of specific emotions, K2, are characteristic for each emotion. In order to study them we need ways to produce emotions reliably and repeatedly in the laboratory. This has been very difficult, particularly so for positive emotions. Mostly, subjects have been exposed to emotional scenes, or are given hypnotic suggestion in order to produce emotion. With the method of generation reported here, however, it is readily possible to generate positive as well as negative emotions in humans, and to study and observe aspects of the cognitive effects (K2) of joy as well as anger; of love as well as hate.

---

* It is proposed that K1 and K2 may also be called "kick -" and "float-cognitive" aspects of emotion, respectively; this suggestion refers to K1's initiating function, and to the K2 effects that are similar regardless of how the emotion was started.

II. Generalised Emotion: Its Production through Repeated Touch Expression

Generalised emotion is emotion generated without K1 i.e. without a cause in the lifeline of an individual. It may be generated either by repeated expression, or by electrical (or chemical) stimulation within the brain. Electrical stimulation has been comparatively widely studied, particularly in animals, but the systematic study of generating emotion through repeated expression is relatively new. Though we first were drawn to the power of precise dynamic expression to generate emotion through music, it became clear that this ability of music is only one example of a wider and fundamental property of the central nervous system and of emotion. It was found first in 1968 that a similarly powerful generation of emotion in this manner is possible through **touch expression** when organized in an appropriate way. Moreover the technique to master this turned out to be extremely simple compared to music, and requires no "musical talent".

To learn what the required organization is for this to occur, sheds light on the nature of emotion and its communication, on personal relationships, and on those arts that use dynamic expression to communicate. We shall describe briefly how we have studied this natural and artistic way of generating emotion over a period of 20 years.

Essentic Form Measurement

That expressions of a particular emotion tend to have a certain dynamic character, i.e. space time form, may be considered common knowledge. For example a sad person might sigh, a person experiencing joy might jump, an angry person may make an angry gesture, a person expressing love may caress, and so on. Such expressions might be carried out by various parts of the body, and various output modalities. One may posit that the expressive nature of the gesture or movement should lie in the *dynamic way* in which the movement conveys the emotional quality, no matter which part of the body or, we might suppose, which output modality may have been used. Making this postulate, one might be able to identify this characteristic dynamic form for a particular emotion (which we may call "essentic form") ideally by using a movement, or motor output, that is confined **virtually to a point** so that non-essential movement would not be conjoined. (Studies of facial expressions, such as those of Ekman and Friesen (1984), do not generally determine dynamic profiles of the expression, but largely use static cross-sections, taken at some "favorable" instant.) In 1967 we decided to search for these forms through expressive pressure of a single finger on a **Sentograph,** an instrument built for this purpose capable of independently measuring vertical and horizontal components of finger pressure (Fig 1).

If we could isolate the specific dynamic forms of the expressions of particular emotions through measures of dynamic finger pressure, it should be possible to apply these forms to other motor outputs and modalities. One could attempt to apply them to sound patterns, for example, and see if these forms transformed into sound indeed conveyed and generated the same emotional qualities as the finger pressure expressions from which they were derived.

Figure 1. Sentograph for measuring dynamic expressive forms. Vertical and horizontal components of finger pressure are measured independently through built-in cantilevered strain guage transducers, and may be recorded on a chart recorder or stored and averaged in a computer. (From Clynes, 1973b).

Generation through Repeated Expression

To be able to do this it was necessary, first of all, to generate the emotions concerned. In the past it had been generally difficult, if not impossible to repeatedly and reliably generate human emotions under laboratory conditions, and particularly positive emotions, such as love and joy. It became apparent quite soon however, that an *emotional expression, repeatedly expressed in an appropriate way would generate its own emotion.* A person required to express a particular emotion by finger pressure could generate that emotion by repeatedly expressing in the appropriate way - and could so to speak, bootstrap his emotion in that manner. This was possible for quite a number of emotions. If this is so, we need to ask, what is the "appropriate way", and what does it mean that there *is* an appropriate way?

1. It became clear that for each emotion there was a characteristic dynamic form of expression, a form with a beginning, middle, and end, and a particular duration. A subject soon discovered what form felt right, and that form was most effective also in generating the emotion (it turned out later that these forms were largely similar for different individuals). The subject could then produce this dynamic form to generate the emotion through repeated expression.

2. It was discovered that the manner of repetition significantly altered the ability to generate the emotion. The repetition had of course to allow each expression to be completed, i.e. a new expression could not start before the previous one had completed its course without blocking the emotion. *Each emotion had a different duration for its expression* , so the maximum repetition rate would be different for each emotion. But it also became apparent that a *precisely regular repetition was counterproductive;* it then quickly became boring. For most emotions a slight pause of *varied* duration between expressions produced more effective emotion generation. That allowed the expression to be renewed and experienced freshly rather than as a mere repetition.

Moreover it was better that timing *when* to begin the next expression was not the responsibility of the person who was expressing but was provided externally, by a soft click. In this way an aspect of dialog is achieved; the small interval between expressions seems to permit one to relate to otherness in a way that is not possible if one produces a self-timed chain of expressions. (The full reason why this is so is still not entirely clear. An interesting clue, however, is that if the initiation cue is provided by the contralateral hand, it goes a considerable way towards achieving the effect of an external cue: activation of the other hemisphere of the brain to give the initiation cues seems to produce some of the "dialog" effect that the external cue provides).

Thus, when the emotion called for was expressed repeatedly with its characteristic dynamic form, and initiated by an external cue (soft click) that allowed a small and variable interval after the completion of each expression, then the expressions were most effective in generating the emotion.

3. It was further found that when the timing cues were *optimised for one individual they appeared to be close to optimal for other individuals.* That is, the timing of these expressions both in regard to their own duration and to the small pauses appeared applicable to subjects in general.

The resemblance here to music is striking: Music would not be possible if the timing effects were not shared by listeners.

It may typically take say 5 - 10 expressions to appreciably generate the emotion. Then there may be 10 - 20 expressions that are felt to adequately or fully express the emotion, with some fluctuations of intensity, and then often there may begin a satiety phase during which the intensity of the emotion gradually diminishes. After the emotion is thus dissipated, it is very significant that the subject is quite unsated towards expressing a different emotion. This *differential satiation* has been suggested as a way of distinguishing basic emotions (Clynes, 1973a, 1977, 1980), and also noted as suggesting the existence of specific receptors and chemical transmitter substances (Clynes, 1973a) that would cause the receptors to be occupied, or clogged, producing satiation.

If the emotion concerned had previously been appreciably repressed, or had been acutely experienced by the subject before beginning the procedure, it would take longer to satiate.

Because the subject *senses the emotional effect of his expression* - as a psycho-biological feedback - he also discerns whether each expressive form he has used is appropriate or not: if not, the emotional effect he otherwise senses is not present. This phenomenon helps him to correct deviations in the expressive form. The experience of the expression is a homing function that leads to executing improved expressive form - it is self teaching. The teaching involved, however, is merely discovery of the natural dynamic form of expression for that emotion - as produced with finger pressure.

This form, corresponding to an inner gesture, is found to be not capable of basic modification in its link to a particular emotional quality. The forms are not arbitrary, but are found to **cohere inherently** with the emotion that they express. Coherence between the dynamic form of expression - capable of many, varied representations in different output modes - and its emotional quality is confirmed in numerous ways by the body of findings of these studies.

III. Experimentation with Essentic Form

1. Isolation of Specific Essentic Forms

With this method of generating emotion, expressive dynamic forms of specific emotions were measured in groups of subjects in different cultures. In these experiments subjects sat in a standardised position and expressed emotions with finger pressure of the middle finger of their dominant hand on the finger rest of the Sentograph, as initiated with a soft click from a timing tape prepared for that purpose according to the principles to be described. 50 expressions of each emotion were measured and averaged for each subject. Subjects readily experienced the emotions concerned (fig. 2). In these studies they were *not* asked to make the emotions as intense as possible, but rather with each expression to express as precisely as possible the emotion asked for. In doing this some subjects imagined scenes and incidents to help them generate the emotion. But most subjects found that soon they could generate the emotion concerned *without the aid of particular fantasies*, merely through the acts of expression. Moreover, having generated the emotion in this way, fantasies might then arise involving the emotion.

Choice of Emotions. The emotions chosen to be studied in this way were anger, hate, grief, love, sex, joy and reverence. These emotions are contagiously communicable - an important criterion for this research, and one that delimits a category of emotions. Concerning this choice , I should add that to a musician of my kind it is clear that love and reverence are communicable basic emotions in great music, such as in the music

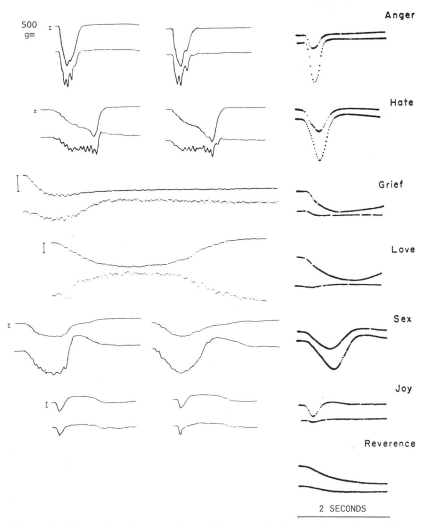

Figure 2. Examples of sentograms of the essentic forms of emotions. The upper trace for each emotion is the vertical component of transient finger pressure; the lower trace is the horizontal component (shown at 3x magnified pressure scale). On the right, each form is an average of fifty expressions, reproduced from Clynes, 1969. On the left, recent recordings of single expressions are shown. An approx. 10 Hz tremor is notable to a various extent in specific portions of the forms, particularly in the horizontal components of hate, anger, and sex. These and some other characteristic details are hidden by the averaging process; the latter however gives quite a good measure of the specific form for most emotions. Subtle differences in forms (e.g. between love and grief) may be as significant as more obvious ones. Reprinted from Clynes and Nettheim, 1982.

of Beethoven, Bach, Mozart, as well as in Indian classical music, for example. The others, except for hate, are generally accepted as belonging to the basic set of emotions (fear was not studied because its expression does not lend itself to be measured in this way, as it is a withdrawing).

In this way we isolated the essentic forms of these emotions, and found, in a limited initial study, that they appeared to be *universal human characteristics;* they varied no more between groups in different cultures than among individuals within one group (Clynes 1973a).

2. Correspondence between Production and Recognition of Essentic Form

Experiments were then carried out to test the correspondence between dynamic emotion expression and its recognition (Clynes and Nettheim, 1982). In a first experimental study, subjects were tested to see whether executing the motoric action of the hand involved in producing expressive finger pressure would be recognised as expressing the particular emotion concerned. In the first of a series of such experiments, 50 subjects (25 male, 25 female) were taught these seven motoric patterns as motor skills, without any indication that they represented emotional expression. Having learned them in a half hour learning session, seeing only the hand of the instructor, they were then asked to assign emotions to the motoric patterns, from a randomly ordered list of these seven emotions as a forced choice test. Results proved to be very successful and significant, with all seven emotions correctly scored by more subjects than any other score, and errors of choice being mainly choosing hate for anger and vice versa. Only 10% of subjects confused love and sex, for example, and each of the seven emotions were recognised correctly by 63-84% of the subjects. Males and females did equally well.

In a second series of experiments subjects watched a film of the hand (and part of the forearm) expressing those emotions with finger pressure, (chart traces of finger pressure were not seen by the subjects). Ten expressions of each of the seven emotions were shown to 232 subjects (116 male, 116 female). Recognition was even better than in the motor skill experiment. Emotions were generally identified correctly in over 80% of the choices, with 40.1 % of the subjects getting all seven emotions correct. 21% of the subjects confused love and reverence. However, only 14% confused anger and hate, and vice versa, about two thirds the figure found with the motoric experiment. Males and females, here too, did equally well. There was no significant difference between males and females in their recognition of any of the emotions, including sex, as also in the motoric experiment. In both sets of experiments, confidence indices obtained showed that subjects were more confident of their choice when it was a correct choice.

These experiments confirmed that the dynamic patterns involved in *expressing* the particular emotions were also *recognized* , i.e. they confirmed the biologic coordination of the nervous system in the production and recognition of dynamic emotion communicating forms.

Transforming Touch Expression to Sound Expression

Transformation of Pressure Essentic Forms to Sound Essentic Forms

The postulate that essentic forms are in a sense more primary in terms of brain function than their realization in any of the sensory output modes was tested by first obtaining transforms of pressure dynamic forms to sound forms that expressed the same emotion, and noting the required nature of that transform. The resultant sounds were tested on subjects to see whether they indeed recognised the corresponding emotions.

The first aspect was solved by making frequency follow the pressure contours - and by shaping the amplitude contour similarly, with the additional constraint that the amplitude had to start and end on zero. The polarity and range of the frequency deflection was different for different emotions. But the dynamic form, i.e. the time course, was preserved inviolate for all emotions.

Details of the transform are given in figures 3 and 4, and Table 1.

Table 1. Transforms of dynamic forms to sound forms of like expression, as amplitude and frequency modulated sinusoids (see Fig. 6): specific scaling parameters.

EMOTION	Sinusoidal base frequency Hz	FREQUENCY MODULATION Depth and Sign	AMPLITUDE MODULATION		
			Propor- tional	Diff. time constant T (seconds)	A
ANGER	110	+ 59%	Prop.		
HATE	106	- 5%	Prop.	1.2	0.05
GRIEF	406	- 21%		3.1	1
LOVE	205	- 2.4%	Prop.		
SEX	228	+ 14%		1.0	
JOY	480	-, one octave: biphasic 20% down then 61% up	Prop.	0.32	0.20
REVERENCE	298	+ 9%		4.0	1

+ means : frequency↑as pressure↑   Differentiation time constant
- means : frequency↑as pressure↓   refers to transfer function
                                      $\frac{A \, Ts}{1 + Ts}$ for ampl. mod. where s is the Laplace Transform.

PARAMETERS FOR TRANSFORMING
TOUCH FORMS TO SOUND FORMS OF LIKE EXPRESSION

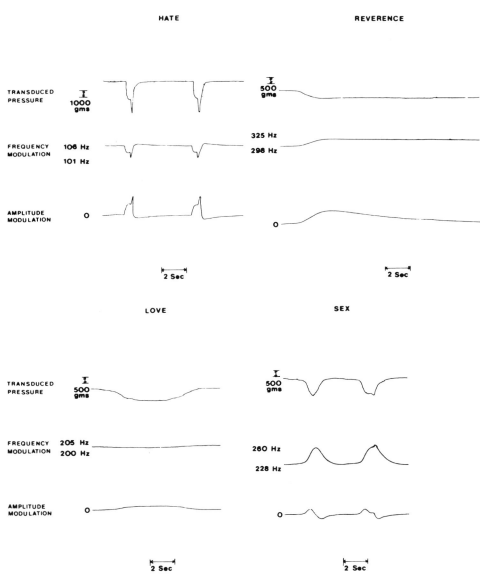

Figures 3 and 4. Examples of transformation of expressive forms of touch to sound that expresses the same feeling. The top trace shows expressive finger pressure (vertical component); the middle the frequency modulation envelope; and the lower trace the amplitude module envelope (time scale is doubled for Joy and Anger). The frequency envelope is the same as the pressure form apart from a vertical scale factor (except for Joy, where the wide dynamic range requires an approximately logarithmic scaling).

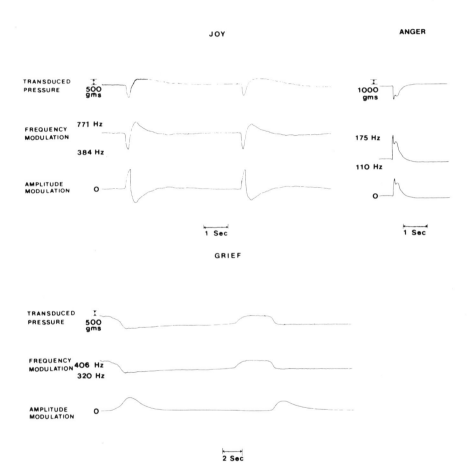

Figure 4. For caption, see previous page.

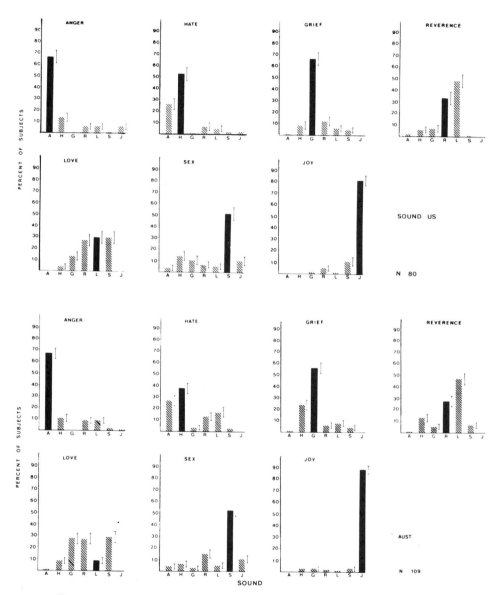

Figure 5. Recognition of sound expressions transformed from expressive touch. This figure shows that recognition of emotions was high for all emotions except for Love and Reverence which were largely confused with each other. A, H, G, R ,L,S and J stand for the names of emotions. 'Correct' identification is shown in solid bars. Shaded bars show errors made. Standard deviations are drawn with each bar.   Top group - students of M.I.T. and University of California, Berkeley. Bottom group - medical students of the University of New South Wales.

These emotionally expressive sounds, transformed from touch expressions were then tested on subjects for recognition using similar forced choice tests as in the visual recognition experiments. With a group of 80 university students from the University of California, Berkeley and another group of 109 medical students from the University of New South Wales recognition was excellent and highly significant as for the visual experiments, except for confusion between love and reverence (Fig.5). It was thus confirmed that the transforms worked: the sound expressed the same emotion as the touch expression from which it was derived (except for confusion between love and reverence). The next step was to test this cross-culturally.

Sound Expression transformed from White Urban Touch tested on Central Australian Aboriginals

To see whether the ability to recognise the emotional expression of the sounds transformed from touch was largely biological, or cultural, these sounds transformed from white urban touch were tested on a goup of 40 Central Australian Aborigines of the Walbiri tribe, in Yuendumu, an Aboriginal settlement of about 800 persons located 200 miles north west of Alice Springs (Clynes and Nettheim, 1982). 20 males and 20 females were tested, with the help of separate interpreters of the same sex - most Aboriginals spoke only little English. The names of the emotions were translated into the Walbiri language. Aboriginals who live under abysmal, subhuman conditions on a "reserve" were highly attentive to the sounds and enjoyed the test - they listened intently, often with memorable expression on their faces.

Results for the Aboriginal subjects (Fig.6) showed very similar performance as the medical students and University of California students, and an even better recognition of joy (88% correct). However, in place of the confusion between love and reverence, there was a statistically significant switch between the two, so that love was significantly recognized as reverence and vice versa. (A possible reason for this was in the translation of the corresponding words.) Again males and females did equally well.

Recognition scores were similar for the other five emotions for both groups, even in terms of the kind of errors made. Clearly, these dynamic forms indeed were recognised cross-culturally. Moreover those sounds that were better realised in the judgement of one group were also judged to be better realised by other groups. That this occurred with sounds transformed from touch expression argues strongly for the primacy of essentic form as a brain program, over its specific realization in one sensory mode.

Application to Emotional Expression of Musical Themes

In further experiments these emotionally expressive sounds transformed from touch expression were then converted to musical themes so that the pitch-time contour of the notes fitted the frequency curve. The amplitude relations of the notes were also adjusted to fit the transform. It could be predicted that any musical theme

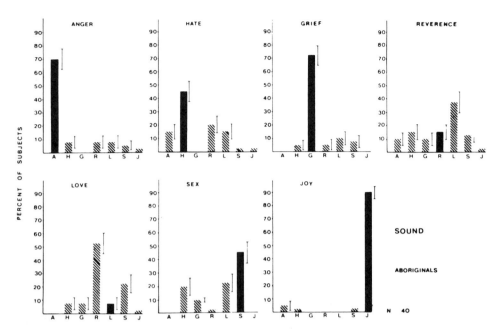

Figure 6. Recognition by a group of 40 Australian Aborigines, of the Warlbiri
Tribe in Central Australia, of sounds produced from white urban touch expression
of finger pressure. Performance is very similar to the high recognition shown by the
M.I.T. and Berkeley students, and by the medical students of the University of New
South Wales. They did somewhat better than those groups in identifying Joy, Anger
and Grief, although differences between groups were not statistically significant.
Instead of confusing Reverence and Love they chose more clearly, but the choice
was opposite of that intended: Love was chosen for Reverence, and vice versa. This
may have been due to subtleties of translation. Differences between male and
female scores were not significant in this group.

that conformed to these requirements would in fact express that particular emotion
(many such themes are of course possible). These predictions (28 such melodies
predicted to sound sad, Clynes & Nettheim,1982) were also confirmed - a phono-
graph record of examples of such sounds and musical themes is included in Clynes,
1982.

Further work with expression in music may be found in Clynes, 1983, 1984, 1985,
1986b, 1987. These studies describe discovery and consequences of two principles of
unconscious musical thought (*Pulse and Predictive Amplitude Shape microstructure*)
that add musical microstructure present in musical thought, but unnotatable, to the
notated score, transforming the 'dead' notes of a score to living, expressive music.

(The above citations, except for 1984 and 1986b, also include musical recordings.) Other relevant studies of brain functions concerned with timing and rhythm are described in Clynes 1986a, and Clynes & Walker, 1986, 1982.

In order to understand the relation of essentic form to music, and to the touch expression mode described here we need to clarify here that in music there are in general *two* parallel processes in time that contribute to its nature. One is the melodic line - the unfolding story of the music that develops as the music proceeds. The other is the 'beat' or 'pulse' which repeats throughout the piece, and has a character or microstructure that is largely maintained throughout the repetitions. The first one of these double processes portrays the emotional qualities of the 'story', their changes and contrasts, and in this process essentic form applies as outlined above to convey the various shades of emotion, using pitch time curves and amplitude contours. One function of the second process, the reiterated beat, can be said to be, in Western classical music, to identify intimately who is telling the story. In other music, the microstructure of the beat may reveal a type of group identity, eg. Hungarian, Spanish etc.

The parallel between the language of music and touch expressions of essentic form described occurs only with the first process - the unfolding of the musicial story. The second music process, the phenomenon of the beat, has no parallel in the generation of emotion described here. That this method can generate emotion like music can but without a 'beat' constitutes a significant and basic difference, and has a number of advantages. (The need for a beat in music is linked to the use of separate 'notes'. These are given a grid in time on which they are dispersed. If continuous forms of expressions rather than discontinuous notes are used, however, as in touch expression, this problem does not arise.)

The Amygdala as a processor of Essentic Form

There is a known structure in the brain which may relate to the primacy of essentic form over particular sensory modalities that our experiments indicate: the function of the amygdala as a "funnel-like gateway between cortical sensory areas and the deep subcortical nuclei responsible for the expression of emotions" (including the hypothalmus) (Aggleton & Mishkin, 1986). In their words "the behavioral and anatomical data reviewed make it evident that the amygdala is a main gateway for the evocation of emotion *by stimuli in all the sensory modalities.*" Further, direct electrical stimulation of the hypothalmus shows that, in cats, mechanisms of emotion are left intact after amygdalectomy (Egger & Flynn, 1967, Fernandez de Molina & Hunsperger, 1962). Recent work shows also that after amygdal lesions in monkeys, the sound frequency trace of their separation distress cries becomes flattened, and loses its normal expressive contour. The amygdala may be regarded as a promising candidate for involvement in the key-lock processing of essentic form in the brain, before it is directed to stimulate the emotion, and also before it is expressed.

IV. Sentic Cycles

Initial Discovery of their Function

Measuring the essentic forms as described, the author was initially often subject for long hours at a time. It was repeatedly noted, after as much as seven hours of experiments, that instead of feeling tired the subject felt refreshed, energized. This good feeling, it soon became apparent, could not simply be due to the satisfaction of a good day's work, and also lasted longer. Clearly it seemed due to the process of repeatedly expressing and experiencing the emotions, and this has been confirmed by further work.

A second important factor observed was the ability to switch from one emotion to another - this was much easier than in life situations, and also invited comparision with performing music, where different movements of a sonata, for example, might require very different emotions to be summoned and expressed.

Thirdly, there was enjoyment in experiencing and expressing each emotion, regardless of whether these were positive or negative emotions - although some emotions were more enjoyable than others.

Even the most enjoyable emotions were not exempt from eventual satiation - the satiation time tended to vary to an extent with different emotions. The human need for variety presented itself in terms of this type of brain function in a very specific manner (one can relate this to the satiation function of neurotransmitters and receptors). The process of recovery from satiation for each emotion also took a certain largely predictable time.

Design and Composition of the Cycle

Using these observations, a cycle of emotions was constructed lasting about 27 minutes. The sentic cycle is a touch composition with a prescribed sequence and duration of emotions. Each emotion phase has a series of expressions, timed in accordance with that emotion. The time for *beginning* each touch expression is provided by a timing click. Usually a tape is used. The sentic cycle tape announces each emotion by a word, and presents the series of soft timing clicks for that emotion, and then announces the next emotion followed by its series of clicks giving the beginning of each expression, and continues in this way through the whole cycle. It contains the following (for further details, see Appendix A):

	Duration of Phase	No. of Expressions
No emotion	2 min 6 sec.	23
Anger	3 min 13 sec.	34
Hate	2 min 33 sec.	27
Grief	4 min 19 sec.	31
Love	4 min 14 sec.	30
Sex	3 min 8 sec.	36
Joy	3 min 31 sec.	40
Reverence	2 min 46 sec.	21

The timing of each click for starting an expression is adjusted to fit the natural duration of the expression for each emotion and *additionally leave a small variable pause between successive expressions*. As a consequence a user cannot predict when the next click would occur even after years of use. Each emotion phase is announced with a word, spoken with a slight degree of expressiveness. 'No emotion' is an initial period during which the user is asked to press on the finger rest with a simple action as when depressing a typewriter key each time they hear a click, without expressing emotion. (This preparatory stage quietens the body. It is then a simple transition in the next phase to express anger with a modification of this pressure-movement when hearing each click. For each emotion, of course, the dynamic form (time course) and intensity of the pressure is suitably modified by the user, according to his or her own feeling.)

Transition between emotions

Special care needs to be taken in designing the timing of the clicks as one emotion phase ends and the next one begins. A short extra interval before the next emotion word is announced suffices to alert the subject that something new is about to happen. After the word is spoken special attention is required in designing the first timing clicks of the new series. In all this, as in music, either too much or too little seems to be irritating and counterproductive.

A second cycle, similar but with somewhat differently proportioned emotion phases was included in the early stages of our experience with sentic cycles. But as this increased the total duration to almost an hour, it was decided to discontinue it for frequent regular use. Although more powerful in its overall effect than a single cycle, it required more time than people could set aside over the longer term. Repeating the 27 minute cycle twice may not be as good as doing the original double cycle, because of its special modification. (A new digital electronic sentic cycler being introduced will make it possible for the user to select differently designed cycles and make modifications for special needs.)

An exact representation of the 27 minute sentic cycle is given in Appendix A.

Physical Setup for Executing Sentic Cycles

A person sits on a hard backed chair without arm rests. A finger rest is mounted on a coffee table or other hard surface, of the same height as the seat of the chair. The middle finger of the dominant hand is used for expression, placed on the finger rest in a natural, relaxed position. Expressive pressure is guided by the whole arm. Using the middle finger provides balance when pressure is exerted; otherwise there is a tendency of the arm to turn inward or outward. For some emotions the fourth finger may be adduced to the middle (third) finger for additional expressiveness, eg. in grief, to provide a greater sense of collapse. Eyes closed and dim light are desirable.

The physical setup and position used is designed with a double purpose:

1.) To permit adequate generation of all the emotions required. Body position and posture may favour certain emotions and hinder others. Anger, for example, is not favoured in a lying down position. Sitting with the spine straight, a small cushion behind the upper back, a cushion on the seat, and thighs supported by the chair, provides a neutral position from which all the emotions can be well realised.

2.) This arrangement also results in the body, other than the expressing arm, becoming exceedingly quiet during the cycle. The quietness - one can almost call it a falling asleep of the rest of the body in a motor sense - allows one to focus on the quality of the emotion and on sensations in the body associated with it. This quietness provides a valued sense of inner freedom - an emotional freedom - and also helps one to be aware of the quality of the expression undistracted by other bodily events.

Finger Rest

For sentographic measurement, the finger rest serves as a mechanical input to the Sentograph. But for doing sentic cycles for emotional well being, expressive forms are *not* as a rule measured - the finger rest here has the purpose of providing appropriately resistive support, a suitable surface on which to express and to avoid that it be touched by other fingers. (The finger rest in sentic cycles is not connected to anything - it does not measure anything.) It fulfils a number of requirements. To suitably accommodate all the emotions called for, the finger rest should have a very slight 'give'. It is quite remarkable how much difference in 'feel' a very slight give makes, even only a fraction of a millimetre. Without such a 'give', the communication is impeded. The finger tip is deformed an order of magnitude more than this when expressing, so that it is quite remarkable that such a small 'give' is sensed so clearly, and given such importance. It actually makes a considerable difference to the quality of touch expression. It would be worthwhile to study this phenomenon by itself.

Too much "give" is undesirable, on the other hand, expecially for anger and hate where resistance provides satisfaction, and permits the exercise of force.

The texture of the finger rest surface is also significant. It should be neither too smooth nor too rough, since both of these attract continuing attention. A surface character that is, as it were, grey to the touch is required; one whose presence one rapidly forgets. With such a surface, one soon is little aware of it - as a musician and his instrument tend to become one in a good performance - and expression may occur without obtrusiveness of the finger rest. Fig.7 shows a person doing sentic cycles.

Rating and Diary

The user is encouraged, about half an hour after doing the cycles to:

1. Rate himself on a scale of 0 - 5 for the intensity of each emotion of the cycle.
2. To write comments concerning each emotion about what he experienced. Comments concern body sensations, images, thoughts, memories and may often be surprisingly eloquent and poetic.
3. Also, later, to write comments on the effects experienced afterwards.

The ratings and comments are useful to the subject, for both short term and long term and also have value for research purposes. Ratings and comments have been collected from over 1,000 subjects and statistically analyzed (Clynes, 1988). A summary of findings is given in Section V. Two typical rating and comments sheets are shown in Appendix B.

Art Form of Touch

The practice of sentic cycles may thus be regarded as a simple art form of touch. The sequence and timing of the emotions and their expressions is given - this represents the composition. However, the emotions are not those of a composer, but those of the individual. Improvisatory and spontaneous expressiveness and thought is combined with a program, or metastructure.

The art consists of the discovery, by each person, of the most appropriate and effective dynamic form of the expression of that emotion, and sensing how that expression generates the emotion. Having found and sensed this, the person can apply it to other situations and modes, increasing the 'livingness' (to use Susan Langer's term) of their communication and experience, and become more authentic.

The art shows the individual how easily they can switch from one emotion to another, at will, and how such a sequence of emotions results in an overall impression greater than the sum of the parts. It impresses on the person how emotions are embedded in time, how time is part of the expression, communication and experience of emotion. And finally it teaches how we may "consider" emotion and its quality, without becoming totally involved bodily, so that its timeless aspects are also perceived, as an existential entity. In this (seemingly uniquely human) mode, called Apollonian, it becomes possible also to view the cognitive substrates K2 of each emotion and become aware of them free from the constraint experienced in every day life. This art, like other true art, can promote empathy and compassion.

Function of the Sentic Cycle, a Summary

I. *Effects of each cycle*

The sentic cycle engages the following functions:

    I. Generating the emotions of the cycle.

    2. Practically effortless switching of emotions.

    3. Catharsis and release of repressed emotions.

    4. Discloses which emotions may be problematic for the individual.

    5. Draws memories to awareness relating to the emotion.

    6. Stimulates fantasy.

    7. Enjoyment of all the emotions of the cycle, with some specially favored.

    8. Makes a person aware of the specific body sensations and changes that each emotion provides.

After doing the cycle:

    9. A sense of well being , peace, energy and centredness lasting typically I0-24 hours.

    10. Dissipates anxiety and nervousness.

    11. Improves sleep.

    12. More creative and spontaneous functioning

II. *Continuing use for "normal" persons tends to:*

1. Even out the intensity of emotions experienced during the cycle; bringing out those that have been repressed and problematic, diminishing the intensity of those that were overly strong (typically, this tends to be noticeable with continuing use of 3-4 times a week, in 2-3 weeks).

2. Develops emotional fluidity - as opposed to being in an emotional rut, being stuck in one emotion.

3. Improves self esteem, confidence, joy of being alive, vitality, better communication with others, better control (2-3 weeks as above).

4. Gives feeling of security in being in touch with the range of human feelings, a sense of belonging and sharing - one becomes better able to give and receive. (2-5 weeks).

5. Gives insight into character structure (6 months +).

6. Improved understanding and enjoyment of the arts and music.

III. *For those suffering from emotional problems it tends to provide:*

1. Assistance for the remission of psychosomatic symptoms of emotional origin (Typical period for noticeable effectiveness 1-4 weeks).

2. The possibility of dealing with specific emotional problems such as phobias (1-2 months).

3. Help against insomnia without medication (1 week).

4. Help for dealing with moderate and light depression (1-3 weeks).

For these several cycles per day may be indicated, according to the severity of the condition.

Other helpful uses of sentic cycles have been as an adjunct to treatment for alcoholism, for combating drug dependence, for emotional care of cancer patients, and in a number of cases, for prevention of suicide.

Figure 7. A person doing sentic cycles, showing proper posture and position. A series of expressive forms for each emotion of the sequence, No Emotion, Anger, Hate, Grief, Love, Sex, Joy and Reverence, are expressed with the pressure of the finger and arm on the finger rest. Timing is guided by soft clicks at arrhythmic intervals of 4-10 seconds, depending on the emotion, from the sentic cycle tape played on a tape recorder. These indicate when to begin each expression. The sequence takes approximately 27 minutes.

Functions of the Sentic Cycle

1. Generating Emotions

It is quite easy for most people to generate emotions in this way on their first try (about three out of four people), even though they have never done it before . This is reflected by their self-ratings and also by concomitant effects on facial expression, subtle changes in posture, flushing of the face and/or of the ears at different parts of the cycle, by crying during grief, a degree of sexual arousal during sex, and by modulation of respiration, changes in heart rate, and in finger temperature at the inactive hand which can be measured. About one in five or six subjects, for example, cry during grief. Individuals are *not asked to maximise the intensity* of each emotion - merely to express as precisely as they can the quality of the emotion with each expression. One may observe that:

a) A person does not generate each emotion with the same intensity. In their first experience of the cycle individuals may have some difficulty with one or two of the emotions - reflected in their low intensity ratings. Which particular emotions these are, varies. Some individuals have difficulty with anger at first, some with joy, others with grief. Still others may have trouble with reverence, or hate, or with love. Rarest of all is the individual who has difficulty with sex in the cycle, be it male or female (this is unexpected). Difficulties with anger generally relate to individuals who have much repressed anger. People who are unusually timid may also have initial difficulty in expressing anger as it is uncommon for them to express anger overtly. Difficulties with hate are initially encountered with people who cannot differentiate between anger and hate, or those who say "I cannot feel hate for anybody", and those who on principle do not wish to feel hate. Repressed hate is, of course, also often encountered. Those who initially have difficulty with grief usually have severe repressed grief, sometimes going back to childhood. Rarely one finds a younger person who is genuinely untouched by grief, and who also is not appreciably affected by the grief of others, initially. Difficulties with love are initially encountered mostly among those who have not felt love for a long time (some of these have indeed included psychiatrists!). Those who have initial difficulty with joy often have lost their natural joi de vivre, are generally somewhat cynical, and may have subclinical, mild depression. Difficulties with reverence initially may be due to unfamiliarity with this feeling (meant not for a person), or, it often is due to an inner fury at the world, a cursing of existence.

b) Some people show unusually high intensity ratings for certain emotions at first. This may indicate an acute life situation relating to that emotion, but may also be an indication of character structure. High initial ratings are often found for anger, grief, love, joy, occasionally for hate and reverence. Sex is seldom given the highest ratings initially.

c) It appears also that here as elsewhere, people to some extent fall into categories of high raters, medium raters and low raters and to that extent their overall ratings might tend to be relatively high, or low, for all emotions, as a rating artifact.

d) Certain professions appear to facilitate   initial ability to generate and experience emotions through the cycle. Musicians, actors, dancers, for example, find it especially easy; others such as engineers or accountants whose work does not provide as much emotional differentiation may find it somewhat less easy, initially. Categories of extrovert versus introvert, however, do not predict relative initial ease or difficulty.

e) Neither the initial ratings nor the quality of the sentic cycle experience appear on the whole to have any marked correlation with intelligence.

f) Obsessive - compulsive and hysterical personalities tend to be low raters and high raters, respectively, initially, for all emotions.

g) The sentic cycle experience and the rating system have not been adequately studied with psychotic individuals, and may not be suitable to them. Such studies could however be revealing and fruitful in a number of ways.

Switching of Emotions

Even at their first try of the cycle, individuals have little difficulty switching emotions. The sequence is constructed so that the juxtaposition of consecutive emotions is not irritating, as alternating anger and joy would be, for example. Even those who experience intense emotions in the cycle rarely find that the previous emotion carries through to the following one for more than a few expressions. Ease of switching increases with use.

With strongly repressed emotions, however, (and with some acute life-situations), it happens on occasion that the emotion first surfaces so strongly that it floods into the remaining parts of the cycle; this may happen with grief, and rarely, with anger. Crying may continue through part of the remainder of the cycle. On such rare occasions, one may wish to prolong the grief phase of the cycle, before continuing with the rest of the cycle. In such instances the outpouring of emotion is felt as a relief, as a fulfilment, and has not led to uncontrollable, or destructive action in any instance. (These individuals do not include psychotics, about whom data are not available.)

Such strong and long repressed emotion is generally less in evidence at the next cycle, done on the following day, and after another two or three cycles settles down to be hardly more prominent than the other emotions, and does not impede switching from one emotion to another.

Achieving emotional fluidity over a period of time liberates persons from being in an emotional "rut"of being stuck in one emotion, as often occurs in their lives.

Interestingly, switching from "sex" - involving a degree of sexual arousal - to joy and then to reverence does *not* bring a sense of frustration, in spite of being an incomplete sexual experience. This contradicts a widely held notion concerning sexual functioning. Nor is there any evidence that "sublimation" is involved in the switching from sex to another emotion. The following emotion is enjoyed, but would have been enjoyed also, had sex not immediately preceded it.

This aspect, and switching are significant and of theoretical interest especially also when couples do sentic cycles together, expressing emotions on each other's hands, a valuable mode, not described further here.

2. Cathartic and Selective Memory Aspects of the Cycle

Going through the emotions of the cycle can be a cathartic experience. It offers an opportunity to express negative emotions without fear of punishment or rejection. Catharsis works directly in relation to current life situations. But the generalised emotions have the special and remarkable property of selective recall: past experiences of similar emotion are readily and spontaneously recalled, while during one emotion memories of a *different* emotion tend *not* to be recalled spontaneously. This is one of the interesting properties of the K2 substrate function of the emotion (see also Bower, 1981, Gilligan & Bower, 1984, Isen et al., 1978, Laird et al, 1982, for similar findings). Further, certain past experiences of that emotion are readily recalled, others less readily, still other instances only with difficulty or not at all, at first. Repression is not necessarily an all or nothing phenomenon: one readily learns in these studies that there are degrees of it. Generating emotions through the sentic cycle serves as an access path to memory. During each emotion phase memories relating to that emotion may spontaneously arise. They can be written down after the cycle and become part of the emotion and rating diary.

A gradual weakening of the operation of Freudian 'censors' involved in repression of certain specific memories and feelings may be observed as the indivdual explores past life situations with this means.

We may view cathartic experience broadly, with conscious and unconscious aspects involving both negative and positive emotions. The expression of positive emotions (which we find can also be repressed, a condition not usually comprised under the concept of catharsis), gives the individual assurance that he or she is capable of these emotions, and that their enjoyment is available to them. (A surprising number of individuals note that they have not experienced love and/or joy for a long time and are greatly relieved to be able to feel these again; sometimes moved to tears by this.)

Sentic cycle experience can be viewed as dis-alienating, as a factor in reintegrating and rejoining the fragmented emotional sphere of the individual, resulting also in greater spontaneity. (Increase in spontaneity is sometimes dramatically evident after the very first experience of the cycles as blockages disappear).

An additional K2 property became evident in the course of teaching this to a group of psychoanalysts at the William Allinson White Institute in New York. Analysts who had their patients do sentic cycles found that they reported dreams about three times as frequently as before - patients remembered their dreams much better. It is well known among psychoanalysts that after starting analysis a client will tend to remember dreams more readily than he had customarily . The sentic cycle experience thus seems to open that path of communication further.

The greater power of sentic cycles as an "emotional lens" than music is due to its ability to focus on one emotion for 3-4 minutes at a time, freed from a composer's personality, idiosynchracies and story telling. While sentic cycles may be viewed as an art form of touch, its therapeutic and integrating functions may be greater and more accessible due to the absence of intellectual construction present in most art forms. Intellectual construction, interesting and valuable though it is, can circumscribe the direct applicability to the individual's own life. Often it is a barrier and a filter which needs to be surmounted by knowledgeable understanding of the art work. For that reason the catharsis of art experience for a *perceiver* of art is not easily applied to analysis of character structure, treatment of phobias and personality disorders. The situation is different when *creating* works of art or poems, or music, where the content and structure more or less directly express thought and feelings of the creator. Compared to this, sentic cycles is direct, with a minimum of symbolic structure. It allows creativity in each expression. A clear link is formed between expressive activity of a person outside their own life-line, and their personal life - a link they can explore themselves, moreover, without necessarily having professional assistance.

For the same reasons, emotion generated through this means, being unencumbered by symbolism and incidental structure, may be a method of choice for studying the nature of K2, the output cognition substrate of a particular emotion.

3. Generating Play of New Fantasies

Individuals doing sentic cycles can and do generate emotion without imagined scenes, either remembered, or newly fantasized. They can choose, however, to "play" with memories, or with new fantasies related to the emotion. This freedom, combined with control, gives the sentic cycle experience a play-like, an almost dream-like quality, where new fantasies *effortlessly stay guided within the context of the particular emotion* - and remain so until a new emotion is called for, with an announced word.

The freedom of association within the context of the quality of the emotion permits the individual also to actually conduct Gedanken-Experiments with his own psyche. For example, when experiencing love, or anger, he or she may deliberately imagine specific other individuals and note to what extent the emotion 'fits' with the imagined person, as a recipient, or even as a sender. (This process is quite different from word association, or free association, and to some extent resembles guided imagery.) In this way they may sometimes surprise themselves at finding that they can or cannot associate that feeling towards the fantasized person. This kind of testing of relationships can be helpful and revealing, and often gives quite a different view than what they would have off-handedly thought. It can be used to probe how the person relates to mother and father, and other long term relationships. Surprisingly, it is easy to separate recent events giving rise to emotion in relation to the imagined individual from a more basic, long term, emotional attitude towards that person.

Such relationship and reality testing with emotion-focused fantasy processes are used in particular therapeutic applications to be described in a later section.

4. Bodily Sensations Experienced During the Cycle

As a person experiences the sentic cycles he has an unusual opportunity to sense bodily effects of each emotion. He sits quietly, and yet has ongoing activity involving motor output. These sensations experienced appear to be part of the total gestalt of the emotion - they cannot be separated from the emotion, although they may often not be noticed as clearly and readily in real life situations, being masked by other ongoing movements and sensations. These sensations are not to be confused with the usually measured autonomic changes such as of heart rate, blood pressure and finger temperature, which are less specific, and not clearly (or not at all) sensed. They tend to continue throughout the emotion phase - they are not separately produced only with each expression. Virtually all individuals experiencing the emotions of the cycle describe such bodily sensations:

1. Anger: clenching of the jaws (moderate), abdominal tension, fixation of the eyes (even with eyes closed), gaze slightly (or 10%) downward from horizontal, breathing in jabs, tendency to lean forward slightly, sense of temporary forcefulness (e.g. territorial defense).

2. Hate: abdominal tension - lower than in anger, involving anal regions also, clenching of jaws, resistive breathing in exhalation. Sense of continuing purposefulness, force.

3. Grief: sensation of heaviness - arm feels heavy, limbs feel heavy, great sense of effort to move, helplessness, breathing tends to stop after exhalation for moments before next inspiration, breathing pattern like a series of sighs, head tends to bow to one side (usually the side of the expressive arm), gaze downward, shoulder and torso tends to bend forward. Abdomen relaxed, but chest constricted. Eyelids heavy. Little energy, weakness, hopelessness, isolation.

4. Love: head level, mouth opened slightly, no clenching of teeth, breathing even and rounded, eyes in soft focus, gaze forward, abdomen relaxed, chest free, sense of quiet strength, contained energy, sending of flow: sensation of flow going outward from torso through limbs, eyes and forehead, a reduced sense of effort, a sense of contact, slight smile.

5. Sex: A degree of sexual arousal and excitement, sensations in the genital areas, and breasts in women, desire, breathing unfree, with some expiration resistance, a diffuse sense of tension, desire for contact, to touch and be touched.

6. Joy: sense of lightness of limbs, bouncy energy, torso upright, head slightly upward, eyes "dancing", soft focus, sense of freedom, carefree, effortless, undirected energy, breathing gasps of inhalation, smile, abdomen relaxed, chest free and expandable.

7. Reverence: sense of expansiveness, of vague or insubstantial body limits, deep slow respiration, head lifted upward slightly, gaze slightly upward, steady, soft focus, no smile, effortlessness, unweightedness (but not bouncy) *, a sense of being a vessel, a receiver of flow.

These are of course only partial descriptions.

A further interesting aspect is that expressing with the right or left hand appears to be differentially effective - certain emotions are more favored with one hand, both with regard to generation and memory recall (cf. Davidson,1984). This links with indications of hemispherical localisation of emotion observed in evoked potentials with expression, using finger pressure (Clynes 1975, 1973). However, interestingly, the body sensations experienced for the various emotions all tend to be symmetrical.

(During the cycle, a smoker does not seem to desire to smoke, nor does a person wish to eat, drink, and it seems one tends to feel less cold than one would otherwise be.)

Effects After Sentic Cycles

After finishing the last emotion, a person sits quietly for a minute or so before getting up and resuming activities. For the next 15 minutes or so there may be little desire to talk, but rather a wish to let the experience sink in, to allow it to transfer to long term memory. A sense of calm and completeness is generally present. This may merge gradually into a feeling of well being, of centredness, of effectiveness in whatever one may be doing. There is flow, lack of hesitation or of conflict. Correspondingly, there is a marked diminution of anxiety, or none at all. There seems often to be more time to do the things one has to do, as well as much less anxiety about getting them done. Even unpleasant chores tend to lose much of their unpleasantness, and there is a sustained sense of quiet energy.

These effects tend to last for a number of hours, up to 24 hours.

If an individual experiences the emotions very intensely he or she may feel drained afterward, but this tends to be the exception rather than the norm, and is rectified as cycles are repeated on other occasions.

If the cycle is done before going to sleep or within an hour or two of going to sleep it tends to improve the quality of sleep - if a person has a sleep deficit, it will tend to make that person sleepy; and will also promote yawning after the cycle in such instances.

(* Recent experiments in our laboratory indicate that feeling reverence can reduce sensations of effort in muscular exertion and can temporarily increase physical strength up to 20%. How these and other effects are mediated neurochemically and neurophysiologically is a challenging question to explore.)

V. Results of Sentic Cycle Ratings and Observations

The following reports on some of the data obtained from the scoring of each emotion phase for intensity (0 - 5), and from written comments concerning each emotion phase and after-effects of sentic cycles, from a sample of 1142 records collected over a ten year period, on sentic cycle diary and rating forms. Subjects were United States and Australian adults, 18-76 years old. The cycles were done by the subjects at home, or in groups supervised by the author.

For some subjects, the scoring and reports available comprise several hundred sentic cycle experiences, over several years, for others, 5-20 sentic cycles, and for most subjects 2-5 sentic cycles.

Intensity

Ratings for intensity were self scored, within 30 minutes of completion of the cycle, on a scale of 0 - 5 (0 no effect, 5 maximal intensity). Among U.S. subjects, mean ratings for the seven emotions were in the range of 2.6 to 3.2. Fig. 8 shows male and female mean ratings in the U.S. and for Australian subjects. Fig. 9 separately compares the females and males of U.S. and Australian subjects. These results show that:

1. Overall, love achieved the highest mean score, next came joy, then sex and grief, anger, reverence and hate lowest, though the values were all in the medium range of intensity. (In this analysis a subject's score is taken as his/her average for the number of cycles done). The conclusion that people tend to experience the emotions with medium intensity under these conditions needs to be tempered by the well known tendency for people to score toward the middle of a presented range. It is interesting and unexpected however that overall, love tended to have the highest score, though not by a great margin.

2. U.S. men and U.S. women scored very similarly for most emotions, but U.S. men scored significantly somewhat higher for anger and hate than women (p <.001). We could consider that these differences indicate somewhat greater open agressiveness among men than women in the U.S., but the difference in means is relatively slight, about 0.4 of a rating point.

3. Australian women scored strikingly similarly to U.S. women, except that they scored significantly lower for hate and somewhat higher for grief (p <.01) than US women. This difference may well relate to sociologic conditions: Australian women are not as emancipated as American women - there is probably a lag of about 30 years in the social effectiveness of the feminist movement, compared with the U.S. Among Australian women perhaps grief has not turned into hate as it often may have for U.S. women; this would be consistent with greater acceptance of repression by Australian women.

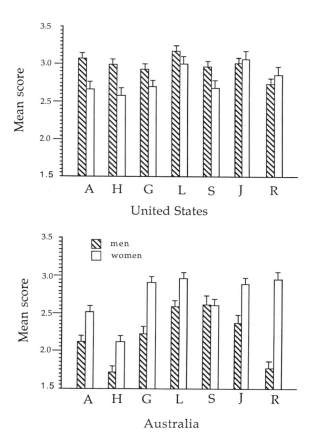

Figure 8. A comparison of mean scores of emotion intensity for United
States and Australian subjects for each emotion phase of the sentic cycle.
Intensity is rated on a scale from 0 to 5. Standard errors of the mean are shown
also (n=216).

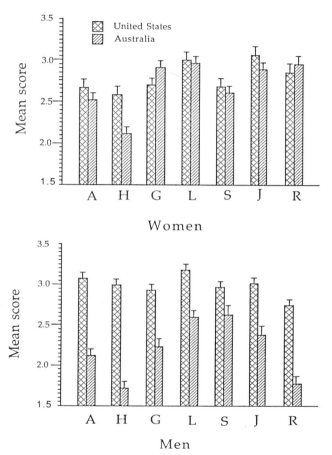

Figure 9. A comparison of mean scores of emotion intensity for men and women for each phase of the sentic cycle. Australian men score notably lower than Australian women.

4. Australian men scored significantly lower for all emotions than Australian women (p <.001), except for sex.

5. Australian men scored significantly lower than American men for all emotions (p <.0001). A remarkable result indeed! This seems to reflect to an extent the prevalent Australian mores and an education system which still considers it unmanly to show emotion, except at football games or races.

6. Variances in the score were in the range of 1.2 - 1.6, and showed largely similar variability for all emotions.

In depicting the relative intensity of the emotions experienced in the sentic cycle, sentic cycle experience data, it can be seen, may also yield socially significant results.

Intensity Changes with Successive Sentic Cycles

Fig. 10 illustrates how the intensity of the emotions averaged across subjects changes with several experiences of the cycle. The various emotions show clearly different progressive courses. Two sets of data are superimposed, one set for a group who have completed four cycles, another for a group who completed five cycles. The two groups show largely overlapping results confirming the reliability of the progressive trends observed. Notable is:

1. A gradual decrease in Anger
2. An increase in Hate, at least for the first 4 cycles
3. A considerable increase in Grief, followed by an apparent attenuation
4. A comparatively steady Love score
5. Increase in Sex scores for the first 4 cycles
6. Gradual increases in Reverence
7. A slight and gradual increase in the mean for all emotions, for the first 4 cycles.

It is striking how anger is gradually reduced, sex gradually build up, and how grief is increasingly tapped and then released over a number of cycles, in a biphasic curve, reaching greatest intensity at the third cycle.

By the fourth cycle, all emotions are scored higher than at the beginning, except anger which is reduced considerably. These increases observed for the first few cycles do not of course continue unabated as more cycles are done; rather they tend to settle at an enjoyable, comfortable level, and fluctuate around that level - a level that varies for different individuals.

Fig. 11 shows changes in the rank order for the intensities of the various emotions as progressively more cycles are done (for the 5 cycle group). Notably, love retains its rank throughout. The prominence of grief and anger are decreased, while that of joy, sex and reverence increases.

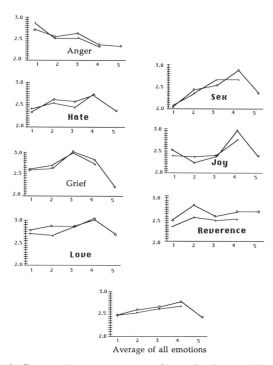

Figure 10. Progressive mean scores for each phase of the sentic cycle showing changes in the scores from the first to the fourth and fifth cycle. Results from two groups are separately drawn, one group who have completed five cycles (n = 24), the other group four cycles (n = 41). Results of the two groups are largely similar and show specific progressive patterns for each emotion discussed in the text. Horizontal axis gives the cycle number.

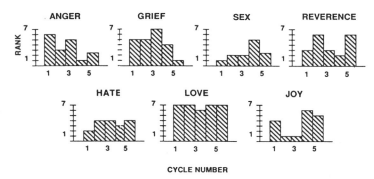

Figure 11. Rank order of intensities of the phases of the sentic cycle with increasing sentic cycle experience. Note progressive changes in the order.

Diurnal Cycle and Intensity Scores

If intensity scores are analysed, in preliminary work, according to two time zones, morning and evening zones (up to midday, and from midday to midnight), significant differences found are: somewhat higher scores for grief, reverence and for sex (surprisingly) in the morning, but a higher score for hate in the evening and afternoon zone - the other emotions show no significant change - which is also interesting. It is theoretically important in terms of circadian neurochemical regulation of peptides and of receptor sensitivity, that we do not see a general diurnal change in intensity affecting all emotions across the board but instead select differences pertaining to specific emotions .

How some After-Effect Comments relate to Scores

The written comments concerning after effects of sentic cycles were not structured - no specific questions were asked, and comments were made spontaneously, in a manner chosen by the user.

These comments were searched according to a number of categories. Did they specifically mention increased (or decreased) a) calmness, b) sense of well-being, c) energy?

When the scores corresponding to the instances where special mention was made of calmness, sense of well-being, or energy were analyzed, a significantly lower level of hate (calmness and well-being), and a higher level of reverence (well-being and energy) was noted with a high level of the 'mentioned' categories. Other emotions were not significantly different. Table 2 shows these effects, and also shows differences in the scores when subjects cried during the grief phase and when they experienced physical discomfort.

Crying during the cycle goes together with a higher score of grief, not surprisingly (mean value of 3.83 compared to 3.01, p<.005). But notably, for none of the other emotions is the mean score significantly different for those who cried during grief. This tends to show that grief was not carried over to alter the intensity of other emotions systematically.

Table 2. Phases of the sentic cycle with significantly increased or decreased mean intensity when comments on the *after-effects* of the cycle included the descriptors shown.

		A	H	G	L	S	J	R
After cycle	Calm			↓				
	Well being			↓				↑
	Energy							↑
	Low energy						↓	↓
During cycle	Crying		↑					
	Physical discomfort		↓	↓	↓	↓	↓	

Physical discomfort experienced by some subjects due to incorrect sitting positions (such as wrong height or position of the finger rest (sore arm), or wrong height of the chair (unsupported thighs (tall people), or no cushions as instructed), resulted in all scores after hate being significantly lower. It is interesting that anger and hate were not scored lower. This could be because discomfort takes a while to be felt - anger and hate are the first two emotions of the cycle - or it could be that discomfort itself is quite consonant with anger and hate, and may help to promote them, or a combination of these two factors.

Notably, a high score of reverence accompanies after-effect comments of a high degree of well-being, of high energy. Lower hate scores accompany after-effect comments that emphasize calmness, and well-being. These findings recall our previous observations that hate and hope tend to be opposites rather than hate and love (Clynes, 1977), here juxtaposing hate and reverence as having opposing influence. It may be pointed out, parenthetically, that those with a strong resentment or hate for existence, encountered often among people subject to great injustice or affliction, often have corresponding difficulty in feeling reverence, and derive special benefit from rediscovering this ability through sentic cycles.

VI. Cognitive Aspects of Generalised Emotion

We may consider specific cognitive effects of generalised emotion on:

    1. memory   - a) as a retrieval lens
                   - b) on the ability to learn, involving both
                        short term and long term memory, and
                        combinatorial thought
    2. perceptual processes
                   - a) narrowing or widening of
                        perceptive fields
                   - b) perceptual alteration and distortion
    3. relationships with those not responsible for its generation
                   - a) how we regard others
                   - b) to whom the emotion may be directed
                        and from whom received
                   - c) how we view ourselves and the world

These effects seem in general not to depend on how the emotions have been stimulated, i.e. they may be independent of K1, and may be thought largely to be K2 functions.

Let us consider each of the emotions of the cycle in turn, and describe some of the effects that have become evident through cumulative reported sentic cycle experience. Some of these qualities seem to agree with common knowledge, others have been expressed by poets, and still others appear to be new insights.

Anger - has a narrowing effect on perception, span of attention, reduces the ability to learn (as noted in unpublished experiments with number sequences presented during the sentic cycle), larger relationships are not readily noted. Anger is readily directed towards any person or object available for its expression (cf. the common phrase "taking it out on someone else"). Concentrates attention on some object of anger at the expense of other competing perceptions. (An important difference between anger and hate may be noted when one realises that one can be angry at a child, say, without hating the child. A pure anger is strong without being nasty, generally involves an aspect of protection, and can be beautiful.) A significant parallel can be pointed out between the narrowed **cognitive focus,** and the **body condition** of abdominal tension described for anger under the Section IV, which feels like a narrow internal body-focus. *(Similar parallels may be drawn for other emotions.)*

Hate - an inner closing off, a sense of a continuing injustice and threat that needs to be removed or avenged (protective measures are no longer sufficient), suspiciousness of anything new, distrust, especially of anything beautiful, a sense of having been essentially violated, a "logical" thought that only destruction is the proper end that will give relief. No restriction by conscience from doing immoral acts in order to satisfy the imperative of the hate, as cognitively the destruction is seen as justifiable. Hate is not quite as easily directly transferable as anger, but when it is, is all the more deadly, and tends to become pathological.

In depressive states in which joy cannot be experienced, a hate of existence is often felt, perhaps conceptualized as hate of God, sometimes even leading to suicidal impulses. (When such a person rediscovers the ability to feel joy through sentic cycles, both depression and hate are reduced or disappear. A factor that may also stimulate such hate, in a circular fashion, is the inability to feel joy in itself.)

Understanding these functions of hate through the sentic cycle also diminishes its power and hold over the individual - the idea is not to teach people to hate, but to understand what it feels like to hate, so that they can recognize it in themselves and understand it in others.

Grief - This appears to affect short-term memory negatively, resulting in part probably from diminished interest (interest enhances memory retention). Somber, dark colors, greys appear consonant with grief, and this appears to be not merely a social convention. A sense of isolation is experienced, and stimuli from other individuals and the environment are not processed cognitively with the usual interest. An irretrievable loss has occured, and hopelessness makes every action effortful, contributing to helplessness. Crying provides a measure of relief from the isolation. This remarkable cognitive function of crying is not well understood and needs to be studied. (cf. also Separation Distress Vocalisation in animals; both crying and SDV are 'help' signals to others (mother) indicating distress. That this is not a simple problem is clear from the facts that the cognitive relief of crying is present when one knows that no one can hear it, and indeed that for human adults, frequently the best way of helping a person who cries is to let them cry.

Love - With love (not in phases of 'being in love'!) we tend to observe a wide attention span, improved memory retention, trust, a widening of interest and improved learning, perception of larger interrelations, a sense of inner freedom combined with responsibility, of giving. Seemingly also increased appreciation of beauty, colors of nature, and other perceptual qualities. But unlike for reverence, individual details (and details of individuals) retain their interest. (Further cognitive aspects of love are given in the following section.)

Sex -   Among the most unresearched but important 'facts of life' are the cognitive transformation of view, and the changes in cognitive function after orgasm as compared to before (to an extent different for men and women), and the neuropeptide and neurohormonal changes that appear to be involved in these. While sentic cycles experience does not tell us about this either since orgasm is not involved (except, quite rarely, in women) it gives us valuable pointers along the way. Cognitively, sexual arousal greatly narrows the focus of perceptual awareness, as sexual feelings 'take over'. Non-sexual environmental stimuli tend to be ignored, while sexually stimulating sounds and images become more potent. (After orgasm, the reverse occurs for a period of time.)

Memory retrieval functions during sexual arousal are highly selective. But the effect of and need for fantasy, of newly imagined scenes may be greater (though not indispensable) for sex than for the other emotions in the cycle. Sexual arousal appears to clearly interfere with learning; not surprisingly.

Another significant cognitive aspect is the degree of attachment that develops as a result of sexual intimacy, a sort of 'imprinting', which varies a great deal depending on the experience and character structure of the persons concerned. This may sometimes lead to power plays. A further cognitive aspect is that some individuals put an unusually great value on sexual intimacy and require or barter other values to be exchanged in relation to it. This, however, conflicts with the aspect that sex tends to be valued far more when it is not available than when it is. As a result serious problems, conflicts, and instabilities arise. (Such potential (systems) conflicts can be explored in the sentic cycle, and related to other emotions.) Sense of power appears to be a cognitive substrate of sex, but it remains to be clarified to what degree this is innate, and to what extent a distortion of natural function, associated with individual character structure and particular culture (cf. also animal dominance patterns in relation to sexual behavior).*

The main cognitive effect remains an attraction, which may lead to a merging of two individuals in which their separateness is partially drowned - and thereby to the procreation of the species.

Joy - care falls away - unburdened, there is sharing and generosity, celebration, exaltation, no hard focusing of attention, some deactivation of memory and of combinatorial thought. As described in Schiller's Ode to Joy, a sense of brotherhood is a cognitive consequence of joy. Joy is a natural 'high'; we may note parenthetically that the actions on particular endorphins and neurohormones of various drugs producing "euphoria" in some ways may appear to mimic the natural process of joy, including some of the cognitive substrates.

---

*This potentiating property of the sexual drive, and its companion, frustration, may well be invoked by advocates of the theory of sublimation advanced by Freud. A different kind of potentiation is observed however, for example, in relation to reverence, one that biochemically and neurohormonally seems not to be deactivated at the times when the sexual potentiation is. The consensus of reported sentic cycle experience accords the sexual drive major importance, and recognizes it also as a hidden (unconscious) factor in much hostility, but does not support the concept that it is the only basically effective 'drive'.

Reverence - infuses a sense of wonder and gratitude to be alive. Triviality in effect vanishes and cannot distract - instead, details, such as ambient sounds and noises, are not as usually tried to be suppressed, but perceived as part of existence, without irritation. The perceptive fields are widened, but interest is quite changed: nothing seems to attract interest merely in itself, only as part of a larger whole. Effort tends to disappear. Rather, there is a sense of receiving and of participation in the larger creative process - paradoxically it makes a person feel both insignificant and secure, and also strong in a way that, unsought, becomes an antidote to depression.

(Ironically, the old notion of religion as the opiate of the people has literally turned itself inside out now as a way to produce endogenous opiates in the brain that appear to be able to lead to greater wisdom, meaning, and satisfaction in life.)

These cognitive functions of reverence, also to be found especially in the late works of Beethoven, seem not to depend on specific personifications, dogma and imagery associated with various religious practices, which in fact largely may be seem to function to cultivate the feelings of reverence.

Experiment on Cognitive Substrates of Emotion:
Even an Insignificant Lie Blocks Love but not Anger

We shall now give an example of experimental studies of the cognitive substrates of specific emotions that have become possible with our method. This particular study addresses the question of an inherent connection between love and truthfulness, and in a larger sense, trust. It shows that even an insignificant, trivial lie temporarily blocks the emotion of love, but not of anger, and demonstrates strikingly that love is incompatible with lying (Clynes, Jurisevic, and Rynn, 1988).

We designed the study to test the effect of a small, insignificant lie, which could be readily and repeatedly produced in the laboratory.

31 subjects were trained to express and generate emotion by means of appropriately repeated dynamic forms of finger pressure on a sentograph pressure transducer, as descibed in previous sections. There were 18 male and 13 female subjects aged 22 - 59. Subjects completed three one-hour long sentic cycle training sessions as well as a number of additional practice sessions at home with a finger rest without a transducer before taking part in the experiment, and had become familiar with and enjoyed this method of generating emotion.

In the experiment subjects were asked to choose one of ten serially numbered tokens and hold it in their closed left hand. They then expressed and generated love, or anger, depending on the experimental run, with their right hand, using the timing clicks, as previously described. After a number of expressions to establish the emotion, for the next ten expressions they were asked with each expression: Do you have a 9? or, Do you have a 4? and so on including all 10 numbers, in randomized latin square order. In one type of run the subject had to answer 'No' every time, concurrently with the expression. In such a run the subject says the truth 9 times out of 10 - but lies for one expression when the number asked is the one he holds in his hand. The other type of run is the converse of this, the subject answers 'Yes' to each question, lying 9 times out of 10, and tells the truth when the number asked is the number holds.

Each expression by the subject was recorded with the sentograph. Two runs of each type were completed for each emotion, altogether eight runs per subject; a total of 248 runs consisting of 2480 separate expressions.

After each run the subject was asked to rate the intensity of the emotion experienced at the end of the base line period, during the question sequence before the singular expression, at the singular expression, and after it, on a scale of 0 - 5. Subjects had no difficulty to rate themselves in this manner. They were able to generate the emotions concerned with an intensity, indicated by self rating on a scale of 0 - 5, of mean level 3.17, s.d. 0.83 for Anger, and mean 3.09, s.d. 0.95 for Love (rated at the end of the base line period). The subjects were not aware of the aim of the experiment, and were told that it concerned the experience of numbers. As an objective correlate, the sentograph tracings were measured to examine differences in the expressive form before, at, and after the singular event (lie, or truth, respectively).

The results showed that for *Love,* there was an increase in intensity of love experienced at the singular event for 23 subjects when saying the truth (*Yes* series), and only 3 subjects for whom the intensity was lower. In the corresponding *No* series there were 21 subjects who experienced decreased intensity when lying was the singular event, and only 5 who experienced increased intensity (Fig. 12a,b). Lying blocked the feeling of love, in a large preponderance of runs: Love intensity was significantly reduced in 'lie' conditions compared to 'truth' conditions ($F(1, 30) = 15.85, p < .001$, *Yes* series, $F(1,30) = 12.65, p < .005$, *No* series; combined for both series $F(1,30) = 20.87, p < .0002$).

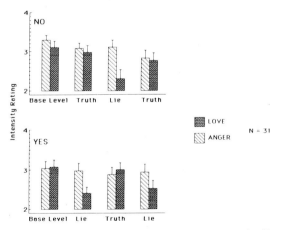

Figure 12 (a). Effects of lying on intensity experienced of love and of anger for two types of runs. In the 'No' series subjects necessarily first told the truth until their number was called, when they had to lie; thereafter they again told the truth for the remaining questions. In the 'Yes' series, the opposite took place, subjects had to lie until their actual number was called, when they necessarily told the truth; thereafter they lied again. Results show that in both kind of runs lying considerably reduced the rated intensity for Love but not for Anger. Mean ratings and standard errors of the mean are shown for 31 subjects.

In the runs with *Anger* the corresponding figures show no significant differences, or directions of change (Figs. 12a,b). Indeed many subjects actually liked to lie when angry; for them the lie seemingly enhanced the expression of anger. (This phenomenon as a cognitive aspect of emotion may warrant separate study.)

Measures of the sentograph forms recorded showed a significant ($p < .02$) shortening of the post peak duration of the love expression when lying, indicating an increased withdrawing after the maximum pressure is reached, compared with the love expressions when telling the truth (mean reduced by 11% from 3.37 sec to 3.03 sec). By contrast the corresponding sentographic expression of anger showed no significant changes.

(It should be mentioned that a related type of withdrawing behavior is often sentographically observed in conditions of expressing shame. See also Lewis(1979).)

The effect that the process of answering itself may have had on the intensity of emotion does not affect the conclusions, which show the differences in intensity experienced under truth and lying conditions. It can be seen from Fig. 12a that there is little difference in the rated mean intensity between the base line period and the first period of questions for which the answer was the truth, indicating that answering the question by itself without lying had apparently little effect on the intensity experienced.

It is possible also that there may be subtle changes in the Anger expression for those who take delight in lying when angry, as compared with those who are indifferent to whether they are lying or not. Such differences could be meaningful in terms of character structure. An unexpected cognitive aspect came to light in a similar experiment involving the emotion of *Grief*, when it was noted that many subjects *forgot*, during the run, what number they had in their hand. Such forgetting happened only rarely with other emotions. It appears likely that the generation of grief, joy and other emotions by the present method can be used advantageously to study how memory functions may be variously affected by specific emotions. Previous such studies used hypnosis to generate emotion (Gilligan and Bower, 1984; Bower, Gilligan and Monteiro, 1981).

The results with *Love* and *Anger* tend to validate some aspects of the popular commonly held view that love is connected with being "open", "sincere" and "guileless". They show a necessary connection, at least at the time of expression, of not lying with the experience of love. (An objection might be that it may sometimes be necessary to lie to persons whom one loves in order to protect them. What is shown here, however, is that at the time of such lying the feeling of love will be temporarily inhibited, or blocked. The liar in this case sacrifices his own momentary feeling of love for the well being of the other). Such a connection, leading to conscious results, can be considered to operate on a neuronal organizational substrate linking the processes of thought and feeling; probably not unlike those that may operate in "instinctive" animal processes. This connection is clearly a significant property of the nature of love. There are of course many other cognitive aspects of this emotion that need to be investigated.

Love has not generally been a popular emotion for study in psychology, with the exception of "being in love" romantically. Often it is not even listed among the basic emotions (Izard, 1977; Plutchik, 1980). As previously suggested, such omission is not shared by musicians however, for whom it may be clearly and specifically found in the works of Mozart, Bach and Beethoven, for example (but without the "love object" of course, i.e. as generalized love).

Apollonian and Dionysian Mode of Expression

A few words should be said about the existence in humans of two different cognitive modes of expressing (and also of experiencing) emotion, both of which may be used in sentic cycles. With the more common one, which we share with animals, called Dionysian, emotion is expressed and experienced as an ego function - it is one's 'own' emotion. In the second mode, called Apollonian, the emotion is expressed (and experienced) as a general or universal quality, is 'quoted' authentically, with a very clear idea of its quality, but not as one's 'own' feeling; in short, as "the emotion" - not as "my emotion" (Clynes, 1977,1980). This mode is very potent when expressed with precision of the dynamic form. But it involves the body less 'viscerally', i.e. its body images, and associated sensations are not projected on one's own body, though experienced mentally. For example, one may be keenly aware of the heaviness of grief, but not feel it in one's own arms and legs.

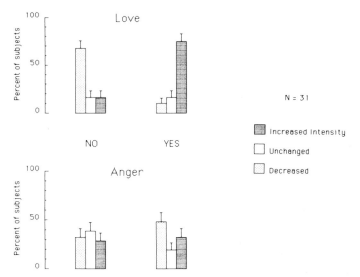

Figure 12 (b). Changes in rated intensity across subjects at the singular event: Lying - in the "No" runs, left; Truth - in the "Yes" runs, right. The singular event occurred when the number held in the hand was called. For Love there was a highly preponderant increase in intensity when subjects spoke the truth, and decrease when they lied (p < .001). For Anger there appeared to be no significant influence. In the experiment the singular event was always preceded by its opposite condition i.e. truth by lying and lying by truth, since the subjects answered No throughout the "No" run and Yes throughout the "Yes" run.

A third mode, mimicry, in which emotional expression is imitated with deliberate disconnection to feeling is of little concern in the present context. Interestingly however, humans are aware, though not necessarily by name, which of the three cognitive modes they are using.

VII. Longterm Effects of Sentic Cycles and Therapeutic Applications

We may consider longterm effects of sentic cycles and generalised emotion as those effects that occur after at least six months of regular use. We shall here briefly summarize observations and appropriate modes of application drawn from 62 subjects of varied age and both sexes who have used sentic cycles from six months to several years. They have reported changes in their ability to communicate in, and the quality of their relationships, feeling of well being, and enjoyment of life.

It has not been practical so far to conduct longterm studies with control subjects; for example, subjects sitting quietly without expressing these particular emotions. Clearly however those who continue to use sentic cycles for a long period find it rewarding, or they would not persist in doing them. (There are a considerable number of long term users with whom there has been no continuing contact, and from whom no reports have been collected. Also, a large percentage of those who have learned to do sentic cycles use them on demand, whenever special needs or stresses arise, rather than systematically.)

We need to distinguish between a general improvement that may happen through doing sentic cycles without being specifically sought and improvement in a particular aspect that is being worked on deliberately. It is not always clear whether to leave a problem to be relieved by the general method, or whether to work on it more single mindedly.

The longterm use of sentic cycles through its focus on specific, pure (rather than mixed) emotions offers preventive and therapeutic effects that cut across a number of established therapeutic disciplines, but it allows the subject to accomplish results by him/herself.

It also has aspects of meditation, as the body becomes very quiet, except for the expressing arm, and the mind enjoys an unusual freedom of thought yet focussed on a specific emotion. (It should be mentioned here that there were ancient Buddhist practices of meditation on emotions, some of which included emotion symbols called Mudras; these however did not include active repeated expression (reserved for dance), the means to generate emotion given here, with its biologically appropriate timing and dynamic forms. The latter of course, make it readily possible for virtually anyone to do this.)

Applications, without claiming rigor throughout, may be summarized under the following categories:

1. Psychosomatic problems

For psychosomatic problems related to repressed or inadequately expressed emotion an initial two to three week period of sentic cycles twice a day seems generally to alleviate or eliminate the psychosomatic symptoms. It will also clarify to the individual what tends to precipitate these symptoms.

Having identified that process the subject can then, as a second stage, if they so wish, as in behavior therapy, associate this stimulus in fantasy with a different emotion of the cycle than the habitual one and thereby establish another associative connection. Once a subject has generated a particular emotion during the sentic cycle, he or she may then at will think of the particular stimuli that previously had evoked the psychosomatic symptom. Bringing this to mind frequently in context of a totally different emotion reduces the power of the original stimulus to evoke the symptoms concerned. After some time, perhaps three to five weeks the same stimulus may be sufficiently associated mentally with the new emotion so as to effectively lose its power to evoke the undesirable emotion and psychosomatic effect.

2. Character Structure

Continuing sentic cycle experience provides a way for a person to become more aware of their own character structure. It allows them to experience in fantasy their emotional reactions to many fantasized and real situations, often bringing to light unexpected emotional reactions which may then be investigated further through sentic cycle experience. Subjects also learn about their central feelings towards members of their family, their circle of friends and relatives.

There are a number of ways in which the longterm practice of sentic cycles crosses into the territory of psychoanalysis. The concept of transference and cross-transference may be readily linked to the concept of generalised emotion. Through generalised emotion it becomes more understandable to the subject how similar emotions may be applied (transfered) to a different person appearing in a similar context as in previous experience. Once this transference is understood by the subject it can also be counteracted to an extent if desired.

Childhood experiences frequently re-emerge from memory while doing sentic cycles and allow the possibility to reintegrate them into the present condition of the subject. Continuing evocation of the particular emotions over a period of time appears to relax the 'censor' function gradually, as previously pointed out, so that more material is released from the unconscious, affecting both dreams and recall during the cycle experience.

In connection with the effect of sentic cycles on the unconscious, *it should be mentioned that even if the mind appears to wander in portions of the cycle, as long as the expressions carried out have appropriate dynamic form an unconscious effect appears to be achieved.* The influence of the word announcing each emotion phase seems also to carry over the period until the next word is announced (cf. Kihlstrom, 1987).

Patterns of dominance and submission are often characteristically changed by longterm sentic cycle experience. Subjects who have been consistently dominated by their spouses lose their submission and become able to achieve equality. This often comes as a surprise to them as well as to their spouses and may call for significant readjustments in their relationship. Increased ego strength is very characteristic of longterm sentic cycle use. Subjects acquire greater self confidence and self esteem. They are able to interact more readily and with greater satisfaction with others. As their anxiety disappears they also become more desirable partners for others in manifold ways; but relationships relying on dependency lose their power correspondingly.

Subjects who are initially fearful and timid tend to lose their timidity and become more self assertive, and in consequence also more attractive. Those who initially are overbearing, or bullies, tend to become less overaggressive and more able to view themselves and others outside the dominance-submission axis. These patterns are related to inner insecurity. As the sentic cycles reduce the insecurity both of these aberrations may tend to fade.

One of personal psychology's basic tenets could be called *"the domino law"*: what someone has done to you, you do to another. If early in life mother, father, brother or sister has consistently done something strongly emotionally provoking to you, you will later tend to do likewise to another person, given the chance. But if through generalised emotion one can realise that the same emotion can be experienced without the original input pattern, then dependency on this kind of imprinting may be reduced, and greater emotional freedom achieved (cf. MacLean,1985). This is one aspect of long term emotional training that sentic cycles makes possible, with wide application.

Unlike many of the 'products' of psychoanalysis, persons tend to become more charismatic through long term use of sentic cycles. Much of charisma consists of ability at will to communicate any desired emotion while remaining in control and making it apparent that this control is exercised in unexpected, playful ways that leave a measure of inscrutability not about the emotional competence of a person, but about how the control is exercised. Ease of switching emotions which sentic cycles provides as well as familiarity with these pure emotions appear to contribute to the increase in charisma found with longterm users. While important analytic processes are engendered, the focus is more directly experiential and the subject is less prone to 'head trips', to dry intellectualising with theory that are often too much part of psychoanalysis, and also tend to give rise to socially boring personalities - being involved with introspection of interest only to the person him- or herself. The introspection of sentic cycles however tends to promote vital sharing, and intimacy, as it concerns active, universal forms of communicating feeling, and also because it deals largely with 'pure' emotions rather than with mixtures, which are not as easily shared.

3. Specific Phobias

In phobias the underlying situation causing the symptom is generally not known at first. The subject generally will describe bodily sensations that accompany the phobia such as constriction in the chest, breathing problems, specific pain and the like. It is then useful to examine the various emotions and see which may cause similar bodily sensations, since these sensations generally represent a partial bodily picture of emotion related to the incident or incidents causing the phobia. We have called these partial emotion body images "virtual body images" (Clynes 1973,1977). Having identified to which emotion the virtual body image representing the phobic symptoms belongs, we may then work especially with that emotion and use it as an emotional lens to draw up memories from the unconscious. A link can be made by the subject between the bodily sensations experienced and the recalled original cause when a situation in the past strongly produced that same emotion. This is experienced as a very significant insight and discovery by the subject.

The next phase of the treatment is to reassociate that memory with a totally different emotion by deliberately recalling it during that emotion phase in the sentic cycle. After some weeks of this the phobia tends to weaken and disappear. Sometimes there may be a mild recurrence in which case the last phase of the treatment is reapplied.

Thus for instance a 23 year old married woman who would not drive a car, or go into an elevator, for several years because of acute symptoms, discovered through sentic cycles that the constriction in her chest and breathing patterns she experienced on such occasions were the same as she felt when experiencing grief in the cycle. She then remembered the intense grief she felt when six years before she was waiting in front of a tall building for her boyfriend to pick her up to take her to live with him, and that instead he came in an old car and told her he would never see her again, and drove off. She then went up this building in an elevator. Having made the connection, and relived the grief, the phobia shortly disappeared with further sentic cycle experience, and other associations of that boyfriend with different emotions.

In other cases however phobias may disappear spontaneously through the general sentic cycle experience over a period of time without any particularly focused procedure. Thus a sixtyseven year old three times married man lost his intense irrational fear of dogs which he had had for decades, after eight months of regular sentic cycle experience, that also removed his submissiveness to his spouse, and restored his potency. Whether in these cases the subject himself might be reassociating his inner experience without particular methodologic instructions is not known.

4. General Anxiety

Freefloating anxiety appears to diminish steadily and consistently with regular use of sentic cycles, as an unsought byproduct. We may speculate that this is brought about both by chemical factors invoving the production of neuropeptides with the various emotions and the total cycle experience, and by mental and unconscious processes relating to being in touch with one's emotional sphere, i.e. losing one's alienation.

These long term effects can generally be distinguished from the efficient use of sentic cycles to decrease anxiety and nervousness before special occasions, such as exams or public appearances, although for regular users the two effects appear partially to merge.

5. Addiction to Alcohol and Drugs

In combatting addiction to alcohol, drugs, or smoking, sentic cycles may be of assistance in two ways:

1. During the cycle a person generally has little or no craving for the addictive substance.

2. The satisfaction of the cycle may enable a person to be less drawn to the addicting stimulus.   One may speculate that neuropeptides and endorphins produced by the processes of the cycle might act in some way to diminish the potency of the addictive desire.

To be continuingly effective against addiction it is generally desirable to use sentic cycles in conjunction with other forms of supportive therapy that provides human interaction. Thus for example the Alcohol Abuse Combatting Center of the Catholic Church in Brisbane has obtained good results using sentic cycles together with psychotherapy in the treatment of 23 alcoholic priests and nuns.

6. Sexual Problems

1. Problems due to general anxiety and lack of self confidence.

As sentic cycles in the longterm are very helpful in diminishing anxiety and self consciousness, sexual function and enjoyment tend to improve considerably. This applies to both males and females. For instance, a female subject reports after eight months "I now have more arguments, but more orgasms". A woman in her fifties (a TM teacher) re-established satisfying and regular sexual relations with her husband after virtually ten years of abstaining.

2. Sexual touch.

With continuing practice of sentic cycles, the sexually arousing form of touch with characteristic dynamic form can be better and more clearly produced and received; and distinguished from other forms of expression. Reports tends to emphasize greater communication, arousal, and responsiveness, more intimacy and less selfconsciousness. Much prevalent confusion is avoided between touch forms of affection and of sexual desire, and yet one form can merge naturally into the other, not unlike how one phase follows another in the sentic cycle, in mutual feeling and action. Ability to express sexuality clearly and appropriately when desired increases confidence in both males and females. While some individuals have this ability seemingly as a gift, others can benefit from acquiring it, as a natural function (rather than as a 'technique').

3. Problems relating to specific childhood experiences or later traumatic events.

With regard to specific problems of a traumatic kind, such as rape or molestation, sentic cycles can be used as with phobias both for abreaction and replacement, that is, reliving the experience with a different emotional background - and do this for scenes before, during, and after the traumatic event. With systematic practice of this, using a number of different emotions, reduction is possible in the prolonged emotional transformation, shame, and change in character structure that these events tend to cause. Sentic cycles have helped to re-establish potency and to overcome frigidity caused by traumatic incidents.

4. Problems of power and dominance in a relationship.

Sexuality often becomes enmeshed in dominance - submission linked to personality structure. Such roles and games can at times degenerate into fixed patterns from which it may be difficult to escape. Sentic cycles permit persons to effectively explore different role functions, and in time incorporate these into practice.

Sado-masochistic tendencies may be rooted in ancient and possibly repressed (psychic ?) pain, which may be rediscovered, and worked on to be restructured by steps similar to those described for phobias. The sense of power, one could propose, may be regarded as an emotion itself, that can combine with other emotions.

5. Constitutional problems.

It would seem sentic cycles can offer merely a confirmation or disconfirmation of what may be regarded as constitutional sexuality, but not change. It may be futile - to the extent that data are available - to attempt to alter established homosexual patterns; but sentic cycles can well be useful for example to re-establish the confidence in heterosexuality of a person who may have been exposed to an isolated incident of homosexuality (or vice versa). An interesting application would be to study whether and for whom bisexuality involves lustfulness without imagery, i.e. is a restriction rather than an expansion of sexuality.

7. Depression

One of the most promising applications of sentic cycles seems to be to provide help for mild to moderate depressions. (The main difficulty is to get a person to do the cycles when seriously depressed. If another person is available to ensure that the cycles are done with some regularity, they offer help to seriously depressed individuals also.) Benefits appear to be provided regardless whether the depression is endemic, biological or reactive in origin. For example, a 63 year old woman who, like her mother had, suffers from periodic six months long serious depressive phases, has used sentic cycles consistently two or three times a day during these phases, for three years. She reports consistently that she is able to bear these phases much better with their use, and has been able to use far less medication, or none at all. Good results are also obtained with reactive depressions, for example those often encountered with divorce situations. These benefits do not require intervention of a therapist; the persons concerned learn how to do the cycles from the instruction booklet provided, quite easily, even though depressed.

Frequently, a depressed subject may not be able at first to experience joy in the cycle, to any degree. To overcome this it is useful to deliberately imagine scenes that would help with the experience of the emotion concerned, for example to imagine being in a beautiful garden, perhaps as a child, and after a number of such tries the subject may be able to feel joy at being in such a garden, in fantasy. As the feeling of joy is gradually rediscovered, the expression gradually assumes a natural vitality and dynamic form that in turn enhances the feeling. (A similar process towards authentic feeling and expression takes place for anger, say, or one of the other emotions, if a person has difficulty with expressing that emotion.) Transfer from fantasy to reality occurs with repeated sentic cycle experience, illustrating one facet of how fantasy and reality are interwoven. But one should not lose sight of the fact that the *total cycle experience and its after effects,* rather than joy by itself, *appears to be the main effective factor in relieving the depression.*

Another aspect of long-term use of sentic cycles may be some increase in awareness of sensory stimuli, colors, sounds, and shapes as well as increased tactile sensation. One also may have the opportunity to observe that acute pain such as a toothache can be reduced while expressing love on one's own body, e.g. on the contralateral hand; and also that such pain is increased while expressing grief.

For General Use by People at Large

But perhaps the most widely useful therapeutic and preventive application of sentic cycles is in overcoming a deadening cynicism, a blunting of sensibilities and depersonalization that tends to spread like an epidemic. Such culturally induced cynicism, alienation and/or mild depression results in inability to feel joy, other than at exceptional circumstances.* But sentic cycles readily transmute that cynicism - and these blase cynics may become glad, perhaps even almost 'young at heart' and grateful for some wonders of existence they can now tap at first hand. That this can be done with such a simple device is merely a compliment to the frugality and harmony of nature. Like music.

---

* In a sense, the effects of the sentic cycle can appear to run counter the prevalent United States cultural milieu. To a cynical mind their effects can seem disturbingly magical, forgetting that even the simplest things are not in essence comprehendible. To such a mind magnetism loses its magic. The emotional freedom that sentic cycles give appears outside the purview of Western culture, although not as much outside the view of other cultures such as the Balinese. Had music and dance not been invented many thousands of years ago, they probably would have difficulty to be accepted gladly in today's pill and pragmatics oriented social environment.

VIII. Generalised Emotion in a Social Context

A few last words may be in order to consider some social aspects.

The rhythms of language, and socially prevalent body language patterns to an extent tend to create a generalised "atmosphere" or ambiance with some emotional overtones characteristic of different countries and cultures (see also Byers, this volume). Sentic cycles permit an individual to be liberated, to a degree, from this immersion. Unlike music which generally is influenced by a nationalistic pulse, the art of sentic cycles is free from nationalistic influence.

Emotions as System Functions

Socially produced anger, and hate incited by injustice and oppression, as well as repressed anger, can, as is well known, readily be manipulated and whipped up by demagogues, generalised and directed at scapegoats of their choosing, and escalated. Of these processes involving "waves" of emotion we see historical as well as current examples.

Fear and the duty of governments to protect their citizens contribute to arms build ups. The desires of the peoples of the world to be friends are in effect trampled on by their governments, who try to produce fear in other governments. Escalating positive feedback is a danger equally manifest in social as well as in individual relationships - and is a *systems property*.

How these emotions are transformed following massacres, the associated satisfactions, and how shame, guilt and triumph spread as social waves of emotion need far greater study. The methods described here make it possible to design some relatively simple experiments involving generalised emotion, to shed light on cognitive aspects of these processes, in a laboratory setting.

The K2 of Love in Social Construction

Sociologically, love has played a major role in establishing and improving societal norms, in the religious sphere, in the pursuit of ethics and justice, of human (and animal) rights. Much of that role can be attributed to the K2 properties of love. The sociologic question is to what extent can love provide a solution - a modus vivendi, if we make better or fuller use of its K2 factor. Different societies have provided different answers to this in the past.

Currently, we ask ourselves - must we fight nature and human nature destructively, to live in accordance with it? There seems to be a natural paradox. We live with a permanent blind spot to our own killing: it is only a matter of the size of the blind spot - either we kill animals in order to eat, (when we don't kill people for our perceived self protection), or at the very least - and are we so sure that it is the least? - we kill insects, and certainly microbes.

The generalised love in music and in sentic cycles has no address though it has a message. It does not supply its own address. It seems part of our freedom, to choose and be responsible for that address. Even Beethoven could eat animals between symphonies and laugh when the Jewish community wanted to commission him.

But not only our inner filing system needs care. The problem needs to be addressed that no-one can love all the time, given the brain's biochemical structure and function.

Need for Variety

It seems that some alternation of emotions, or variety is a necessity for maintaining aware vitality - to avoid saturation of the receptors and resulting staleness. No one has yet adequately studied boredom as an emotion. The need for variety is fundamental, born directly from the way the brain is constructed. Channels of communication by design tend to be more sensitive to change than to continuing conditions, and relatively desensitize sooner or later for any particular steady condition (cf. also Clynes 1969b, 1961, 1962). This is one reason why we prize creativity, which banishes boredom without trying - as also we are never bored when we dream.

Emotion, Knowledge and Reality

How real is the knowledge (K2) of emotion? Obviously we often view matters with considerable distortion depending on emotion. But in another sense, viewing something without emotion is not viewing it at all. Interest itself may well be considered to be an emotion (Izard, 1977) (what then is the K2 of Interest? cf. Clynes, 1977, where the special emotion when searching for an idea was named "apreene").

Strangely the practice of sentic cycles makes us remember, to an appreciable degree, what we are. The neurohormonal substances it presumably releases may help this to occur. We may hope that chemical intervention too, in the future will not lead to another round of horrors such as Aldous Huxley, however well meaningly, helped to precipitate, but to progress in what a human can be - towards a world Beethoven opened up for us in his last quartets that so few people have heard to this day. That which music has given us - "eine bessere Welt" (A better world - Schubert's song, "An die Musik") need not now remain outside our life-lines as a recreation . Knowing essentic forms consciously we may, all of us, use them as creation, without the dictates of composers, according to their natural properties, to form our own life-lines.

Toward a new social integration of emotion

We may see that the misuse of the knowledge of emotion leads to emotional bias, but its constructive (Apollonian) use leads to understanding of oneself and of others; to humaneness and empathy. The "knowledge" of emotion, its cognitive output substrate (K2), has in the past been largely neglected as scientific study - but is of great consequence - probably the most important aspect of emotion affecting individuals and society. On one hand the K2 of love largely constitutes the basis of systems of ethics, the K2 of reverence the fundamentals of religion; on the other, the K2 of hate and fear are manifest in the genesis of war and organization of persecution.

In personal life and in the function of society, as well as in art, emotion's K2 includes a way of viewing others as well as oneself. We do animals injustice when we call ourselves "beastly". But how may we justly view ourselves? Man will be the only animal that knows about the knowledge of his emotions, and will be able to use that knowledge for ends of his choice. Will these ends be tinged with emotion? Necesssarily so, for sociopolitically, and individually, man cannot escape the prison of his emotions: the "pursuit of happiness" is, so it goes, guaranteed by the constitution - and 'the peace achieved by being in harmony with the universe is both emotion and knowledge past our understanding'.

Indeed, psychopathology of emotion may become clear only to the extent that emotions are understood, individually and socially. Here we have described a theory and method derived from experiment that provides a small, intriguing step toward this. Much indeed remains to be discovered on that road, concerning these unique entities with built-in windows across the mind body barrier, and their tappable power for the development of the individual, of society, and even for the now self-conscious evolution of man.

Summary

The nature and production of generalised emotion is discussed. A theoretical distinction is introduced between cognitive factors giving rise to the emotion, K1, and cognitive factors or substrates affected by the generalised emotion as output functions, K2. A new easily learned touch art form of expressing and generating emotion is described, and a 27 minute long touch composition called sentic cycles, performed by finger and arm pressure in a sitting position, with the rest of the body quiet, which effectively generates the emotions of anger, hate, grief, love, sex, joy, reverence in turn. The ability to generate emotions in this way is seen to rest on the innate coherence between the dynamic form of the expression and the emotion it expresses. The 'better' (or more authentic) the expressed form, the more powerfully does it act to generate - and this is felt as a biologic feedback. Results from a large number of subjects are shown that compare intensity ratings for different emotions for men and women, and for United States and Australian subjects, and also with repeated sentic cycle experience. Preventive and therapeutic applications are given for emotional balance, integration and wellbeing through home use by subjects of sentic cycles and this method of generating unmixed or 'pure' emotions. These are seen to rest on cognitive, memory, and cathartic functions of the specific emotions. Applications relate to psychosomatic problems, character structure, phobias, general anxiety, sexual problems, drug and alcohol addiction, and depression. Sociologic aspects are discussed briefly.

Acknowledgement

Special thanks are due to Sharon Steller for much painstaking work in the analysis of sentic cycle data and reports, and also to William Thompson, Michael Rynn, and Stoyan Jurisevic for help in the statistics, in the preparation of the manuscript, and for many helpful suggestions. Support from Grants of the New South Wales Government is acknowledged, as well from the New South Wales State Conservatorium of Music. A substantial part of the data analysis was carried out while at the Department of Psychology, Bowling Green State University, and the author is grateful for use of the statistical and computer facilities there, as well as for Jaak Panksepp's invaluable support and encouragement.

References

Aggleton, J.P., & M. Mishkin, 1986, The Amygdala: sensory gateway to the emotions, in R. Plutchik and H. Kellerman, eds., "Emotion: Theory,

Research and Experience", Vol.3, Academic Press, New York.

Bower, G.H. Gilligan, S.G., & Monteiro, K.P., 1981, Selectivity of learning caused by affective states, *Journal of Experimental Psychology, General*, 110, 451-473.

Bower, G.H., 1981, Mood and memory, *American Psychologist,*, 36, 129-148.

Clynes, M., 1961, Unidirectional rate sensitivity: a biocybernetic law of reflex and humoral systems as physiologic channels of controls and communications,*Annals N.Y. Acad.Sci*, 92(3): 946-969.

Clynes, M., 1962, The nonlinear biological dynamics of unidirectional rate sensitivity illustrated by analog computer analysis, pupillary reflex to light and sound, and heart rate behavior, *Annals N.Y. Acad.Sc.* 98(4): 806-845.

Clynes, M., 1968, Essentic form - aspects of control, function and measurement, Proceedings of 21st Annual Conference of Engineering in Medicine and Biology, Houston, Texas.

Clynes, M., 1969a, Towards a theory of Man: Precision of essentic form in living communication, in: "Information Processing in the Nervous System," K.N. Leibovic, and J.C. Eccles, eds., Springer, New York, pp.177-205.

Clynes, M., 1969b, Cybernetic implications of rein control in perceptual and conceptual organization, *Annals of the N.Y. Acad. Sci.*, 156 (2), 629-671.

Clynes, M., 1970, Toward a view of Man, in M.Clynes & J.H. Milsum, eds., "Biomedical Engineering Systems," McGraw-Hill, New York, 272-358.

Clynes, M., 1973a, Sentics: Biocybernetics of emotion communication, *Annals N.Y. Acad.Sci.*, 220(3): 55-131.

Clynes, M., 1973b, Sentography: Dynamic forms of communications of emotion and qualities, *Computers in Biol. and Med.* 3: 119-130.

Clynes, M. 1975, Communication and generation of emotion through essentic form, in: "Emotions - Their Parameters and Measurement," L. Levi, ed., Raven Press, New York, pp. 561-601.

Clynes, M., 1977, "Sentics: The Touch of Emotions," Doubleday/Anchor, N.Y. p. 249.

Clynes, M., 1980, The communication of emotion: theory of sentics, in: "Theories of Emotion," Vol 1., R. Plutchik, and H. Kellerman, eds., Academic Press, New York.

Clynes, M. & Walker, J. 1982, Neurobiologic functions of rhythm, time and pulse in music, in M. Clynes, ed., "Music, Mind amd Brain, The Neuropsychology of Music." Plenum Press, New York, pp. 176-216. (Includes sound record.)

Clynes, M. & Nettheim, N. 1982, The living quality of music, neurobiologic patterns of communicating feeling, in M. Clynes ed., "Music, Mind and

Brain: The Neuropsychology of Music", Plenum Press, New York, pp. 47-82. (Includes sound record.)

Clynes, M. 1983, Expressive microstructure in music, linked to living qualities, in J. Sundberg ed., "Studies of Music Performance," Publications Issued by the Royal Swedish Academy of Music, No. 39, Stockholm, pp. 76-181. (Includes music record.)

Clynes, M. 1984, Music beyond the score, Somatics V, No.1, 4-14, and Communication and Cognition, 19, No 2, pp. 169-194.

Clynes, M. 1985, Secrets of life in music, in "Analytica: Studies in the Descriptionand Analysis of Music in Honour of Ingmar Bengtsson". Publications issued by the Royal Swedish Academy of Music, No. 47, Stockholm,pp. 3-15. (Includes music record.)

Clynes, M., & Walker, J. 1986, Music as time's measure, *Music Perception*, Vol. 4, 85-120.

Clynes, M., 1986, When time is music, in J.R. Evans & M. Clynes eds., "Rhythm in Psychological, Linguistic and Musical Processes", Charles C. Thomas, Springfield, Illinois.

Clynes, M., 1986, Generative principles of musical thought: Integration of microstructure with structure, *Communication and Cognition, CCAI*, Vol 3, pp.185-223.

Clynes, M., 1987, What a musician can learn about music performance from newly discovered microstrucure principles, in "Action and Perception in Rhythm and Music", A. Gabrielsson ed., Publications issued by the Royal Swedish Academy of Music, No. 55, pp. 201-233.

Clynes, M., Jurisevic, S. & Rynn, M. 1988, Cognitive substrates of emotion: Love is blocked by lying but anger is not, (in press).

Clynes, M., 1988, in preparation.

Darwin, C., 1872, The expression of the emotions in man and animals, Murray, London.

Davidson, R.J., 1984, Affect, cognition and hemispheric specialization, in C.E. Izard, J. Kagan & R. Zajonc eds., "Emotion, Cognition and Behavior", Cambridge University Press, New York.

Egger, M.D., & J.P. Flynn, 1967, Further studies on the effects of amygdaloid stimulation and ablation on hypothalamically elicited attack behavior in cats, in W.R. Adey and T. Tokizane, eds.,*Progress in Brain Research*, Vol. 27, 165-182, Elsevier, Amsterdam.

Ekman, P., 1984, Expression and the nature of emotion, in K.R. Scherer and P. Ekman eds., "Approaches to Emotion", Erlbaum, Hillsdale, New Jersey.

Ekman, P., Levenson, R.W., & Friesen, W.V. 1983, Autonomic nervous system activity distinguishes between emotions, *Science*, 221, 1208-1210.

Fernandez de Molina, A. & R.W. Hunsperger, 1962, Organization of the subcortical system governing defence and flight reactions in the cat, *Journal of Physiology*, Vol 160, 200-213.

Gilligan, S.G. & Bower, G.H., 1984, Cognitive consequences of emotional arousal, in C. Izard, J. Kagan, & R.B. Zajonc eds., "Emotions, Cognition and Behavior", Cambridge University Press, New York.

Isen, A.M., Shalker, T.E., Clark, M., & Karp, L. 1978, Affect, accessibility of material in memory and behaviour: A cognitive loop? *Journal of Personality and Social Psychology,* 36, 1-12.

Izard, C.E., 1977, "Human Emotions", PlenumPress, New York.

Izard, C.E., 1984, Emotion-cognition relationships and human development, in C.E. Izard, J. Kagan, & R. Zajonc eds., "Emotions, Cognition and Behavior", Cambridge University Press, New York.

Kihlstrom, J.F., 1987, The cognitive unconscious, *Science,* Vol 237, 1445-1451.

Laird, J.D.Wagener, J.J., Halal, M., & Szegda, M. 1982, Remembering what you feel: the effects of emotion on memory, *Journal of Personality and Social Psychology,* 42, pp 646-657.

Leventhal, H., 1984, A perceptual-motor theory of emotion. In L. Berkowitz ed., *Advances in experimental social psychology,* 17, pp. 117-182.

Leventhal, H., & K. Scherer, 1987, Relationship of emotion to cognition: a functional approach to a semantic controversy, *Cognition and Emotion,* Vol. 1, 3-28.

Lazarus, R.S., 1984, On the primacy of cognition, *Amercan Psychologist,* 39,124-129.

MacLean, P.D., 1985, Brain evolution relating to family, play and the separation call, *Arch. Gen. Psychiatry,* 42, pp 405-417.

Minsky, M., 1987, "The Society of Mind", Simon and Schuster, New York.

Oatley, K., & P.N. Johnson-Laird, 1987, Towards a cognitive theory of emotions, *Cognition and Emotion,* Vol 1, 29-50.

Panskepp, J., 1982, Toward a general psychobiological theory of emotion, *The Behavioral and Brain Sciences,* 5, 407-468.

Panksepp, J., 1986, The anatomy of emotions, in R. Plutchik & H. Kellerman, eds., "Emotions: Theory, Research and Experience", Vol 3, The Biologic Foundations of Emotion", Academic Press, NewYork.

Ploog, D. 1981, Neurobiology of primate audio-vocal behaviours, *Brain Res. Rev.,*3, 35-61.

Plutchik, R. 1980, A general psychoevolutionary theory of emotion, in R. Plutchik, R. and H. Kellerman eds., "Theories of emotion", Vol.1, Academic Press, New York.

Plutchik, R. 1980, Emotion: A psychoevolutionary synthesis, Harper and Row, New York.

Schiller, Friedrich, 1793, Uber Anmut und Wurde.

Simon, H.A., 1979, Information processing models of cognition, in M.R. Rosenzweig & L.W.Porter eds.,*Annual Review of Psychology,* Vol. 30, pp. 363-396.

Weiner, B., 1985, An attributional theory of achievement motivation and emotion, *Psychological Review,* Vol. 92, 548-573.

Zajonc, R.B. 1980, Feeling and thinking: Preferences need no inferences. *American Psychologist,* Vol. 35, 151-175.

Zajonc, R.B. & Markus, H. 1984, Affect and cognition: the hard interface, in C.A. Izard, J. Kagan, & R.B. Zajonic eds., "Emotions, Cognition and Behavior", Cambridge University Press, New York.

Appendix A

Timings for the Start of Expressions for Sentic Cycles (soft clicks)

Next click occurs after an interval of: No. of seconds		
	5.322	5.839 ***
	6.941	
	6.451	9.465
	4.722	0.137 Spoken: *GRIEF*
Spoken: *NO EMOTION*	5.643	3.908
5.269	4.777	7.403
5.619	7.269	8.732
6.208	4.844	8.501
4.360	6.288	8.467
6.873	6.266	8.564
5.487	6.405	7.539
5.138	6.209	7.421
4.359	4.256	8.786
5.107	5.878	8.274
5.455	4.952	7.694
5.413	6.359	7.484
4.718	4.352	8.106
4.284	5.048 ***	7.972
5.104		7.960
4.089	7.271	8.348
5.550	0.140 Spoken: *HATE*	8.604
5.650	3.767	7.403
4.228	4.261	8.781
5.765	5.183	8.425
5.269	5.354	8.798
6.499	5.328	7.876
4.206	4.212	7.318
4.548 ***	5.759	8.833
	5.513	8.142
6.883	4.276	8.271
0.445 Spoken: *ANGER*	5.880	8.566
4.391	5.506	8.918
4.179	6.378	7.744
4.616	4.767	8.718
5.483	5.566	8.172 ***
4.354	5.891	
5.253	5.364	11.729
5.272	6.799	0.136 Spoken: *LOVE*
5.781	5.643	9.136
6.515	4.046	8.898
5.338	4.749	7.479
5.811	5.841	9.301
6.039	5.979	7.382
6.377	5.723	8.339
6.660	5.630	8.642
4.399	5.731	7.838
5.148	6.085	8.738

8.680	5.799	6.748
7.873	4.248	4.447
9.151	4.866	4.254
8.933	4.539	7.168
7.351	5.702	5.386
7.957	4.232	6.217
8.256	4.958	4.657
7.227	5.336	4.412
9.047	5.637	4.212
9.604	4.032	4.771
8.332	5.201	5.469
8.722	5.448	5.660
7.465	4.238	4.050
8.227	5.413	4.829
7.948	5.222	5.369
8.594	4.732 ***	4.117
8.504		5.414 ***
8.205	5.503	
7.477 ***	0.346 Spoken: *JOY*	6.448
	4.656	0.408 Spoken: *REVERENCE*
10.028	6.681	5.443
0.068 Spoken: *SEX*	4.903	6.382
5.332	5.504	7.479
4.310	4.688	7.068
4.772	5.665	7.663
5.575	5.169	7.151
4.152	4.910	7.628
5.572	5.439	6.813
5.515	4.220	7.953
5.669	5.540	7.790
6.546	5.493	8.700
4.863	5.812	6.499
4.142	5.769	6.833
5.318	4.214	7.580
5.147	4.734	7.291
5.003	5.959	6.668
5.594	4.824	7.578
4.760	4.366	7.716
4.223	5.367	8.158
5.551	5.522	8.056
5.925	5.136	7.696 ***
5.850	4.606	

*** Indicates the last click for that emotion. The following timing interval is from this click to the announcement of the next emotion.

These timings are available recorded on tape, together with a finger rest and instruction booklet for doing Sentic Cycles, from the American Sentic Association, Box 2176, La Jolla, Ca. 92037, ($ 32.50). Information on Sentographs may be obtained from the author.

Appendix B

Sentic Cycle Worksheet

This is an example of a sentic cycle worksheet, completed for each cycle, about half an hour after the experience, except for the after-effects comments, which are filled in later. This particular example is after the first cycle completed by the subject, a 37 year old Australian female hospital aide.

While the contents of reports vary so that no single report may be described as typical, it may yet be called typical in the following ways:

1. The remarks indicate clearly that the emotions were experienced.
2. The emotions were experienced the very first time the cycle was done.
3. The after-effects described are typical.
4. Specific body effects described are typical.

It is atypical as it contains less than usual reference to old memories, and other people.

ANGER   *Intensity Rating 2*

I was greatly involved physically in this emotion, more so than for any other in the cycle - particularly the clenching of my jaw and mouth and the tightening of my abdomen and shoulders. I seemed to move my head holding it sometimes sideways, then partly lowered. I was very alert and keyed up for each signal. Yet while I was ready to act immediately the signal went, like a starter's pistol, I also found myself hanging on to the last thrust, like a bulldog. I felt hot . There was no particular image involved, more the emotional process itself. My breathing built up markedly and became strong to my ears, so that I became momentarily selfconscious.

HATE   *Intensity Rating 2*

This experience came on more slowly than did anger, but built to an intensity that seemed to go into some 'cold' stage beyond the former hot one. The hatred seemed to pour from my eyes, so that my head was held straight, perhaps slightly raised, as if I was glaring fixedly at whatever I was confronting. I felt I was confronting various anti-life forces, and images of evil then began to flow in the form of destrucive possessiveness or parasite life-styles.

GRIEF   *Intensity Rating 2*

A vast sadness flooded over me and I felt physically reduced in size and lacking in shape. I felt I had shrivelled up, or that I wanted to curl up and cut off. I did not want to look outwards and in fact had difficulty in keeping in contact with the 'here and now' sufficiently to hear the signals (clicks). I felt that I may have let a couple of beats pass unnoticed. I remembered how I had felt when I lost my own Paradise - when I had the shocking awareness that the world I have loved and frolicked in was largely a social concensus reality. Then, the memory became an affectionately viewed foible, and I was content to move on again.

LOVE   *Intensity Rating 4*

I was filled with a great tenderness and a beauty that hinted elusively at something exquisite. There was a stillness and peace. My finger pressure seemed slow and gentle, but so powerful. I enjoyed each beat (expression started by a click) and took each renewed chance to exerience and express this wonderful feeling. It culminated in an image of the few ...people I know and of my own unconditional love for them - a feeling that suggested freedom the same way as the feeling of anger had suggested the tyranny of hanging on. I thought of a man I love.

SEX *Intensity Rating 2*
This triggered off a train of sensual imagery - particularly smells and sounds. I saw part of a sweaty body, and heard the panting sounds of breathing. My own body responded. My finger movements were at first sharp and rapid and tended to prematurely anticipate the signal. They then became co-ordinated with the beat, and became slower and more subtle, to the point of barely touching the finger rest. I became aware of a mounting excitement in my vagina, along with almost holding my breath. I was not ready for the directive to change emotions, and felt left up in the air.

JOY *Intensity Rating 4*
My initial hesitation at leaving the last emotion vanished the instant I realized that it was joy that I was to express. I lept at this opportunity and the feeling came to me more readily than any other emotion. My neck seemed elongated and my body felt skinny and nimble. It was beautifully sunny I seemed to be trotting along on a horse, on some voyage of self-discovery. I was thrilled at finding life even more wonderful than my optimistic expectations had led me to believe. I felt naive. I could hear Keith Jarrett playing his Cologne Concert as an affirmation of life. I was filled with a sense of trust and lept simplemindedly into the next emotion.

REVERENCE *Intensity Rating 4*
A powerful feeling slowly gripped me. A strong sensation came into the pit of my stomch. My body was still - suspended. I seemed to hold my breath and search the sky of my mind with my eyes. An overwhelming expansiveness filled me, and I had intimations of being initiated into some profound mystery. Time and place became irrelevant, and while I was aware that the session had ended, I remained in that state for some minutes.

GENERAL COMMENTS AND EXPERIENCE AFTER DOING CYCLES
I opened my eyes to find that people seemed more self-contained than when I had closed them, and that a certain sensitivity reigned in voices and movements, where before there had been a coarsened joi de vivre. I felt reluctant to get involved with any immediate conversation, preferring to stay with my own feelings. However, when someone initiated contact with me, I responded with a greater readiness than I had expected.
At bedtime, I felt highly alert and so prepared to lie awake and absorb my experience further, whereas in fact I fell straight to sleep.
Next morning, I was filled with a sense of well-being,... with a heightened sense of awareness and sense of satisfaction, both of which seemed to come from having been intimately in touch with another part of myself.

To give the reader a feeling for the development of insight into each emotion as more cycles are done, we shall here show the remarks by the same subject for the second and third cycle, done within one week of the first cycle, for Grief, Love and Joy only (in view of space limitations). (For further contrasted examples, see Clynes 1977.)

SECOND CYCLE

GRIEF Intensity Rating 3   (Three days later)
I felt a great loss, as if I had not only been drained of everything inside me but had also lost my framework, my orientation, ... I felt unresponsive. There was a sameness, and endlessness about everything, like a decot. Even individual images did not bring about an individual experience. My finger seemed to have nothing to express that was in any way different to the all pervading greyness about me. All subtleties and nice differences in values seemed to vanish, and I had to periodically force myself to get involved almost mechanically, in what was happening at the moment.

LOVE Intensity Rating 4

Love flowed in and filled the hollowness of my grief. I became self-regenerating, reborn. My face melted with softness, and my touch was gentle and rich. I felt receptive and responsive and capable of true fellowship. I felt in no hurry to express my feelings as already I felt effective. I felt the sure hand of integrity, and was filled with a simple honesty that brought me face to face with my love, with little need for supporting acts. My body listened quietly to the beautiful flow within me.

JOY Intensity Rating 3

I felt myself growing taller and lighter. This quality had a higher pitch, and rose to that pitch, rapidly. A jubilant bub-bubbling up from within called for more movement than did love. This feeling was unable to contain itself, and was uncontained. My touch was perky with vitality. I had the sensation of floating over the roofs of houses on Mercury's winged heels, as in some Chagall painting.

THIRD CYCLE

GRIEF Intensity Rating 4   (One week later)

My shoulders sagged, my cheeks and jaw fell, and all remaining life drained out of me in a heavy sigh. A heavy left hand fell upon heavy thighs above heavy feet. The right hand would rather have hung than have lifted a finger, but did so mechanically because it had been directed to and did not have enough initiative to decide otherwise. Each touch was inconsistent within itself, ambivalent, as if saying something and then retracting it. While I went through the motions, still the act of pressing on the finger rest seemed pointless: my cry had no voice, and there seemed no one out there who could hear - and even if there was, I felt incapable of responding to any input. I was caught in some terrible inertia. My eyes seemed now to look without seeing. This state was interminable. All past losses seemed cumulative and all the present contaminated.

LOVE Intensity Rating 3

I welcomed love like a dear friend, I felt at home. I affirmed and was reaffirmed. My finger softly told of my love with a touch that was gentle but sure. My quiet breathing echoed my trust. If not complete it did not matter. I was free, and yet related.

JOY Intensity Rating 3

A light tripping motion took hold of me. I tapped gracefully at the finger rest. I felt buoyant and pure in heart. My finger movement seemed deceptive in its simplicity, but my touch expressed a feeling for life that had little need to plumb the depths of any deeper understanding. I was uncomplicated and contagious.

GENERAL COMMENTS AND EXPERIENCE AFTER DOING CYCLES   *(Second Cycle)*

After doing the cycle I felt a sense of equanimity and calm. I felt content to be alone and to continue experiencing my fullness. The next day I felt my usual sense of well-being but with a difference. My feelings were more differentiated and throughout the day I found myself responding more spontante-ously and being more aware of the nuances of each response. In particular, I was markedly more aware of the physical side of my "inner" experiences. I found the writing up of my experiences to be a most clarifying aspect of doing sentic cycles.

(Third Cycle)

Doing sentic cycles is like walking the dog: my emotions look forward to getting exercised. I am particularly surprised at the amount of body-awareness that I have developed, and I have a growing appreciation of the extent to which an emotional experience is a total experience. Having my feeling at my finger-tips has not made my daily life any easier but it has certainly made it livelier, more honest than conventional. On occasions, when responding "colorfully" to a situation that I have not been accustomed to responding to in this way, I have gone away like a child with a secret, feeling that only I knew that my sentic cycles were behind this storm in the teacup. Doing sentic cycles, for me, is both a clarifying and a purifying experience.

Emotions and the Society of Mind

Marvin Minsky

Department of Computer Science
Massachusetts Institute of Technology
Cambridge, Massachusetts

What on Earth could emotions be, if they aren't thoughts and they aren't things? What enables a mind to thrill to the sound of a trumpet or be jealous of a rival? And what makes such matters so hard to understand? Certain problems are hard to solve because they are genuinely intricate but, sometimes, when a subject seems intractably mysterious, the difficulty stems instead from flaws in our own attitudes. The problem itself might not be so hard, but if the way we've framed it is wrong, then we may find clues by studying the character of our own confusion. Emotions seem mysterious for both kinds of reasons. There can be no doubt that emotions come from truly intricate machinery. But we then proceed to make matters worse because our own emotions interfere with how we think about them. For any problem so complex, we must do what science always does: propose a model with simple parts - setting aside, at least at first, all but their most essential details.

> **Mini-Theory 1**. The brain consists of several nearly separate thinking machines; we'll call them "protospecialists". Usually, in infancy, only one of them is active at a time, while the others tend to be suppressed. Each protospecialist is a highly evolved goal-mechanism concerned with some important need such as nutrition, reproduction, or defense. The psychological conditions that correspond to those activities are what we recognize as emotions such as hunger, affection and attachment, or anger and fear, and so forth. Each of our most basic emotions involves the activity of a distinct division of the brain, as suggested in section 16.3 of *Society of Mind* (*SOM*, Minksy, 1987).

Each emotion thus imposes a different personality on the mind as a whole. Once we understand this, it is easier to see why it is so difficult to think clearly about our emotions. For if each emotion is virtually a separate mind, and if none of those protospecialists knows much about the other ones, then, naturally, emotions will seem mysterious. "Mysterious to whom?" one is tempted to ask - and then we fall into a fatal trap: the Fallacy of the Single Self. For, as adults, we feel compelled to think that somewhere, deep down in the mind, exists some central entity that experiences all of our feelings and thoughts. But nothing of that sort exists. As infants, our minds have separate parts; then they develop closer ties; but never are all those different thoughts all shared by any particular part of the mind.

Some readers may be horrified at picturing a baby's mind as made of nearly-separate agencies. But we'll never understand how emotions grow, without some theories of how they start. One evidence for separateness is the suddenness with which our infants switch from contentment or calmness to anger or rage. Older children show less sudden and drastic changes in mood, and their expressions suggest more complex mixtures of emotions and dispositions. This suggests that we begin composed of almost separate "protospecialists" that each accumulate their private memories. Then, through the course of infancy and childhood, these fragments of the mind learn various ways to exploit the others. But because they each evolved to use rather different processes for different kinds of purposes, they are each endowed with somewhat different ways to represent the knowledge that they acquire. In section 6.12 of SOM we explain why makes it hard for there ever to be good communication among the different protospecialists.

> **Mini-theory 2.** As the child grows, each primitive protospecialist grows level after level of new memory and management machinery. One result of this process is to make those specialists become less separated. This is because those newer levels tend to be shared. But those primitive perspectives still remain in place below the managers of the adult mind, and are used for many purposes - and each division of the mind has its own particular view of what the other divisions do. Now, whenever we experience a substantial change in emotional state, this involves a substantial transfer of control from one division to another. Naturally, that will alter what we think and, in particular, it will alter what we think about what emotions are and what they do. So naturally, emotions seem mysterious.*

The remainder of this article consists of several disconnected vignettes, each illustrating how the *Society of Mind* viewpoint might illuminate an emotional phenomenon.

---

* As scientists, we can set ourselves to work toward constructing a unified view of what emotions are and do. However, in our daily lives, there are reasons why this is not feasible. Section 29.6 of SOM conjectures that a child who tried too hard to maintain too unified a view might risk the loss of ability to distinguish between physical and psychological phenomena - and that could result in autism.

Pleasure, Pain, and Plan

What is pain, and why does it make us hurt? What is pleasure, and why do we like it? The trouble with such questions is that they are formulated in terms of a single self that feels pain and dislikes it. However, words such as hurt and like do not refer to simple, elemental entities. I suspect, indeed, that "pain" is used to describe a large variety of different processes involved with lowering the level-bands of our momentary goals. (Chapter 8 of SOM has more details on what I mean by level-band.) Because of this, when you're in pain, it's hard to maintain your interest in higher level goals - and that is why pain makes you feel that there's nothing more important than to find some way to stop the pain. That is why pain makes it so hard to think of anything else. Pain's power to distract evolved because our bodies are endowed with special sensors that detect impending injuries - and because those signals are wired up to disrupt our concerns with long-term goals. This enables our lowest-level agencies to concentrate on immediate, urgent problems. This usually helps one to survive - but it certainly can do more harm than good when one actually needs more complex plans for removing what is causing the pain.

When something causes pleasure, too, it is hard to think of other things. You feel that nothing's more important than to find a way to make that pleasure last. Thus pleasure and pain tend to seem opposed, since pleasure makes us draw things near while pain impels us to push things away. But they also tend to seem similar, in that they both tend to simplify one's view - by making rival goals seem small and turning us from other interests. However, they do this in different ways: pleasure, in its simplest forms, involves a vertical sort of narrowing of interest at every level, whereas pain involves a horizontal sort of narrowing that focuses concern on the lowest levels. Pleasure and pain are also involved in how we learn but, again, although in some respects they seem simply opposed, they also engage fundamentally different types of processes. For example, pain and punishment do not merely cancel learning or induce forgetfulness but are involved in the construction of systems for active suppression and censorship.

Which comes first: the emotion or the accompanying change in level of activity? This is a wrong kind of question because we can understand the particular characteristics of each emotion only by understanding the processes that constitute it - that is, through constructing a cognitive theory of why each emotional configuration produces its own peculiar effects. The simplest stimuli that we recognize as physically painful are based upon inborn mechanisms like those that, in simpler animals, result in withdrawal from sources of irritation. When we see that happen in, say, a crab, we tend to assume that the crab experiences the same feeling that a person would. But such a sympathetic inference would be based on a superficial resemblance because withdrawing a claw, in the case of the crab, involves mechanisms that are similar only at the very lowest level. It might make sense to say that crabs react to pain, but to claim that pain hurts crabs (the way it hurts us) might make no more sense than to say that heat must hurt a thermostat.   It might make sense in that way to us, merely because of that particular resemblence to the thermostat. It is more complicated than that. Even animals with brains much simpler than ours appear to have evolved pain mechanisms with priorities or intensities powerful enough to disrupt all other activities. The way in which pain makes people hurt is much more complicated than that because, when pain threatens to distract other parts of the mind, by altering their higher levels of activity, each of many agencies must anticipate the postponement of most of their goals and long range plans. This initiates many other kinds of activities that we tend to describe in negative terms such as frustration, impotence, distraction, apprehension, and loss of goal. The reason pain hurts us so much - is that we have such complex systems to disrupt.

Reason, Fantasy, and Exploitation

The growth of every individual involves constructing agencies with different goals and processses. As time goes on each agency learns various ways to control and exploit some of the others. It is the resulting complex of relationships that becomes the personality. In *SOM* I used thew following anecdote to illustrate how agencies can interact.

I was trying to concentrate on a certain mathematical problem, but was getting bored and sleepy. Then I imagined that my competitor, Professor Challenger, was about to solve the same problem. An angry wish to frustrate Challenger then kept me working for a while longer. The strange thing was that this problem was not the kind that interested Challenger.

A psychoanalyst might suggest that the conflict with Challenger represents some underlying drive or wish that serves as as source of energy. No matter that this conflict is a fantasy; it might only disguise some other, sublimated urge that momentarily penetrates a transiently weakened barrier. But I prefer a more pragmatic interpretation: the fantasy represents a simpler, practical strategy in which my agency for Work exploits the ability of Anger to inhibit Sleep. Why use a scheme so devious as to invent an outright lie? Why can't we simply tell ourselves to do the things we want to do? Why cannot Work simply turn off Sleep? To see the answer, consider the alternatives. If work could simply turn sleep off Sleep, we'd quickly wear our bodies out. If Work could directly switch Anger on, we would all be fighting all the time. Directness is too dangerous; we would die if we could suppress all the vital systems involved with hunger and fatigue. Instead, our brains have evolved systems of checks and balances that prevent any single agency from controlling the others.

Direct connections have been weeded out. Consequently, in order for our agencies to exploit one another's skills , they must discover and use indirect pathways. Our fantasies provide these missing paths. You cannot make yourself angry simply by deciding to be angry, but it remains possible for you to learn to imagine things or situations to make yourself angry.

This is one reason why emotion and reason are so intertwined. Logic alone is incomplete. It can help us decide when our deductions are properly based on our assumptions, but we cannot employ it to decide which directions of thought to pursue. The Challenger scenario shows how indistinct is that boundary between reason and emotion. We usually think of anger as irrational. But here, if we take Work's point of view, it seems just as rational to use Anger to inhibit sleep as to use a stick to move something out of reach. Anger is merely a tool Work can use to solve one of its problems. No matter that such states of mind may be what people call emotional; to Work the use of fantasy is merely a way to accomplish a goal.

Disappointment, Fear, and Shame; Attachment, Love, and Reverence

Our most powerful emotions involve the bonds that link parent and child. We tend to regard as positive what we call love, affection, and reverence. We tend to regard as negative the emotions we call embarrassment, shame, and guilt. What functions do those emotions serve? The obvious roles of attachment are in the areas of nutrition and defense because they favor the evolution of mechanisms that keep infant animals close to their parents. But attachment also serves learning and education. Imagine a child playing with mud, perhaps with the goal of filling a pail, and consider how disappointment, fear, and shame affect how and what that child learns. I submit that each of those emotions may play fundamentally different roles.

DISAPPOINTMENT: What would happen if a certain strategy fails to get mud into the pail. The child will be disappointed - and probably try a different technique. Usually, the emotion of disappointment will lead to a change in technique: a certain strategy failed for a goal, so try a different strategy. In the case of a simple failure, the learner maintains the current goal but makes a change on the level below by adopting a different sub-goal.

FEAR: What would happen if a stranger appeared and started to scold and criticize. The child would be likely to experience fear, and try to escape, to seek a parent's protection. The apprehension of possible harm will not much affect the current goal, although our child may subsequently somewhat less inclined to play with mud. Fear-provoking disturbances affect how we learn to classify situations, but have less effect on how we choose goals.

SHAME: What if it were a parent who proceeded to censure and complain? That would have a very different effect on the child: it would produce, not fear, but shame - an emotion that usually involves a person to whom one is attached. Shame tends to cause the child to learn, "I ought not want that sort of goal."

Thus attachment has a profound effect. Simple failure and success merely affect how we learn subgoals - that is, how we learn which means to adopt for achieving goals we already want. But attachment affects the goals themselves, by making us change in various ways how we select which goals to pursue. Shame results in repression of goals, whereas reverence promotes them. What could be the mechanical cause of such an important phenomenon? Section 17.2 of *SOM* proposes a theory of how this might work: the detectors which recognize the presence of an attachment-person are directly connected so as to raise the locus of the effects of reinforcement signals. Then, where success and failure signals ordinarily affect the learning of "means", they now apply to the learning of ends, simply by switching their effects on them from the level of sub-goal to that of supergoal. This conception of the effect of attachment suggest a mechanistic embodiment of Freud's idea that child can "introject" the values of their parents.

Sympathy, Gesture, and Trajectory

How do we construct attachment bonds? In some species of animals, it occurs so rapidly that scientists call it "imprinting." In human infants the development of attachment appears to be a complex, many stage process in which various inborn systems learn to distinguish the parents' individual peculiarities - first by senses of touch, taste and smell, and then by Voice and sight of face. But attachment is more than simply to distinguish parents from other things; once those attachment bonds are formed, the child will react in different ways to the presence of strangers and parents. As we saw just above, these have different effects on how and what the child will learn. Furthermore, the effect of attachment depends not only on the presence of the parent, but on which particular "expression" the parent presents. Smiles and caresses have what we call positive effects, while frowns and scowls have negative effects.

To help their offspring grow and learn, social animals evolve complementary schemes: attachment is a two-way street. Babies are born equipped with shrieks that arouse their parents far away or fast asleep. Adults, on the other side, are made to find those signals irresistible. What special systems in our brains assign to those cries such high priorities? I conjecture an evolutionary trick in which our adult cry-detectors are connected to the remnants of the very same protospecialists that caused us to make those same types of cries when we were infants. The result would be to make us respond to those sounds by attributing to them the same sorts of feelings that would drive us to shriek with similar intensity. This drives the baby's caretakers to respond to its needs with urgent sympathy (for a summary of some recent empirical work and related ideas in this area see Panksepp, 1986). To fill this out in more detail we first would have to understand how our brains distinguish the external signs of different emotional states. Then we would need a theory of how the output of each detector is connected to the correct brain center - namely, one that can reproduce the appropriately sympathetic effect. How does a child learn to recognize another person's mental state of being angry or affectionate?

Consider the hypothesis that this is largely based on how we recognize and classify trajectories. Just as we learn to interpret spatial change as motions of things in the physical realm, we also learn to classify certain other types of changes as signifying mental events: namely, as what we call "gestures" and "expressions." For example, consider speech. Some of the meaning comes just from the words. But we also find significance in the shape of a sequence of vocal sounds. Each envelope of tone and phrase leads us to interpret each utterance as having emotional character. Now, certain features of vocal sounds seem almost universally to signify specific emotional qualities. For example, the more abrupt trajectories seem angry or imperative. Perhaps they tend to evoke alarm by inducing the kind of narrowing of interest that accompanies pain; usually, a sudden change demands our full attention. In contrast, we react to "gentle" sounds in ways we label more positive" because of how those smoother time-trajectories arouse affection, love, or reverence. Manfred Clynes's experiments certainly appear to show that people react in similar ways to certain types of trajectories, no matter in which sensory domain they may happen to occur. For example, we consistently identify certain rapid, jerky gestures as angry - regardless of whether they are expressed in the form of visible thrusts, abrupt sounds, or tactile jabs. The same seems equally clear in the case of gestures that we recognize as gentle or affectionate. Clynes (1973,1977) concludes that at least half a dozen distinct trajectory-types are universally associated with particular emotions.

What kind of brain-machinery could make us respond in such similar ways to similar trajectories in such diverse domains? I propose a three-part hypothesis. First, each of our sensory systems is genetically equipped with agents that detect certain particular types of time-trajectories. Second, the outputs of all the agents that detect corresponding "trajectory-types" - in all those sensory domains - are wired up to converge upon a corresponding central "gesture-recognizing" agency.

FIGURE: trajectory-layer agencies

According to this hypothesis, each sensory agency contains agents specialized to react to various particular expressions - that is, trajectory-types. One type of agent might react only to signals that increase slowly and then decrease quickly; another might react only to signals that increase quickly and decay slowly, and so on. The important thing is for the detection of each type of trajectory is transmitted to the same central place, no matter where it was detected. This will make it easy for that central agency to learn to react in similar ways to a snarl, grimace, or shaken fist - and thus to construct an "anger-recognizing" agent whose function is abstract - in the sense of being detached from any particular sensory mode.

We need a third hypothesis to account for that sense of "sympathy". Merely to distinguish a particular gesture-type does not, by itself, enable us to identify another person's "anger-type" trajectory with our own personal experience of being angry. Simply recognizing anger is not the same as comprehending or sympathizing with it. So our diagram also suggests how certain genetically established nerve bundles might connect each central gesture-recognizing agency to a particular "protospecialist" of the sort we described above. (For more detail, see the Appendix of *SOM*.). These cause each particular gesture-type to activate a corresponding protospecialist - and, hence, a particular kind of emotional response. A direct connection of this sort cause us to experience elation in response to another person's joyous gesture. (We would also need a theory of how arousing a particular protospecialist - that is, of a particular primitive emotion - might produce a particular type of trajectory.) A "cross-wired" connection of this sort could make us tend to retreat from threatening gestures, or to attack in response to signs of fear. The behavior of animals reflects genetically constructed machinery through which particular gesture types evoke "instinctive" reactions, as when a sudden motion toward a bird provokes a fear-reaction flight. Human brains are also endowed with much instinctive wiring. But more than any other animal, we also have machinery that can learn to bridge across those built-in links, to bury ancient instincts under modern social disciplines.

Emotion and Thought

I've often heard the view expressed that it must be easy to build machines that do our ordinary sorts of reasoning, whereas it would be impossible to build machines that experience pain, or affection, ambition, fear, or shame. Such subjects are often considered beyond what science can ever hope to explain because emotions are nonphysical. Yet when we examine this common belief, that thinking is easier to explain than emotion, we find that this has things reversed. For when we get right down to it, it is very hard to make machines that reason well. I think the distortion comes form a tradition that informs us that reasoning involves little more than logical principles. However, experience with research on Artificial Intelligence seems to show that this is far from true. It has turned out very difficult to express the seemingly simplest forms of commonsense knowledge in logical form. Furthermore, this is only a small part of the problem because logic can tell us only which inferences are correct, but says nothing at all about what inferences to make, which goals how to select, or how to avoid meandering into endless amounts of futile, useless reasoning.

On the other side, the rules of emotion are rather more easy to see and describe; we all know well how, usually, threats evoke fear, frustrations evokes aggression, competition (in love) leads to jealousy, and disapproval (in the context of attachment) leads to shame. To be sure, such regularities apply only to primitive states and, as we grow and develop and learn, the interactions among such mental states can become arbitrarily subtle and complex. But it is important to recognize that this, in itself, is not peculiar to emotion in particular; the complexity of our reasoning, too, can grow beyond bounds in complexity.

Our traditional concepts of psychology are too confused to help us understand how emotions work. We have all been told that emotions are separate from reason. We also learn that machines are inherently reasonable and cannot have emotions. Consequently, we are forced to believe, there can never be a mechanistic explanation of emotion. What makes our task so difficult is that the same tradition also assumes that inside the mind is something else: a separate Self inside the self that thinks and feels what we feel and think. The actual problem is hard enough: to understand a complex brain composed of thousands of agencies. That myth of the single, central Self starts us out in the wrong direction.

References

Clynes, M. (1973), Sentics: Biocybernetics of emotion communication, *Annals N.Y.Acad. Sci.*, 220(3): 55-131.
Clynes, M. (1977), "Sentics, the Touch of Emotions", Doubleday, New York.
Minsky, M. (1987) "The Society of Mind", Simon and Schuster, Heinemann & Co., New York.
Panksepp, J. (1986) The psychobiology of prosocial behaviors: separation distress, play and altruism. In: "Altruism and Aggression: Biological and Social Origins," C. Zahn-Waxler, E.M. Cummings & R. Iannotti (Eds.) Cambridge: Cambridge Univ. Press. pp. 19-57.

Emotions, Brain, Immunity, and Health:
A Review

Theodore Melnechuk

Neuroimmune Physiology Laboratory
Helicon Foundation
4622 Santa Fe Street
San Diego, CA 92109
and
Department of Neurosciences, A-001
School of Medicine
University of California San Diego
La Jolla, CA 92093

In this review of research on emotions and immunity, in the context of psychobiology and psychosomatic medicine, emphasis is placed as much as possible on the physiological mechanisms whereby emotional responses and attitudes appear to affect disease resistance.

I. Historical and Physiological Background

1. Major Steps in Western Research on Emotions and Health

Early Ideas

In their perennial search for a general theory of health, people in all cultures have observed that, along with heredity, intake, and activity, emotions can affect health. In the fourth century BC, the father of scientific medicine, Hippocrates, stated that all body functions were influenced by the passions, as emotions used to be called. Moreover, he put forth the "psychogenicity doctrine" that emotions could actually cause disease (Ackerknecht, 1982). In the second century AD, Galen asserted the "specificity doctrine" that specific personality types correlate positively with specific disease susceptibilities - e.g., that melancholy women are more apt than sanguine women to develop cancer (Gordon, 1935). Like so many Greco-Roman ideas, these two doctrines were influential through the subsequent centuries. They are still entertained in medical science, but in modified forms discussed below. Galen's specificity doctrine postulated as mediators of its correlations a simplistic system of excess amounts of substances called humors that led to debilitating regimens of bloodletting, cupping, purging, and vomiting (Thomas, 1987).

A major theoretical advance was made in 1859, when Claude Bernard advanced his idea that it was essential for life that the "milieu interieur" (internal environment) be stable, at least within a permissible range of fluctuation (Halberg, 1967). One implication of Bernard's idea was that medical science should study the effects of emotions on this fluctuating stability and its regulatory mechanisms - its "homeostatic" mechanisms, as they were later called by Cannon (1932).

However, the success of the Pasteur-Koch germ theory of infectious diseases soon encouraged medical science in its now century-long concentration on small-scale pathogens, the "seeds" of disease, and not on its "soil", the internal environment. The relative etiological importance of seed and soil was the subject of a lifelong dispute between pro-seed Pasteur and pro-soil Bernard reminiscent in fatuity of the parallel dispute over the relative developmental importance of nature and nurture. Despite Pasteur's overgenerous deathbed concession - "Bernard was right; it is the soil" (Gordon, 1980) - emotions as modifiers of the internal environment, and perhaps even as pathogens, were largely ignored by physiologists, with the notable exceptions of Pavlov (1902) and Cannon (1914).

Stress Responses

Cannon (1914) discovered what he later called the "fight or flight" response to challenge (Cannon, 1932). It mobilizes the body for exertion with the feelings of anger or fear and the concomitant activation of the arousing sympathetic branch of the autonomic nervous system (Brooks, 1987). Sympathetic arousal in turn stimulates the medulla of the adrenal gland to release the catecholamine hormones epinephrine and norepinephrine, since found to have different time courses and functional consequences (Henry, 1980).

Cannon's study of the role of the adrenal medulla in mediating bodily effects of some major emotions and pain began a new field of inquiry devoted to the physiology of what came to be called "stress". A complementary discovery, made by Selye (1936), was of what he called at first the "general adaptation syndrome" (Selye, 1946) and later the "stress response" (Selye, 1956). It includes feelings of anxiety or distress and the release of corticosteroid hormones such as cortisol from the cortex of the adrenal gland.

Both the catecholamine and the corticosteroid stress hormones are catabolic: they create muscle fuel by breaking down protein and carbohydrate. Thus they have been thought to be most damaging when conjoint, because of the increased risk of exhausting reserves (Frankenhaeuser, discussed in Theorell, 1986). Frankenhaeuser (1982) has also thought it better to call the "fight or flight" response the "effort" response and the "general adaptation syndrome" the "distress" response, a practice adopted in this review except when the effort response is further discriminated.

Cannon did not distinguish between the physiological concomitant of the feelings of anger and fear, but when they were later found to be different (Ax, 1953), his discovery became consistent with a current emphasis on the multiplicity of specific responses to different stressors, whereas Selye insisted to the end on the reality and clinical importance of a general adaptive response to all stressors.

For example, Selye (1946) postulated that such disorders as allergy, collagen disease, and rheumatic diseases were caused by an abnormal or excessive stress response. However, the next 40 years produced no evidence that chronic stress causes destruction of any tissue (Stein, 1986), although Sapolsky (1987) reported that exposure of aging rats to glucocorticoid hormones at high physiological concentrations like those seen after exposure to major stressors accelerates degeneration of the hippocampus, a brain region crucial for memory (Squire, 1987). Moreover, the corticosteroids were later found to be not pro- but anti-inflammatory, counter to an implication of Selye's postulate (Stein, 1986). Nevertheless, in the final form of his hypothesis, Selye (1976) again posited a general stress response, this time comprising his and Cannon's original discoveries, despite their different conditions, feelings, mediators, and effects (Henry, 1982), but he at last distinguished this composite from a set of specific stress responses whose existence he conceded.

The diversity of the specific stress responses can be judged from the finding of Liebeskind et al. (1983) that in the rat, equal amounts but different patterns of electric footshock evoke at least three different endogenous pain-suppression systems, one not mediated by opioids, another that seems to be mediated by central opioids, and a third apparently mediated by adrenal enkephalin-like opioids. The simplicity of earlier thinking about "stress" was perhaps appropriate at a time when only a few kinds of catecholamine and steroid molecules were known to mediate stress responses. Current models can and should be complex, now that the several opioids and others of the scores of recently discovered neuropeptides are also known to be involved in emotional responses to stressors, as discussed below in section 3. Bohus et al. (1987) proposed that activation (or inhibition) of behavioral, physiological, and endocrine systems represents the nonspecific component of the stress response, whereas its specific character is the result of interactions between the environment (controllability/predictability), the coping strategy (i.e., passive vs. active), the properties of the stressor, and the system (cardiovascular, metabolic, etc).

Psychobiology, Holism, and Psychosomatic Medicine

In the early years of this century, a "psychobiological" movement led by Meyer (1957) argued for discarding mind vs. body dualism. This dualistic view had dominated scientific thinking since Descartes had proposed it in 1637. Back then, dualism made the body as a ghost-free machine of mere meat a permissible object of empirical investigation at a time when the Inquisition was dangerous to scientists, as shown by the contemporaneous trial of Galileo. In modern times, it reinforced the biomedical avoidance of studying emotions as factors in health and disease.

The view of mind and body as complementary aspects of a single underlying entity was called "holism" by Smuts (1926). It soon became a tenet of a new movement of research and treatment that came to be known as "psychosomatic medicine". This term was discussed in the first issue of *Psychosomatic Medicine* by a founder of the field, the psychoanalyst Franz Alexander (1939), who expressed a concern that the term "may imply a dichotomy between psyche and body....If however we understand psychic phenomena as nothing but the subjective aspect of certain bodily (brain) processes this dichotomy disappears".

Lipowski (1986) has called psychosomatic medicine a movement of explicit opposition to biomedical reductionism. This reductionism was incomplete, as mentioned above; despite the high general interest of biomedicine in cellular and molecular phenomena, it had little interest in the specific subset of those phenomena that comprised the somatic correlates of conscious and unconscious feelings. The new psychosomatic movement did not try to remedy this omission. Alexander and his school felt that they had other things to do than to delineate the physiology of emotions (Weiner, 1985a) and they accepted Cannon's emphasis on autonomic arousal.

For 25 years, psychosomatic medicine was dominated intellectually by Freudian psychoanalytic ideas. These included the ages-old doctrines of emotional psychogenesis and emotion-disease specificity, but also the new idea that the pathogenic emotions arose from conflicts between a patient's forbidden wishes and the patient's conscience and realism. The more radically Freudian therapists thought that every physical illness was a case of hysterical conversion of unconscious conflict into symbolic physical symptoms. However, the prevailing psychosomatic concept was that of the more moderate Alexander (1950), who distinguished such hysterical disorders - nowadays called conversion reactions and somatization disorders (Shapiro and Rosenfeld, 1987; Lipowski, 1987) - from the majority of disorders. The latter he considered to be "organ neuroses" that were not symbolic, though indeed initiated by chronic emotions arising from tensions involving psychological defense mechanisms.

Alexander and his school concentrated on bronchial asthma and six other disorders they associated with autonomic arousal - essential hypertension, hyperthyroidism, rheumatoid arthritis, neurodermatitis, peptic duodenal ulcer, and ulcerative colitis. These came to be called the "big seven psychosomatic disorders". In his version of the specificity doctrine, Alexander (1950) linked each of the "big seven" to a specific emotional constellation that he thought tended to afflict specific internal organs. For example, "inhibited rage seems to have a specific relationship to the cardiovascular system," "dependent help-seeking behavior seems to have a specific relationship to functions of nutrition," and "a conflict of sexual wishes and dependent tendencies seems to have a specific influence upon respiratory function" (Alexander, 1950). Alexander recognized the involvement of other than emotional factors in the causation of diseases but insisted on the primacy of the predisposing emotion.

Alexander's formulation of psychosomatic medicine prevailed through the 1950's, despite calls by Wolff (1953) for study of conscious emotions and by Engel (1954) for study of such socially evoked emotions as grief and of such diseases as cancer, all largely ignored by the psychoanalytic school. That school finally lost influence as the result of many severe criticisms (Wallerstein, 1983), including those of therapeutic overoptimism and methodological weakness (Grinker, 1973). It was said that Alexander's form of the specificity doctrine could not be validated (Wallerstein, 1983; Lipowski, 1986), although Weiner (1985a) has cited five confirmations of Alexander's formulations in prospective and blind studies. The disjunction between psychosomatic and other disorders was seen as false; all disorders were now thought to involve emotional factors, but along with other factors (Engel, 1967). Despite Alexander's concession that other factors, then undetermined, were involved with the predisposing emotion in causing disease, his linear view of psychogenic causality was judged inadequate.

About 1960, a transition occurred in the main stream of psychosomatic medical science from a psychoanalytical to a psychosocial view of emotion and from a psychogenic to a multifactorial view of etiology.

Studies of Stressful Life Changes

As the emphasis shifted from inner conflicts to environmental stressors as the source of pathogenic emotions, a wide variety of situations that can be called "stressful" were associated with subsequent diseases (summarized by Meyer and Haggerty, 1962; Rahe, 1972; Cassel, 1973; Dohrenwend and Dohrenwend, 1974; Levi and Andersson, 1975; Wolf and Goodell, 1976; Jenkins, 1977; Klerman and Izen, 1977; Levine and Ursin, 1980; Miller, 1980, and Hamburg et al., 1982).

Some of the disorders reported to follow "stress" are not obviously immune-related - for example, cardiac fibrillation, diabetes, gastrointestinal disorders, headaches, hypertension, insomnia, myocardial infarction, and stroke. Others are related to immune function. Mononucleosis (Kasl et al., 1979), colds, influenza, pneumonia, and tuberculosis are infections (Plaut and Friedman, 1981, 1985) and, with cancer, reflect immune hypoactivity, while arthritis (Baker and Brewerton, 1981; Solomon, 1981a), multiple sclerosis, and other autoimmune diseases, along with allergies, reflect immune hyperactivity (Barnes, 1986).

The relative power of various stressful life events to predispose to disease was calibrated by Holmes and Rahe (1967) in their Social Readjustment Rating Scale and their Schedule of Recent Experience (Rahe, 1975). For example, they found that the single life change most likely to be followed by the onset of disease was the death of a spouse. They also found that experiencing several weak stressors closely in time could have a cumulative effect equal to that of one powerful stressor. A recent review by Connolly (1985) of their and related research discusses criticisms of it, especially doubts expressed by Brown and Harris (1978) about retrospective judgements of life events and the assumed linear additivity of stressfulness scores.

Hinkle (1974) found two distinct populations: people who become ill frequently, and others who remain relatively healthy despite experiencing stressful life events. In 10% of the latter group, there is no relationship between life changes and illness.

Nevertheless, there are those people whose health does reflect their emotions. In some, strong emotions can actually kill, as for example by triggering cardiac death

(Engel, 1971; Reich, 1981). When induced by suggestion in non-Western cultures, this phenomenon has been called "voodoo" death (Cannon, 1942). Its equivalent in contemporary Western culture may be induced by the thoughtless physician's authoritative categorization of a disease as terminal and the explicit prediction of how much time a patient has to live (Cousins, 1984). The converse of voodoo death - the apparent curative power of suggestions made by physicians even when the patients are consciously skeptical - was recently discussed in a report with the title "Which doctor is not a witch doctor?" (Saver and Denlinger, 1985). In a similar vein, one might ask "Which companion is not a healer?" because of the reported salutary effects, discussed below, of social support (Berkman and Syme, 1979; Coe et al., 1987; Glaser, Kiecolt-Glaser, Speicher, and Halliday, 1985; Kiecolt-Glaser, Glaser, Williger et al., 1985; Monroe et al., 1986). One might ask also "Which personality is not a self-healer?" because of the reported salutary effects, discussed below, of certain feelings, attitudes, life styles, and coping techniques (Simonton et al., 1978; Cousins, 1976, 1979; Kobasa et al., 1985; Siegel, 1986).

Popular interest in such questions has helped to animate a multifaceted movement called "holistic medicine" (Hastings, 1980) and sustains the monitoring by the quarterly *Advances* (1983-current) of mind-brain-body- health research conducted in Western and in non-Western countries (Temoshok and Fox, 1986).

The Multifactorial Approach and Behavioral Medicine

In reaction against the emphasis of early psychosomatic medicine on emotions as the prime cause of disease, another countervailing trend began, this one toward the use of a multifactorial etiological model, later called "biopsychosocial" by Engel (1977). This model of disease causation assumed that social, psychological, and physiological factors interact in pathogenesis. The life-change and biopsychosocial revisions of psychosomatic medicine did not satisfy investigators of a behavioristic cast of mind. In 1977, they launched a new movement called "behavioral medicine" at a convention at Yale University (Weiss, 1983). As its name indicates, the new field emphasizes the effects of lifestyle on health, although some of its members are interested in emotions as precursors of disease. The two approaches " do not always work in concert" (Dreher, 1986).

Within the doubly revised paradigm of psychosomatic medicine, Weiner (1977) advocated studying the etiology of disease in terms of the interplay between a patient's emotions considered as neural phenomena and the patient's genetic endowment. Today, Alexander's organ neurosis of bronchial asthma appears to be a biopsychosocial disorder in those individuals who have both an allergic disorder and a genetic predisposition to respond with bronchospasm to intense emotional stimuli or conflict (Locke and Gorman, 1987). However, the predisposition may not be genetic but learned (Stein, 1986).

Meanwhile, as psychosomatic medicine enlarged its view of causal factors, so also did biomedicine, which came at last to recognize that seed and soil interact in pathogenesis, so that even tuberculosis, the classic infectious disease of the last century, is now thought in biomedicine to be determined not only by the tubercle bacillus but also by genetic factors that modulate immunity (Diamond, 1987). Remaining at issue between the biopsychosocial approach and the biomedical approach is whether in addition, to quote Alexander (1950), "specific and nonspecific immunity, the resistance of the organism to infection, is a complex phenomenon which may depend on emotional factors".

2. The Immune System in Disease Resistance

Since Alexander's day, the role of the immune system in health has been shown to go beyond resistance to infection.

Importance of Optimal Responsiveness

Four types of disorders can occur if immune responsiveness is not kept within an optimal range, as shown in Table 1.

Immune responses that are too weak to nonself entities from outside the body permit infections; responses too weak to nonself entities from within the body permit cancers; responses too strong to harmless nonself entities from outside the body permit allergies and anaphylactic shock, and responses too strong to harmless nonself entities from within - i.e., self entities misperceived as nonself - permit autoimmune disorders, which destroy tissue and organs (Talal and Hadden, 1985). All of these disorders of defective immune regulation can be fatal.

Thus the proper regulation of immune responsiveness is crucial for physical health. The question arises: how is immune responsiveness normally regulated? The answer is, by a complex intrinsic system, partly determined by antigens and partly not, which involves interactions between several kinds of white blood cells. Even a greatly oversimplifed explanation requires describing the major kinds of immunity and their effector and regulatory cells (for more details of mentioned aspects, and for aspects not mentioned, see Stites et al., 1987, or an equivalent up-to-date textbook).

Table 1. Disorders Caused by Improperly Regulated Immune Responses

These disorders occur if immune responses to nonself antigens are...

	too weak...	or too strong...
to those from outside...	Infections	Allergies
or from inside the body...	Cancers	Autoimmune disorders

Immune Effector Cells

The effectors of immune responses are white blood cells of two main types - lymphocytes and phagocytes. These cells can detect and destroy alien and thus potentially harmful substances, called "nonself" antigens, both when the nonself antigens are free-floating and when they are borne by cells. In the latter case, the antigen-bearing cells can also be destroyed, whether such cells are alien microbes or the organisms's own "self" cells that have become infected, cancerous, or otherwise deleteriously altered.

The immune system has two main branches. Its nonspecific branch attacks all nonself entities in general, recognizing them because they become tagged with constituents of blood called opsonins. The effector cells of nonspecific immunity are a subclass of the lymphocytes called natural killer (NK) cells and two types of phagocytes, the mononuclear monocytes that when activated become macrophages, and the polymorphonuclear leukocytes also called neutrophils. All of these cells go into the tissues (Stossel, 1987), where NK cells kill virus-infected and tumor cells (Herberman and Ortaldo, 1981).

In the immune system's specific branch, which attacks nonself elements on an individual basis, the effector cells are B and T lymphocytes, which circulate in the blood and lymph. Specific immunity has two main arms, called humoral and cell-mediated.

In humoral immunity, a B-cell, when stimulated by a free-floating antigen whose shape happens to fit the receptor type on the B-cell, becomes receptive to differentiative and growth factors (monokines and interleukins) secreted by macrophages and inducer/helper T cells. These induce it first to turn into a plasma cell and then to clone into a multitude of plasma cells that secrete free-floating replicas of its receptor, called antibody molecules. These antigen-specific antibodies then bind to all the instances they find of their complementary antigen, marking those replicas for destruction by phagocytes.

In cell-mediated immunity, a killer (cytotoxic) T-cell, when stimulated through having its specific receptor bind to an antigen presented by a macrophage, becomes responsive to interleukins that clone it into a multitude of identical T-killers that attack all self-cells they find displaying replicas of the triggering antigen.

The literally vital importance of the normal functioning of this intrinsic immune regulation has been made clear by the current plague of acquired immune deficiency disease (AIDS). The AIDS viruses invade several immune cell types, including not only B-cells and macrophages (Marx, 1987b) but also and most devastatingly the regulatory helper/inducer T-cells that normally enhance immune responsiveness by secreting interleukins. In the AIDS-caused lack of sufficient helper T-cell function, the normally opposing regulatory effect of suppressor T cells prevails, and proper immune responses can not be mounted against the AIDS virus and other microbes.

In both a humoral and a cellular immune response, some lymphocytes in the clone linger as long-lived immunological memory cells, giving the body an effective head-start ("immunity") toward attacking any future incursion by replicas of the particular antigen that evoked the clone.

At any given time, there is an enormous diversity of the shapes of the antigen receptors on an individual's B-cells and T-cells; even a mouse weighing only an ounce has the capacity to make 100 million different antibody shapes (Jerne, 1984). Therefore it is likely that a given antigen will be matched closely enough to trigger an immune response by the receptor type on at least one B-cell or T-cell. To further increase this probability, the set of lymphocyte receptors is continuously changing its range of antigen-binding shapes as new, differently shaped receptors are synthesized through a process of somatic mutation involving genes that immunologists call the "generator of diversity" or GOD (Cohn, 1985). Of course the immune system, being biological, is imperfect, and other factors not altogether understood can also induce tolerance to an antigen (Cohn, 1985). The immune system is not preprogrammed to distinguish between self and non-self, but learns to do so as a result of exposure to self-molecules during early development.

Thus an individual's immune system evolves during the lifespan through the development of new sensors, somewhat as the mind evolves during an individual's lifespan through the development of new concepts (Minsky, 1986). Cohn (1968) pointed out how both the nervous and the immune systems are concerned with adaptive responses to "unexpected" (i.e., unpredictable) environmental stimuli. This functional similarity between the two systems is not evidence for a functional link between them but is certainly consistent with the possibility of such a link.

3. Neural and Molecular Aspects of Emotional Responses

If emotions fine-tune (Melnechuk, 1985d) or override the intrinsic regulation of immune responses, the modulation is presumably mediated by the nervous system. Emotions are evolved, species-specific patterns of behavior (Plutchik, 1980), and behavior comprises all neurally mediated responses whether of the whole organism or of its parts (Engel, 1986). Therefore emotions include not only affective feelings and facial expressions and other overt expressive and communicative behaviors but also covert physiological changes. In order to discuss whether these covert aspects of emotions include changes in the state of the immune system, it is useful to clarify the main points of current thinking about the neuroanatomical and biochemical correlates of emotion. Previously held ideas about these correlates have been revised and augmented by recent progress in neuroscience and psychoneuroendocrinology.

Focus on the Hypothalamus

The main neuroanatomic basis of emotion was previously thought to be a variously defined set of brain structures called the limbic system. That system now seems best thought of as essentially a two-way gate between two main brain regions involved in emotion, the frontal cortex and the hypothalamus (Swanson, 1987). Linking the frontal cortex, with its cognitive, imaginative, and intentional information (Nauta,1971) and the hypothalamus, with its body-state information (Moore, 1987), is the amygdala (Nauta, 1973; Price, 1987), a core region of the limbic system by all definitions (Nauta, 1973; Smith, 1987). Because the amygdala also receives information from each of the senses, it may be a site where both real and hallucinatory sensory information can influence the emotion-computing transactions of the other two regions. Contributions of other cortical and limbic regions and of transcerebral modulatory circuits to human emotions have been discussed by Mandell (1980), Mueller (1983), Benson (1984), and Smith (1987).

The hypothalamus is doubly central to emotion. First, it is central to the subjective experience of such basic emotions as those called (in a review of their neural command systems by Panksepp, 1986a) anger-rage, anxiety-fear, grief-panic, and curiosity-desire, the fulfillment of which Panksepp thinks may be joy. Second, the hypothalamus is also central to the different integrated behaviors and body states associated with these emotions (Panksepp, 1981, 1986a,b; Smith and DeVito, 1984). As the hypothalamus evokes the effort, distress, and other adaptive responses to physical and psychological stressors, it directly signals a two-branched, coordinated effector system (Swanson et al., 1986). The two branches of the effector system regulated by the hypothalamus are the endocrine system, as established by the groups of Guillemin (Burgus et al., 1970) and Schally (Nair et al., 1970), and the autonomic nervous system, as established by Saper et al. (1976).

For example, in the case of the distress response, the hypothalamus sends a chemical factor called "corticotropin releasing factor" (CRF), discovered by Vale et al. (1981), to the master gland of the endocrine system, the pituitary. There, CRF is one of several neurotransmitters and hormones that can cause the dispatch of ACTH (corticotropin) to the adrenal cortex, to evoke in turn the release of the corticosteroids (Axelrod and Reisine, 1984).

Of the many distinct nuclei comprised by the hypothalamus, one, the paraventricular nucleus, is essential in stress responses (Swanson et al., 1986; Palkovitz, 1987), for it is the one from which signal molecules go both to the pituitary gland and to autonomic nervous system. Each of its neurons can release not only CRF but also at least six other neuropeptide signal molecules, and each neuron seems to have its own ratio of these neuropeptides. Also, different paraventricular neuron types appear to affect different autonomic neurons (Swanson et al., 1986).

Here then is at least some of the neural machinery needed for sending any of a variety of specific signals via the two parallel regulators of the body's state.

The only other requirement is a mechanism for differentially prescribing the signals. Such a selective mechanism exists in the set of inputs that bring different kinds of relevant information to the paraventricular nucleus from various parts of the body and brain, including other hypothalamic nuclei, as each person fantasizes or interprets each successive experience with his or her individual temperament. The incoming information is represented in the form of catecholamine (Mezey et al., 1984), cholinergic (Gilad, 1987), steroid (McEwen, 1980), and neuropeptide signal molecules (Lightman and Young, 1987). Their individual effects on the neurons of

the paraventricular nucleus interact to specify its appropriate neuropeptide outputs
to the glandular and nervous regulators of homeostasis (Guidotti and Grandison,
1979; Swanson et al., 1986; Palkovits, 1987).

Lateralization of Emotion

The human cerebral hemispheres develop at different rates and ages (Thatcher
et al., 1987). Much evidence indicates that some brain functions are lateraliz
more so in males and righthanders, less so in females and lefthanders, and v
individual differences (reviewed by Milner, 1973; Corballis, 1983; Benson and Zai
1985; Geschwind and Galaburda, 1985, 1987; Glass, 1987; Kimura, 1987; Ottos
1987; Whitaker, 1987; Witelson, 1987). For example, the left cerebral hemispher
strongly dominant for language, whereas the right hemisphere is dominant
music, though less strongly so (Melnechuk and Zatorre, 1985). Most relevant
this review, there appears also to be a complex lateralization of emotional rej
sentation and regulation in the brain.

According to evidence from many methodologically diverse studies, reviev
by Silberman and Weingartner (1986), there are two aspects to the lateralizatior
emotion. First, an idea prevalent not long ago, that the right cerebral hemisph
is emotional but that the left hemisphere is not, seems now to be only partly tr
in the sense that the forebrain of the left hemisphere can inhibit emotionality a
sexual drive, which, with orgasm, are lateralized to the right hemisphere (Fl
Henry, 1983). This asymmetry in degree of emotionality is consistent with
asymmetry of the cerebral cholinergic neurotransmitter system, associated w
memory and cognitive functions, which has higher concentrations of a mar
enzyme in the left hemisphere (Amaducci et al., 1983).

One dimension of personality seems also to be related to this hemisphe
difference in degree of emotionality: greater activation of the left hemisphere
associated with an obsessive, compulsive personality, greater activation of the ri
with a hysterical personality (Mandell, 1980a; Flor-Henry,1983). However, introv
sion, now often called "neuroticism" by psychologists of personality (Tellegen, ci
by Holden, 1987), is associated with right hemisphere activation, and extrovers
with left hemisphere activation, because of a second kind of hemispheric later
zation of emotion (Flor-Henry, 1983).

The second aspect of emotional lateralization is that positive emotions, defir
as those associated with approach behavior, and thus including anger along w
elation, now seem to be processed in the left cerebral hemisphere, whereas
pleasant negative emotions associated with withdrawal behavior, such as sadn
fear, and guilt, seem to be processed in the right cerebral hemisphere (Gainc
1972; Campbell, 1982; Sackheim et al., 1982; Davidson, 1983; Robinson et al., 1ᵌ
Silberman and Weingartner, 1986).

Whether this emotional asymmetry is cortical, as generally believed (Silbern
and Weingartner, 1986), or subcortical, as claimed by Tucker (1981), is unresoli
(Panksepp, 1985). However, it is consistent with some asymmetries in the he:

spheric concentrations of several neurotransmitters associated with negative emotions. Thus the right thalamus has higher concentrations than does the left hemisphere of norepinephrine (Oke et al., 1978), which is associated with agitated anxiety, although the right hemisphere has higher concentrations of serotonin (Serafetinidea, 1965; Mandell and Knapp, 1979), which is associated with mania. Glick et al. (1979) found a sex-dependent asymmetry in rat caudate nucleus of dopamine, which is associated with activity, pleasure, and reinforcement. Also, Gerendai (1984) reported that in the rat, and presumably also in the human, there is a morphological and functional asymmetry of nerve pathways to and from the hypothalamus and in its control of endocrine hormone secretions.

Normally, reciprocal inhibition seems to prevent either hemisphere's emotional tone from predominating too much (Flor-Henry, 1983). However, there is evidence that, in quiet circumstances, the hemispheres take 90-minute turns at dominating with each one's characteristic attentional style (Kripke and Sonnenschein, 1978) and cognitive style (Klein and Armitage, 1979). This alternation is apparently regulated by the hypothalamus, perhaps by the control of differential blood flow to the hemispheres, as the alternation is in synchrony with alternations of lateral dominance in the body periphery between the sympathetic and parasympathetic branches of the autonomic nervous system. These shifts are manifested in right-left differences in nasal vasodilation (Werntz et al., 1983) and catecholamine blood levels (Kennedy et al., 1986). The induction of lateralized sympathetic input to the heart by the central nervous system during strong emotional arousal has been suggested as a possible neurophysiological trigger of sudden cardiac death (Lane and Schwartz, 1987).

These findings are consistent with the earlier emphasis of Hess (1957) and, millenia earlier, of Kundalini Yogic medicine (Shannahoff-Khalsa, 1987) on the centrality to health and even to life of the reciprocal relationship between the divisions of the autonomic nervous system - the joy-related and rage-related, activity-mediating sympathetic, and the withdrawal-related, rest- mediating parasympathetic, the role of which in stress and the emotions was described by Vingerhoets (1985). Gellhorn (1967) independently discovered evidence that both internal and environmental perturbations of homeostasis evoke reciprocal systems that activate and inactivate the organism. He thought that sympathetic-parasympathetic reciprocity broke down in altered states of consciousness and mental disorders. However, evidence is increasing that the sympathetic and parasympathetic systems function not only reciprocally but also nonreciprocally, with the latter function organized at the levels both of the hypothalamus (Kollai and Koizumi, 1981) and of the brainstem (Langhorst et al., 1981).

Specificity of Physiological Correlates of Feelings

There has been a dogma in cognitive psychology, based essentially on the data from one experiment (Schachter and Singer, 1962) interpreted in a way that has been criticized (Plutchik and Ax, 1967; Stricker, 1967). This dogma asserts that emotions differ cognitively but not in their peripheral physiological representations and effects, which are all merely instances of general arousal (Mandler, 1983). This dogma seems to be as inaccurate as, and related to, Cannon's failure to distinguish the physiological correlates of anger from those of fear and Selye's original insistence on the existence of only a general stress response.

It seems true that mere changes in the degree of stimulation can evoke physiological changes (Frankenhaeuser, 1975, 1982). However, Hallam (1985) and Liebowitz (elsewhere in this volume) have given evidence for differences between the central biochemical representations of subtly different forms of similar negative emotions, and the different emotions have different cross-cultural muscular expressions in the face (Ekman et al., 1972) and fingers (Clynes, 1977). Likewise, Ax (1953), Lacey (1967), Mason (1974, 1975), and Ellendorf and Parvizi (1980) found that neural and hormonal correlates of different emotions have patterns specific to each emotion. Also, with regard to the autonomic nervous system, Ekman (1983) found specific differences among autonomically mediated body changes brought about by expressing happiness, surprise, fear, anger, disgust, and sadness. This is consistent with the discovery that the autonomic nervous system releases not only a few catecholamine neurotransmitters but also many neuropeptides. For example, sympathetic neurons in the superior cervical ganglion of the rat synthesize both norepinephrine and the neuropeptides substance P and somatostatin (Bohn et al., 1984).

Neuropeptides are found both in the brain and in the peripheral nervous systems (Martin et al., 1987). Since Hokfelt et al. (1984; Hokfelt, 1987) began showing that every autonomic neuron examined contained not only a classical neurotransmitter such as a catecholamine or acetylcholine but also a neuropeptide, neuropeptides have been thought perhaps to modulate the postsynaptic effects of the classical neurotransmitters coreleased with them (Cooper et al., 1986) or even to mediate parallel and independent regulation of smooth muscle (Bitar and Makhlouf, 1982).

About 50 neuropeptides are now known and more are expected to be discovered (Gainer, 1987). Their numerosity, their distribution pattern (and that of their receptors) both centrally and peripherally in such emotionally sensitive organs as the lungs, stomach, and intestines, and the ability of most if not all of them to alter mood and behavior have led Pert et al. (1984) to propose them as the major molecular mediators of the emotions. For example, the endogenous opioid peptides have been implicated in euphoria (Goldstein, 1976) and dysphoria (Pfeiffer et al., 1986), the sensation of musical and other thrills (Goldstein, 1980), and the modulation of incoming pain messages, which, with other sensory inputs, are conveyed or enhanced by another neuropeptide, substance P (Jessel and Womack, 1985). With regard to health, opioid peptides are also involved in cardiovascular control (Holaday, 1983) and can modulate the responsiveness of immune effector cells to substances (mitogens) that induce cell division analogously to antigens and interleukins (Heijnen and Ballieux, 1986).

The selectivity of release of different neuropeptides is complemented by a target-cell receptive specificity (Goetzl et al., 1985). Altogether, the molecular means seem to be in place for the variety of different emotions to include specific effects on the various tissues and homeostatic mechanisms of the body, including the immune system.

4. Psychoneural Modulation of Immune Responsiveness

Growth of the Field

For more than half a century, first in Europe (Ader, 1981a; Spector and Korneva, 1981), then increasingly in North America (Garfield, 1986), evidence has been accumulating at an accelerating pace for the reality both of psychological influences on immune responses and of neural and neuroendocrine mechanisms appropriate for the mediation of such influences.

The first volume to give an overview of the emerging field was originally published in Russian in 1978; its English translation appeared seven years later (Korneva, 1985). Meanwhile, the first overview in English had appeared (Ader, 1981b). Its coverage has been successively updated and augmented by the proceedings of a series of wide-ranging conferences (Goetzl, 1985; Guillemin et al., 1985; Spector, 1985; Jankovic et al., 1987). Presentations at some of these and other relevant conferences were summarized (Berkman et al., 1983; Melnechuk, 1983; Lloyd, 1984; Melnechuk, 1984d; Melnechuk, 1985b; Williams, 1987), as were psychoneuroimmunological sessions at annual meetings of the Society for Neuroscience (Melnechuk, 1984a; Melnechuk, 1985a; Melnechuk, 1986). Also published were a bibliography of 1453 publications that came out between 1976 and 1982, annotated with their abstracts if any (Locke and Hornig-Rohan, 1983), an anthology of classic papers in the field (Locke et al., 1985), and a special issue of a journal devoted to the subject (Raine, 1985).

Recently there have been at least three reviews (Baker, 1987; Dorian and Garfinkel, 1987; Solomon, 1987), an overview volume (Lloyd, 1987) and three articles in one encyclopedia (Hall and Goldstein, 1987; Solomon, 1987; Spector, 1987). The volume of psychoneuroimmunological research is now large enough that a new quarterly journal, *Brain, Behavior, and Immunity* began publication in 1987. In addition, the semimonthly *International Journal of Neuroscience* established a new section on neuroimmunomodulation in May 1987, and in the autumn of 1987 the *Journal of Neuroscience Research* published a special issue (vol. 18, no. 1) on "neuroimmunomodulation". Said to be in preparation are the proceedings of two 1987 conferences, one on "Nervous System Aspects of Nervous System-Immune System Interactions" held at St. George's Medical School on Grenada, West Indies, on June 9-11, and a NATO Advanced Research Workshop on "Neuroimmunomodulation: Interventions in Aging And Cancer," held at Stromboli, Sicily on June 7-11. A FASEB-sponsored conference on neuroimmunomodulation is scheduled for June 26-July 1, 1988 at Copper Mountain, Colorado.

Major Claims

Research on the psychoneural modulation of immunity has been conducted at and between levels that range from the psychological to the molecular. Therefore it has generated evidence for several important claims. One of these is that the physiological correlates of negative and positive feelings and attitudes do indeed include changes in immune responsiveness. Evidence for this claim will be summarized in subsequent sections of this review. However, that evidence can best be judged in the context of other major claims, which include the following (see Solomon, 1985, 1987 for additional claims):

(1) Immune responses can be suppressed and enhanced by Pavlovian conditioning. The evidence has been most recently reviewed by Ader (1985), Ader and Cohen (1985), and Ader et al. (1987). Subsequent studies have been reported by Hiramoto et al. (1987) and Neveu et al. (1987), the former reporting the one-trial conditioning of natural killer cell activity.

(2) Stimulation or lesion of several brain regions, including the cerebral cortex (Biziere et al., 1985; Nance et al., 1985, Neveu et al., 1986; Renoux et al., 1987), hypothalamus (Stein et al., 1981; Roszman et al., 1985; Katayama et al., 1987), and midbrain raphe nuclei (Eremina and Devoino, 1973), has specific effects on several immune functions. Effects of cortical lesions are lateralized, which is consistent with neurological evidence for a relationship between human hemispheric laterality and immune disorders (Behan and Geschwind, 1985; Geschwind and Galaburda, 1985, 1987). In the hypothalamus, lesioning of the paraventricular area results in immune suppression (Adams et al., 1987).

(3) Solid tissues of the immune system—including the bone marrow, where blood cells arise and B-cells differentiate; the thymus, where T-lymphocytes differentiate; the spleen, the lymph nodes, and other lymphoid tissues, where macrophages present antigens for recognition to lymphocytes—contain a marker for the diffuse neuroendocrine system (Angeletti and Hickey, 1985) and are innervated by the autonomic nervous system (Bulloch, 1985; Felten et al., 1985; Livnat et al., 1985; Blennerhassett et al., 1987). Noradrenergic nerve fibers actually contact lymphocytes in the spleen (Felten et al., 1987). The sympathetic nervous system seems to have an inhibiting effect on immune responsiveness, as sympathectomy enhances the severity of experimental autoimmune myasthenia gravis (Agius et al., 1987) and of experimental allergic encephalomyelitis (Chelmicka-Schorr et al., 1987). The mouse thymus also receives a cholinergic innervation during fetal and postnatal development (Bulloch and Bossone, 1987), suggesting neural regulation of thymus maturation as well as of mature thymic function.

(4) Immune solid tissues, regulatory cells, and effector cells display receptor molecules for binding many classical and peptide neurotransmitters and hormones, including those released during the effort and distress responses - e.g., beta-adrenergic receptors (Williams et al., 1976; Pochet et al., 1979; Miles et al., 1984) and receptors for acetylcholine (Lopker et al., 1980; Shapiro and Strom, 1980); dopamine (Ovadia et al., 1987); benzodiazepines (Zavala and Lenfant, 1987), thought to be agonists

of an endogenous modulator of GABA activity (Tallman and Gallagher, 1985); ACTH (Johnson et al., 1982); opioids (Hazum et al., 1979; Wybran, 1985); substance P (Payan et al., 1984; Wiedermann et al., 1987), neurotensin (Bar-Shavit et al., 1982); vasoactive intestinal peptide (Beed, 1983; Danek et al., 1983; Ottaway et al., 1983); calcitonin gene related peptide (Popper et al., 1987), and growth hormone (Arrenbrecht, 1974).

(5) Many classical and peptide neurotransmitters and hormones influence the numbers and responsiveness of lymphocytes and other aspects of immune responses (reviewed by Hall, 1985; subsequent studies included those by Devoina and Alperina, 1985; Haijnen and Ballieux, 1986; Plotnikoff et al., 1986; Hadden, 1987; Payan et al., 1987; Peck, 1987; Stanisz et al., 1987, and Werner et al., 1987). Of the neuropeptides, substance P stimulates T lymphocytes, whereas somatostatin is inhibitory (Goetzl, cited in Barnes, 1986).

(6) As is required for a neural regulatory system, the hypothalamus and pituitary gland receive feedback messages from the immune system (Besedovsky et al., 1985; Blalock and Smith, 1985; Hall et al., 1985; Besedovsky et al., 1986; Del Rey et al., 1987). One source of this feedback is the bone marrow (Petrov et al., 1987), factors from which also affect tissue regeneration (Pierpaoli et al., 1987). Korneva (1987) has reviewed studies of changes in hypothalamic electrophysiology following peripheral administration of antigens. Ablation of the immune system affects brain waves in the ventromedial hypothalamus and the cerebral cortex (Dafny, 1985).

II. Emotions and Immune Responsiveness

Studies of emotions and immunity can be grouped in more than one way. Because the main subject of this volume is emotions and psychopathology, studies of abnormal emotions and immunity will be discussed first, in section 5. I have found no studies of mania and immunity, so sections 5 will deal only with negative abnormal emotions. Negative normal emotions will be discussed in sections 6 and 7, positive normal emotions in sections 8 and 9.

5. Abnormal Emotions

If emotions affect immunity, people with major emotional abnormalities could reasonably be expected to have immune abnormalities. Such abnormalities have been reported, as summarized below. However, the results of many studies are conflicting. One problem is that of telling whether any immune abnormality found in a patient is indeed a direct effect of the psychosis or whether it is a cause of the psychosis, or a parallel consequence with psychosis of some third factor, genetic or experiential, or an indirect effect. By "indirect effect" is meant that the immune system can be influenced by a behavior caused by the psychosis, such as the use of various drugs (Tennenbaum et al., 1969; Sherman et al., 1973; Baker et al., 1977), changes in nutrition (Bistrian, 1975), changes in activity (Eskola, 1978), and deprivations of sleep (Palmblad et al., 1979).

Schizophrenia

Goldstein et al. (1980) summarized and discussed almost 20 years of reports that schizophrenia is associated with abnormal immune function. The topic has been controversial because many of the findings have not been reproducible. Interpretation has been complicated by evidence that the antipsychotic drug chlorpromazine has direct immunosuppressive effects *in vitro* and *in vivo* (Ferguson et al., 1976; Lovett et al., 1978). In their own work, Goldstein's group found a significant immunological imbalance in some schizophrenic patients, namely an abnormally high responsiveness of lympocytes to mitogens, along with the presence in blood serum of a cytotoxic factor directed against thymic lymphocytes. Solomon (1981b), in another review, concluded that trends were not clear, as some studies found immune hyperactivity, whereas others found immune hyporeactivity.

In considering such conclusions, it is important to distinguish the activity of T-helper/inducer cells from the activity of T-suppressor cells, for a selective enhancement of suppressor activity will lower helper/induction activity and thus lower overall immune responsiveness, just as selective enhancement of helper/inducer activity will raise overall immune responsiveness.

Recently, Villemain et al. (1987) reported that in affective forms of schizophrenia they found decreased production of interleukin-2, a factor released by antigen-stimulated lymphocytes that enhances the proliferation and differentiation of cytotoxic T-cells. Mueller et al. (1987) and Ganguli et al. (1987) reported finding reduced T-suppressor activity in schizophrenic patients, which the latter group interpreted as evidence of an autoimmune etiology of acute schizophrenia. Kronfol et al. (1987) found a significant reduction in natural killer cell activity in 49 schizophrenic patients, in 28% of whom the reduction was greater than 50% compared to their normal controls. However, it is not clear whether these findings reflect a fundamental immunological abnormality in schizophrenia or such other factors as hospitalization, nutrition, and infection.

Depression

There have been about a dozen recent studies of altered immune function in patients with major depressive disorder, including those by Cappel et al. (1978), Nasr et al. (1981), Gottschalk et al. (1983), Kiecolt-Glaser, Ricker et al. (1983), Kronfol, House et al. (1984), Krueger et al. (1984), Schleifer et al. (1984), Mann et al. (1985), Schleifer et al. (1985), Darko et al. (1986), and Kronfol et al (1986). Some of these studies have been reviewed by Schindler (1985) and Locke and Gorman (1987).

Most of these studies found lower lymphocyte responsiveness to mitogens in unmedicated depressed patients, with the degree of immune suppression apparently proportional to the degree of emotional depression. Krueger et al. (1984) found a lower than normal number of helper/inducer T-lymphocytes in depressed patients, with no change in the suppressor/cytotoxic T-cells (at least some T-cells are both suppressors and killers).

In other studies a decrease in sensitivity of lymphocyte receptors for norepineph-rine was reported, correlated however more closely with severity of psychomotor agitation than with that of depression (Mann et al., 1985). Gottschalk et al. (1983) reported that the three most depressed or hostile of seven depressed patients had a significant inhibition of a normal response of neutrophils that was not mediated by cortisol. However, Irwin, Daniels et al. (1987) found that in 19 hospitalized depressed men the absolute number of neutrophils was greater, while NK cytotoxicity was significantly lower, than in matched controls.

Clinically, affective patients and their relatives were found to have a significantly higher incidence of allergies and asthma than did schizophrenic patients and their relatives (Nasr et al., 1981). Nemeroff et al. (1985) found antithyroid antibodies in depressed patients.

Multiple Personality

A third kind of psychopathology has also provided some relevant evidence. Cases have been reported (Braun, 1983; Braun, 1986) of people with multiple person-alities who have specific allergies when one personality is in control but who lack those allergies when another personality is in control. The transition from one kind of personality to another, and thus from one state of allergic sensitivity to the other, can be almost instantaneous (Ischlondsky, 1955).

At least 90% of patients with multiple personality disorder were abused as children (Kluft, 1985). Shanahoff-Khalsa (1987) has suggested that in order to endure their psychic pain, such children accommodate in their right hemispheres the personality that fantasizes the self in a way necessary to survive. The switch between allergic and nonallergic personalities would then be a switch between temporary hemispheric dominances of the sort mentioned above in section 3. In this connection recall the findings of hemispheric differences in effects of cortical lesions on immune responses, mentioned above in section 4.

6. Negative Emotions

As shown by discussions elsewhere in this volume, research on normal emotions relevant to health is animated by a number of perplexing issues - for example, the number of emotions. This issue (with others) has been discussed by Plutchik (1980), Heller (1983), Knapp (1983), and Panksepp (1986).

Emotional States and Traits

Especially relevant to the subject of this review is the issue of whether the most rewarding emotions to study in relation to health are short-term or long-term—that is, ephemeral feelings and somewhat longer moods or much longer-lasting attitudes amounting to personality traits.

To some investigators, emotions are subjective experiences and physiological events that are essentially brief. Thus Clynes (1977) reported that the feelings of anger, hate, grief, love, sex, joy, and reverence have characteristic forms of expression with specific durations that average about six seconds, although each feeling can last longer than its brief expression. Similarly, Ekman (1983) distinguished different autonomic correlates of relived feelings of surprise, disgust, sadness, anger, fear, and happiness that were only 30 seconds long.

The problematical relationships between these brief forms of feeling and longer attitudinal forms can make analysis of an emotion's correlates difficult, as for example when a confirmed optimist feels temporary discouragement. For another example, discussed by Clynes elsewhere in this volume, Clynes (1973, 1977) reported that in some people a good mood that lasts for hours can be induced by repeated brief expressions of each of the seven feelings listed in the paragraph above, clustered in the stated sequence from negative to positive affective tone, and preceded by the repeated expression of no emotion - a half-hour-long series that he called a "sentic cycle". Clynes (1981) has since found that a series of brief expressions of only positive emotions can also induce a much longer-lasting good mood, albeit of different quality.

Solomon (1985), in reviewing evidence for psychoneural modulation of immunity, distinguished studies of emotional "states" of feeling and mood from studies of emotional "traits" of coping style and enduring personality. Following Solomon's example, this review will consider the physiological and clinical correlates of both forms of emotion, because there are findings with regard to both.

Grief

Studies investigating whether normal emotions have effects on immunity began with grief, an emotion that resembles depression but is distinguished from it by several criteria discussed in a review by Van Dyke and Kaufman (1983).

A correlation of grief with subsequent illness has long been noted anecdotally. A century ago, an editorial in the *British Medical Journal* (Anonymous, 1884; cited in Baker, 1987) said that at funerals, "the depression of spirits under which the chief mourners labour at these melancholy occasions peculiarly predisposes them to some of the worst effects of chill".

Such observations were largely ignored and the psychobiology of correlated grief and illness was not much studied until a few decades ago. Cross-cultural studies confirmed the finding (Holmes and Rahe, 1967; Rahe, 1975) that the life change most likely to be followed by the onset of disease was the death of a spouse. This was consistent with much other evidence (reviewed by Jacobs and Ostfeld, 1977) that conjugal bereavement is associated with increased medical morbidity and excess mortality. As Shuchter (1986) wrote in his study of adjustment to spousal death, "dying of a broken heart" can occur, and almost literally in those cases where strong grief precipitates life-threatening ventricular arhythmias (Reich et al., 1981).

For example, Parkes et al. (1972) reported data from a nine-year follow-up of 4,486 widowers 55 years old or older. Their excess mortality peaked at 40% during their first six months of bereavement, then declined to normal five years later. Though the deaths had various causes, almost half were certificated to be the result of heart disease. A more recent study (Helsing et al., 1981) found none of these details, only the excess mortality. Lundin (1984) concluded from a controlled study of 32 people who had suddenly and unexpectedly lost a close relative that such survivors are a high-risk group at least for increased psychiatric morbidity. A similar adverse effect of bereavement on mental health was found by Parkes (1984) and an adverse effect on health in general by Osteweis et al. (1984). In a multivariate analysis of 1,447 post-bereavement interviews, Mor et al. (1986) found that having been married to the deceased and previous health problems were the two strongest predictors of morbidity and medical care use.

Although 2/3 of widows suffer a decline in health within a year of bereavement (Weiner, 1985a), most studies have generally found a greater decline in the health of widowers, a sex effect reviewed by Stroebe and Stroebe (1983). Widowers have an excess mortality of about 40% over age-matched husbands (Young et al., 1963; Parkes et al., 1972), but widows die at about the same rate as age-matched wives (Rees et al., 1967; Helsing et al., 1981). Suggested explanations for this sex effect (Kahn et al., 1987) include a greater reliance of men than of women on spouses for emotional support (Stoddard and Henry, 1985).

In view of the excess mortality of widowers over husbands, several groups have examined immune parameters in widowers. Bartrop et al. (1977) studied the stimulation of lymphocytes by mitogens in 26 widowers. They found lower lymphocyte responsiveness than in controls matched for race, sex, and age, but found no differences in T-cell and B-cell numbers or plasma levels of various hormones, including cortisol, known to modulate immune responsiveness. Medically, they found no differences in autoantibody counts, which would have indicated a B-cell mediated immune disorder, and no difference in delayed hypersensitivity, which is a T-cell mediated immune response.

In a prospective but otherwise similar study of 15 husbands before and after the death of their wives from advanced breast carcinoma, Schleifer et al. (1983) also found a significant suppression of lymphocyte responses to mitogens for the first two months after bereavement and intermediate levels of mitogen responsivity during the four-to-14-month period after bereavement. However, they found no change in the number of lymphocytes circulating in peripheral blood and in the percentage and absolute numbers of T-cells and B-cells. For technical reasons, effects on the health of the widowers were not measured.

Stein (1985) pointed out that the links between bereavement and changes in lymphocyte responsiveness remained to be determined. However, the 15 subjects in his group's study (Schleifer et al., 1983) reported no major or persistent changes in diet or activity or in the use of medicines, alcohol, tobacco, or other drugs, and no significant changes in weight were noted. In the absence of evidence that subtle changes in those parameters were related to the effect of bereavement on lymphocyte responsiveness, Stein supposed that the effect could result from centrally mediated immunosuppression by any of several possible pathways still to be determined.

Stein (1986) has since noted that a small subset of the subjects whose lowered mitogen responses occurred not in the first two months but in the latter half of the postbereavement year were younger than the majority of the sample. Individuals also differed in the profiles of their responses to the three different mitogens used to test lymphocyte responsiveness. Stein concluded that further systematic investigation is required to consider age, biological predisposition, personality, and changes in life-style and behavior related to bereavement, as well as consideration of the stability of the measures used.

In a controlled study of 37 women with husbands who were dying or had just died of inoperable lung cancer, Irwin, Daniels et al. (1987) found significantly lower activity of NK cells and lower numbers of suppressor/cytotoxic T-cells in the soon-to-be-widowed and widows, proportional both to the severity of their anticipatory and post-bereavement grief as measured by the Hamilton Rating Scale for Depression and also to their positive scores on the Social Readjustment Rating Scale. However, the low values were within the normal range and did not necessarily have clinical significance.

In discussing the possible mechanisms of the immune cell inhibition by grief, the authors mentioned a number of neurotransmitters and neurohormones known to suppress NK cell activity, including central CRF (Irwin, Vale et al., 1987) and two hormones commonly found with high levels in the plasma of distressed people (Rose, 1980), cortisol (Parrillo and Fauci, 1978) and norepinephrine (Hellstrand et al., 1985).

Marital Distress and Loneliness

As marital happiness contributes more to overall happiness than does job satisfaction, friendships, or other sources (Glenn and Weaver, 1981), marital disruption is among the life events that are the most stressful (Bloom and Asher, 1978). Separated and divorced individuals are at greater risk than married, widowed, or single adults both for mental (Bachrach, 1975) and for physical illness (Somers, 1979), with higher rates of mortality from infectious diseases, including six times as many deaths from pneumonia (Lynch, 1977) and a significantly higher incidence of cancer (Ernster et al., 1979).

To investigate whether the immune system might be a mediator of these epidemiological findings, Kiecolt-Glaser, Fisher et al. (1987) collected self-report data and blood samples from 3 married and 38 separated or divorced women. In married subjects they found that the poorer the marital quality, the greater the depression and the poorer the immune responsiveness on three qualitative measures. In women separated one year or less, they found significantly poorer qualitative and quantitative immune function than in married counterparts; in them, as in the divorced women, the shorter the separation and the greater the attachment to the (ex) husband, the greater the depression and the poorer the immune function, including lower percentages of NK cells.

Although the immune suppression could have been caused by preexisting depressive symptoms that then caused marital disruption, the authors cited evidence (Menaghan, 1985; Monroe, 1986) suggesting that depression is more likely to be the result than the cause of marital disruption. Earlier studies showing that loneliness is associated with poorer immune function (Kiecolt-Glaser, Ricker et al., 1984; Kiecolt-Glaser, Garner et al., 1984) and also with changes in herpesvirus latency (Glaser, Kiecolt-Glaser et al., 1985) led the authors to conclude that the quality of interpersonal emotions appears capable of having immune-mediated clinical consequences.

Academic and Occupational Stress

In the last five years, several studies have examined various immune measures in students undergoing academic stress and found or assumed to be experiencing appropriate negative emotions. Dorian et al. (1982) found impaired lymphocyte responsiveness to mitogens in the five most stressed of eight psychiatric trainees taking a final oral examination, compared to the nine least stressed of 16 trainees not taking an exam. In other medical students, Baker et al. (1985) found that levels of anxiety, serum cortisol, and T-helper/inducer cells were higher during their first week in the training hospital than a few months later or in second year students.

Four of the studies came from one collaboratively led group. In a study of stressor effects on immunity, Kiecolt-Glaser, Garner et al. (1984) twice drew blood from 75 first-year medical students. On the first occasion, one month before final examinations, baseline values of immune parameters were obtained, along with estimates of recent symptoms, distress, life events, and loneliness. The second blood drawing was on the first day of final exams. From the first to the second blood sample, total plasma immunoglobulin A increased, while NK cell activity decreased and was significantly lower in students who scored high on loneliness and stressful life events. In two similar studies of 34 twice-sampled medical students, Kiecolt-Glaser, Glaser et al. (1984) found in the exam-day samples significant declines in the number of helper/inducer T-cells, in their ratio to suppressor/ cytotoxic T-cells, and in NK activity, and Glaser, Rice, Speicher et al. (1987) found significantly lower levels of NK cells and of interferons released by mitogen-stimulated white cells in exam-day samples.

The clinical significance of such changes was investigated in a fourth study, which used a year-long prospective design. In blood samples drawn from 40 medical students during the first, third, and fifth examination periods, which were compared with samples drawn one month before exams, Glaser, Rice, Sheridan et al. (1987) found significant decrements in production by mitogen-stimulated lymphocytes of gamma interferon, an antiviral factor, along with higher titers of antibody to Epstein-Barr virus, suggesting reactivation of latent virus and therefore weaker cell-mediated immunity. Because the incidence of self-reported symptoms of infectious illness rose during examinations, the authors conclude that their data support a connection between stress, suppression of cellular immunity, and viral infection. In an earlier study of military cadets, Kasl et al. (1979) similarly found a greater likelihood of contracting infectious mononucleosis in those undergoing greater academic pressure.

A prospective study of occupational stress was made by Dorian et al. (1985) in 21 healthy licensed tax accountants (A's) and 12 age-and-sex-matched controls (C's) at four times in the tax year: February, April, July, and November. Although A's and C's had the same total number of life events, A's suffered more distress, including anxiety, depression, somatic symptoms, compulsiveness, and interpersonal sensitivity at all times, and especially when they were overworked helping clients with annual income tax returns. They found differences in some immune parameters between A's and C's that changed with time, and also complementary changes in some immune parameters over time in A's, NK activity being higher when the ratio of helper/inducer to suppressor/cytotoxic T-cells was lower. Lymphocyte responsiveness to mitogens was lowest in the most distressed A's. Marked impairment of lymphocytic responsiveness to mitogens has also been shown in two studies of the effects of working on rotating shifts (Curti et al, 1982; Nakano et al., 1982), but interpretation of these findings is complicated by the possible effects of sleep losses, which affect immunity (Palmblad, 1979).

In a prospective study of immune function in unemployed women, Arnetz et al. (1987) found that lymphocyte responsiveness to mitogens and to a tuberculin antigen decreased significantly in unemployed women, compared to employed women, nine months after their job loss.

7. Negative Attitudes and Cancer

Studies of long-term emotional attitudes or personality types in relation to immunity and immune-related diseases have focused largely on cancer, the incidence of which is highest in the developed countries (Cox and Mackay, 1982).

In a critical discussion of psychooncologic research, Locke and Gorman (1987) made several important points - that cancer is a set of different though similar diseases; that emotional states and traits might affect the initiation and the progression of cancer(s) differentially; that the effects might be direct or indirect, and that the psychometrics used need to be standardized. Because their review is a textbook chapter, they could refer explicitly to only a few suggested readings, including a book by Cohen et al. (1982) and a collection of reviews edited by Greer and McEwan (1985), but research reports discussed in those and other reviews cited below are among the 20 reports published between 1976 and 1982 for which abstracts were given by Locke and Hornig-Rohan (1983).

Until recently, most studies were retrospective and therefore subject to several methodological biases and contaminations (Grossarth-Maticek et al. 1982). Therefore recent reviews tend to distrust the findings of earlier investigations.

Stress and Cancer Initiation

In animal studies of cancer initiation, investigators are obviously unable to measure attitudinal variables and can study only the effects of stressors on the development of cancer. From their review of such animal studies, LeBarba (1970) concluded that stress does have a carcinogenic effect. Riley et al. (1981), who devised techniques for quantitating laboratory stress effects, concluded that their own review "demonstrated the tangible increased risk of the stressed subject with regard to either incipient or overt malignancies", but were impressed by the finding of Monjan and Collector (1977) that chronic stress caused initial immunosuppression followed by immunoenhancement.

In a review, Peters and Mason (1979) concluded that there is support for both negative and positive views concerning the effects of stress on oncogenesis, depending on the choice of animal for carcinogenesis or as donor or recipient of tumor transplants, the parameters of applied stressors, the timing of the stress with regard to carcinogen exposure or tumor tranplantation, and the outcome measures - tumor incidence or growth rate or animal survival.

A review of studies of stress and cancer in human subjects by Anisman and Zacharko (1983) similarly concluded that the studies "at best provided a mixed bag of results, and the factors contributing to the diverse outcomes across studies have yet to be identified. In general, the approaches...adopted have frequently lacked experimental sophistication....Well-controlled prospective and prognostic studies, and analysis based on types of tumors, social, cultural, and demographic variables, would be helpful."

Attitudes and Cancer Initiation

With regard to specific emotional attitudes and cancer initiation in people, a depressive personality has long been linked with cancer. As mentioned at the outset, Galen reported in the second century AD that melancholic women were more likely than sanguine women to develop cancer (Gordon, 1935). From 1700 through the 1960's, several similar correlations of a depressive temperament and cancer proneness were published (reviewed in Cox and Mackay, 1982). However, because it is difficult to determine the onset of cancer accurately, occult cancers may have been the cause and not the consequence of the depressions, for cancer can produce mood-influencing amines such as norepinephrine and serotonin.

At least four recent studies have looked at cancer mortality rates in patients with clinical depression. Two of the studies found higher than expected death rates (e.g., Whitlock and Siskind, 1979), but two studies found no increase (e.g., Niemi and Jaaskelainin, 1978). Most prospective studies have also failed to find a significant correlation between high scores on the depression subscale of the Minnesota Multiphasic Personality Inventory (MMPI), which is being restandardized (Holden, 1986), and later deaths from cancer (e.g, a study of medical patients of both sexes by McCoy, 1978). However, Shekelle et al. (1981) tested 2020 randomly selected middle-aged men with the MMPI and after 17 years found that those who had scored as depressed had twice the normal probability of death from cancer, after allowing for family history, occupation, and alcohol and tobacco use.

Other emotional traits have been nominated as oncogenic from both the psychoanalytic and the psychosocial points of view. Reviewing studies that were clinical, anecdotal, cross- sectional, and retrospective, and therefore largely uncontrolled, LeShan and Worthington (1956) concluded that four recurrent emotional and personality factors were found in cancer patients - grief, repression of anger, unresolved tension regarding a parental figure, and sexual problems. In the psychoanalytic vein, Bahnson and Bahnson (1966) saw the ego defenses of denial and repression as predisposing to cancer. More recently, Bahnson (1981) still thought that when adaptation breaks down in the face of various stressors, those people who use projection as the preferred defense mechanism tend to have psychopathologic symptoms, whereas those who prefer repression as a defense mechanism tend to have somatic symptoms, most noticeably cancer, which by this scheme is the somatic equivalent of and alternative to psychosis.

In contrast to most research, a controlled study by Greer and Morris (1975) found no relationship between breast cancer and depression, denial, stressful life events, sexual inhibition, or extraversion, but did find one with the extreme suppression of anger; their patients also had more frequent temper outbursts than did the controls. Fox (1978) first thought that two personality types predisposed to cancer - "extraverted, nonneurotic people," who had pathogenic styles of diet and drug uses, and "yielding, compliant, eager to please, 'good' people", who had repressed disgruntlement. Later, he was much more tentative (Fox, 1981), concluding that although personality factors, both state and trait, probably do affect the probability of cancer, both damagingly and protectively, their contribution to cancer incidence is probably small, and that the effect of psychological factors if real is specific to organ sites and dependent on several factors, and less important in people than in animals.

Repression of emotional expression was also found to be the most likely attitudinal factor in the etiology and development of cancers in reviews by Greer and Watson (1985) and Cox and Mackay (1982). However, Grossarth-Maticek et al. (1983) found in a longitudinal prospective study of 1335 males and females in the Yugoslavian community of Crvenka that those who repressed emotions were more apt to develop cardiovascular and other circulatory diseases, while those who passively received emotional repression from others were more apt to develop cancers. These authors related active repression to a personality prone to the "challenge" response and the receipt of repression to a personality prone to the "distress" response. Beliauskas (1983) also concluded that a depressive-like, probably chronic state of mild "distress" may indeed be the measured risk factor for cancer. However, in a reexamination of the Crvenka data, Grossarth-Maticek et al. (1985) found that all 38 lung cancer deaths occurred in people with high scores for rationality and antiemotionality, a factor related to the suppression of aggression. Jansen and Muenz (1984) compared women with breast cancer to women with fibrocystic disease to determine differences in their self-perceptions. The healthy controls called themselves calm, relaxed, outgoing, and able to express anger; the fibrocystic group called themselves tense, restless, outgoing, and expressing anger; the breast cancer group called themselves timid, nonassertive, noncompetitive, calm, easy-going, and as keeping anger inside.

In a review, Cunningham (1985) concluded, "it is suggested that depression and repressive tendencies are among those [emotional] characteristics favoring [i.e., predisposing to] cancer, although there is great variation of results between studies." In their review, Locke and Gorman (1987) concluded that impaired ability to express emotion, especially anger, may be a risk factor for cancer, or a marker of its presence.

Attitudes and Cancer Progression

With regard to the effects on survival of an organism's psychological and behavioral response to the onset and diagnosis of cancer, Levy (1984) concluded from a review of animal and human studies that "feelings of depression and helplessness appear to be associated with a shorter survival period, and feelings of anger and expressions of coping appear to be associated with longer survival periods". The strongest psychological predictor of mortality in women with a recurrence of breast cancer was denial of distress and worry; such patients tended to be dead within a year. However, the relationship of denial and breast cancer is complex and may also depend upon the stage of the disease. Levy has speculated that denial soon after diagnosis of breast cancer may keep distress from suppressing body defense systems but that later on, complaining may mobilize body defense systems. This idea was cited in a paper on denial by Goleman, 1985; denial has also been discussed in the proceedings of a conference (Breznitz, 1983, reviewed by Borysenko, 1984).

In a study of psychosocial correlates of survival in 359 male and female patients with advanced cancers, Cassileth et al. (1985) concluded that "although these factors may contribute to the initiation of morbidity, the biology of the disease appears to predominate and to override the potential influence of life-style and psychosocial variables once the disease process is established". This conclusion seems controversial in the light of reports (discussed in section 8 of this review) of spontaneous and faith-associated remissions even of advanced cancers (Boyd, 1966; Everson and Cole, 1966; Dowling, 1984; Lerner and Remen, 1985; Siegel, 1986).

Regarding cancer progression, Locke and Gorman (1987) concluded that the role of behavior is still unknown and therefore agreed with Cassileth et al. (1985) that cancer patients should not be burdened with responsibility for illness outcome. However, other cancer physicians believe strongly that "in the absence of certainty, there is nothing wrong with hope" (Simonton et al., 1978) and they counsel cancer patients to accept the diagnosis but not the verdict (Lerner and Remen, 1985) and to change their attitudes toward life in order to improve and even to lengthen it (Siegel, 1986).

Intervening Biological Variables

There have been few studies of the biological variables intervening between emotions and cancers. At the neural level, the predominance of left-sided breast tumors (McManus, 1977) seems consistent with the cerebral lateralization of emotions and of lesions that affect immune regulation (Biziere et al, 1985; Nance et al., 1985). Grossarth-Maticek et al. (1983), who linked distress responses to cancer, suggested that "frequency, duration, and high intensity of these reactions may trigger pathological developments in peripheral tissues via enhanced biosynthesis and release of related neurohormones." The impact and possible mechanisms of psychoendocrine effects in cancer and immunity were discussed in a book by Fox and Newberry (1984) and in reviews by Cox and Mackay (1982) and Pettingale (1985).

At the effector-cell level, the majority of studies have turned away from a previous emphasis on cytotoxic T cells as the agents of the immune surveillance for cancer cells that was theorized by Burnet (1965). Burnet's theory has been generally accepted, though disputed by some (Prehn, cited favorably by Davies, 1987). Pettingale (1985) commented that "even if the proposed system of immunosurveillance does not detect the very earliest malignant change, the immune system is likely to be involved at various stages in the growth and development of human tumors." Burnet's theory assumes that all tumor cells, at their very inception, display nonself antigens that evoke a cytotoxic response. If this were true, patients with immunodeficiency diseases or immunosuppression induced to permit transplantations ought to have an increased incidence of cancer. This is so, but the cancers observed are limited to unusual types, including lympho- proliferative tumors, Kaposi's sarcoma, and some tumors thought to be related to oncogenic viruses (Hoover and Fraumeni, 1973). The implication is that nonspecific immunity plays a major role in tumor control. Therefore the new emphasis is on natural killer (NK) cells, which do not depend on antigenic cues but are nevertheless important in destroying virally infected and cancerous cells (Herberman and Otaldo, 1981). NK cell activity was related to psychological health in a study by Heisel et al. (1986) of healthy college students, 33 female and 77 male. A weak but statistically significant inverse correlation was found between psychopathology and NK activity. Students who had high levels of NK activity had a psychologically healthier profile on 10 of the 12 scales of the MMPI than did students with NK values below the sample median. An earlier study by members of the same group (Locke and Kraus, 1982) obtained similar findings.

In a study of 13 patients with malignant melanoma, Levy (1986) used a logistic regression equation calculated to relate emotional and physical factors in survival. She found a positive association between survival and both NK cells and total score on the Profile of Mood States Scale, and a negative correlation with the belief called "negative attribution", that whatever happens will be for the worst. Together, the three factors of NK cells, positive mood, and absence of belief in negative attribution predicted survival in nearly half of the patients. The sample was small but the correlation is impressive.

8. Positive Emotions and Attitudes

The possibility that negative emotions and attitudes can affect immunity naturally suggests the possibility that positive emotions and attitudes also may affect immunity. Clinically, it would be desirable that positive emotions modulate immune reactivity in the specific sense of enhancing it when it is hyporeactive, as in the case of cancers and infections, and inhibiting it when it is hyperreactive, as in the case of autoimmune and allergic disorders. There is some evidence for both forms of modulation.

Positive Emotions and Immune Modulation

The placebo response(s) may include the modulation of immune responses by positive emotions (White et al., 1984). The reality of the placebo effect, which in pain relief is 56% as effective as morphine (Evans, 1984), has been widely though reluctantly recognized in biomedicine, more as a nuisance variable that confounds measurements of the effectiveness of new drugs than as a potent therapeutic intervention in its own right (Benson and Epstein, 1975). The many disorders for which placebo has been useful include cancer, infections like the common cold, allergic disorders like asthma, and autoimmune disorders like multiple sclerosis and rheumatoid arthritis (Beecher, 1955).

Expectation based on religious belief may sometimes induce regression of cancers, other hyperplasias, and some serious autoimmune disorders. Several instances were given in a physician's report of rapid, complete cures judged medically inexplicable by a commission of physicians charged by the Vatican with scientifically evaluating candidate miracle cures in patients who made pilgrimages to the Shrine of Bernadette in Lourdes (Dowling, 1984). About 65,000 pilgrims are registered and documented as sick annually. Since 1858, more than 2 million pilgrims have visited Lourdes; about 6,000 claiming to have been cured have been examined by doctors; 64 cures have been judged miraculous by the Roman Catholic church. Since 1954, an International Medical Commission of Lourdes has judged 19 cures to be medically and scientifically inexplicable; 13 have been judged miraculous by the Church, including the cures of 1 sarcoma, 3 other hyperplastic disorders, 2 cases of tuberculosis, and 3 cases of multiple sclerosis.

Like Dowling, Siegel (1986) made the point that physicians perplexed by inexplicable remissions do not usually report them in the literature, so that the statistics on recovery are skewed negatively. Even so, it has been possible to compile a forthcoming bibliography of more than 3,000 abstracts of reports from more than 830 medical journals (O'Regan and Hirshberg, 1987) that will describe many spontaneous (i.e., inexplicable) remissions of cancers, autoimmune disorders, and other diseases involving hypo- and hyper-reactivity of the immune system. As Siegel (1986) tells his cancer patients, there seems to be no "incurable" disease from which someone has not recovered even at the threshold of death. It is possible that positive emotions played a role in these recoveries.

Modulation of Immune Hyporeactivity

The possible effects of hope and the will to live were considered in a volume devoted to the question of the mind and cancer prognosis (Stoll, 1979b). In it, Stoll (1979a) concluded that "we have no incontrovertible scientific evidence that emotional factors can influence the prognosis in the cancer patient - that is a question that remains to be answered. However, to deny that such links exist is to deny numerous clinical observations in individual cases."

Positive feelings may have contributed to at least some of the documented spontaneous remissions of cancers. Two critical discussions of such cases have been published. Boyd (1966) discussed 23 cases, Everson and Cole (1966) discussed 176 (out of 1,000 claimed cases). None of these authors explicitly considered emotions as possible factors in remission, although Boyd suggested that psychosocial factors might affect susceptibility, and Everson and Cole suggested that the remissions were attributable to factors that included endocrine influences and immune reactions.

Cunningham (1984) reviewed several clinical studies suggesting that interventions that arouse or reinforce hope and other positive emotions and attitudes increase not only the quality of life but also the longevity of cancer patients, presumably at least in part through the enhancement of specific or nonspecific immune responses. These studies are methodologically questionable, because they were not controlled. However, as some earlier empirical treatments turned out to be, they may be reliable; if so, they are important medically and call for explanation in terms of physiological mechanisms.

Simonton et al. (1978) augmented medical treatment with positive adjustments of life-style and emphasized the patients' use during periods of relaxation of positive mental imagery (described by Achterberg, 1985) to visualize the success of their immune systems in removing their tumors. A large group of patients using this approach had a mean survival time about twice that of similar patients receiving only traditional treatment at major American centers (Simonton et al., 1980). Nevertheless, the American Cancer Society (1982) found no evidence that the Simonton program provided "objective benefit," conceding however that it promoted relaxation and a sense of control.

Newton (1982-83) described a program like the Simonton's that emphasized hypnosis. Depending on the sites of the cancers, patients had median survival times 2-1/2 to 4 times the national medians. Earlier, Meares (1978) reported that regression of several metastatic sarcomas were associated with intensive daily meditation. Meares later reported (1980, 1982) that of 73 patients treated, 5 had complete regressions unattributable to any organic treatment and 5 others appeared to be well on the way to similar regression. Benson (1975) thought that meditation was effective because it evoked what he called the "relaxation response," since reported by his colleague Borysenko (in Melnechuk, 1984c) to lower blood levels of immunosuppressive epinephrine and norepinephrine as well as the insulin requirement in insulin-dependent diabetics who are achievement-oriented.

Grossarth-Maticek (1980) gave 24 cancer patients "social psychotherapy" emphasizing a healthy lifestyle, natural piety, expression of goals and hopes, and trust in and support from the physician and other people important to the patient. Patients so encouraged had median survival times 2 years longer than controls matched for cancer type, age, sex, and social class.

Cunningham (1984) reported an early impression that of 9 patients given 1-1/2 hours per week for up to 10 weeks of training in relaxation, medication, mental imagery, stress handling, and goal definition, "those patients who do well medically are often among those most involved in their meditation and imagery."

Siegel (1986) gave no data but reported many anecdotes of patients in whom deliberately evoked feelings of self-love and love of others were soon followed by at least temporary and sometimes permanent regressions even of apparently terminal cancers. Like the Simontons by whose program he was inspired, Siegel found that no more than a fifth of his patients already were or were willing to become "exceptional" in the sense of taking the initiative in working hard to have their every thought and deed manifest the will to live and advance the cause of life.

Before these reports, Maguire (1979) had concluded that "a multidisciplinary approach in which surgeons, physicians, biochemists, immunologists, psychiatrists and psychologists work together closely, is the most likely to determine if the will to live really does affect length of survival in the cancer patient." After the publication of all but the latest of these anecdotal and clinical reports had suggested that positive emotions can have a beneficial effect on health, Miller (1985) deplored the scarcity of experimental studies of the effects of positive factors. There have indeed been only a few such studies with regard to immune enhancement in itself and in relation to infections and cancers.

Jemmot et al. (1983) followed 64 dental students for an academic year, assayed their personalities with the Thematic Apperception Test, and measured the amount secreted in their saliva of immunoglobulin A, an antibody type involved in defense against respiratory infection. Antibody secretion fell before examinations. However, antibody secretion was higher at all times in those students deemed to have a "relaxed affiliative" personality than in those judged to have "an inhibited power motive," who, in a preliminary retrospective study, reported more severe upper respiratory infections than did those with other personality characteristics (McClelland et al., 1980).

H. H. Hall (1983) reported that, in blood drawn from young, highly hypnotizable, but otherwise normal subjects given the suggestion under trance that their white cells were like "powerful sharks" consuming "weak germs", there was an *in vitro* increase of the proliferative response of lymphocytes to pokeweed mitogen, which stimulates both B-cells and T-cells.

At a conference with the title "How might positive emotions affect physical health?" (Melnechuk, 1984c), two speakers discussed enhancement of immunity by positive emotions. Coe, presenting results later published (Coe, 1987), reported that in post-weaning squirrel monkey infants, the immunosuppression that followed separation from their mothers for seven days was much weaker in the consoling presence of familiar monkeys from whom the infants received social support.

N. R. Hall reported findings from two studies since informally discussed in a published interview (Hall, 1987). He first conducted an unfunded and therefore simple study initiated by a single patient - a physician with metastatic cancer who had been inspired to practice positive imagery by reports of its effectiveness in prolonging the life of cancer patients (Simonton et al., 1978). During periods when the patient would repeatedly visualize in imagination his immune system attacking his tumor, Hall found that the metastases regressed, as shown by bone scans. There was also a synchronous rise both in the numbers of lymphocytes circulating in the peripheral blood and in blood serum levels of the thymic hormone thymosin alpha 1, believed to play a role in the differentiation of T-cells. During periods when the patient did not practice positive imagery or thought he did it poorly, metastases returned and the previously increased immune values declined. The patient died soon after the death of his wife.

Intrigued by this suggestive clinical experience, Hall has since obtained support for a collaboration with psychiatrists and psychologists on a year-long double-blind study of the effects of positive imagery in 5 male and 5 female patients with different kinds of cancers. A battery of five psychological tests is being given and 18 immune parameters are being measured in frequent blood samples.

Hall's preliminary findings are of imagery-correlated increases in lymphocyte responsiveness to the mitogen concanavalin-A, in immunoglobulin G, and in the mixed lymphocyte (T-cell) response, along with a 20% rise in NK cells. However, relaxation seems to be as effective as positive imagery.

As already mentioned, other investigators have also reported immunoenhancing effects of the positive emotions associated with relaxation. At the opposite end of the life-span from Coe's infant primate subjects, Kiecolt-Glaser, Glaser, Williger et al. (1985) reported the psychosocial enhancement of immunocompetence in a geriatric population of 45 subjects given relaxation training, social contact, or no contact. At the end of the intervention, the relaxation group showed a significant increase in NK activity and decrease in antibody titers to herpes simplex virus, both signs of enhanced cellular immunity, along with a significant decrease in self-rated distress. Earlier, Kiecolt-Glaser, Glaser, Strain et al. (1984) found that in medical students assigned to a relaxation group that met between blood- samplings a month before and on the first day of final examinations, the frequency of relaxation practice was a significant predictor of the amounts of helper/inducer T-cells in the examination-day sample.

Dillon et al. (1985-86) reported that salivary immunoglobulin A concentrations did not change in subjects shown a didactic videotape but increased significantly when the subjects viewed a humorous and presumably relaxing videotape. Jasnoski (1986) reported a preliminary finding that relaxation increased the level of salivary immunoglobulin A, whereas imagery had a greater effect on raising the number of helper/inducer T-cells, which help to regulate both B-cell and T-killer responses.

Modulation of Immune Hyperactivity

In an influential article (Cousins, 1976), later expanded into a book (Cousins, 1979), a patient reported that his deliberate assumption of responsibility for his own therapeutic regimen was followed by regression of a serious autoimmune disease, ankylosing spondylitis, in which the spinal ligaments ossify. His account has often been oversimplified as claiming that he laughed himself well.   In fact, Cousins reported that, with the approval of his cooperative physician, he moved from a hospital to a hotel. He did this partly to control his food intake, in order to enjoy better cooking, to avoid chemical additives, and also to take large amounts of vitamin C, because of reports that it modulated immunity. He also moved to the hotel to get more and uninterrupted healing sleep, both by avoiding routine awakenings by hospital staff and by laughing at funny movies as his only possible tiring and thus sleep-inducing physical exercise.

Cousins concluded in this case, as in his later successful self-treatment of a heart attack (Cousins, 1983), that he did not know which, if any, of these steps had been effective, and if so by what physiological mechanism(s), or whether instead or in addition the effective step had been his adoption of a hopeful attitude and an active role, or even his prior possession of a positive character that could and would adopt them. Thus his actual experience has been a mandate to explore all of these potentialities.

Swedish patients with chronic rheumatoid arthritis, who were given six weeks of treatment in a warm climate, experienced immediate benefit, which the investigators concluded was probably caused by the diversion from familiar problems (Johansson and Sullivan, 1975). Udelman and Udelman (1985) reported beginning a year-long study of the impact of new hope on the course of rheumatoid arthritis in patients receiving their first course of remission-inducing therapy.

9. Coping and Hardiness

The concept of coping has become scientifically popular in the decade since it was advanced (Levine et al., 1978). One scheme that uses coping as an explanatory variable proposes that after a stressor is perceived and appraised and while tentative emotions are felt, an individual tries to deal with the stressor by means of a coping strategy, either altering or eliminating the stressor's danger or revising its meaning for the individual. When the coping strategy succeeds, positive emotions are felt, but when it proves to be inadequate, inappropriate, or too long, negative emotions of grief, anxiety, anger, panic, etc., are felt as part of a physiological response to the stressor (Zegans, 1983).

This formulation suggests that there are no universal stressors, other perhaps than certain threats to life, because the meaning of a situation can be different for different individuals (Barnard, 1985). Recall that some soldiers welcome receiving battlefield wounds, perceived as tickets home.

In a book on stress, appraisal, and coping, Lazarus and Folkman (1984) define psychological stress as "a particular relationship between the person and the environment that is appraised by the person as taxing or exceeding his or her resources and endangering his or her well-being." As the Greek stoic philosopher Epictetus noted, we are disturbed not by events but by our opinions of events; an event is a stressor only if some mediator of meaning converts it into a noxious stimulus (Hamburg and Elliot, 1981). Thus, in 50 males with periodontal disease, Green et al. (1986) found that as the number of what many observers would consider to be stressors in their lives increased, the severity and spread of the disease increased in most of the subjects, but not in all, for some of the patients did not feel threatened by experiences that others did feel threatened by.

The concept of coping, under the name of "control", was linked with the characteristics of "commitment" and "challenge" in a compound personality attribute called "hardiness" by Kobasa and Maddi (1982). By commitment they meant the opposite of alienation; by control, the opposite of powerlessness, and by challenge, the anticipation of change. They found that such hardiness, as measured on a scale (Kobasa, 1978), appears to be a buffer against the power of stressful life events to predispose to illness, although Kobasa recently stated that the experimental evidence is firmest for commitment and control (Wood, 1987). One factor influencing survival among AIDS patients was reported to be the degree of control they perceived over their lives; those who felt they could exert little control died more quickly (Temoshok, 1986).

Studies of Intervening Biological Variables

Vogel (1985) reviewed a number of animal experiments suggesting that biochemical, physiological, or pathological changes in an organism are caused not by the aversive or noxious nature of a stressor but by the ability or inability of the organism to cope with it. For example, Sklar and Anisman (1979) found that in mice given a series of escapable or inescapable electric shocks, larger tumors developed faster in the inescapable shock group than in the escapable shock group. A psychoimmunomodulatory mechanism for this effect was suggested by the outcome of a similar experiment with rats, in which Laudenslager et al. (1983) found that lymphocyte proliferation in response to mitogens was suppressed in the inescapable shock group but not in the escapable shock group.

The physiological mediators of coping effects on immunity have been investigated in a number of human studies. A biochemical correlate of the feeling of self-efficacy was reported by Bandura et al. (1985). In 12 women with a spider phobia, a rise in the feeling of being able to cope with spiders was paralleled by a fall in the blood levels of their catecholamines. However, Frankenhaeuser (1982) associated catecholamine secretion with the positive aspect ("effort") of arousal, in contrast to the negative aspect ("distress") associated with cortisol secretion. She saw controllability as reducing the negative aspect and enhancing the positive aspect of arousal.

A further discrimination between hormones associated with coping emotions was made at the conference on positive emotions and health (Melnechuk, 1984c), when Henry summarized his published account (Henry, 1982) of hormone changes associated with positive and negative emotions related to different forms of coping. As an individual moves along the emotional dimension that ranges from relaxation to extreme concern with maintaining status, there is an increase in the blood plasma levels of the catecholamines epinephrine (if angry) or norepinephrine (if anxious). As one moves from the elation of security to the dejection of helplessness, there is a rise in the plasma levels of the adrenal corticoids. As one moves from social success to social failure, there is a fall in the plasma levels of the gonadotrophins, which regulate reproductive and parenting drives. Because these chemical correlates of negative emotions can, over time, override the neuroendocrine feedback controls that normally restore homeostasis, they can lead to pathophysiological changes and even to disease. Henry thus saw the role in health of the positive emotions associated with success at various forms of coping as that of preventing different kinds of illness by preempting the deleterious effects of negative motions.

In addition to affecting cells that make up such solid tissues as vascular linings, all of the hormones mentioned above as related to coping and control affect lymphocytes and NK cells. Solomon et al. (1987) found in both young and old subjects a very strong psychoimmunological correlation between psychological hardiness as measured on the Kobasa (1978) scale and the ability of NK cells to be stimulated.

10. Conclusions Regarding Emotional Immunomodulation

Contemporary textbooks of basic and clinical immunology (e.g., Stites et al,. 1987) ignore the findings of psychoneuroimmunology. However, from the evidence cited in this review, it seems clear that the immune system is responsive to psychosocial factors. It appears that several immune parameters, especially the numbers and responsiveness of regulatory and effector lymphocytes and NK cells in peripheral blood, can be lowered by short and long experiences of the negative withdrawal emotions and raised by short and long experiences of the positive approach emotions.

In the case of emotional immunosuppression, experiments in which it was possible to control rigorously such confounding factors as the effects of stress on hygiene, sanitation, and diet have confirmed a causal effect (Miller, 1985). Miller (1985) has also been able to account for at least some of the contradiction between the findings that stress suppresses immunity, has no effect on immunity, and enhances immunity (e.g., Newberry et al., 1976) in terms of the type of tumor implanted and of nonmonotonic dose-response and time-response curves.

Nevertheless, "the relation between emotional factors and immunity is complex and diverse" (Kronfol and House, 1984). As Williams (1987) put it, "[knowledge about] the interactions of the neuroendocrine and the immune systems must become a lot more complex before a coherent pattern can emerge."

In the case of emotional immunoenhancement, the enhanced regulatory T-cells are sometimes helpers/inducers and sometimes suppressors. Another source of complexity is the fact that response patterns can change as subjects adapt to a stimulus situation or can even differ between phases of an experience, as Mason et al. (1972) showed in monkeys whose hormonal responses were different in the learning and retention phases of an operant learning procedure.

The complexity derives also from sex differences. Some of these are in the endocrine responses to stressors. For example, Frankenhauser (1982) found a sex difference in the "effort" response, in that females were less prone than males to respond to achievement demands with increased catecholamine secretion. A study by Matheny and Cupp (1983) of 126 subjects of both sexes found that the relationship between life change and illness was much stronger for females than for males, and that desirable events were positively related to illness for females only. They attributed this finding to different degrees of control between the sexes. Differences between the sexes in physiological responses to stress were reviewed by Stoney et al. (1987). There are also sex differences in immunity, reviewed in connection with differences in cerebral lateralization by Geschwind and Galaburda (1985).

Another source of difficulty in interpretation of findings lies in ethnic and individual genetic differences, such as those in cardiovascular reactivity to stress (Ditto, 1987) and in enzyme profiles (Kalow et al., 1986). The biochemical heterogeneity of cancer cells, which can produce inhibitory and necrotic as well as mitogenic and trophic factors (Pettingale, 1985), makes it difficult to attribute to positive emotions all regressions preceded by them.

It is also clear that most of the many studies that have established the reality of some emotional suppression and enhancement of immune parameters have not also established their clinical significance. Only a few studies have proposed these effects as the intervening variable between correlations of emotion and illness, such as those of academic stress with mononucleosis (Kasl et al., 1979), of loneliness with herpes virus latency (Glaser, Kiecolt-Glaser, Speicher et al., 1985) and of positive mood and attribution with cancer survival duration (Levy, 1986). However, as Plaut and Friedman (1985) pointed out, the relationships between emotional factors and immune parameters are largely correlative, and thus only suggest possible mechanisms.

Criticisms of Psychoneuroimmunological Research

Many suggestions for future research on the role of emotions in immunity and health are made explicit or implied in published criticisms of psychoneuroimmunological investigations. In addition to criticisms already cited in this review, here are several more.

Skeptical immunologists at an international conference on the subject made the following criticisms in the postpresentation and general discussions (Guillemin et al., 1985; Melnechuk, 1985e). They could produce an immune response *in vitro* in cloned cell lines without the need for any substances of neural origin. They found it hard to imagine how conditioned immunosuppression could work. They criticized the unsophisticated sampling of stress-evoked changes in blood hormone levels because the samples were taken only once a day, when it is known that the secretion of some stress-related hormones is pulsatile, with circadian or ultradian rhythms. They criticized the common practice of assaying the effects of emotions on immunity in terms of changes in lymphocyte responses to mitogens, both because the mitogens commonly used are not the physiological growth factors endogenous to the specific animal species and lymphocyte class (B or T) used, and also because sensitive assays exist for many other important parameters of immune function. They claimed that no investigator had yet delineated a complete causal chain showing that a particular neural manipulation, psychological or physical, caused a particular change in some intermediary that then brought about a particular change in an immune response, which then made a clinical difference.

Adding to the criticisms of commonly used assays, Stone et al. (1987) presented three reasons why total secretory IgA protein may not be a reasonable measure of immune system functioning and suggested an alternative method that focuses on secretory IgA antibody response to a novel antigen.

Doherty et al. (1986) commented that the many immune measures have not been integrated into a pattern of immunosuppression following stress. A temporal sequence is lacking; the various immune measures sample different times following the stressor. However, immune variables are at least clearly conceptualized and defined; social and psychological variables are not. Few studies use direct or multiple measures of social interaction, relying only on the report of a single individual or on a structural indicator like marital status. Terms like stress, coping, control, and personality differ in definition from study to study, and are not always well defined even within a given study.

Nevertheless, the authors of two current critical reviews conclude that in spite of the mixed findings, the small number of prospective studies, the scarcity of well-controlled research designs, and the virtual lack of replications, there is an intriguing body of scientific evidence consistent with the notion that emotional, personality, and other psychological and behavioral factors influence the onset and course of immune-associated diseases (Locke and Gorman, 1987), and that the overall weight of the available evidence supports the theory that the nervous, endocrine, and immune systems constitute one integrated suprasystem for maintaining homeostasis (Gorman and Locke, 1987) and therefore health.

However, important as psychoneuroimmunology is in itself, it is also important as the first well-investigated instance of a more general phenomenon (Melnechuk, 1985c) discussed in the final sections of this review—namely the psychoneural (and other signal-molecule mediated) modulation of all defensive and repair systems.

III. Toward a General Theory of Health

11. Emotions and Other Defense and Repair Systems

The organism's attempt to maintain homeostasis is made in the face of an everpresent burden of inherited and acquired biochemical microlesions, as pointed out by Huemer (1977). Therefore one's state of health reflects in part the varying success not only of the immune system but also of nonimmunological defense systems (some of which were reviewed by Apffel, 1976), as well as repair systems, in preventing and correcting further damage to one's structural, functional, and, above all, informational molecules.

The information in the DNA of a just-fertilized ovum is there to specify not only its development into a new organism but also the subsequent moment-to-moment biochemistry in every eventual cell of that organism during its lifetime. Therefore the most vital species of biomolecule is the DNA in one's somatic cells— that is, cells other than gametes, for in gametes DNA damage is deleterious only to the next generation. In a somatic cell, damage to DNA is either lethal to the cell or causes a mutation that is passed on to the descendants of that cell. Except for nerve cells, polymorphonuclear leukocytes, and keratinized cells of the epidermis, which do not divide, other cells divide either slowly or continuously, passing on to their descendants whatever sublethal load of genetic defects they have accumulated.

Antioxidant and Other Defenses

One of the most important systems for defending molecules protects DNA and other vital biomolecules from damage by oxygen-centered free radicals. These negatively ionized forms of oxygen are generated by radiation and radiomimetic compounds in air and food (Ames, 1983). The oxygen radicals then react destructively with DNA, which, being rich in electrons, is especially vulnerable to oxidation (Simic et al., 1986). The resulting damage to DNA is thought to be one of the major causes of aging (Harman, 1981; Gensler and Bernstein, 1981; Tice and Setlow, 1985; Warner et al., 1987). Perhaps through the conversion of protooncogenes to oncogenes (Pryor, 1986; Cerutti, 1986), oxidant radical reactions are thought to be a cause also of the age-related proliferative diseases—cancers, atherosclerosis, which is now thought to involve endothelial hyperplasia (Penn et al., 1986), and, as a consequence of the latter, heart attack and stroke (Armstrong et al., 1984; Marx, 1987a). These diseases account for a large proportion of all deaths.

Before most life became aerobic, anaerobic life evolved a defense system of enzymes and other chemicals to neutralize what was then the poison gas oxygen. Because oxygen free radicals are still poisonous, such substances are still in place even in aerobic life forms such as human beings. The endogenous antioxidants include the enzymes superoxide dismutase, catalase, and glutathione peroxidase, the nonprotein sulfhydrils glutathione, cysteine, and cysteineglycine and urate, supplemented by dietary vitamins C and E, and beta-carotene (Cerutti, 1985).

No research on the effects of emotions on the antioxidant defense systems was presented at the recent 4th International Congress on Oxygen Radicals (National Bureau of Standards, 1987) and I am unaware of any such past or current research. I also know of no research yet on the effects of emotions on other molecular defense systems, such as the cytochrome p450 liver enzymes that metabolize drugs and many other ingested substances (Strobel et al., 1986) or the "heat shock" proteins, induced by many stressors, which confer resistance to heat and oxidative stress and may play a role in growth and development and thus in healing (Lindquist, 1986). Mammalian, especially human, analogs have not yet been found of the antimicrobial peptides called magainins newly discovered in frog skin (Zasloff, 1987). Research on the emotional modulation of such defense systems is clearly indicated, especially in the light of several reports, discussed next, that distress both damages DNA and inhibits DNA repair.

Effects of Negative Emotions on DNA Repair

When oxygen free radicals evade antioxidant defenses and damage DNA bases and strands, a DNA repair system is evoked (Collins et al., 1987). In humans, it comprises at least 15 enzymes, which, after breaking the DNA chain to which an oxidant-damaged nucleotide is attached, remove the damaged nucleotide and hundreds of surrounding nucleotides. Then the missing section of DNA chain is resynthesized from one end of the break, using the complementary chain as a template for the insertion of replacement nucleotides, until the remaining nick is ligated. Because Nature is noisy, incorrect nucleotides are inserted at a low rate, causing somatic mutations that are perpetuated in each succeeding round of cell division (Burnet, 1974). Most mutations are deleterious. Thus the DNA repair system is intrinsically mutagenic and cancerogenic. However, it presumably causes far fewer mutations than would unrepaired DNA damage, for even small declines from its normal level of activity may have serious pathophysiological consequences (Setlow, 1983).

According to Fischman et al. (1987), distress causes DNA damage, which consequently evokes an increase in DNA repair. In four animal experiments, it was found in rats that a variety of stressors including forced swims in cold water significantly increased the number of sister chromatid exchanges, an indicator of chromosome damage, in proportion to the severity of the stressors. DNA repair subsequently increased. Rats exposed only to the physical environment in which conspecifics had been stressed also showed significant intermediate elevations of the damage marker. Fischman (1985) has discussed possible mediating mechanisms of both effects, noting in effect that the stressors applied were such as to evoke not the Cannon "effort" but the Selye "distress" response, thereby increasing ACTH and opioid release and decreasing norepinephrine release.

Like the neuropeptide substance P (Levine et al., 1984), the above-mentioned emotion-expressing signal molecules can affect the phagocytic activity of monocytes/macrophages and neutrophils, the effectors of inflammation, both directly (Leme, 1985) and through evoking inflammatory intermediaries (Flohe et al., 1985). Phagocytes release "oxidative bursts" of oxygen free radicals in order to destroy alien entities and debris (Stites et al., 1987). There is always some damage to surrounding healthy self cells. Perhaps stress may damage DNA in this way, by means of oxidant radicals.

Another collaborative team has reported that distress lowers DNA repair enzyme levels and activity. In an animal experiment, Glaser, Thorn et al. (1985), exploring mechanisms to account for the relationship between distress and cancer development, used rotation to stress 22 of 44 rats given a carcinogen in drinking water. The levels of methyl transferase, a damage-induced DNA repair enzyme, were lower in spleen cells from the stressed animals. In an experiment with human subjects, Kiecolt-Glaser, Stephens, Lipets et al. (1985) assessed differences in DNA repair in X-rayed lymphocytes from 28 individuals with high and low levels of distress as judged by a median split on Scale 2 of the Minnesota Multiphasic Personality Inventory. The high-distress subjects had significantly poorer DNA repair than did the low-distress subjects.

The mechanism of this stress effect on DNA repair is unknown. DNA repair can be inhibited by a number of pharmacological agents (Collins et al., 1984), some of which may mimic endogenous inhibitors affected by or consisting of neurotransmitters and hormones; insulin for example delays DNA repair (Johnson et al., 1987). All genes, including those that dictate the biosynthesis of DNA repair enzymes, neurotransmitters, and all of the estimated 90,000 other specific gene products in the cells of a human body (Markert, 1987) are ultimately regulated by signals derived from the environment, expressed as neurotransmitters (Hunt et al., 1987; Roach et al., 1987) and hormones (McEwen, 1980; Woo and O'Malley, 1975). Since changes in the profiles of at least some of these signal molecules represent emotions, it makes sense to look for emotional effects on the biochemical constituents of all defense and repair systems.

Effects of Positive Emotions on Wound Healing

With regard to other repair systems besides that of DNA repair, emotional effects on wound healing seem indicated by several reports. For example, Boltwood (1986) was cited in a medical newsmagazine article as saying that the level of burn recovery was linked to the attitude of the patient. In a refereed paper, Ulrich (1984) reported investigating whether assignment to a hospital room with a view of a natural setting might have restorative effects on surgery patients. He found that after gall bladder removal, 23 patients whose windows looked out on a natural scene had shorter postoperative hospital stays and took fewer potent analgesics than 23 matched patients in rooms similar except for having windows facing a brick wall.

As in the case of Cousins' recovery from ankylosing spondylitis, discussed in section 8, the nature of the effective stimulus in the surgery patients studied by Ulrich is uncertain. For example, it could be the pleasure evoked by a natural scene, but it could be the emotional attitude that demanded the sight of such a scene. Clearly, something made a difference to the rate of healing and it seems quite possible that something was emotional.

How might emotions affect wound healing? The healing of an injured tissue resembles in many ways the original developmental growth of that tissue. Sensory and autonomic nerves are known to play an important and in many cases essential part in the development of many and perhaps all tissues. For example, sensory nerves are known to be essential for the embryonic development of many tissues and organs in higher animals and to exert a trophic influence on peripheral sensory cells (Jessel, 1985). Not only sensory nerves affect growth, differentiation, and maintenance: autonomic nerves are essential to normal development of the salivary gland and have trophic actions (Brooks, 1987). More immediately relevant to wound healing, sensory nerves are known to be essential for the "regeneration" (really only compensatory hyperplasia) of injured organs in higher animals and for true limb regeneration in amphibians and lower animals (Guth, 1987). During wound healing, they regulate peripheral vasculature and capillary permeability, and thus the magnitude of the healing phase of the inflammatory response to injury (Jessel, 1985).

Inflammation has already been mentioned as being modulated by neurotransmitters that can be representative of emotions. Inflammation is also affected by several classical hormones, chiefly the corticosteroids and sex steroids (Ahonen et al., 1980). However, the main biochemical regulators of wound healing and development appear to be a recently discovered, increasingly numerous group of locally released polypeptide factors collectively called "growth factors" (Massague, 1987). Actually, these factors differentially control the growth (i.e., first an increase in cell size and then cell division), differentiation, trophic (metabolic) maintenance, and programmed death of specific types of cells (James and Bradshaw, 1984). Like excitatory and inhibitory neurotransmitters and neuromodulators (Schmitt, 1984), these various mitogenic, maturational, maintenance, and and necrotic factors modulate one another's effects (Zoon et al., 1986). Their major sources during wound healing and tissue repair are both injured cells and inflammatory cells, including the platelets, macrophages, and lymphocytes (Sporn and Roberts, 1986), of which at least the latter two types of white cell are known to be affected by neurotransmitters. By means of genetic engineering, growth factors can now be produced synthetically and their potential medical use in wound healing treatments is being tested (Bronson, 1987).

It has been pointed out (Melnechuk, 1985b) that neuropeptide and other neurotransmitters appear to modulate the activity of many growth, differentiation, and trophic factors; moreover, in some cases, neurotransmitters, especially peptides, themselves appear to act as such factors (Hanley, 1985; Bartolome et al., 1986). Some of these neurotransmitters are released by sensory nerves not only at their spinal cord end, to inform the brain of an injury, but also simultaneously at their sensory receptor end (Jessel, 1985), as if in a reflex response to start healing as soon as possible. Such a reflex action may be considered the first part of an emotional response to injury of which the immediately subsequent parts are the pain and affective feeling evoked by the injury. These centrally mediated parts of the emotion are then expressed by means of the autonomic nerves that release catecholamine and peptide neurotransmitters at the site of an injury. Ruff et al. (1987) reported that human neuropeptides are chemotaxic for monocytes/macrophages, inducing them to migrate into specific areas of pathology. This is especially relevant for potential emotional effects on wound healing if, as Pert (1984) suggested, the neuropeptides are the major biochemical representatives of the emotions.

Second Messengers and Bioelectricity

When signal molecules affect cells, they do so by binding transiently to specific receptor molecules on the cell surface or, if they are steroids that can dissolve through the cell membrane, they bind to the chromosomes of the cell. In the first case, the transient binding triggers the dispatch to an appropriate part of the cell of one of several kinds of "second messenger" molecules. It has been recently reported that the activities of molecular components of such second messengers - e.g., calcium ions and certain enzymes - adenylate cyclase, protein kinases, and an enzyme essential for normal and abnormal growth, ornithine decarboxylase - can be affected through nonlinear reactions at the cell membrane by extracellular oscillating electromagnetic fields as weak as brain waves, in which tissue heating is therefore not the essential stimulus (Adey, 1987). This phenomenon conceptually couples the biochemical approach of the sections above to a bioelectrical approach that is beyond the scope of this review but which may be of great importance for understanding the role of emotions in health.

12. Synthetic Perspectives

The span from social events and human feelings to DNA and microbioelectric fields may seem long to some readers but to those who seek a comprehensive understanding of health the analytical levels are as close together as a nested set of hollow Russian dolls. The polarization of mind vs. body has, like many other polarizations, been shown by closer study to be a series of discrete levels of biological organization. At the top end of the series, a human being is a social and psychological person. At the bottom end, a human being is a biochemical and biophysical organism.

One can prefer to focus on a given level of this series and yet perceive the series as a ladder that can be climbed holistically up as well as reductionistically down by those (Grossman, 1985) who wish to help integrate psychosomatic medicine with biomedicine. Only the delineation of physiological mechanisms will convince the skeptical that the reported correlations express causal relationships and only mechanistic knowledge will permit the fullest therapeutic exploitation of phenomenological discoveries. Thus it seems fair to quote Dr. Orpheus (cited in Melnechuk, 1984b) to the merely psychologically minded: "Back to Eden, on to Zion/Via molecule and ion!"

Two conceptualizations of this series of levels seek to find unity within its diversity by emphasizing similarities between phenomena at the various levels. One approach, urged by Engel (1977), is that of general systems theorists, one of whom (Miller, 1978) described the analogous functional essentials of living systems at major levels of organization from single cell up to world society. According to this view, the understanding of pathology at one level will give insights into pathologies at the other levels, but there is no strong coupling across all of the levels.

The other approach is that of investigators of nonlinear dynamics (Mandell et al., 1982; Mandell, 1986; Babloyants, 1987), who confine themselves to individual health and assume the centrality in it of the nervous system. They are applying to neural function from psychological down to biophysical levels the recent physico-mathematical discovery that there can be cross-scale self-similarity and coupling between the different levels of turbulent phenomena that have fractal (nonintegral) dimensionalities. In this scheme, pathology at any level is a narrowing of a broad band of oscillational frequencies to over-orderliness, recovery a return to healthy variegation. Unlike the general systems approach, this approach holds that a therapeutic intervention at any level ought to be able in principle to effect recovery at other levels.

Whatever the scientific fruit of these conceptualizations, deeper and richer understanding of the effects of emotions on health will require a more detailed analysis of the exogenous and endogenous stimuli of emotions, the specific biochemical and biophysical changes evoked by them centrally and peripherally, and the specific contributions of these changes to all of the homeostatic, defense, and repair systems known and not yet known.

One possible source of relevant new knowledge comprises the medical systems of non-Western cultures. Already Western science and medicine has benefitted from the attempt to explain Chinese acupuncture in terms of the endogenous opioids discovered in the West (Liebeskind et al., 1983). Important enrichments of our understanding of emotion's effects on health may come from further attempts on the part of Western medical science to integrate its hard-won findings with the phenomenological and theoretical claims of non-Western medical science. Two examples of such integrative potentialities follow.

Possible Connections of Western and Non-Western Findings

The first example involves emotions in the sense of fairly transient feelings and moods. The particular emotion is one not often mentioned in physiological literature, that of the creative state in relation to health.

The creative emotional state of active serenity that nurtures the quest for new ideas has been a nameless state for which Clynes (1977, pp 204-206) coined the term "apreene". This state has great social importance, because the ever-evolving problems of the world require a steady stream of new solutions, as argued for example by Salk (1972). Besides being a resource for the prevention of social and physical threats to human life, the creative state can also foster individual health by enabling the adaptive reconception of one's self and of one's supposed stressors, an aspect of coping that Barnard (1985) has called "the construction of meaning".

The emotion of creativity may also express a neural state that is intrinsically salutary (Cousins, 1985).

The neural mechanisms of creativity are obscure. In apparent contradiction to modern versions (Prentky, 1979) of a Shakespeare character's claim that "The lunatic...and the poet/Are of an imagination all compact", studies of regional blood flow in schizophrenic brains show a paucity of neuronal activity in the frontal areas (Ingvar, 1980) associated with planning and imagination (Nauta, 1971). However, some association of creativity has been claimed with a tendency toward mania and depression (Holden, 1986a; Andreasen, 1987) and artists have been articulate about the relationships of their physical illnesses to their creativity (Sandblom, 1985). Nonverbal creativity has been postulated to involve the right hemisphere and a method of encouraging people to draw has been based on the assumption (Edwards, 1979). However, the sign languages of the congenitally deaf - in which poetry comprises beautiful lines in the sense of graceful spatial trajectories - are controlled by the linguistic areas of the left hemisphere (Klima and Bellugi, 1979; Poizner et al., 1987), the right hemisphere has considerable linguistic powers (Zaidel, 1985), and music involves both hemispheres (Melnechuk and Zatorre, 1987).

Ancient Yogic medicine reported discoveries about this question. It teaches that the creative state involves the balance of cerebral hemispheric activations. Such a balance is usually experienced only briefly in the transition described in section 3 from the temporary dominance of one hemisphere to that of the other. As far as I can tell, brainwaves of creative people have not been localized during the process of creating, although Jasper (1965) reported that creative thinking was signaled by low-amplitude, high-frequency EEG waves (theta) and not by high-amplitude, low-frequency waves (alpha). However, in one woman found by chance who was able to shift dominance between hemispheres at will with no neurological or Yogic knowledge, assymetries of EEG activity and correlated differences in task efficiencies were measured by Gott et al. (1984). The subject said that she found this "skill" useful in adapting to different life situations and for entering moods that were the most comforting in various situations. However, she was incapable of stabilizing the transition state of balance. Yogis report achieving hemispheric balance and voluntary control of hemispheric dominance by means of various peripheral exercises involving feedback to the brain from deliberate control of nasal airflow (Shannahoff-Khalsa and Bhajan, 1986), the effects of which have been experimentally supported (Werntz et al., 1987).

The second example involves emotions in the sense of traits. Recently, instead of seeking to associate a particular illness with one or more personality traits, Stanwyck and Anson (1986) looked for relationships between such traits and groups of disorders. From 68 published reports, they subjected data from the MMPI for 194 groups to cluster analysis. Their statistical analysis tentatively indicated that specific personality profiles are consistently associated with clusters of physical illnesses. Five clusters appeared to identify the most distinctive set of profiles. The major disorders in the five clusters are (1) alcoholism, eating disorders, (2) heart disease, asthma, general medical disorders, some multiple sclerosis, headache, cancer, (3) narcotic addiction, rheumatic fever, delivery complications, (4) nonorganic back pain, pain, intestinal disorders, some multiple sclerosis, and (5) allergy, myocardial infarction.

Stanwyck and Anson speculated about the biological basis of their personality-disease clusters in histological terms: "It may be that certain psychological dynamics affect body chemistry in such a way that only certain types of tissue - epithelial, or striated muscle, or autonomic nervous system - are predisposed toward abnormality." However, it would be interesting to consider the authors' findings in relation to the claims of traditional Chinese medicine that certain widely different illnesses are connected and that such clusters are associated with personality attributes (Requena, 1986). The Chinese clusters are arranged along 12 vertical meridians, each keyed to a major function associated with a major organ. In another context, Pettingale (1985) pointed out that the kidney, the lung, and the gastrointestinal tract are sources of major regulatory peptides and other hormones, and so is the heart, which secretes atrial natriuretic peptide. O'Regan (1986) reported informally that the first evidence for the physical existence of the Chinese meridian system was recently found at the Necker Hospital near Paris, where radioactive isotopes were injected into humans at acupuncture points and traced as they moved along a meridian at 3-6 cm/min. The electrical environment did not affect the motion, as shown by control injections of inert and ionic materials, and the motion was not along the vascular or lymphatic system.

Overall Conclusion

Heredity provides a person with an idiosyncratic constitution that has specific vulnerabilities. The physical environment is the source of such major modifiers of health as nutrients, toxic substances, and microbes. As this review has evidenced, the social environment evokes emotions that can affect defense and repair systems as well as other tissues.

Two burgeoning integrations—that of the sociopsychobiological and biomedical approaches within Western medical science, and that of all Western medical science with the medical sciences of other cultures—will speed the achievement of further understanding of how the biochemical and biophysical aspects of emotions affect and perhaps are affected by the body's defense and repair and other homeostatic mechanisms. This scientifically and medically desirable understanding can only foster the eventual human achievement of a general theory of health.

Acknowledgment

Parts of this review have been derived from a review in progress commissioned by the Institute for Noetic Sciences and the Kroc Foundation, which I thank for their support. For helpful discussions and materials, I thank W. Ross Adey, Morris H. Aprison, Claude F. Baxter, Dale Bloom, Floyd E. Bloom, Thomas Brod, Karen Bulloch, Manfred Clynes, Melvin Cohn, Norman Cousins, Dennis F. Darko, Joel Elkes, David L. Felten, Ronald Glaser, Nicholas R. Hall, James P. Henry, Michael R. Irwin, Gerald Kersenbrock, Janice K. Kiecolt-Glaser, Daniel Kripke, Seymour Levine, Steven E. Locke, Arnold J. Mandell, Neal E. Miller, James G. Miller, Walle J. H. Nauta, Brendan O'Regan, Thomas L. Roszman, Jonas Salk, David Shannahoff-Khalsa, George F. Solomon, Stephen R. Shuchter, N. Herbert Spector, Marvin Stein, Larry W. Swanson, Lydia Temoshok, Charles A. Thomas, and Harold W. Ward.

226

T. MELNECHUK

References

Achterberg, J., 1985, Imagery in Healing: Shamanism and Modern Medicine. *New Science/Shambala*, Boston.

Ackerknecht, E.H., 1982, The history of psychosomatic medicine. *Psychol Med, 12:* 17-24.

Adams, E.M., Richardson Morton, K.D., Van de Kar, L.D., and Sanjal, M., 1987. The paraventricular nucleus modulates immune function. [Abstract] *J Immunol, 16* : 11.

Adelman, G., (Ed.), 1987. "Encyclopedia of Neuroscience," 2 vols. Birkhaeuser, Boston.

Ader, R., 1981a, "A Historical Account of Conditioned Immunobiologic Responses," In: Ader, (Ed.), op cit, pp 321-352.

Ader, R., (Ed.), 1981b, "Psychoneuroimmunology," Academic Press, New York.

Ader, R., 1985, "Behaviorally Conditioned Modulation of Immunity," In: Guillemin, et al, (Eds.), op cit, pp 55-69.

Ader, R., and Cohen, N., 1985, CNS-immune system interactions: conditioning phenomena. *Behav Brain Sci, 8:* 379-426.

Ader, R., Grota, L.J., and Cohen, N., 1987, "Conditioning Phenomena and Immune Function," In: Jankovic, et al, (Eds.), op cit, pp 532-544.

Adey, W.R., 1987, "Electromagnetic Fields and the Brain Cell Microenvironment in Transmembrane Signaling," In: Adelman, G., (Ed.), op cit, pp 376-378.

Advances. Published quarterly by the Institute for the Advancement of Health, 16 East 53rd St., New York, NY 10022.

Agius, M.A., Checinski, M.E., Richman, D.P., and Chelmicka-Schorr, 1987, Sympathectomy enhances the severity of experimental autoimmune myasthenia gravis (EAMG). [Abstract] *J Immunol, 16:* 11-12.

Ahonen, J., Jibom, H., and Zederfelt, B., 1980, "Hormone Influences on Wound Healing," In: "Wound Healing and Wound Infection," Hunt, T.K., (Ed.), Appleton-Century-Crofts, New York, 99-104.

Alexander, F., 1939, Psychological aspects of medicine. *Psychosom Med, 1:* 17-18.

Alexander, F., 1950, "Psychosomatic Medicine," Norton, New York.

Amaducci, L., Bracco, L., Sorbi, S., Albanese, A., and Gainotti, G., 1983, Right and left differences of cholinergic system in the human temporal lobes. *Int J Psychophysiol, 1:* 108.

American Cancer Society, 1982, Unproven methods of cancer management: O. C. Simonton. *CA-A Cancer J for Clinicians, 32:* 58-61.

Ames, B.N., 1983, Dietary carcinogens and anticarcinogens. *Science, 221:* 1256-1264.

Angeletti, R.H., and Hickey, W.F., 1985, A neuroendocrine marker in tissues of the immune system. *Science, 230:* 89-90.

Anisman, H., and Zacharko, R.M., 1983, Stress and neoplasia: Speculations and caveats. *Behav Med Update, 5:* 27-35.

Anonymous, 1984, [Editorial.] *Br Med J, 1:* 1163.

Apffel, C.A., 1976, Nonimmunological host defenses: A review. *Cancer Res, 36:* 1527-1537.

Armstrong, D., Sohal, R.S., Cutler, R.G., and Slater, T.F., (Eds .), 1984, "Free Radicals in Molecular Biology, Aging, and Disease," Raven, New York.

Arnetz, B.B., Wasserman, J., Petrini, B., Brenner, S.O., Levi, L., Eneroth, P., Salovaara, H., Hjelm, R., Salovaara, L., Theorell, T., and Petterson, I.L., 1987, Immune function in unemployed women. *Psychosom Med, 49:* 3-12.

Aronowski, J., Dougherty, P.M., Samorajski, T., Pellis, N.R., and Dafny, N., 1985, Irradiation modifies the analgesic effects of morphine. *Soc Neurosci Abstr, 11:* 1200.

Arrenbrecht, S., 1974, Specific binding of growth hormone to thymocytes. *Nature (London), 252:* 255-257.

Ax, A.F., 1953, The physiological differentiation between fear and anger in humans. *Psychosom Med 15:* 433-442.

Axelrod, J., and Reisine, T.D., 1984, Stress hormones: Their interaction and regulation. *Science, 224:* 452-459.

Babloyantz, A., 1986, "Molecules, Dynamics, and Life: An Introduction to the Self-Organization of Matter," Wiley, New York.

Bachrach, L.L., 1975, Marital Status and Mental Disorder: An Analytical Review," U.S. Printing Office, Washington, DC.

Bahnson, C.B., 1981, Stress and cancer: The state of the art. Part 1. *Psychosomatics, 21:* 975-981. Part 2. *Psychosomatics, 22:* 207-220.

Bahnson, C.B., and Bahnson, M.B., 1966, Role of the ego defenses: Denial and repression in the aetiology of malignant neoplasm. *Ann N Y Acad Sci, 125:* 827.

Baker, G.A., Santalo, R., and Blumenstein, J., 1977, Effect of psychotropic agents upon the histogenic response of human T-lymphocytes. *Biol Psychiatry, 12:* 159-169.

Baker, G.B.H., 1987, Psychological factors and immunity. Invited review. *J Psychosom Res, 31:* 1-10.

Baker, G.B.H., and Brewerton, D.A., 1981, Rheumatoid arthritis: A psychiatric assessment. *Br Med J, 282:* 2014.

Baker, G.B.H., Irani, M.S., Byrom, N.A., Negvekar, N.M., Wood, R.J., Hobbs, J.R., and Brewerton, D.A., 1985, Stress, cortisol concentrations, and lymphocyte subpopulations. *Br Med J, 290:* 1393.

Bandura, A., 1985, Catecholamine secretion as a function of perceived coping self-sufficiency. *J Counseling Clin Psychol, 58:* 406-414.

Barnard, D., 1985, Psychosomatic medicine and the problem of meaning. *Bull Menninger Clin, 29:* 10-28.

Barnes, D.M. 1986), Nervous and immune system disorders linked in a variety of diseases. *Science, 232:* 160-161.

Bar-Shavit, Z., Terry, S., Blumberg, S., and Goldman, R., 1982, Neurotensin- macrophage interaction: Specific binding and augmentation of phagocytosis. *Neuropeptides, 2:* 325-335.

Bartolome, J.V., Bartolome, M.B., Daltner, L.A., Evans, C.J., Barchas, J.D., Kuhn, C.M., and Schanberg, S.M., 1986, Effects of beta-endorphin on ornithine decarboxylase in tissues of developing rats: A potential role for this endogenous neuropeptide in the modulation of tissue growth. *Life Sciences, 38:* 2355-2362.

Bartrop, R.W., Luckhurst, E., Lazarus, L., Kiloh, L.G., and Penny, R., 1977, Depressed lymphocyte function after bereavement. *Lancet, 1:* 834-836.

Beecher, H.K., 1955, The powerful placebo. *JAMA, 159:* 1602-1606.

Beed, E.A., O'Dorisio, S., O'Dorisio, T.M., and Gaginella, T.S., 1983, Demonstration of a functional receptor for vasoactive intestinal polypeptide on Molt 4b T lymphoblasts. *Regul Pept, 6:* 1-12.

Beliauskas, L.A., 1983, Considerations of depression and stress in the etiology of cancer. *Behav Med Update, 5:* 23-26.

Benson, D.F., ⹁984, The neurology of human emotion. *Bull Clin Neurosci, 49:* 23-42.

Benson, D.F., and Zaidel, E., (Eds.), 1985, "The Dual Brain: Hemispheric Specialization in Humans," Guilford, New York.

Benson, H., 1975, "The Relaxation Response," Morrow, New York.

Benson, M., and Epstein, M.D., 1975, The placebo effect. A neglected asset in the care of patients. *JAMA, 232:* 1225-1227.

Berkman, L., Borysenko, J., Locke, S.E., Rogers, M., and Partridge, A., 1983, Psychosocial determinants of immunologically mediated diseases. Boston, Apr 15, 1983. [Conference report.] *Advances 1(Intro):* 27-29.

Berkman, L., and Syme, S., 1979, Social networks, host resistance, and mortality: A nine-year follow-up study of Alameda County residents. *Am J Epidemiol, 109:* 186-204.

Besedovsky, H., del Rey, A., and Sorkin, E., 1985, Immunological- neuroendocrine feedback circuits. In: Guillemin, et al, (Eds.), op cit, pp 163-177.

Besedovsky, H., del Rey, A., Sorkin, E., and Dinarello, C.A., 1986, Immunoregulatory feedback between interleukin-1 and glucocorticoid hormones. *Science, 233:* 652-654.

Bistrian, B.R., Blackburn, G.L., and Scrimshaw, N.S., 1975, Cellular immunity in semistarved states in hospitalized adults. *Am J Psychiatry, 28:* 1148-1155.

Bitar, K.N., and Makhlouf, G.M., 1982, Relaxation of isolated gastric smooth muscle cells by vasoactive intestinal peptide. *Science, 216:* 531-535.

Biziere, K., Guillaumin, J.M., Degenne, D., Bardos, P., Renoux, M., and Renoux, G., 1985, Lateralized neocortical modulation of the T-cell lineage. In: Guillemin, et al, (Eds.), op cit, pp 81-94.

Blalock, J.E., 1984, The immune system as a sensory organ. *J Immunol ,132:* 1067-1070.

Blalock, J.E., and Smith, E.M., 1985, A complete regulatory loop between the immune and neuroendocrine systems. *Fed Proc 44:* 108-111.

Blennerhassett, M.G., Stead, R.H., and Bienenstock, J., 1987, Association and interaction between sympathetic neurons and mast cells in vitro. [Abstract] *Biophys J ,51:* 65a.

Bloom, B.L., Asher, S.J., and White, S.W., 1978, Marital disruption as a stressor: A review and analysis. *Psychol Bull 85:* 867-894.

Bohn, M.C., Kessler, J.A., Adler, J.E., Markey, K.A., Goldstein, M., and Black, I.B., 1984, Simultaneous expression of the SP-peptidergic and noradrenergic phenotypes in rat sympathetic neurons. *Brain Res 298:* 378-381.

Boltwood, M., 1986, Cited in: Level of burn recovery linked to attitude of patient. *Am Med News, May 9:* 32.

Borysenko, J., 1984, "Review of The Denial of Stress, edited by Schlomo Breznitz. *Advances 1(4):* 74-77.

Boyd, W., 1966, "The Spontaneous Regression of Cancer," Thomas, Springfield, Illinois.

Braun, B., (Ed.), 1986, "Treatment of Multiple Personality Disorder," American Psychiatric Press, Washington, D.C.

Braun, B.G., 1983, Psychophysiological phenomena in multiple personality. *Am J Clin Hypn 26 :* 124-137.

Breznitz, S., (Ed.), 1983, "The Denial of Stress," International Universities Press, Madison, Connecticut.

Brittain, R.W., and Wiener, N.I., 1985, Neural and Pavlovian influences on immunity. *Pavlovian J Biol Sci 20:* 181-194.

Bronson, G., 1987, Beyond the band-aid. *Forbes June 1:* 160-161.

Brooks, C.M., 1987, Autonomic nervous system, nature and functional role. In: Adelman, (Ed.), op cit, pp 96-98.

Brown, G.W., and Harris, T.O., 1978, "Social Origins of Depression," Tavistock, London.

Bulloch, K., 1985, Neuroanatomy of lymphoid tissue: A review. In: Guillemin et al, (Eds.), op cit, pp 111-141.

Bulloch, K., and Bossone, S.A., 1987, Nerve-related 3S acetyl-cholinesterase in murine thymus. In: Jankovic et al, (Eds,.) op cit,pp 338-345.

Burgus, R., Dunn, T.F., Desiderio, D., Ward, D.N., Vale, W., and Guillemin, R., 1970, Characterization of ovine hypothalamic hypophysiotropic TSH-releasing factor. *Nature 226:* 321-325.

Burnet, F.H., 1965, Somatic mutations and chronic disease. *Br Med J 1:* 338-342.

Burnet, S.M., 1974, "Intrinsic Mutagenesis: A Genetic Approach to Ageing," Wiley, New York.

Campbell, R., 1982, The lateralization of emotion: A critical review. *Intern J Psychol 17* : 211-229.

Cannon, W.B., 1914, The emergency function of the adrenal medulla in pain and the major emotions. *Amer J Physiol 33:* 356-372.

Cannon, W., 1932, (2nd ed. 1963), "The Wisdom of the Body," Norton, NY.

Cannon, W., 1942, "Voodoo" death. *Am Anthropol 44:* 169.

Cappel, R., Gregoire, F., Thiry, L., and Sprecher, S., 1978, Antibody and cell mediated immunity to herpes simplex virus in psychotic depression. *J Clin Psychiatry 39:* 266-268.

Cassel, J., 1973, The relation of the urban environment to health: Implications for prevention. *Mt Sinai J Med 40 :* 539-550.

Cassileth, B.R., Lusk, E.J., Miller, D.S., Brown, L.L., and Miller, C., 1985, Psychosocial correlates of survival in advanced malignant disease? *N Engl J Med 312:* 1551-1555.

Cerutti, P., 1985, Prooxidant states and tumor promotion. *Science 227:* 375-381.

Cerutti, P., 1986, The role of active oxygen in tumor promotion. In: "Biochemical and Molecular Epidemiology of Human Cancer," C. Harris (Ed.), Liss, New York, pp 167-176.

Chelmicka-Schorr, E., Checinski, M.E., and Arnason, B.G.W., 1987, Sympathectomy augments the severity of experimental allergic encephalomyelitis (EAE) in rats. [Abstract.] *J Immunol 16:* 30-31.

Clynes, M., 1973, "Sentics: Biocybernetics of emotion communication" Annals NY Acad Sc 220, (3), 55-131.

Clynes, M., 1977, "Sentics: The Touch of the Emotions", Anchor Press/Doubleday, New York, pp 1-243.

Clynes, M., 1983, Personal communication.

Clynes, M., 1987, On music and healing. In: "Music and Medicine," R. Spintke & R. Droh (Eds.), Springer Verlag, Berlin, pp 13-31.

Coe, C., Rosenberg, L.T., and Levine, S ., 1987, Immunological consequences of psychological disturbance and maternal loss in infancy. In: "Advances in Infancy Research," C. Rovee-Collier & L.P. Lipsitt (Eds.), Ablex, Norwood, New Jersey, in press.

Cohen, J., Cullen, J.W., and Martin, L.R., 1982, "Psychosocial Dimensions of Cancer," Raven, New York.

Cohn, M., 1968, Molecular biology of expectation. In: "Nucleic Acids in Immunology," I.J. Plescia & W. Brown (Eds.), Springer, New York, pp 671-715.

Cohn, M., 1985, What are the "must" elements of immune responsiveness? In: Guillemin, et al, (Eds.), op cit, pp 3-25.

Collins, A., Downes, C.S., and Johnson, R.T., 1984, "DNA Repair and Its Inhibition," IRL Press, Oxford, England.

Collins, A., Johnson, R.T., and Boyle, J.M., 1987, Molecular biology of DNA repair. *J Cell Sci suppl 6:* 1-353.

Connolly, J., 1985, Life happenings and organic disease. *Br J Hospital Med 33:* 24-27.

Cooper, E.L., (Ed.), 1984, "Stress, Immunity, and Aging," Dekker, New York.

Cooper, J.R., Bloom, F.E., and Roth, R.H., 1986, "Neuroactive Peptides. The Biochemical Basis of Neuropharmacology," (5th ed.), Oxford University Press, New York, pp 352-393.

Corballis, M.C., 1983, "Human Laterality," Academic, New York.

Cousins, N., 1976, The anatomy of an illness (as seen by the patient). *N E J Med 295:* 1458-1463.

Cousins, N., 1979, "The Anatomy of an Illness," Norton, New York.

Cousins, N., 1983, "The Healing Heart," Norton, New York.

Cousins, N., 1983, Personal communication.

Cousins, N., 1985, Can creativity heal? [Review of Sandblom, P., 1985, Creativity and Disease.] *Advances 2(3):* 69-72.

Cox, T., and Mackay C., 1982, Psychosocial factors and psychophysiological mechanisms in the aetiology and development of cancers. *Soc Sci Med 16:* 381-396.

Cunningham, A.J., 1984, Psychotherapy for cancer: A review. *Advances 1(4):* 8-14.

Cunningham, A,J., 1985, The influence of mind on cancer. *Canadian Psychology 26:* 13-29.

Curti, R., Radice, L., Cesana, G.C., Zanettini, R., and Grieco, A., 1982, Work, stress and immune system: Lymphocyte reactions during rotating shift work. Preliminary results. *Med Lavoro 290:* 1393.

Dafny, N., Dougherty, P., and Pellis, N.R., 1985, The effect of immunosuppression and opiates upon the visual evoked responses of cortical and subcortical structures. *Soc Neurosci Abstr 11:* 907.

Danek, A., O'Dorisio, M.S., O'Dorisio, T.M., and George, J.M., 1983, Specific binding sites for vasoactive intestinal polypeptide on nonadherent peripheral blood lymphocytes. *J Immunol 131:* 1173-1177.

Darko, D.F., Lucas, A.H., and Gillin, J.C., 1986, Replication of lower lymphocyte blastogenesis in depression [letter]. *Am J Psychiat 43:* 1492-1493.

Davidson, R.J., 1983, Affect, repression, and cerebral asymmetry. In: Temoshok, et al, (Eds.), op cit, pp 123-135.

Davies, T., 1987), Peculiar progress. [Review of Paradoxes in Immunology, Geoffrey W. Hoffman, Julia G. Levy, & Gerald T. Nepom (Eds.).] *Nature 327:* 110-111.

Del Rey, A., Besedovsky, H., Sorkin, E., and Dinarello, C.A., 1987, Interleukin-1 and glucocorticoid hormones integrate an immunoregulatory feedback circuit. In: Jankovic, et al, (Eds.), op cit, 85-90.

Devoino, L.V., and Alperina, E.L., 1985, Stimulation of the immune response by activation of dopaminergic system: Interaction with serotonergic system in neuroimmuno-modulation. In: Spector, (Ed.), op cit, pp 124-128.

Diamond, J.M., 1987, Infectious, genetic, or both? *Nature 328:* 199-200.

Dillon, K.M., Minchoff, B., and Baker, K.H., 1985-86, Positive emotional states and enhancement of the immune system. *Int J Psychiatry Med 15:* 13-17.

Ditto, B., 1987, Sibling similarities in cardiovascular reactivity to stress. *Psychophysiology, 24:* 353-360.

Doherty, W.J., Baird, M.A., and Becker, L.A., 1986, Family medicine and the biopsychosocial model: The road toward integration. *Advances 3(3):* 17-28.

Dohrenwend, B.S., and Dohrenwend, B.P., (Eds.), 1974, "Stressful Life Events: Their Nature and Effects," Wiley, New York.

Dorian, B., Garfinkel, P., Brown, G., Shore, A., Gladman, D., Keystone, E., 1982, Aberrations in lymphocyte subpopulations and function during psychological stress. *Clin Exper Immunol 50:* 132-138.

Dorian, B., Garfinkel, P., Keystone, E., Gorczynski, R., Darby, P., and Garner, D., 1985, Occupational stress and immunity [abstract]. *Psychosom Med 47:* 77.

Dowling, S.J., 1984, Lourdes cures and their medical assessment. *J Roy Soc Med 77:* 634-638.

Dreher, H., 1986, The perspectives and programs of behavioral medicine. *Advances 3(1):* 8-21.

Eccles, R., and Lee, R.L., 1981, The influence of the hypothalamus on the sympathetic innervation of the nasal vasculature of the cat. *Acta Otolaryngol 91:* 127-134.

Edwards, B., 1979, "Drawing with the Right Side of the Brain.,"Tarcher, Los Angeles.

Ekman, P., Freisen, W.V., and Ellsworth, P., 1972, "Emotion in the Human Face," Pergamon, New York.

Ekman, P., Levenson, R.W., and Friesen, W.V., 1983, Autonomic nervous system activity distinguishes among emotions. *Science 221:* 1208-1210.

Ellendorf, F., and Parvizi , N., 1980, The endocrine function of the brain. In: "Role of Extrahypothalamic Centers in Neuroendocrine Integration," M. Motta (Ed.), Raven, New York, pp 297-325.

Engel, B.T., 1986, An essay on the circulation as behavior. *Behav Brain Sci 9:* 285-318.

Engel, G.L., 1954, Selection of clinical material in psychosomatic medicine. *Psychosom Med 16:* 368-373.

Engel, G.L., 1967, The concept of psychosomatic disorders. *J Psychosom Res 11:* 31-39.

Engel, G.L., 1971, Sudden and rapid death during psychological stress. *Ann Intern Med 74:* 771-782.

Engel, G.L., 1977, The need for a new medical model: A challenge for biomedicine. *Science 196:* 129-136.

Eremina, O.F., and Devoino, L.V., 1973, Production of humoral antibodies in rabbits following destruction of the nucleus of the midbrain raphe. *Byull Eksp Biol Med 74:* 258-261.

Ernster, B.L., Sacks, S., Selvin, S., and Petrakis, N.L., 1979), Cancer incidence by marital status: U.S. third national cancer survey. *J Natl Cancer Inst 63:* 578-585.

Eskola, J., Ruuskanen, O., Soppi, E., Viljanen, M.K., Jarvinen, M., Toivonen, H., and Kouvalainen, K., 1981, Effect of sport stress on lymphocyte transformation and antibody formation. *Clin Exp Immunol 32:* 339-345.

Evans, F.J., 1984, Unravelling placebo effects: Expectations and the placebo response. *Advances 1(3):* 11-20.

Everson, T.C., and Cole, W.H., 1966, "Spontaneous Regression of Cancer," Saunders, Philadelphia.

Felten, D.L., Felten, S.Y., Carlson, S.L., Olschowka, J.A., and Livnat, S., 1985, Noradrenergic and peptidergic innervation of lymphoid tissue. In: Goetzl, (Ed.), op cit, pp 755s-765s.

Felten, S.Y., Olschowka, J.A., and Felten, D.L., 1987, Tyrosine hydroxylase positive nerve terminals contact lymphocytes in the periarteriolar lymphatic sheath of the rat splenic white pulp. *Soc Neurosci Abstr 13:* 1379.

Ferguson, R.M., Schmidtke, J.R., and Simmons, R.L., 1976, Differential effects of chlorpromazine on the in vitro generation and effector function of cytotoxic lymphocytes. *J Exp Med 143:* 232-237.

Fischman, H.K., 1985, Personal communication.

Fischman, H.K., and Kelly, D.D., 1987, Sister chromatid exchanges induced by behavioral stress. In: Jankovic, et al, (Eds.), op cit, pp 426-435.

Flohe, L., Giertz, H., and Beckmann, R., 1985, Free radical scavengers as anti-inflammatory drugs? In: "Handbook of Inflammation, Vol 5: The Pharmacology of Inflammation," I.L. Bonta, M.A. Bray, & M.J. Parnham (Eds.), Elsevier, New York, pp 255-270.

Flor-Henry, P., 1983, "Cerebral Basis of Psychopathology," Wright/PSG, Boston.

Fox, B.H., 1978, Premorbid psychological factors as related to cancer incidence. *J Behav Med 1:* 45-113.

Fox, B.H., 1981, Psychosocial factors and the immune system in human cancer. In: Ader, (Ed.), op cit, pp 103-157.

Fox, B.H., and Newberry, B.H., 1984, "Impact of Psychoendocrine Systems in Cancer and Immunity," Hogrefe, Toronto, Canada.

Frankenhaeuser, M., 1975, Experimental approaches to the study of catecholamines and emotion. In: "Emotions, Their Parameters and Measurement," L. Levi (Ed.), Raven, New York.

Frankenhaeuser, M., 198,) Challenge-control interaction as reflected in sympathetic-adrenal and pituitary-adrenal activity: Comparison between the sexes. *Scand J Psychol suppl 1:* 158-164.

Gainer, H., 1987, Neuropeptide precursors. In: Adelman, (Ed.), op cit, pp 834-835.

Gainotti, G., 1972, Emotional behavior and hemispheric side of lesion. *Cortex 8:* 41-45.

Ganguli, R., Rabin, B.S., Kelly, R.H., Lyte, M., and Ragu, U., 1987, Clinical and laboratory evidence of autoimmunity in acute schizophrenia. In: Jankovic, et al, (Eds.), op cit, pp 676-685.

Garfield, E., 1986, Psychoneuroimmunology: A new facet of the mind-body dialogue. *Current Contents 1986 (May5):* 3-11.

Gellhorn, E., 1967, "Principles of Autonomic Somatic Integrations," University of Minnesota Press, Minneapolis, Minnesota.

Gensler, B., and Bernstein, H., 1981, DNA damage as a primary cause of aging. *Q Rev Biol* 56: 279-303.

Gerendai, I., 1984, Lateralization of neuroendocrine control. In: "Cerebral Dominance: The Biological Foundations," N. Geschwind & A.M. Galaburda (Eds.), Harvard University Press, Cambridge, Massachusetts, pp 167-178.

Geschwind, N., and Galaburda, A.M., 1985, Cerebral lateralization. Brain mechanisms, associations, and pathology: A hypothesis and a program for research. *Pt I Arch Neurol* 42: 428-459. *Pt II Arch Neurol 42:* 521-552. *Pt III Arch Neurol 42:* 634-654.

Geschwind, N., and Galaburda, A.M., 1987, "Cerebral Lateralization: Biological Mechanisms, Associations, and Pathology," MIT Press, Cambridge, Massachusetts.

Ghanta, V.K., Hiramoto, R.N., Solvason, H.B., and Spector, N.H., 1985, Neural and environmental influences on neoplasia and conditioning of NK activity. In: Goetzl, (Ed.), op cit, pp 848s-852s.

Gilad, G.M., 1987, The stress-induced response of the septo-hippocampal cholinergic system. A vectorial outcome of psycho-neuroendocrinological interactions. *Psychoneuroendocrinology, 12:* 167-184.

Gilman, S.C., Schwartz, J.M., Milner, R.J., Bloom, F.E., and Feldman, J.D., 1982, Beta-endorphin enhances lymphocyte proliferative responses. *Proc Natl Acad Sci USA, 79:* 4226-4230.

Glaser, R., Kiecolt-Glaser, J.K., Speicher, C.E., and Holliday, J.E., 1985, Stress, loneliness, and changes in herpesvirus latency. *J Behav Med, 8:* 249-260.

Glaser, R., Kiecolt-Glaser, K.C., Stout, J.C., Tarr, K.L., Speicher, C.E., and Holliday, J.E., 1985, Stress-related impairments in cellular immunity. *Psychiatry Res, 16:* 233-29.

Glaser, R., Rice, J., Sheridan, J., Fertel, R., Stout, J., Speicher, C., Pinsky, D., Lotur, M., Post, A., Beck, M., and Kiecolt-Glaser, J., 1987, Stress-related immune suppression: Health implications. *Brain Behavior Immunity,* in press.

Glaser, R., Rice, J., Speicher, C.E., Stout, J.C., and Kiecolt-Glaser, J.K., 1987, Stress depresses interferon production by leukocytes concomitant with a decrease in natural killer cell activity. *Behavioral Neurosci,* in press.

Glaser, R., Thorn, B.E., Tarr, K.L., Kiecolt-Glaser, J.K., and D'Ambrosio, S.M., 1985, Effects of stress on methyltransferase synthesis: An important DNA repair enzyme. *Health Psychol, 4:* 403-412.

Glenn, N.D., and Weaver, C.N., 1981, The contribution of marital happiness to global happiness. *J Marriage Fam, 43:* 161-168.

Glick, S.D., Meibach, R.C., Cox, R.D., and Maayani, S., 1979, Multiple and interrelated functional asymmetries in rat brain. *Life Sci, 25:* 395-400.

Goetzl, E.J., (Ed.), 1985, Neuromodulation of immunity and hypersensitivity. *J Immunol, 135(suppl).*

Goldstein, A., 1976, Opioid peptides (endorphins) in pituitary and brain. *Science, 193:* 1081-1086.

Goldstein, A., 1980, Thrills in response to music and other stimuli. *Physiol Psychol, 8:* 126-129.

Goldstein, A.L., Rossio, J., Kolyaskina, G.I., Emory, L.E., Overall, J.E., Thurman, G.B., and Hatcher, J., 1980, Immunological components in schizophrenia. In: "Perspectives in Schizophrenia Research," C. Baxter & T. Melnechuk (Eds.), Raven, New York, pp 249-267.

Goleman, D., 1935, Opioids and denial: Two mechanisms for bypassing pain. *Advances, 2(3):* 35-45.

Gorczynski, R.M., Kennedy, M., and Ciampi, A., 1985, Cimetidine reverses tumor growth enhancement of plasmacytoma tumors in mice demonstrating conditioned immunosuppression. *J Immunol, 134:* 4261-4266.

Gordon, B.L., 1935, "Medicine Throughout Antiquity," Macmillan, New York.

Gordon, J.S., 1980, The paradigm of holistic medicine. In: "Health for the Whole Person: The Complete Guide to Holistic Medicine," A.C. Hastings, J. Fadiman, & J.S. Gordon (Eds.), Westview, Boulder, Colorado, pp 3-27.

Gorman, J.R., and Locke, S.E., 1987, Neural, endocrine, and immune interactions. In: "Comprehensive Textbook of Psychiatry," H. Kaplan & B. Sadock (Eds.), Williams & Wilkins, Baltimore. In press.

Gott, P.S., Hughes, E.C., and Whipple, K., 1984, Voluntary control of two lateralized conscious states: Validation by electrical and behavioral studies. *Neuropsychologia, 22:* 65-72.

Gottschalk, L.A., Welch, W.D., and Weiss, J., 1982, Vulnerability and the immune response. *Psychother Psychosom, 39:* 23-35.

Green, L.W., Tryon, W.W., Marks, B., and Huryn, J., 1986, Periodontal disease as a function of life events stress. *J Human Stress, 12:* 32-36.

Greer, S., and McEwan, P.J.M., (Eds.), 1985), Cancer and the mind. *Soc Sci Med, 20:* 771-853.

Greer, S., and Morris, T., 1975, Psychological attributes of women who develop breast cancer: A controlled study. *J Psychosom Res, 19:* 147-.

Greer, S., and Watson, M., 1985, Towards a psychobiological model of cancer: Psychological considerations. *Soc Sci Med, 20:* 773-777.

Grinker, R.R., 1973, "Psychosomatic Concepts," Revised ed. Jason Aronson, New York.

Grossarth-Maticek, R., 1980, Social psychotherapy and course of the disease. First experiences with cancer patients. *Psychother Psychosom, 33:* 129-138.

Grossarth-Maticek, R., Bastiaans, J., and Kanazir, D.T., 1985, Psychosocial factors as strong predictors of mortality from cancer, ischaemic heart disease and stroke: The Yugoslav prospective study. *J Psychosom Res, 29:* 167-176.

Grossarth-Maticek, R., Siegrist, J., and Vetter, H., 1982, Interpersonal repression as a predictor of cancer. *Soc Sci Med, 16:* 493-498.

Grossman, R., 1985, Ecumenical medicine. *Advances, 2(4):* 39-50.

Guidotti, A., and Grandison, L., 1979, Participation of endorphins in the regulation of pituitary function. In: "Endorphins in Mental Health Research," E. Usdin, W.E. Bunney Jr., & N.S. Kline (Eds.), Macmillan, New York, pp 416-422.

Guillemin, R.G., Cohen, M., and Melnechuk, T., (Eds.), 1985, "Neural Modulation of Immunity," Raven, New York.

Guth, L., 1987, Trophic effects. In: Adelman, G., (Ed.), op cit, pp 1237-1238.

Hadden, J.W., 1987, Neuroendocrine modulation of the thymus-dependent immune system: Agonists and mechanisms. In: Jankovic, et al, (Eds.), op cit, pp 39-48.

Halberg, F., 1967, Claude Bernard and the "extreme variability of the internal milieu". In: "Claude Bernard and Experimental Medicine," F. Grande & M.B. Visscher (Eds.), Shenkman, Cambridge, Massachusetts, pp 193-210.

Hall, H.H., 1983, Hypnosis and the immune system: A review with implications for cancer and the psychology of healing. *Am J Clin Hypnosis, 25:* 92-103.

Hall, N., 1987, Imagery does affect aspects of our physiology. The question is, can it be used to stimulate the immune system? (Interview.) *Advances, 4(1):* 3.

Hall, N.R., and Goldstein, A.L., 1985, Neurotransmitters and host defense. In Guillemin, et al, (Eds.), op cit, 143-156.

Hall, N.R., and Goldstein, A.L., 1987, Immune system, modulation by the central nervous system. In: Adelman, (Ed.), op cit, pp 523-524.

Hall, N.R., McGillis, J.P., Spangelo, B.L., Healy, D.L., Chrousos, G.P., Schulte, H.M., and Goldstein, A.L., 1985, Thymic hormone effects on the brain and neuroendocrine circuits. In: Guillemin, et al, (Eds.), op cit, 179-193.

Hallam, R.S., 1985, "Anxiety—Psychological Perspectives on Panic and Agoraphobia," Academic, Orlando, Florida.

Hamburg, D., and Elliott, G., 1981, Biobehavioral sciences: An emerging research agenda. *Psychiatr Clin North Am,* 407-421.

Hamburg, D.A., Elliott, G.R., and Parron, D.L., 1982, "Health and Behavior: Frontiers of Research in the Biobehavioral Sciences," Nat Acad Press, Washington, D.C.

Hanley, M.R., 1985, Neuropeptides as mitogens. *Nature, 315:* 14.

Harman, D., 1981, The aging process. *Proc Natl Acad Sci USA, 78:* 7124-7128.

Hastings, A.C., Fadiman, J., and Gordon, J.S., (Eds.), 1980, "Health for the Whole Person: The Complete Guide to Holistic Medicine," Westview, Boulder, Colorado.

Hazum, E., Chang, K.G., and Cuatrecasas, P., 1979, Specific non-opiate receptors for beta-endorphin. *Science, 205:* 1033-1035.

Heijnen, C.J., and Ballieux, R.E., 1986, Influence of opioid peptides on the immune system. *Advances, 3(4):* 114-121.

Heisel, J.S., Locke, S.E., Kraus, L.J., and Williams, R.M., 1986, Natural killer cell activity and MMPI scores of a cohort of college students. *Am J Psychiat, 143:* 1382-1386.

Heller, B.W., 1983, Emotion: Toward a biopsychosocial paradigm. In: Temoshok, et al, (Eds.), op cit, pp 189-194.

Hellstrand, K., Hermodsson, S., and Strannegard, O., 26, Evidence for a beta-adrenorecep-tor-mediation regulation of human natural killer cells. *J Immunol, 134:* 4095-4099.

Helsing, K.J., Szklo, M., and Comstock, G.W., 1981, Factors associated with mortality after widowhood. *Am J Public Health, 71:* 802-809.

Henry, J.P., 1980, Present concept of stress theory. In: "Catecholamines and Stress: Recent Advances," E. Usdin, R. Kvetnansky & I.J. Kopin (Eds.), Elsevier, New York, pp 557-570.

Henry, J.P., 1982, The relation of social to biological processes in disease. *Soc Sci Med, 16:* 369-380.

Herberman, R., 1982, Possible effects of central nervous system activity on natural killer (NK) cell activity. In: S. Levy, (Ed.), op cit.

Hess, W.R., 1957, "Functional Organization of the Diencephalon," Grune and Stratton, New York.

Hinkle, L.E., Jr., 1974, The effect of exposure to cultural change, social change, and changes in interpersonal relationships on health. In: Dohrenwend & Dohrenwend, (Eds.), op cit, pp 9-44.

Hiramoto, R.N., Hiramoto, N.S., Solvason, H.B., and Ghanta, V.K., 1987, Regulation of natural immunity (NK activity) by conditioning. In: Jankovic, et al, (Eds.), op cit, pp 545-552.

Hokfelt, T., 1987, Neuronal mapping by transmitter histochemistry with special reference to coexistence of multiple synaptic messengers. In: Adelman, (Ed.), op cit, pp 821-824.

Hokfelt, T., Johansson, O., and Goldstein, M., 1984, Chemical anatomy of the brain. *Science, 225:* 1326-1334.

Holaday, J.W., 1983, Cardiovascular effects of the endogenous opiate system. *Ann Rev Pharmacol Toxicol, 23:* 541-594.

Holden, C., 1986a, Manic depression and creativity. *Science, 233:* 725.

Holden, C., 1986b, Researchers grapple with problems of updating classic psychological test. *Science, 233:* 1249-1251.

Holden, C., 1987, Measuring personality. *Science, 237:* 599.

Holmes, T.H., and Rahe, R.H., 1967, The social readjustment rating scale. *J Psychosom Res, 11:* 213-218.

Hoover, R., and Fraumeni, J.F., 1973, Risk of cancer in renal transplant recipients. *Lancet, 2:* 55-57.

Huemer, R.P., 1977, A theory of diagnosis for orthomolecular medicine. *J Theoret Biol, 67:* 625-635. (1983) [Reprinted with a new footnote.] *Advances, 1(3):* 52-59.

Hunt, S.P., Pini, A., and Evan, G., 1987, Induction of c-fos-like protein in spinal cord neurons following sensory stimulation. *Nature, 328:* 632-634.

Ingvar, D.H., 1980, Abnormal distribution of cerebral activity in chronic schizophrenia: A neurophysiological interpretation. In: "Perspectives in Schizophrenia Research," C.F. Baxter & T. Melnechuk (Eds.), Raven, New York, pp 107-130.

Irwin, M., Daniels, M., Bloom, E.T., Smith, T.L., and Weiner, H., 1987, Life events, depressive symptoms, and immune function. *Am J Psychiatry, 144:* 437-441.

Irwin, M., Vale, W., and Britton, K., 1987, Central corticotrophin- releasing factor suppresses natural killer cytotoxicity. *Brain Behavior Immunity, 1:* 81-87.

Ischlondsky, N.D., 1955, The inhibitory process in the cerebro-physiological laboratory and in the clinic. *Am J Med Sci, 174:* 231-244.

Jacobs, S., and Ostfeld, A., 1977, An epidemiological review of the mortality of bereavement. *Psychosom Med, 39:* Z344-357.

James, R., and Bradshaw, R.A., 1984, Polypeptide growth factors. *Ann Rev Biochem, 53:* 259-292.

Jankovic, B.D., Markovic, B.M., and Spector, N.H., (Eds.), 1987, Neuroimmune Interactions: Proceedings of the Second International Workshop on Neuroimmunomodulation. *Ann N Y Acad Sci, 496:* 1-756.

Jansen, M.A., and Muenz, L.R., 1984, A retrospective study of personality variables associated with fibrocystic disease and breast cancer. *J Psychosom Res, 28:* 35-42.

Jasnoski, M.L., 1986, Presentation at the Society for Behavioral Medicine 7th Annual Scientific Sessions, San Francisco, March 5-8.

Jasper, H.H., 1965, Pathological states of brain mechanisms in different states of consciousness. In: "Brain and Conscious Experience," J.C. Eccles (Ed.), Springer, New York, pp 256-282.

Jemmot, J.B., Borysenko, J.Z., Borysenko, M., McClelland, D.C., Chapman, R., Meyer, D., and Benson, H., 1983, Academic stress, power motivation and decrease in secretion rate of salivary secretory immunoglobulin A. *Lancet, 1:* 1400-1402.

Jenkins, C.D., 1977, Epidemiological studies of of the psychosomatic aspects of coronary heart disease. *Adv Psychosom Med, 9:* 1-19.

Jerne, N.K., 1984, Idiotypic networks and other preconceived ideas. *Immunol Rev, 79:* 5-24.

Jessel, T.M., 1985, Cellular interactions at the central and peripheral terminals of primary sensory neurons. *J Immunology, 135:* 746s-749s.

Jessel, T.M., and Womack, M.D., 1985, Substance P and the novel mammalian tachykinins: A diversity of receptors and cellular actions. *Trends In NeuroScience, 8:* 43-45.

Johansson, M., and Sullivan, L., 1975, Influence of treatment and change of climate in women with rheumatoid arthritis. *Scand J Rheumatol, suppl 9:* 1-193.

Johnson, H.M., and Torres, B.A., 1985, Regulation of lymphokine production by arginine vasopressin and oxytocin: Modulation of lymphocyte function by neurohypophyseal hormones. In: Goetzl, (Ed.), op cit, pp 773s-775s.

Johnson, H.M., Torres, B.A., Smith, E.M., Dion, L.D., and Blalock, J.E ., 1984, Regulation of lymphokine (gamma-interferon) production by corticotropin. *J Immunol, 132:* 246-250.

Johnson, R.T., Collins, A.R.S., Squires, S., Mullinger, A.M., Elliott, G.C., Downes, C.S., and Rasko, I., 1987, DNA repair under stress. In: Collins, et al, (Eds.), op cit, pp 263-288.

Kahn, R.L., Wethington, E., and Ingersoll-Dayton, 1987, In: "Life-Span Perspective and Social Psychology," R. Abeles, (Ed.), Erlbaum, Hillsdale, New Jersey, in press.

Kalow, W., Goedde, H.W., and Agarwal, D.P., 1986, "Ethnic Differences in Reactions to Drugs and Xenobiotics," Liss, New York.

Kasl, S.V., Evans, A.S., and Niederman, J.C., 1979, Psychosocial risk factors in the development of infectious mononucleosis. *Psychosom Med, 41:* 445-446.

Katayama, M., Kobayashi, S., Kuramoto, N., and Yokoyama, M.M., 1987, Effects of hypothalamic lesions on lymphocyte subsets in mice. In: Jankovic, et al, (Eds.), op cit, pp 366-376.

Kennedy, B., Ziegler, M.G., and Shannahoff-Khalsa, D.S., 1986, Alternating lateralizaton of plasma catecholamines and nasal patency in humans. *Life Sci, 38:* 1203-1214.

Kiecolt-Glaser, J.K., Fisher, L.D., Ogrocki, P., Stout, J.C., Speicher, C.E., and Glaser, R., 1987, Marital quality, marital disruption, and immune function. *Psychom Med, 49:* 13-34.

Kiecolt-Glaser, J.K., Garner, W., Speicher, C.E., Penn, G., and Glaser, R., 1984, Psychosocial modifiers of immunocompetence in medical students. *Psychosom Med, 46:* 7-14.

Kiecolt-Glaser, J.K., Glaser, R., Strain, E.C., Stout, J.C., Tarr, K.L., Holliday, J.E., and Speicher, C.E., 1984, Modulation of cellular immunity in medical students. *J Behav Med, 9:* 5-21.

Kiecolt-Glaser, J.K., Glaser, R., Williger, D., Stout, J., Messick, G., Sheppard, S., Ricker, D., Romisher, S.C., Briner, W., Bonnell, G., and Donnerberg, R., 1985, Psychosocial enhancement of immunocompetence in a geriatric population. *Health Psychol, 4:* 25-41.

Kiecolt-Glaser, J.K., Ricker, D., George, J., Messick, G., Speicher, C.E., Garner, W., and Glaser, R., 1983, Urinary cortisol levels, cellular immunocompetency, and loneliness in psychiatric inpatients. *Psychosom Med, 46:* 15-24.

Kiecolt-Glaser, J.K., Stephens, R.E., Lipetz, P.D., Speicher, C.E., and Glaser, R., 1985, Distress and DNA repair in human lymphocytes. *J Behav Med, 8:* 311-320.

Kimura, D., 1987, Sex differences, human brain organization. In: Adelman, (Ed.), op cit, pp 1084-1085.

Klein, R., and Armitage, R., 1979, Rhythms in human performance: (1) 1- 1/2 hour oscillations in cognitive style. *Science, 204:* 1326-1328.

Klerman, G.L., and Izen, J.E., 1977, The effects of bereavement and grief on physical health and general well-being. *Adv Psychosom Med, 9:* 63-104.

Klima, E.S., and Bellugi, U., 1979, "Signs of Language," Harvard University Press, Cambridge, Massachusetts.

Kluft, R., (Ed.), 1985, "Childhood Antecedents of Multiple Personality," American Psychiatric Press, Washington, DC.

Knapp, P.H., 1983, Emotions and bodily changes: A reassessment. In: Temoshok, et al, (Eds.), op cit, pp 15-27.

Kobasa, S.C., 1979, Stressful life events, personality and health: An inquiry into hardiness. *J Pers Soc Psychol, 37:* 1-11.

Kobasa, S.C.O., Maddi, S.R., Puccetti, M.C., and Zola, M.A., 1985, Effectiveness of hardiness, exercise, and social support as resources against illness. *J Psychosom Res, 29:* 525-533.

Korneva, E.A., 1987, Electrophysiological analysis of brain reactions to antigen. In: Jankovic, et al, (Eds.), op cit, pp 318- 337.

Korneva, E.A., Klimenko, V.M., and Shkhinek, E.K., 1985, "Neural Maintenance of Immune Homeostasis," [Translated by S and E Corson from the Russian original published in 1978.] University of Chicago Press, Chicago.

Kripke, D., and Sonnenschein, D., 1978, A biological rhythm in waking fantasy. In: "The Stream of Consciousness," K.S. Pope & J.L. Singer (Eds.), Plenum, pp 321-332.

Kronfol, Z., and House, J.D., 1984, Depression, cortisol, and immune function [letter]. *Lancet*, 1: 1026-1027.

Kronfol, Z., House, J.D., Silva, J. Jr., Greden, J., and Carroll, B.J., 1986, Depression, urinary free cortisol excretion, and lymphocyte function. *Br J Psychiatry*, 148: 70-73.

Kronfol, Z., Nair, M.P.N., Soudah, H., Rhodes-Reed, G., Barucha-Reid, R., Schwartz, S.A., and Hawthorne, V.M., 1987, Natural killer cell activity in schizophrenia. *Soc Neurosci Abstr*, 13: 1583.

Kronfol, Z., Turner, R., Nasrallah, H., and Winokur, G., 1984, Leukocyte regulation in depression and schizophrenia. *Psychiat Res*, 13: 13-18.

Krueger, R.B., Levy, E.M., Cathcart, E.S., Fox, B.H., and Black, P.H., 1984, Lymphocyte subsets in patients with major depression: Preliminary findings. *Advances*, 1(1): 5-9.

LaBarbra, R.C., 1970, Experimental and environmental factors in cancer. A review of research with animals. *Psychosom Med*, 32: 259-276.

Lacey, J.I., 1967, Somatic response patterning and stress. In: "Psychological Stress," M. Appley & R. Trumbull (Eds.), Appleton- Century-Crofts, New York.

Lane, R.D., and Schwartz, G.E., 1987, Induction of lateralized sympathetic input to the heart by the CNS during emotional arousal: A possible neurophysiologic trigger of sudden cardiac death. *Psychosom Med*, 49: 274-284.

Laudenslager, M., Capitanio, J.P., and Reite, M., 1985, Possible effects of early separation experiences on subsequent immune function in adult Macaque monkeys. *Am J Psychiatry*, 142: 862-864.

Laudenslager, M.L., Ryan, S.M., Drugan, R.C., Hyson, R.L., and Maler, S.F., 1983, Coping and immunosuppression: Inescapable but not escapable shock suppresses lymphocyte proliferation. *Science*, 221: 568-570.

Leme, J.C., 1985, The endocrine and nervous systems in inflammation: Pharmacological considerations. In: "Handbook of Inflammation, Vol 5: The Pharmacology of Inflammation," I.L. Bonta, M.A. Bray & M.J. Parnham (Eds.), Elsevier, New York, pp 195-234.

Lerner, M., and Remen, N., 1985, A variety of integral cancer therapies. *Advances*, 1(1): 10-15.

LeShan, L.L., and Worthington, R.E., 1956, Personality as factor in pathogenesis of cancer: Review of literature. *Br J Med Psychol*, 29: 49-56.

Levi, L., and Andersson, L., 1975, "Psychosocial Stress—Population, Environment, and Quality of Life," Spectrum, New York.

Levine, J.D., Clark, R., Devor, M., Helms, C., Moskowitz, M.A., and Basbaum, A.I., 1984, Intraneural substance P contributes to the severity of experimental arthritis. *Science*, 226: 547-549.

Levine, S., and Ursin, H., (Eds.), 1980, Coping and Health. NATO Conference Series. Plenum, New York.

Levine, S., Weinberg, J., and Ursin, H., 1978, Definition of the coping process and statement of the problem. In: "Psychobiology of Stress," H. Ursin (Ed.), Academic, New York.

Levy, S., 1982, "Biological Mediators of Behavior and Disease Neoplasia," Elsevier, North Holland, New York.

Levy, S.M., 1984, Emotions and the progress of cancer: A review. *Advances*, 1(1): 10-15.

Levy, S.M., 1985, "Behavior and Cancer," Jossey-Bass, San Francisco.

Levy, S.M., 1986, Presentation at the Society for Behavioral Medicine 7th Annual Scientific Sessions, San Francisco, March 5-8.

Liebeskind, J.C., Lewis, J.W., Shavit, Y., Terman, G.W., and Melnechuk, T., 1983, Our natural capacities for pain suppression. *Advances, 1(intro):* 8-11.

Lightman, S.L., and Young, W.S. III, 1987, Changes in hypothalamic preproenkeophalin A following stress and opiate withdrawal. *Nature, 328:* 643-645.

Lindquist, S., 1986, The heat-shock response. *Ann Rev Biochem, 55:* 1151-1191.

Lipowsky, Z.J., 1986, Psychosomatic medicine: Past and present (3 parts). *Can. J. Psychiatry, 31J:* 2-7 (Part I), 8-13 (Part II), 14-21 (Part III).

Lipowski, Z.J., 1987, Somatization: Medicine's unsolved problem. *Psychosomtics, 28:* 294-297.

Lloyd, R., 1984, Stress-induced immunomodulation and cancer: Mechanisms and consequences. Fort Lauderdale, Florida, Jan 28-29, 1984. [Conference report] *Advances, 1(3):* 60-64.

Lloyd, R., 1987, "Explorations in Psychoneuroimmunology," Grune & Stratton, Orlando, Florida.

Locke, S.E., and Gorman, J.R., 1987, Behavior and immunity. In: "Comprehensive Textbook of Psychiatry," H. Kaplan & B. Sadock (Eds.), William & Wilkins, Baltimore. In press.

Locke, S.E., and Hornig-Rohan, M., (Eds.), 1983, "Mind and Immunity: Behavioral Immunology," Institute for the Advancement of Health, New York.

Locke SE, Kraus L (1982) Modulation of natural killer cell activity by life stress and coping ability. In: Levy, ed, op cit, pp 3-28.

Locke, S.E., Ader, R., Besedovsky, H., Hall, N., Solomon, G., and Strom, T., (Eds.), 1985, "Foundations of Psychoneuroimmunology," Aldine, Hawthorne, New York.

Lopker, A., Abood, L.G., Hoss, W., and Lionetti, F.J., 1980, Stereoselective muscarinic acetylcholine and opiate receptors in human phagocytic leukocytes. *Biochem Pharmacol, 29:* 1361-1365.

Lovett, C.L., Ulrich, J.T., and Simms, B.G., 1978, Effects of chlorpromazine on antibody production in vitro. In: "Neurochemical and Immunologic Components in Schizophrenia," D. Bergsma & A.L. Goldstein (Eds.), Liss, New York, pp 407-422.

Lundin, T., 1984, Morbidity following sudden and unexpected bereavement. *Br J Psychiatry, 144:* 84-88.

Lynch, J., 1977, "The Broken Heart," Basic, New York.

McClelland, D.C., Floor, W., Davidson, R.J., and Saron, C., 1980, Stressed power motivation, sympathetic activation, immune function, and illness. *J Hum Stress, 6:* 11-19.

McCoy, J.W., 1978, Psychological variables and onset of cancer. *Diss Abstr Int, 38:* 4471B.

McEwen, B.S., 1980, Steroid hormones and the brain: Cellular mechanisms underlying neural and behavioral plasticity. *Psychoneuroendocrinology, 5:* 1-11.

McManus, I.C., 1977, Predominance of left-sided breast tumors. *Lancet, 2:* 297-298.

Maguire, P., 1979, The will to live in the cancer patient. In: Stoll, (Ed,.) op cit, pp 169-182.

Mandell, A.J., 1980, Toward a psychobiology of transcendence: God in the brain. In: "The Psychobiology of Consciousness," J.M. Davidson & R.J. Davidson (Eds.), Plenum, New York, pp 379-464.

Mandell, J., 1986, Toward a neuropsychopharmacology of habituation: A vertical integration. Review article. *Math Modeling, 7:* 809-888.

Mandell, A.J., and Knapp, S., 1979, Asymmetry and mood, emergent properties of serotonin regulation. *Arch Gen Psychiatr,y 36:* 909-916.

Mandell, A.J., Russo, P.V., and Knapp, S., 1982, Strange stability in hierarchically coupled neuropsychiobiological systems. In: "Evolution of Order and Chaos in Physics, Chemistry, and Biology," H. Haken (Ed.), Springer, New York, pp 270-286.

Mandler, G., 1983, Emotion and stress: A view from cognitive psychology. In: Temoshok, et al, (Eds.), op cit, pp 195-205.

Mann, J.J., Brown, R.P., Halper, J.P., Sweeney, J.A., Kocsis, J.H., Stokes, P.E., and Bilezikian, J.P., 1985, Reduced sensitivity of lymphocyte beta-adrenergic receptors in patients with endogenous depression and psychomotor agitation. *N Engl J Med, 313:* 715-720.

Markert, C.L., 1987, Isozymes and the regulatory structure of the genome. In: "Isozymes: Current Topics in Biological and Medical Research Vol 14: Molecular and Cellular Biology," M.C. Rattazzi, J.G. Scandalios & G.S. Whitt (Eds.), Liss, New York, pp 1-17.

Martin, J.B., Brownstein, M.J., and Krieger, D.T., 1987, "Brain Peptides Update," Wiley-Interscience, New York.

Marx, J.L., 1987a, Oxygen free radicals linked to many diseases. *Science, 235:* 529-531.

Marx, J.L., 1987b, The AIDS virus—well known but a mystery. *Science, 236:* 390-392.

Mason, J.W., 1972, Organization of psychoendocrine mechanisms. A review and a reconsideration of research. In: "Handbook of Psychophysiology," N.S. Greenfield & R.A. Sternbach (Eds.), Holt, Rinehart, and Winston, New York, pp 3-91.

Mason, J.W., 1974, Specificity in organization of neuroendocrine response profiles. In: "Frontiers in Neurology and Neuroscience Research," P. Seeman & G.M. Brown (Eds.), University of Toronto, Toronto, pp 68-80.

Mason, J.W., 1975, Emotions as reflected in patterns of endocrine integration. In "Emotions: Their Parameters and Measurement," L. Levi (Ed.), Raven, New York, pp 143-181.

Massague, J. 1987), The TGF-beta family of growth and differentiation factors. Minireview. *Cell, 49:* 437-438.

Matheny, K.B., and Cupp, P., 1983, Control desirability and anticipation as moderating variables between life change and illness. *J Human Stress, 9:* 14-23.

Meares, A., 1978, Regression of osteogenic sarcoma metastases associated with intensive meditation. *Med J Aust, 2:* 433.

Meares, A., 1980, What can the cancer patient expect from intensive meditation? *Aust Family Physician, 9:* 322-325.

Meares, A., 1982, A form of intensive meditation associated with the regression of cancer. *Am J Clin Hypnosis, 25:* 114-121.

Melnechuk, T., 1983, Neuroimmunomodulation. University of Kentucky, *Advances, 1(introductory):* 29-31.

Melnechuk, T., 1984a, Society for Neuroscience 13th annual meeting, Boston, Massachusetts, Nov 6-11, 1983. *Advances, 1(1):* 39-41.

Melnechuk, T., 1984b, A diagnosis and a prescription. [Commentary in verse.] *Advances, 1(2):* 61-63.

Melnechuk, T., 1984c, How might positive emotions affect physical health? [Conference report.] *Advances, 1(3):* 4-8.

Melnechuk, T., 1984d, Neural modulation of immunity. University Foundation, Brussels, October 27-28, 1983. [Conference report.] *Advances, 1(4):* 56-59.

Melnechuk, T., 1985a, Society for Neuroscience 14th annual meeting, Anaheim, California, Oct 10-14, 1984. *Advances, 2(1):* 58-63.

Melnechuk, T., 1985, Neuroimmunology: Crossroads between behavior and disease. New York, April 15-16. [Conference report.] *Advances, 2(3):* 54-58.

Melnechuk, T., 1985c, Progress toward a general theory of health. [Commentary.] *Behav Brain Sci, 8:* 406-407, 421-426.

Melnechuk, T., 1985d, The biology of music-making. University of Colorado, July 8-12, 1984. [Conference report.] *Advances, 2(2):* 53-59.

Melnechuk, T., 1985e, Why has psychoneuroimmunology been controversial? Proponents and skeptics at a scientific conference. [Annotated selections from conference discussions.] *Advances, 2(4):* 22-38.

Melnechuk, T., 1986, Society for Neuroscience 15th annual meeting, Dallas, Texas, Oct 20-25, 1985. *Advances, 3(1):* 46-51.

Melnechuk, T., and Zatorre, R.J., 1987, Music. In: Adelman, (Ed.), op cit, pp 724-725.

Menaghan, E.G., 1985, Depressive affect and subsequent divorce. *J Fam Issues, 6:* 295-306.

Meyer, A., 1957, "Psychobiology: A Science of Man," Thomas, Springfield, Illinois.

Mezey, E., Reisine, T.D., Brownstein, M.J., Palkovits, M., and Axelrod, J., 1984, Beta-adrenergic mechanism of insulin-induced adrenocorticotropin release from the anterior pituitary. *Science, 226:* 1085-1087.

Miles, K., Atweh, S., Otten, G., Arnason, B.G.W., and Chelmicka-Schorr, E., 1984, Beta-adrenergic receptors on splenic lymphocytes from axotomized mice. *J Immunopharm, 6:* 171-176.

Miller, J.G., 1978, "Living Systems," McGraw-Hill, New York.

Miller, N.E., 1985, Effects of emotional stress on the immune system. *Pav J Biol Sci, 20:* 47-52.

Milner, B., 1973, Hemispheric specialization: Scope and limits. In: "The Neurosciences: Third Study Program," F.O. Schmitt & F.G. Worden (Eds.), MIT Press, Cambridge, Massachusetts, pp 75-89.

Minsky, M., 1986, ,"The Society of Mind. Simon and Schuster, New York.

Moertel, C.G., 1986, On lymphokines, cytokines, and breakthroughs. *JAMA, 256:* 3141.

Monjan, A.A., and Collector, M.I., 1977, Stress-induced modulation of the immune response. *Science, 196:* 307-308.

Monroe, S.M., Bromet, E.J.m., Connell, M.M., and Steiner, S.C., 1986, Social support, life events, and depressive symptoms. A one-year prospective study. *J Consult Clin Psychol, 54:* 424-431.

Moore, R.Y., 1987, Hypothalamus. In: Adelman, (Ed.), op cit, pp 317-318.

Mor, V., McHorney, C., and Sherwood, S., 1986, Secondary morbidity among the recently bereaved. *Am J Psychiatry, 143:* 158-163.

Mueller, J., 1983, Neuroanatomic correlates of emotion. In: Temoshok, et al, (Eds.), op cit, pp 95-121.

Mueller, N., Ackenheil, M., Eckstein, R., Hofschuster, E., and Mempel, W., 19897, Reduced suppressor cell function in psychiatric patients. In: Jankovic, et al, (Eds.), op cit, 686-690.

Nair, R.M.G., Barrett, J.F., Bowers, C.Y., and Schally, A.V., 1970, Structure of porcine thyrotropin-releasing hormone. *Biochemistry, 9:* 1103- 1106.

Nakano, Y., Miura, T., Hara, I., Aono, H., Miyano, N., Miyajima, K., Tabuchi, T., and Kosaka, H., 1982, The effect of shift work on cellular immune function. *J Hum Ergol, 11 suppl:* 131-137.

Nance, D.M., Carr, R., and Nance, P.W., 1985, Effects of unilateral brain damage on the immune system in mice and men. *Soc Neurosci Abstr, 11(pt2):* 860.

Nasr, S., Altman, E.G., and Meltzer, H.Y., 1981, Concordance of atopic and affective disorders. *J Affect Disord 3:* 291-296.

National Bureau of Standards (1987) Abstracts. 4th International Congress on Oxygen Radicals, La Jolla, California, June 27-July 3.

Nauta, W.J.H., 1973, Connections of the frontal lobe with the limbic system. In: "Surgical Approaches in Psychiatry," L.V. Laitinen & R.E. Livingston (Eds.), University Park Press, Baltimore, pp 303-314.

Nauta, W.J.H., 1971, The problem of the frontal lobe: A reinterpretation. *J Psychiat Res, 8:* 167-187.

Nemeroff, C.B., Simon, J.S., Haggerty, J.J., Jr., et al, 1985, Antithyroid antibodies in depressed patients. *Am J Psychiatry 142:* 840-843.

Neveu, P.J., Taghzouti, K., Dantzer, R., Simon, H., and Le Moal, M., 1986, Modulation of mitogen-induced lymphoproliferation by cerebral neocortex. *Life Sci, 38:* 1907-1913.

Neveu, P.J., Crestani, F., and Le Moal, M., 1987, Conditioned immunosuppression: A new methodological approach. In: Jankovic, et al, (Eds.), op cit, pp 595-601.

Newberry, B.H., Gildow, J., Wogan, J., and Reese, R.L., 1976, Inhibition of Huggins tumors by forced restraint. *Psychosom Med, 38:* 155-162.

Newton, B.W., 1982-83, The use of hypnosis in the treatment of cancer patients. *Am J Clin Hypnosis, 25:* 104-113.

Niemi, T., and Jaaskelainin, J., 1978, Cancer morbidity in depressive persons. *J Psychosomat Res, 22:* 117-120.

Oke, A., Keller, R., Mefford, I., and Adams, R.N., 1978, Lateralization of norepinephrine in the human thalamus. *Science, 200:* 1411-1413.

O'Regan, B., 1987, Healing, remission, and miracle cures. [Lecture, Dec 5, 1986.] Special Report. Institute of Noetic Sciences, Sausalito, California.

O'Regan, B., and Hirshberg, C., (Eds.), 1987, "Spontaneous Remission," Institute of Noetic Sciences, Sausalito, California, in preparation.

Ottaway, C.A., Bernaerts, C., Chan, B., and Greenberg, G.R., 1983, Specific binding of vasoactive intestinal peptide to human circulating mononuclear cells. *Can J Physiol Pharmacol, 61:* 664-671.

Ovadia, H., Lubetzki-Korn, I., and Abramsky, O ., 1987, Dopamine receptors on isolated membranes of rat thymocytes. In: Jankovic, et al, (Eds.), op cit, 211-216.

Palmblad, J., Petrini, B., Wasserman, J., and Akerstedt, T., 1979, Lymphocyte and granulo-cyte reactions during sleep deprivation. *Psychosom Med, 41:* 273-278.

Panksepp, J., 1981, Hypothalamic integration of behavior: Rewards, punishments, and related psychological processes. In: "Handbook of the Hypothalamus, Vol 3, Pt B, Behavioral Studies of the Hypothalamus," P. Morgane & J. Panksepp (Eds.), Dekker, New York, pp 289-431.

Panksepp, J., 1985, Mood changes. In: "Handbook of Clinical Neurology, Vol 1 (45), Clinical Neuropsychology," JAM Frederiks (Ed.), Elsevier, New York, pp 271-285.

Panksepp, J., 1986, The anatomy of the emotions. In: "Emotion: Theory, Research, and Experience, Vol 3.," R. Plutchik (Ed.), Academic, New York, pp 91-124.

Panksepp, J., 1986, The neurochemistry of behavior. *Ann. Rev. Psychol., 37:* 77-107.

Parkes, C.M., 1972, "Bereavement: Studies of Grief in Adult Life," International Universities Press, New York.

Parkes, C.M., 1984, Recent bereavement as a cause of mental illness. *Brit J Psychiatry, 110:* 198-204.

Parrillo, J.E., and Fauci, A.S., 1978, Comparison of the effector cells in human spontaneous cellular cytotoxicity and antibody-independent cellular cytotoxicity: Differential sensitivity of effector cells to in vivo and in vitro corticosteroids. *Scand J Immunol, 134:* 4095-4099.

Pavlov, I.P., 1902, "The Work of the Digestive Glands," Translated by W.H. Thompson. Lippincott, Philadelphia.

Payan, D.G., Levine, J.D., and Goetzl, J.E., 1984, Modulation of immunity and hypersensi-tivity by sensory neuropeptides. *J Immunol, 132:* 1601-1604.

Payan, D.G., McGillis, J.P., Renold, F.K., Mitsuhashi, M., and Goetzl, E.J., 1987, Neuropep-tide modulation of leukocyte function. In: Jankovic, et al, (Eds.), op cit, pp 182-191.

Peck, R., 1987, Neuropeptides modulating macrophage function. In: Jankovic, et al, (Eds.), op cit, pp 264-270.

Penn, A., Garte, S.J., Warren, L., Nesta, D., and Mindich, B., 1986, Transforming gene in human atherosclerotic plaque DNA. *Proc Natl Acad Sci, 83:* 7951-7955.

Pert, C.B., Ruff, M.R., Weber, R.J., and Herkenham, M., 1984, Neuropeptides and their receptors: A psychosomatic network. *J Immun, 135:* 820s-826s.

Peters, L.J., and Mason, K.A., 1979, Influence of stress on experimental cancer. In: Stoll, (Ed.), op cit, pp 103-123.

Petrov, R.V., Mikhailova, A.A., and Zakharova, L.A., 1987, Myelopeptides: Mediators of interaction between the immune system and the nervous system. In: Jankovic, et al, (Eds.), op cit, pp 271-277.

Pettingale, K.W., 1985, Towards a psychobiological model of cancer: Biological considerations. Soc Sci Med, 20: 779-787.

Pfeiffer, A., Brantl, V., Herz, A., and Emrich, H.M., 1986, Psychotomimesis mediated by kappa opiate receptors. Science, 233: 774-776.

Pierpaoli, W., Balakrishnan, J., Sche, E., Choay, J., and Maestroni , G.J.M., 1987, Neuroendocrine and bone marrow factors for control of marrow transplantation and tissue regeneration. In: Jankovic, et al, (Eds.), op cit, pp 27-38.

Plaut, S.M., and Friedman, S.B., 1981, Psychosocial factors, stress, and disease processes. In: Ader, (Ed.), op cit, pp 3-30.

Plaut, S.M., and Friedman, S.B., 1985, Biological mechanisms in the relationship of stress to illness. Pediatr Ann, 14: 563-567.

Plutchik, R., 1980, "Emotion: A Psychoevolutionary Synthesis," Harper & Row, New York.

Plutchik, R., and Ax, A.F., 1967, A critique of determinants of emotional state by Schachter and Singer. Psychophysiology, 4(1): 79-82.

Pochet, R., Delespesse, G., Gausset, P.W., and Collet, H., 1979, Distribution of beta-adrenergic receptors on human lynmphocyte subpopulations. Clin Exp Immunol, 38: 578-584.

Prentky, R.A., 1979, Creativity and psychopathology: A neurocognitive perspective. Prog Exp Personality Res, 9: 1-39.

Price, J.L., 1987, The amygdaloid complex. In: G. Adelman (Ed.), op cit, pp 40-42.

Pryor, W.A., 1986, Cancer and free radicals. In: "Antimutagenesis and Anticarcinogenesis Mechanisms," D.M. Shankel, P.E. Hartman, T. Kada, & A. Hollaender (Eds.), Plenum, New York, pp 45-59.

Rahe, R.H., 1972, Subjects' recent life changes and their near-future illness susceptibility. Adv Psychosom Med, 8: 2-19.

Rahe, R.H., 1975, Epidemiological studies of life change and illness. Intern J Psychiatry Med, 6: 133-146.

Raine, C.S., (Ed.), 1985, Special issue on neuroimmunomodulation. J Neuroimmunol, 10: 1-99.

Rees, W.D., and Lutkins, S.G., 1967, Mortality of bereavement. Br Med J, 4: 13-16.

Reich, P., DeSilva, R., Lown, B., and Murawski, J., 1981, Acute psychological disturbances preceding life-threatening ventricular arrythmias. JAMA, 246: 233-235.

Reilly, V., Fitzmaurice, M.A., and Spackman, D.H., 1981, Psychoneuroimmunologic factors in neoplasia: Studies in animals. In: R. Ader (Ed.), op cit, pp 31-102.

Renoux, G., Biziere, K., Renoux, M., Bardos, P., and Degenne, D., 1987, Consequences of bilateral brain neocortical ablation on imuthiol-induced immunostimulation in mice. In: Jankovic, et al, (Eds.), op cit, pp 346-353.

Requena, Y., 1986, Acupuncture's challenge to Western medicine. Advances, 3(2): 46-55.

Roach, A., Adler, J.E., and Black, I.B., 1987, Depolarizing influences regulate prepro-tachykinin mRNA in sympathetic neurons. Proc Natl Acad Sci USA, 84: 5078-5081.

Robinson, R.G., Kubos, K.L., Starr, L.B., Rao, K., and Price, T.R., 1984, Mood disorders in stroke patients: Importance of location of lesion. Brain, 107: 81-93.

Rose, R.M., 1980, Endocrine response to stressful psychologica events. Psychiatr Clin North Am, 3: 251-276.

Rossi, G.F., and Rosadini, G., 1967, Experimental analysis of cerebral dominance in man. In: "Brain Mechanisms Underlying Speech and Language," F.L. Darley (Ed.), Grune and Stratton, New York, pp 167-184.

Roszman, T.L., Cross, R.J., Brooks, W.H., and Markesbery, W.R., 1985, Neuroimmu-
    nomodulation: Effects of neural lesions on cellular immunity. In: Guillemin, et al,
    (Eds.), op cit, pp 95-109.
Ruff, M.R., Hill, J.M., and Pert, C.B., 1987, Neuropeptides (lymphokines, growth factors,
    and classical hormones) as the biochemicals of emotion: Implications for the biology
    of cancer. In: NATO Advanced Research Workshop: Neuroimmunomodulation.
    Interventions in Aging and Cancer. Stromboli, Sicily, Italy, June 7-11. Abstracts of
    the Reports, p 18.
Sackheim, H.A., Greenberg, M.S., Weiman, A.L., Gur, R.C., Hungerbuhler, J.P., and
    Geschwind, N., 1982, Hemispheric assymmetry in the expression of positive and
    negative emotions. Arch Neurol, 39: 210-218.
Salk, J., 1972, The mind of man. In: J. Salk, "Man Unfolding," Harper & Row, New York, pp
    107-112.
Sandblom, P., 1985, "Creativity and Disease: How Illness Affects Literature, Art, and
    Music," Stickley, Philadelphia.
Saper, C.B., Loewy, A.D., Swanson, L.W., and Cowan, W.M., 1976, Direct hypothalamo-
    autonomic connections. Brain Research, 117: 305-312.
Sapolsky, R.M., 1987, Glucocorticoids and hippocampal damage. Trends in NeuroScience, 10:
    346-349.
Saver, J., and Denlinger, S., 1985, Which doctor is not a witch doctor? Advances, 2(1): 20-30.
Schachter, S., and Singer, J.E., 1962, Cognitive, social, and physiological determinants
    of emotional state. Pyschol Rev, 69: 379-399.
Schindler, B.A., 1985, Stress, affective disorders, and immune function. Med Clin North
    Am, 69: 585-597.
Schleifer, S.J., Keller, S.E., Camerino, M., Thornton, J.C., and Stein, M., 1983, Suppression of
    lymphocyte stimulation following bereavement. JAMA, 250: 374-377.
Schleifer, S.J., Keller, S.E., Meyerson, A.T., Raskin, M.J., Davis, K.L., and Stein, M., 1984,
    Lymphocyte function in major depressive disorder. Arch Gen Psychiatr, 41: 484-486.
Schleifer, S.J., Keller, S.E., Siris, S.G., Davis, K.L., and Stein, M., 1985, Depression and
    immunity: Lymphocyte function in ambulatory depressed patients, hospitalized
    schizophrenic patients, and patients hospitalized for herniography.   Arch Gen
    Psychiatry, 42: 129-133.
Selye, H., 1936, A syndrome produced by diverse nocuous agents. Nature, 138: 32.
Selye, H., 1946, The general adaptation syndrome and the diseases of adaptation. J Clin
    Endocrinol, 6: 117-196.
Selye, H., 1956, "The Stress of Life," McGraw-Hill, New York.
Selye, H., 1976, "Stress in Health and Disease," Butterworth, Boston.
Serafetinides, E.A., 1965, The significance of the temporal lobes and of hemispheric
    dominance in the production of LSD-25 symptomatology in man. Neuropsychologia,
    3: 69-79.
Setlow, R.B., 1983, Variations in DNA repair among humans. In: "Human Carcinogene-
    sis," C.H. Curtis & N.A. Herman (Eds.),Academic, New York, pp 231-254.
Shannahoff-Khalsa, D., 1987, A contemporary view of life force biology: The merging
    of Kundalini Yoga and the neurosciences. Presented at the First International
    Conference for Energy Medicine, Feb 27-Mar 1, Madras, India. In: T.M. Srinivasan
    (Ed.), Proceedings of, etc. Fetzer Energy Medicine Research Institute, Phoenix, Arizona,
    in press.
Shannahoff-Khalsa, D.S., and Bhajan, Y., 1986, Sound current therapy and self-healing: The
    ancient science of Nad and Mantra Yoga. Presented at the Third International
    Symposium for Music in Medicine, Ludenscheid, Federal Republic of Germany, Oct
    11-12. In: R. Spintge & R. Droh R, (Eds.), Proceedings of, etc. Springer, Heidelberg,
    in press.

Shapiro, E.G., and Rosenfeld, A.A., 1987, "The Somatizing Child: Diagnosis and Treatment of Conversion and Somatization Disorders," Springer, New York.

Shapiro, H.M., and Strom, T.B., 1980, Electrophysiology of T lymphocyte cholinergic receptors. *Proc Natl Acad Sci USA, 77:* 4317-4321.

Shekelle, R.B., Raynor, W.J. Jr., Ostfeld, A.M., Garron, D.C., Bieliauskas, L.A., Liu, S.C., Maliza, C., and Paul, O., 1981, Psychological depression and 17- year risk of death from cancer. *Psychosom Med, 43:* 117-125.

Sherman, N.A., Smith, R.S., and Middleton, E., Jr., 1973, Effect of adrenergic compounds, aminophylline and hydrocortisone, on in vitro immunoglobulin synthesis by normal human peripheral lymphocytes. *J Allergy Clin Immunol, 52:* 13-22.

Shuchter, S., 1986, "Dimensions of Grief: Adjusting to the Death of a Spouse," Jossey-Bass, San Francisco.

Siegel, B.S., 1986, "Love, Medicine, and Miracles," Harper & Row, New York.

Silberman, E.K., and Weingartner, H., 1986, Hemispheric lateralization of functions related to emotion. *Brain Cogn, 5:* 322-353.

Simic, M.G., Grossman, L., and Upton, A.C., 1986, "Mechanisms of DNA Damage and Repair," Plenum, New York.

Simonton, O.C., Matthews-Simonton, S., and Creighton, J., 1978, "Getting Well Again," Tarcher, Los Angeles.

Simonton, O.C., Matthews-Simonton, S., and Sparks, T.F., 1980, Psychological intervention in the treatment of cancer. *Psychosomatics, 21:* 226- 233.

Sklar, L.S., and Anisman, H., 1979, Stress and coping factors influence tumor growth. *Science, 205:* 513-515.

Smuts, J.C., 1926, "Holism and Evolution," Macmillan, New York.

Smith, O.A., 1987, Emotion, neural substrates. In: Adelman, (Ed.), op cit, pp 385-386.

Smith, O.A., and DeVito, J.L., 1984, Central neural integration for the control of autonomic responses associated with emotion. *Ann Rev Neurosci, 7:* 43-65.

Snow, E.C., 1985, Insulin and growth hormone function as minor growth factors which potentiate lymphocyte activation. In: Goetzl, (Ed.), op cit, pp 776s-778s.

Solomon, G.F., 1981a, Emotional and personality factors in the onset and course of autoimmune disease, particularly rheumatoid arthritis. In: Ader, (Ed.), op cit, pp 159-182.

Solomon, G.F., 1981b, Immunologic abnormalities in mental illness In: Ader, (Ed.), op cit, pp 259-278.

Solomon, G.F., 1985, The emerging field of psychoneuroimmunology— with a special note on AIDS. *Advances, 2(1):* 6-19.

Solomon, G.F., 1987, Psychoneuroimmunology. In: Adelman, (Ed.), op cit, pp 1001-1004.

Solomon, G.F., and Amkraut, A.A., 1983, Emotions, immunity, and disease. In: Temoshok, et al, (Eds.), op cit, pp 167-186.

Solomon, G.F., Fiatarone, M.A., Benton, D., Morley, J.E., Bloom, E., and Makinodan, T., 1987, Psychoimmunologic and endorphin function in the aged. In: *Ann N Y Acad Sci,* in press.

Somers, A.R., 1979, Marital status, health, and use of health services. *J Marriage Fam, 41:* 267-285.

Spector, N.H., (Ed.), 1985, Neuroimmunomodulation: Proceedings of the First International Workshop on Neuroimmunomodulation. International Working Group on Neuroimmunomodulation (WGN), c/o Fundamental Neurosciences Program, NINCDS, NIH, Rm 916, Federal Bldg, Bethesda, Maryland.

Spector, N.H., 1987, Neuroimmunomodulation. In: Adelman, (Ed.), op cit, pp 798-799.

Spector, N.H., and Korneva, E.A., 1981, Neurophysiology, immunophysiology, and neuroimmunomodulation. In: Ader, (Ed.), op cit, pp 449-473.

Sporn, M.B., and Roberts, A.B., 1986, Peptide growth factors and inflammation, tissue repair, and cancer. *J Clin Investigation, 78:* 329-332.

Squire, L.R., 1987, "Memory and Brain," Oxford University Press, New York.

Stanisz, A.M., Scicchitano, R., Payan, D.G., and Bienenstock, J., 1987), In vitro studies of immunoregulation by substance P and somatostatin. In: Jankovic, et al, (Eds.), op cit, 217-225.

Stanwyck, D.J., and Anson, C.A., 1986, Is personality related to illness? Cluster profiles of aggregated data. *Advances, 3(2):* 4-15.

Stein, M., 1985, Bereavement, depression, stress, and immunity. In: Guillemin, et al, (Eds.), op cit, pp 29-44.

Stein, M., 1986, A reconsideration of specificity in psychosomatic medicine: From olfaction to the lymphocyte. *Psychosom Med, 48:* 3-22.

Stein, M., Schleifer, S.J., and Keller, S.E., 1981, Hypothalamic influences on immune responses. In: R. Ader, (Ed.), op cit, pp 429-473.

Stites, D.P., Stobo, J.D., and Wells, J.V., 1987, "Basic & Clinical Immunology 6th ed.," Appleton & Lange, Norwalk, Connecticut.

Stoddard, J.B., and Henry, J.P., 1985, Affectional bonding and the impact of bereavement. *Advances, 2(2):* 19-28.

Stoll, B.A., 1979, Is hope a factor in survival? In: B.A. Stoll (Ed,.) op cit, pp 183-197.

Stoll, B.A., (Ed.), 1979, "Mind and Cancer Prognosis," Wiley, Chichester, England.

Stone, A.A., Cox, D.S., Valdimarsdottir, and Neale, J.M., 1987, Secretory IgA as a measure of immunocompetence. *J Hum Stress, (Fall):* 136-140.

Stoney, C.M., Davis, M.C., and Matthews, K.A., 1987, Sex differences in responses to stress and in coronary heart disease: A causal link? *Psychophysiology, 24:* 127-131.

Stossel, T.P., 1987, The molecular biology of phagocytes and the molecular basis of nonneoplastic phagocyte disorders. In: "The Molecular Basis of Blood Diseases," G. Stamatoyannopoulos A.W. Nienhuis, P. Leder & P.W. Majerus (Eds.), Saunders, Philadelphia, pp 499-533.

Stricker, G., 1967, A pre-experimental inquiry concerning cognitive determinants of emotional state. *J Gen Psychol, 76:* 73-79.

Strobel, H.W., Fang, W-F., Takazawa, R.S., Stralka, D.J., Newaz, S.N., Kurzban, G.P., Neslon, D.R., and Beyer, R.S., 1986, Cytochromes p-450 and the activation and inactivatiion of mutagens and carcinogens. In: "Antimutagenesis and Anticarcinogenesis Mechanisms," D.M. Shankel, P.E. Hartman, T.A. Kada & A. Hollaender (Eds.), Plenum, New York, pp 61-71.

Stroebe, M.S., and Stroebe, W., 1983, Who suffers more? Sex differences in health risks of the widowed. *Psychol Bull, 93:* 279-301.

Swanson, L.W., 1987, The limbic system. In: Adelman, (Ed.), op cit, 589-591.

Swanson, L.W., Sawchenko, P.E., and Lind, R.W., 1986, Regulation of multiple peptides in CRF parvocellular neurosecretory neurons: Implications for the stress response. In: T. Hokfelt, K. Fuxe & B. Pernow (Eds.), "Prog Brain Res, Vol 68," Elsevier, New York, pp 169-90.

Tallal, N., and Hadden, J., 1985, Hormones, immunomodulating drugs and auto-immunity. In: "Handbook of Inflammation, Vol 5: The Pharmacology of Inflammation," I.L. Bonta, M.A. Bray & M.J. Parnham (Eds.), Elsevier, New York, pp 355-369.

Tallman, J.F., and Gallagher, D.W., 1985, The GABA-ergic system: A locus of benzodiazepine action. *Ann Rev Neurosci, 8:* 21-44.

Temoshok, L., 1986, Presentation at the Society for Behavioral Medicine 7th Annual Scientific Sessions, San Francisco, March 5-8.

Temoshok, L., and Fox, B.H., (Eds.), 1986, International issue. *Advances, 3(4):* 1-179.

Temoshok, L., Van Dyke, C., and Zegans, L.S., (Eds.), 1983, "Emotions in Health and Illness," Grune and Stratton, New York.

Tennenbaum, J.I., Ruppert, R.D., and St. Pierre, R.L., et al, 1969, The effect of chronic alcohol administration on the immune responsiveness of rats. *J Allergy, 44:* 272-281.

Thatcher, R.W., Walker, R.A., and Giudice, S., 1987, Human cerebral hemispheres develop at different rates and ages. *Science, 236:* 1110-1113.

Theorell, T., 1986, Research on stress and health in Sweden from 1950 to 1985. *Advances, 3(4):* 92-104.

Thomas, L., 1987, What doctors don't know. [Review of Becoming a Doctor: A Journey of Initiation in Medical School, by Melvin Konner.] *N Y Rev Bks, 34(Sep 24):* 6-11.

Tice, R., and Setlow, R., 1985, DNA repair and replication in aging organisms. In: "Handbook of the Biology of Aging," C.E. Finch & E.L. Schneider (Eds.), Raven, New York, pp 173-224.

Tucker, D., 1981, Lateral brain function, emotion and conceptualization. *Psychol Bull, 89:* 19-46.

Udelman, H.D., and Udelman, D.L., 1985, Hope as a factor in remission of illness. *Stress Med, 1:* 291-294.

Ulrich, R.S., 1984, View through a window may influence recovery from surgery. *Science, 224:* 420-421.

Vale, W., Spiess, J., Rivier, C., and Rivier, J., 1981, Characterization of a 41-residue ovine hypothalamic peptide that stimulates secretion of corticotropin and beta-endorphin. *Science, 213:* 1394-1397.

Van Dyke, C., and Kaufman, I., 1983, Psychobiology of bereavement. In: Temoshok, et al, (Ed.), op cit, pp 37-49.

Villemain, F., Chatenoud, L., Guillibert, E., Pelicier, Y., and Bach, J.F., 1987, Decreased production of interleukin-2 in schizophrenia. In: B.D. Jankovic, et al, (Eds.), op cit, pp 669-685.

Vingerhoets, A.J., 1985, The role of the parasympathetic division of the autonomic nervous system in stress and the emotions. *Int J Psychosom, 32:* 28-34.

Vogel, W.H., 1985, Coping, stress, stressors, and health consequences. *Neuropsychobiology, 13:* 129-135.

Wallerstein, R.S., 1983, Historical perspective. In: Temoshok, et al, (Eds.), op cit, pp 3-5.

Warner, H.R., Butler, R.N., Sprott, R.L., and Schneider, E.L., (Eds.), 1987, "Modern Biological Theories of Aging," Raven, New York.

Weiner, H., 1977, "Psychobiology and Human Disease," American Elsevier, New York.

Weiner, H., 1985a, Psychosomatic medicine and the mind-body problem in psychiatry. In: "Handbook of the History of Psychiatry," Wallace, E IV, (Ed.), Yale University Press, New Haven, Connecticut, in press.

Weiner, H., 1985b, The concept of stress in the light of studies of disasters, unemployment, and loss: A critical review. In: "Stress in Health and Disease," M.R. Zales (Ed.), Brunner-Mazel, New York, pp 24-94.

Weiss, S.M., 1983, Health and illness: The behavioral medicine perspective. In: Temoshok, et al, (Eds.), op cit, pp 7-14.

Werner, H., Paegelow, I., Meyer-Rienecker, H., and Bienert, M., 1987, Interaction between lymphocytes and neurotransmitters. In: Jankovic, et al, (Eds.), op cit, pp 312-315.

Werntz, D., Bickford, R.G., Bloom, F.E., and Shannahoff-Khalsa, D., 1983, Alternating cerebral hemispheric activity and the lateralization of autonomic nervous function. *Human Neurobiology, 2:* 39-43.

Werntz D, Bickford RG, Shannahoff-Khalsa D (1987) Selective hemispheric stimulation by unilateral forced nostril breathing. *Human Neurobiology,* in press.

White, L., Tursky, B., and Schwartz, G.E., 1984, Possible determinants of placebo response: A list. *Advances, 1(3):* 25.

Whitlock, F.A., and Siskind, M., 1979, Depression and cancer: A follow-up study. *Psychol Med*, 9: 747-752.

Wiedermann, C.J., Sertl, K., and Pert, C.B., 1987, Neuropeptides and the immune system: Substance P receptors in bronchus-associated lymphoid tissue of rat. In: Jankovic et al, (Eds.), op cit, pp 205- 210.

Williams, C.A., 1987, The second international workshop on neuroimmunomodulation: A report. *J Immunol*, 13: 343-348.

Williams, L.T., Snyderman, R., and Lefkowitz, R.J., 1976, Identification of beta-adrenergic receptors in human lymphocytes by (-)[3H] alprenolol binding. *J Clin Invest*, 57: 149-155.

Witelson, S.F., 1987, Brain asymmetry, functional aspects. In: G. Adelman, (Ed.), op cit, pp 151-156.

Wolf, S.G., and Goodell, H., 1976, "Behavioral Science in Clinical Medicine," Thomas, Springfield, Illinois.

Wolff, H.G., 1953, "Stress and Disease," Thomas, Springfield, Illinois.

Woo, S.L.C., and O'Malley, B.W., 1975, Hormone inducible messenger RNA. *Life Sci*, 17: 1039-1048.

Wood, C., 1987, Buffer of hardiness: An interview with Suzanne C. Ouellette Kobasa. *Advances*, 4(1): 37-25.

Wybran, J., 1985, Enkephalins, endorphins, Substance P, and the immune system. In: Guillemin, et al, (Eds.), op cit, pp 157-161.

Young, M., Benjamin, B., and Wallis, C., 1963, Mortality of widowers. *Lancet*, 2: 454-456.

Zaidel, E., 1985, Right hemisphere language. In: Benson & Zaidel, (Eds.), op cit, pp 205-236.

Zasloff, M., Magainins: A class of antimicrobial peptides from Xenopus skin: Isolation, characterization of two active forms, and partial cDNA sequence of a precursor. *Proc Natl Acad Sci USA*, 84: 5449-5453.

Zavala, F., and Lenfant, M., 1987, Benzodiazepines and PK 11195 exert immunomodulating activities by binding to a specific receptor on macrophages. In: Jankovic, et al, (Eds.), op cit, pp 240-249.

Zegans, L.S., 1983, Emotions in health and illness: An attempt at integration. In: Temoshok, et al, (Eds.), op cit, pp 235-256.

Zoon, K.C., Karasaki, Y., zur Nedden, D.L., Hu, R., and Arnheiter, H., 1986, Modulation of epidermal growth factor receptors by human alpha interferon. *Proc Natl Acad Sci USA*, 83: 8226-8230.

Toward a Cultural Epidemiology of Emotion

Paul Byers

Teachers College
Columbia University
New York, N.Y.

From what little we know of the relationship between the fine details of human interaction and the longer cycles of the career line, there is reason to expect that the longer cycles will always be enlarged repetitions or repeated re- flections of pattern contained in the fine detail. Indeed, *this assumption that the microscopic will reflect the macroscopic is a major justification of most of our test procedures.* A major function of the techniques of microanalysis is, therefore, to obtain from small quantities of data, accurately and completely recorded, insights into human relationship which could otherwise only be obtained either by long-time observation or from the notoriously unreliable data of anamnestic reconstruction (Bateson, 1971).

Introduction

In this chapter I will display and discuss data records of human interaction in which the sharing of "emotion" is seen as a necessary concomitant of communication. The records I will display are magnified traces of interpersonal talk events in which the structurally significant units have durations of only small fractions of a second. Such micro-events are not in the explicit awareness of the participants not available to observers until they are elec- tronically magnified.

———

Epidemiology is concerned with the diffusion of pathogens through and across populations. **Immunology** is concerned with the biological processes which destroy or deflect pathogens in individuals. **Anthropology** is concerned with the learned and shared organization of a social whole called a culture. And the anthropological study of **communi- cation** is concerned with the processes underlying the sharing of the organization - the culture.

Each of these specialized foci of research into man's adaptive (self-correcting) capacities and behavior recognizes, implicitly or explicitly, that the survival of individuals, societies, or cultures requires continuous adaptive change and that the same (cybernetic) design which permits self-correction also carries the possibility for "positive feedback" or cumulative error. In immunology this may appear as an inappropriate (upside down) immune response and in human social terms it can emerge as marital or family disorder, mass hysteria, lynch mobs, or assorted addictions such as the arms race. In either case our sciences look for the processes which lead, alternatively, to adaptive reorganization or to pathology.

My sub-discipline is the anthropological study of communication and my relation to "Emotions and Pathology" arose from two claims:

- that diseases related to immune dysfunction are increasing,
- that emotions may affect the immune system.

Since emotions are variously attributed to psychological, neurological, or biochemical factors and are now a concern of the immunologist, I will describe anthropological view of emotions and present data related to the epidemiology - i.e. the diffusion or transmission - of emotions. I am not concerned with either the validity of the above two claims or with an analysis of emotions per se. My goals, here, are to place the *idea* of emotions in a multi-level cultural context (which is required to give them anthropological meaning) and to describe a process design that underlines the several disciplines involved in the intertwined matter of emotion-immunity-epidemiology-pathology. All disciplines ultimately rest on the same *fundamental* natural principles. Since my sub-discipline is the anthropological study of communication, I will begin with a much-abbreviated description of parallel developments in the study of disease and the study of communication. At the end I will propose that extending this parallel will lead to questions that may be as interesting to those interested in emotion or immunology as they are to my own sub-discipline.

The microscope enabled the biologist to discover and study an otherwise unseen world of microorganisms and physiological processes. This led to a new understanding of illness and to the common view that germs are transmitted to people and cause disease. Communication study began with the observation that messages are transmitted from person to person and carry meaning. Thus the biologist studied germs as disease carriers and communication research studied messages as meaning carriers.

Then the observation that "getting the germ" was not the same as "getting the disease" led to the concept of the immune system, which at first was seen as a fixed, genetically inherited screen which could also manufacture antibodies. This enabled us to introduce antigens and exercise an extended measure of control over illness. Communication researchers, having observed that prople did not always get the same meanings from messages, introduced various forms of "communication skills" for message senders and receivers as a way to manage or control human access to meaning.

The anthropological study of communication is no longer the study of messages with implied meaning but has become the study of the processes by which human relationships are implemented, maintained, or changed. Human relationships can no more be fully explained in terms of messages than illness can be explained in terms of germs. Communication, like the immune system, is the study of multiple levels of organization or process. Immunology has been concerned with physical bodies and anthropology with the *social* body - which extends beyond the skins of the interactants.

I have begun with this thumbnail-sketched parallel so that I can describe the matters of emotion or state diffusion and epidemiology as analogs - as variant codings or transforms of parallel phenomena in our two disciplines. To carry this still further I must make some further observations about the nature of culture:

- Culture is sometimes defined as that aspect of human society that is learned (i.e. acquired) and *shared*. The anthropological study of communication is, in one definition, the study of the processes of sharing.
- Since cultural configurations are unique to a culture but shared by its members, culture is *endemic*. When new ideas or arrangements enter a culture, they may be *epidemic*. Examples: war hysteria, the "sexual revolution," the present fear of AIDS (as distinguished from the epidemic proportions of the biological condition). The anthropological study of communication is, again, the study of the processes of sharing. Whereas the biological epidemiologist begins with an identified pathogen and studies its transmission, my science studies the sharing process and finds, without preconceptions, whatever is shared.
- The meanings (of anything) in a culture are continuously in the process of construction - and reconstruction, otherwise there could be no change, growth, or development. That process is embraced by the word interaction. Here, the anthropological study of communication recognizes the self-evident condition required for meaning or sharing or for anything to have "information" significance: that there must be a common (fixed) reference or comparator that is shared by the interactants.

Implicit in this epistemological construction is an *apparent* paradox: that sharing must precede sharing. It is not a paradox, however, when it is seen cybernetically - i.e. organized on successive levels of organization. Two people must share a language before they can share ideas expressed in it. Game players must share the rules of the game before they can play (share a game) together. And when people talk to each other, each must continuously and progressively 'know' that the other has 'followed' and 'understands' - and, hopefully 'agrees' and 'feels good about' it. The words in quotes all imply forms of sharing.

The anthropological study of communication is not directly concerned with the meaning of talk or behavior. It is concerned with the underlying (and usually unrecognized) premises or rules which must be shared for the talk to have meaning to the talkers. This is analogous to watching a game (chess, tennis, etc.) in order to discover the rules of the game. It is in this sense that culture can be seen as a set of rules which must be shared in order for the members of the culture to play the"game" - i.e. to behave appropriately. All information or meaning requires an underlying reference or comparator. For *semantic* meaning that reference or comparator, on examination, will be an organized, multi-level hierarchy of shared configurations that disappear into history in one direction (e.g. the "meanings" of words or symbols) and into a microscopic but precisely organized biology (of neurones, muscle arrangements, etc.)

in another. This is the basic paradigm that has emerged from the anthropolical study of communication. It is within this (cybernetic) paradigm that I will look for "definitions" of emotion and of pathology.

Emotion and Levels of Organization

When we examine talk or any human interaction by looking progressively at the layers of shared organization that I have called premises above, we immediately move away from words or "semantic" meaning. A familiar equivalent: When one looks for the organization that underlies and is required for the recognizable and "meaningful" experience of being hungry, he quickly moves away from "hunger" and toward muscular and biochemical activity.

Pathology in my paradigm is the disorganization of self-correcting process which has led to unwelcome distortions at higher levels or organization. In human affairs it is possible for interaction to proceed as though the underlying foundation layers were appropriately shared (*as though* the underlying organization were intact) when they were not. Under some circumstances this organizational flaw can engender cumulative error and become pathology. Pathology is a "lie" in a process which distorts the higher order organization in which it is embedded - as a defect in immunological integrity will ultimately distort the health-maintaining capacity of the larger organism. Believing a lie can lead the believer to inappropriate (pathological) behavior. There are two significant points underlying this pathology - lie parellel: 1) the "seed" from which pathology develops is a mismatch or non-sharing, when a match or sharing is presumed; 2) the *visible* pathology (the system) is usually far removed, organizationally, from the "seed" which engendered it. We tend to look for and "blame" immediate and visible "proximal causes," which is ultimately futile (and which, because it is the equivalent of another "lie," may be the seed of another pathology). I will connect this matter with my data at the end of this paper, but some examples will be illustrative here. We know, of course, that some microorganisms can "lie" to body processes with subsequent pathological consequences. We know that some predators succeed by "lying" to their victims. Shakespeare's *Othello* (and much other literature) is the story of the pathological consequences that began with a mistaken assumption that information was shared when, in fact, it was not. And while we assign blame to Iago, who was a "proximal cause," the *organizational* seed was the unshared information ("truth") which cumulatively distorted the subsequent relationships.

Culture and Communication

Although my chart data are from microscopic slices of behavior, I will begin with large-scale cultural data, i.e. recognizable events with recognizable human emotions. Here the consequences of "emotional epidemiology" can been recognized along with the cultural elaboration. But useful *explanation* will require an examination of the small-scale underlying processes. I will, then, present two kinds of data: 1) ethnographic descriptions of whole cultures, group behavior, and conversation; 2) strip chart recordings of four different kinds of interaction talk:

1. Two Kung Bushmen of Southwest Africa telling a story,
2. Two Yanomamo (South American) headmen in a ritual "shouting match",
3. A movie joke with the subsequent audience laughter, and
4. Artificial speech generated by a Kurtzweil reader.

The chart data will show that:

- There is a fixed rhythm underlying and pacing the *motor* activity of all human talk.
- That two or more people in conversation synchronize their underlying rhythms, i.e. they share the same rhythm.
- That the underlying rhythm is fixed and mechanically regular.
- That the individual *behaved* rhythm is not fixed or mechanically regular but is a modulation of the fixed underlying rhythm.
- That the relation between the fixed rhythm and the variable behaved rhythm of each speaker carries information available to the other speaker.
- That the information carried by the rhythm relationship (between the fixed and the variable rhythms) in speech is information about the *state* of the speaker.
- That persistence of the rhythm-sharing moves the interactants toward a commonly shared state. It is this which led to the definition of communication as "state sharing" and, by extention, to the idea of an "epidemiology of emotion."

This interpersonal rhythm matter will be shown as described in detail by examining chart traces of speech below. But if there is validity to the state-sharing or "emotional epidemiology" idea at the level of conversation, we can expect that, as a consequence, whole cultures should tend to have unique affective or state characteristics. I will begin my presentation of anthropological data by citing a few examples of this.

Whole-Culture Characterization

The Yanomamo of Venezuela and Brazil are described by their ethnographer, Napoleon Chagnon (1968), as *Yanomamo: The Fierce People*. This ferocity is such normal Yanomamo behavior that it not only produces much inter-tribal and interpersonal violence but is reflected in two kinds or aspects of customary behavior that have been recorded on sound film, one of which I have examined in some detail. The first of these, seen in the film *The Feast* (Asch and Chagnon, 1968), documents the occasion of a feast prepared by one group and to which another group is invited. At this ceremonious event the host village has prepared the food and the compound, which is an open plaza partly surrounded by living quarters open to a plaza.

On the day of the feast the visitors come as a group, stop outside the compound and send a messenger to announce their arrival. Then the visiting group puts a showy garb on their painted bodies and faces, and the headmen of the two groups meet face-to-face for a ritual "shouting match" in which they brag and shout insults at each other simultaneously. Then, on signal, the visitors rush "fiercely" into the compound with spears raised in mock attack and threaten to run their spears through their hosts. The hosts, however, lie relaxed and unarmed in their hammocks pretending to be undisturbed by the ferocious mock threats of the visitors. Eventually both groups turn to eating and drinking.

If ferocity is a character of these people in ritualized behavior, it is also near the surface in everyday interpersonal behavior and we can expect to find social control mechanisms to limit what otherwise could become widespread lethal mayhem. I will present strip chart records of the "shouting match" and the microanalysis of these data to demonstrate how full-tilt ferocity is vented in words but within an underlying, closely shared organization which effectively displaces physical violence.

Elizabeth Marshall has called her ethnography of the Bushmen of Southwest Africa *The Harmless People* (1959). Although these people have disputes, they spend much time in playful game-like activity, ritualized storytelling, and in a nighttime chanting-clapping-dancing activity which is synchronous, reverential (they say that it beings them closer to their equivalent of God), and which produces trance in some.

In *Patterns of Culture* (1934) Ruth Benedict described the Dobu of the South Pacific as "paranoid" (they were much involved in working sorcery against others or in avoiding the sorcery of others) in contrast to the Hopi Indians of the American Southwest who were characteristically peaceful and harmonious. Benedict suggested that cultures could be seen as organized around central organizing "themes." American culture, she wrote, is organized around the basic theme of competition and ownership. Later, when the idea of "systematic opposition" within cultures emerged, Benedict wrote *The Chrysanthemum and the Sword: Patterns of Japanese Culture* (1946).

Anthropology provides ample evidence that whole cultures have characteristic profiles of emotional emphasis. I am citing this only to show that large numbers of people in that system of interaction called a culture come to *share states* as a consequence of that ineraction. Or, to be more cautious, they learn to behave *as though they do*. It is the process underlying this sharing (or the choice not to share) that is my concern in this paper. But we can make the inference from these ethnographies that the generalized, shared cultural emotions are aspects of the cultural context which frames or organizes the behavior of the members of the culture and that human interaction within a culture maintains the affect or state aspect - a circular and self-correcting arrangement.

Group Sharing Behavior

Although each of us lives in and participates in a culture, our full immediate awareness of it is akin to the awareness a fish might have of water. But our participation in groups is more explicit to us. In every society there are occasions when a relatively large number of people come together in the same place at the same time to do the same thing in an organized, often synchronized way. The number of people, frequency of the occasions, and the nature and complexity of the events vary around the world, but without group interaction it would not be possible to say "we" with multiple levels of organized inclusion - e.g. couple, family, church, business, nation.

For my purposes here there are a few characteristics of groups I want to point to: A group is both individual members and a set of underlying but shared rules (the "organization") which also enables the members to behave as a single collectivity. This collectivity is sufficiently explicit to be namable (peace marchers, lynch mob, army, party, wake, audience, family, rally, football game, wedding, funeral, etc.). And at many of such occasions there are "synchronizers" which serve to bring the participants toward the same *state:* cheer leaders, church choirs, dirges, marching bands, fife-and-drum corps, disco bands, participatory rituals such as moments of silence, opening prayers, pledges of allegiance, Indian war dances, bugle calls, the "shouting matches" preceding the Yanomamo feast, the chanting-clapping-dancing of the Bushmen, the summoning of ancestors to many primitive ceremonies, or simply culturally pre-scribed "commonsense" behavior that everyone is supposed to know as "manners". In all cases there is a relationship between the affect or state implicit in the synchroniz-ing event or its equivalent and the state deemed appropriate for the larger occasion.

Now I want to describe two of such occasions or events. The first is a shamanistic healing ceremony and the second is a brief event at a comic movie showing.

In 1972 Coberly wrote "Ten Shamanistic Curing Ceremonies in Ten Different Societies". She described the common sequence found in those ceremonies in which the ethnographer had carefully described the sequence of behaviors. Although the cultural content of each ceremony was unique, all had the following sequence in common:

1. Someone brought a "patient" to the shaman who diagnosed the patient as treatable, or not, by his procedure. (On one ocasion, documented on film by a British team concerned with practices among the West African Ashanti, the shaman smelled the patient's scalp and declared him untreatable. The observing western psychiatrists made a provisional diagnosis of schizophrenia.)

2. If the shaman agreed to a curing ceremony, he asked that a large number of people related to the patient assemble for the ceremony at a particular place and time. (Among the Navaho dozens of people may come from long distances and stay for several days.)

3. At the appointed time and place the shaman "synchronized" the assembled people (with the patient absent). Synchronization procedures varied widely and could include singing, chanting, dancing, drumming, or praying - sequentially or in combination.

4. When the group reached an appropriate degree of synchrony (rhythmic rate, loudness, simultaneity) the patient was brought in to experience the (entraining) occasion.

5. As the patient's behavior changed toward a match or harmony with the others, he was seen as "healing". This change may require a long ceremony or several "treatment" ceremonies, and sometimes included various forms of "adjunct therapy".

I want to call attention to only a few observations and inferences from these ethnographic data:

- that a commonality in these ceremonies is the rhythmic synchronization of the group,

- that a synchronized group will act as an entrainer for the patient,
- that a rhythmic matching of patient with the group is equated with successful treatment,
- that not all illnesses are treatable in this way.

There are, however, more precise recordings of an ostensibly different kind of group occasion. Carl Jones, whose media-oriented research into audience behavior is in progress, recorded many audience reactions at different theaters and at different times to the same motion picture comedy, *All of Me*. I will examine, below, a particular aspect of the relationships between a comic line or joke in the movie and the audience laughter that followed it. While we know or assume that a group chant is organized, synchronized, and rhythmic, I will show that so, too, is group laughter. Apart from calling attention to the group-organizing significance of cheer leaders, armies marching together, disco bands, etc. I will describe an occasion that I recall from childhood.

In about 1930 I visited relatives in Florida who listened each week at the same time to a favourite radio program. After the program announcement, there were no spoken words. There was, first, a chuckle, then more chuckles by more people. The chuckles grew into laughter, more and louder laughter, etc. Soon everyone present was convulsed with laughter. I was ten years old and it was "fun." The "fun" was clearly in the participation in the organized process since there was nothing to laugh *at*. No proximal cause. Nothing "caused" the laughter.

Conversation

Now I will turn to interaction in which the number of people is small enough for that class of events we call conversation. When we examine the details of this minimal human interaction, we find a basic process configuration, an abstract design, which underlies and illuminates the epidemiological aspect of group communication events and which is characteristic of other process relationships in nature. I will describe, first, two familiar versions of this design and then the background research and thinking behind the analyses of the strip-chart records.

1. When two (or more) people play ping pong (or other games), they must first share the same "rules of the game". Without this there would be confusion - which arises when even a single rule is remembered or interpreted "incorrectly" by one of the players. The rules are one level of shared organization. When the game begins, the play of each player "organizes" that of the next player. That is, each play partially determines the next but each "next" is also partly unpredictable (a stochastic relationship). We can predict, roughly, what the "next" will try to do, but we cannot predict precisely what it will be.

2. The second example concerns the performance of two-person chamber music in which: a) both players share the written score (which organizes the performance on

one level) and, b) each player, on the next level, is organized by the other player. Each must fit the other in loudness, tempo, etc. In each of these two examples the second level of organization requires that there be sharing on the first.

In order to recognize the events and relationships as they appear in the micro-analyses of conversation, the concept of the motor syllable is necessary.

In *Motor Phonetics* R.H. Stetson (1951) reported on the relation of ballistic motor impulsing of the diaphragm and intercostal muscles to the stream of discrete "motor syllables" that emerged as speech. He used electromyographic sensors and displayed many "kymographs" of short stretches of speech. Since he was interested in the intonational patterns of languages, he focused on the aggregation of syllables into such patterns, using the motor syllable as his behavioral unit.

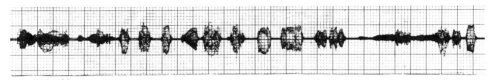

Figure 1: Trace of Bushman Storytelling talk.

To visualize Stetson's motor syllables I have made a chart trace (Fig. 1 above) of talk between two Kung Bushmen of Southwest Africa. On the chart the motor syllables resemble beads on a string. Each small cluster reflects the sound from a single ballistic motor impluse. The larger clusters are over lapped motor syllables of two voices. I will examine this talk in detail below. Some years later Frieda Goldman-Eisler (1956, pp. 136-143) looked at "articulation rate" as a possible correlate of the emotional state of a speaker. Her lineal, quantitative, and statistically smoothed measurements showed (to her) that "articulation rate" was invariant and therefore of no significance to her as a correlate of emotion.

In my research (Byers 1972,1976,1979) I examined the micro-organization of talk (and movement behavior) between speakers, i.e. conversation. The ballistic impulsing underlying speech production is, indeed, an underlying "fixed rhythm train" in all speech in all languages. But as the charts below will illustrate, all speech (indeed all human behavior) is organized and, in conversation or other interaction, each interactant participates in organizing the other interactants *within a larger shared frame* or organization. To put this another way, everyone in interaction "organizes" everyone else, and a fixed, shared underlying oscillation or rhythm is the structural frame for that organization.

Chart Data

The first three talk events were recorded by anthropogical field workers. The "field" for the movie joke and audience laughter was a movie theater. The sounds were copied onto reel-to-reel audiotape at 7 1/2 ips. tape speed. The tape recorder playback speed was slowed to 15/16 ips. (an eighth normal speed) and the output signal was fed to a chart recorder with a chart travel speed of, usually, 10mm/sec. With these settings one second of real time is 80 mm on the chart record. For greater "magnification" the chart travel can be increased to 25 or 50 mm/sec so that one second of real time becomes 200 or 400 mm on the chart. Since the most common significant interval in this research is a tenth of a second, this interval can be displayed as 8, 20, or 40 mm on the chart. The chart trace in Fig 1, where detail is unimportant, was made with a chart travel speed of 5mm/sec. For all the other charts, a diode was inserted in one leg of the circuit and a .2 mfd capacitor across the legs. This rectifies and filters the speech frequencies and converts the output signal to a DC analog of the speech amplitude across time. (This is not the same as subjective loudness, since different frequencies occur with different speech sounds - ed.)

Bushman Storytelling

The Bushman ("The Harmless People") enjoy telling and listening to stories. The stories are traditional and are ideally recited (performed) in the same way with the same words and gestures. The stories are so old that the storytelling language is an obsolescent form of their present language. Storytelling requires a skilled "teller" and a skilled "listener". Our Western concept of teller-listener (i.e. active-passive) is strange to Bushmen and to many other peoples in the world, who see storytelling or conversation as joint co-participation.

In the event from which the Bushman charts were taken two men sat cross-legged facing each other. One man was acclaimed as their best story teller and the other as their best story "listener". The listener's part is more analogous to that of the Western music accompanist than passive listener. He repeats the last part of gestural sequences and frequently (once or more per second) interjects repetitions of the teller's words. These semi-ritualized performances involve considerable skill. There is commonly an "audience" of perhaps a dozen people who sit in a semi-circle and perform "listener" behavior in unison. John Marshall made a sound film record of Bushman storytelling with a microphone hidden in the sand between them. The charts in Fig. 2 represent the first "sentence" of the first story. I will use the identical charts in Fig. 2 to demonstrate the chart-analysis procedure and the configurations or relationships that are characteristic of *all* human conversation records that I have examined - dozens of records from eleven languages.

In the top chart (A) in Fig. 2 there is some evidence that the sound is emerging in somewhat discrete bursts - the "beads-on-a-string" of Fig. 1. There are motor syllables and I have marked, below the trace, the places where the syllables seem to begin or onset. In many places it is not clear where the syllable begins since 1) some syllables begin with sibillant or unvoiced consonants and the recordable sound follows the onset on the trace, 2) sometimes two voices overlap, and 3) sometimes there is no

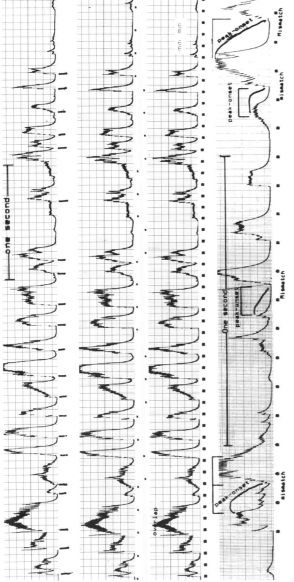

Figure 2. Bushman Storytelling. The marks below the top chart are at points where there are sharp rises in the trace. They are tentative, 'best-guess,' points of motor syllable onset. Under the second chart these same marks have been sorted into sequences of same-spaced intervals. Now that a regular sequence spacing is emerging, other trace rises have been added. There is a rhythmic regularity emerging but in out-of-phase sequences. Under the third chart the marks represent a ±10 cps rhythm train across the entire chart. It was derived by a non-mathematical 'averaging' of the intervals in the chart above and by recognizing: 1) that motor syllables must be at least .2 sec between onsets but 2) that interjected onsets (i.e., those of another person) will begin .1 or .2 sec after a preceding stress peak. This can account for the intermittent mismatches between onsets and the underlying rhythm train in the third chart. In the bottom (magnified) trace the peak-to-onset phenomenon is noted for four instances. When the talk-sound is heard, these are, indeed, points of voice overlap or interjection. When the entire talk unit (sentence?) is seen in relation to the underlying rhythm, it becomes evident that there is an internal self-correcting process--i.e., the rhythm is preserved across the sentence, which begins and ends 'on the beat,' despite the interjected deflections.

silence between syllables and an onset can be seen only as a further rise from continuous voicing. The marks, then, are only "best guesses" at first and have no clear, even spacing that would demonstrate a rhythm. If, however, we compare the marked intervals by laying a strip of paper under them, copying the marks on the paper, and sliding the paper back and forth, we can easily discover that *some* of the intervals (the time between onsets) are the same. And if we take another strip of paper and mark it with a continuous series of these intervals (i.e. a rhythm) and lay this under the trace, quite a few of the presumed onset points fit. Now we can make two observations: 1) some of the rises in the trace that were not marked by the first guesses (because they didn't rise from the baseline) now coincide with the "superimposed" rhythm, and 2) those which do not fit the superimposed rhythm sometimes are spaced the same but are out of phase with the other equal-spaced trains. In Chart B in Fig. 2 I have marked a rhythm series across the chart, but it has gaps. And I have marked some places where trace rises seem to show the same interval spacing but are out-of-phase with the other marked rhythm series.

The sets of marks in (B) are all same-spaced intervals even though they are not continuous across the entire chart or all phase-matched. If we translate the marked rhythm interval into time, the interval is about 16mm on the trace or about two tenths of a second. A motor syllable requires about two tenths of a second of time-space, a syllable may be longer than .2 sec such as a vowel that can be prolonged as long as a lungful of air lasts, but 3) the following onset will fall on a rhythm beat-point. If, then, a syllable is slightly longer then .2 sec, the following onset will be found midway between the points of the .2 sec train we have been marking. From this it follows that the underlying rhythm is actually a one tenth train as is the brainwave pacer.

In chart (C) I have superimposed the 10 cps rhythm across the entire chart. The rhythm was not superimposed but was *derived from the chart*. It is absolutely necessary, when replicating this work, to derive the rhythm interval from the data since the rhythm may never be exactly 10 cps, the tape may have stretched, or the intervening machines may vary in speed. In chart C there are 43 rhythm beats from the first to the last onset and the total distance on the chart is 350mm. Therefore each interval is not 8mm (.1sec) but 8.14mm or about 2% longer. On close examination of the match between the trace rises and the marked rhythm, there is an overall integrity to the rhythm. Despite some "defections", the onsets continue to fit the marked rhythm and the final ones are clearly on it (and the next "sentence" will begin and continue on this same continuing train). It is the process which organizes the "defections" and yet maintains the overall rhythmic integrity that is important to this research.

In chart (C) I have marked two places of clear mismatch. In chart (D) I have "magnified" these for closer examination.

If we listen carefully to the taped sound (perhaps slowing it down) it is possible to *see* the sound-chart relationship and to discover that the onsets that are not on the marked rhythm are those of the listener, who interjects sounds (one or two syllables) and, in two places repeats the speaker's syllables. I am told that it is standard practice among Bushmen for people in conversation to repeat the last words of the previous speaker. In the film of this interaction it looks as though the listener is mimicking the speaker since he also repeats gestures.

The second, interjecting, listener-speaker does not have reliable access to the storyteller's underlying rhythm since the onsets come from the motor impulsing of the diaphragm and intercostal muscles. He can infer it as we first inferred it on the trace, but what is more accessible are stress-peaks of the speaker's syllables. If, then, we look closely at the out-of-phase onsets of the interjected syllables, we can see that those onsets are an exact number of tenths of a second (rhythm units) after a *preceding stress peak* of the storyteller. That is, his onset is entrained by the speaker's preceding stress peak. This resets or recalibrates the rhythm. In chart (D) I have marked this relationship with a curved line from stress-peak to onset.

In all conversations I have examined the turn-taking between (or among) alternating speakers always follows this pattern. Each speaker's beginning onset is entrained by the preceding speaker's stress peak and is a finite number of rhythm unit from it. This accounts for those occasions when two people simultaneously begin to reply to a speaker in group conversation. In some speech or conversational styles the between-speaker interval is brief (in the examples here it is always one tenth of a second) but in other conversations (typical among Eskimos) the interval may be a long pause of seconds. But invariably, in an intact conversational flow, the peak-to-onset interval will be a precise multiple of rhythm units.

In ordinary conversation we do not pay attention to the "degree of precision" of these intervals, but we *feel* them. This emerges as feeling comfortable or uncomfortable about a conversation, feeling that someone "wasn't really paying attention", that a person's "mind had wandered", that his (ill-timed) interruption implied that he didn't hear what the other was saying, that the other person was getting tired, etc. Although I have limited the observation of these relationships to recorded vocal behavior here, they are also present in visible movement behavior. Body parts cannot move as quickly as mouth parts and the easily-visible changes in gestural movement are usually .4 sec apart. In interacting groups it is possible, using analyzer projectors, to discover that everyone's movement onsets (i.e. changes in direction of postural or gestural movement) fall on a shared rhythm train that tends to be the same as military march rate (about 144 steps per minute) or double that of the common heart-rate at rest (72 per minute). When speakers are invisible to each other (on the telephone) or when they are inaudible to each other (deaf), the information sharing is essentially available and ongoing.

Since I am saying that an onset that is mis-timed by about one-fortieth of a second is feeling-significant to the person hearing it, and since this may sound implausible, I will suggest a faily simple way to test this: Find a piece of natural, unrehearsed, "comfortable" conversation on audiotape (recorded at 7 1/2 ips). Copy it and from the copy cut out about a fifth of an inch of tape from the interspeaker silence (the peak-to-onset interval). That will shorten the interval about a fortieth of a second. Listen and compare.

I have focused, here, on the peak-to-onset relationship, which represents one level or part of the whole (in this case the reproduced chart), but there is a higher level or larger whole inferrable from the earlier observation that the underlying shared rhythm was not lost but maintained across the entire sentence and beyond. So, again, there is another apparent paradox: the rhythm is both broken, reset, or recalibrated by the listener and yet it is maintained across the sentence. There is a parallel here with the tightrope walker (or, indeed, with life itself) who is subjected to intermittant small "perturbations" which are corrected in order to maintain the larger balance. That is, the larger organization is self-corrected. If it were not self-correcting i.e. if the underlying rhythm were not shared across the sentence-whole, the conversation would become increasingly uncomfortable, the relationship between the talking interactants would worsen (i.e. become pathological), or the interactants would terminate the interaction. It is the detailed understanding of the self-correcting process which maintains the "health" of the interaction by the continuous sharing of an underlying rhythm and the concomitant sharing of states that will inform other self-correcting processes (and the pathological consequences of their disorganization).

There is an interesting two-level relationship in the Bushman self-regulating process: The underlying shared rhythm is, on one hand, the fixed shared (biological) comparator for the variable, unpredictable information - the modulations of that rhythm. But, at the moment of the interjected perturbation which disturbs (disorganizes) the sharedness of the underlying rhythm is a sudden switch or inversion of "logical type" in which the variable item becomes the fixed comparator and (until corrected) redefines or recalibrates the underlying sharedness. *I am calling attention to this fixed-variable switch because I believe that it is the defining characteristic underlying all pathology.* I will return to this matter as its affects human relations, societies, and emotional epidemiology (the "epidemic" is a disorganizing intrusion but is called "endemic" when it is accomodated into the baseline state of things).

The last observation to make before summarizing the significance of these data is inherent in Fig. 2. The listener-interjector has disturbed the speaker's rhythm four or five times with one, two, or three syllable interjections. Each time a correcting process restored the original rhythm. One might suppose that these perturbations and corrections would have a cumulative or long-range effect on the fixed mechanical rhythm since this is what we infer from most life events. One recovers from assorted trauma (illnesses, accidents, etc.) but the new "norm" is not the same as the previous "norm". But in Fig. 2, where the underlying rhythm is projected across the entire sentence (and it could be continued into the next sentence), it has not been visibly changed. The last syllable onset on the chart is clearly "on target". But there is a change that is not apparent from the chart. At the end of the sentence the listener repeats the last syllables of the speaker and the last syllables are the spoken repeats by the listener. At the end of the sentence represented on the chart, with the listener speaking last, the speaker utters a quiet "ummm" which is followed by and overlaps the listener's "ummm" (.1 or .2 sec later). Since "ummm" is quiet and without a stress peak (it is almost invisible on the chart although it is quite audible), it has no effect on the underlying rhythm - except, perhaps to "reaffirm" it. This overlapping "ummm" is evidently also an end-of-sentence marker since it occurs in this position throughout the half hour of recorded storytelling (and has a gestural concomitant).

I have displayed and described visible process components of this interaction using only the sounds of speech although my investigation began by studying movement relationships without sound. The underlying rhythm was first identified in the movements, but film of body movement has severe limitations. Body parts have differenct inertias and their movements do not start with equal onset clarity. Cameras generally record movement sequences as 24 frames-per-second still photographs with no continuity between. One can slow down the frame rate but cannot retrieve the between-frame flow. By using talk records it is possible to vary the "magnification," to make much more precise measurements, and - most of all - chart records of vocal behavior through time can be produced in written reports. But insofar as the film

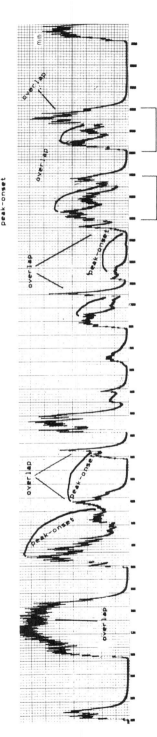

Figure 3. Bushman storytelling, second sentence. As in the first sentence the listener frequently interjects syllables, beginning them a tenth of a second after a preceding stress peak. When more than single syllables are interjected, or when one speaker follows another, the peak-to-onset syllable placement recalibrates the rhythm temporarily. But across a larger stretch of speech a self-correcting process returns the rhythm underlying the talk to the underlying shared rhythm, which is always the same ($\pm$ 10 cps). In other kinds of talk it can be $\pm$ 71/2 cps. At the end of these Bushman storytelling sentences, the listener repeats the last few syllables of the speaker, and at the end each intones an "mm" sound on the shared rhythm. Each following sentence begins on the beat of the rhythm. Since the repeated 'mm' sound is often too soft to appear visibly in traces, the volume of the signal going into the chart recorder was turned up and exaggerated the last trace configuration, the 'mm' sound, in this chart.

The following charts will illustrate the persistence of rhythm sharing in human interaction in different cultural contexts and will show the self-correcting process in more detail. The same self-corrected rhythm-sharing can be found in film or video records without sound. Both the vocal and the movement behavior share the same underlying rhythm in interaction. There is no evidence that the vocal and movement behaviors are separable but are interdependent as a jointly organized communication system.

record permits, the same processes, relationships, and organization that I have described for talk are found in movement with one important caveat: they are not separate but organizationally integrated into our system - communications. In familiar American conversation the "interjections" take the form of head nods, eye blinks, etc.

Before examining the next three examples of trace data there are some summarizing inferences to be made from the Bushman traces.

1. The Bushman interaction unit that I have called a sentence (without linguistic evidence) requires two persons to construct in a process that permits continuous self-correction, in which there are at least two levels of temporal organization, and which is independent of but adaptable to the language words involved.

2. The elements organized in the sentence include both "biological" and "cultural" items but the biology-culture distinction could not be made from *within* the sentence. The internal self-correcting process requires a distinction between fixed and variable items (i.e. the entrainer and the entrained or the shared and the unshared) at any given point in the process. But at the point of speaker-switch or interjection, there is an inversion and the stress-peak in the "cultural" item (the syllable shape) becomes the fixed entraining point for the following syllable onset. I have described this above and I mention it again because 1) pathology in social or interpersonal relationships appears to begin as an unrecognized and therefore uncorrected error in making the fixed-variable (digital-analogic) distinction and 2) immune function (if related to "emotion") may also involve an interplay between fixed-biological and variable-emotional items which can trigger pathology if self-correcting processes become disorganized. The matter is not as simple as making an erroneous distinction. It is complex because the reversal crosses two levels in the organization, is inherently expectable but unpredictable in interactional processes, and may appear paradoxical - as paradoxial as acquiring immunity *from* the disease once seemed, or as cultural-emotional effects on biological systems still seems to many.

3. The psychologist may find no recognizable emotion embedded in the Bushman interaction data I have described. But he may recognize that participants enjoy the interaction or "have fun". I insist that the "fun" is inherent in the participation in a self-organized, self-corrected, precisely organized process. It is curious to me that the interpersonal processes underlying "fun" are ignored until the consequences become visible "joy". Then the "emotion" is examined and the engendering process discarded or subjectively ascribed to one or another cultural "thing".

4. Probably everything I have described in my analysis of the Bushman data is below or beyond the explicit awareness of the participants who, nonetheless, enjoy the interaction in relation to the intactness of its organization but have their own cultural ascription for their feelings. Is it a necessary condition for emotions that access to the inner relational or interactional processes which engender them is denied, requiring humans to ascribe them to external "things" as "causes"? This is an essential question to consider.

The rather detailed description of Bushman storytelling talk was derived from a single "sentence". In order to provide a small measure of perspective I have reproduced the chart tracing of the second "sentence" in Fig. 3 and included the underlying rhythm, the points of listener-interjection, the curving peak-to-onset indicators, the listener repeat at the end, and then the two overlapping "Mmmm" sounds.

The Yanomamo "Shouting Match"

Earlier in this chapter I described occasions in which the "shouting match" occurs. I use "shouting match" as a descriptor only because that is the immediate impression one might form from hearing only the sound. The ethnographer Chagnon (1968) speaks of "chanting". Chagnon writes, "Yanomamo culture calls forth aggressive behavior, but at the same time provides a regulated system in which expressions of violence can be controlled" (p.118), but he does not specifically describe the "shouting match" or "chant" as a violence regulator.

In this Yanomamo interaction each man shouts three syllables, the second person starting (onsetting) one-tenth of a second after the first. They seem to be shouting at the same time - or interrupting each other. The following diagram will illustrate this overlap relationship.

The diagram represents the "ideal", which is only occasionally realized. Unlike the Bushman "storytelling", the Yanomamo chant-talk words are apparently improvised, although set in a traditional talk-structure. If the Bushman story telling interaction parallels the performance of a classical duet (or solo with accompaniment), the Yanomamo shouted "chant" parallels jazz improvisation - in which the structural (temporal) frame is known to both (i.e. shared), but the content is not. In the taped records I have (of two occasions), the men make a few "false starts" before they achieve the precision I have described with the diagram above.

Since each man is shouting, his onsets are also likely to be his stress peaks. Insofar as that happens they are in a mutually entraining vocal juggling performance that requires considerable skill. Fig. 4 is an example, as with Fig. 1, that visualizes the sound as it is formed into the packages I have just described. Above this the same sound is traced out showing the relationships.

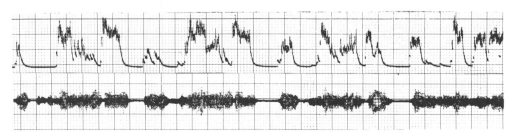

Figure 4: Traces of Yanomamo "shouting match".

On the opposite page (Fig. 5) are three identical traces of three six-syllable, interlocked packages. These will illustrate what I believe to be the tightly interlocked "intimacy" inherent in the conjoint participation of a complex but precisely organized relationship. I have marked a .1 sec. train across the bottom. It is not easy to distinguish each speaker in the traces because of the almost continuous overlap. But as each successive speaker begins, his onset is usually distinguishable as a rise in the trace. Once the interlock pattern is familiar, it becomes easier to find the overlapped onsets since they are usually quite accurately set in the ongoing pattern. The vertical divider separates one package from those before and after.

In the center chart I have circled two places where there are two possible onset points. These are the double onsets I described above, and in Fig. 5 I have marked both the underlying fixed rhythm while the other falls on the appropriate interval after the other speaker's last stress peak.

The basic design elements of the Bushman storytelling are also in this Yanomamo performance: The same underlying rhythm, the same peak-to-onset phenomenon, the same requirement for two speakers conjointly to maintain the pattern, and the readily inferrable self-correcting nature of the complex performance (i.e. the underlying, organizing rhythm is not lost).

But there are differences that make the Yanomamo vocal juggling performance more difficult - and more interesting for my present purposes. Whereas the Bushmen words or script was known in advance to both "performers" and audience so that fitting the words to the interaction pattern had been rehearsed many times, the Yanomamo do not have pre-memorized script to work from. There is considerable (semantic) improvisation which complicates the matter. But, as the chart tracings show, even though they do not always achieve the "ideal" organization of the earlier diagram (the three-syllable overlapped units with a tenth-of-a-second offset), they do not lose the underlying organizing rhythm.

For purposes of this paper there is another and most important observation to be made about this Yanomamo matter. The interaction design or process is characteristic of intimacy - a close, tight, multi-level sharing. But the words and the tone of voice are explicitly intended to convey hostility, ferocity, challenge, bragging about one's self and demeaning the other, etc. That is, there are two levels of meaning, each with emotional implications, but they are diametrically opposed.

The question arises: Which emotion are they "really" feeling? If one were to examine the biochemical or neurological states of these men, which configuration would we find?

In Chagnon's (1968) ethnography of the Yanomamo he includes a photograph of two nearly naked warriors sitting on the ground face to face in a close embrace. The caption reads

> These two men were pounding each other's chest a few minutes before this photo was taken. Here, they embrace each other intimately, vowing eternal friendship, and ask each other for specific trade goods. (p. 116)

I am not concerned with the apparent contradictions since, seen in a larger perspective or context, they are not equivalents but belong to different logical domains (even though one is nested inside the other). The Yanomamo know that feasts (social

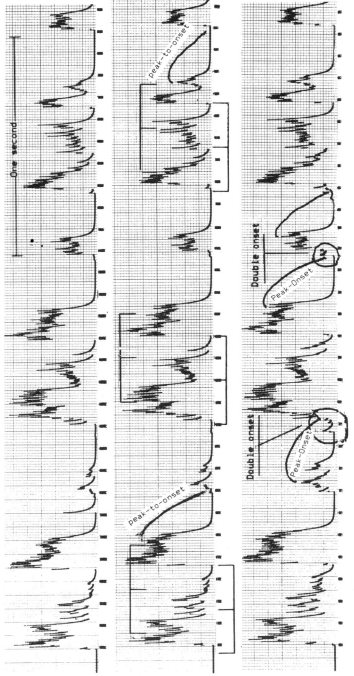

Figure 5. Yanomamo "shouting match." These charts illustrate the way two Yanomamo men brag and shout insults at each other in a highly organized (intimate) way. Although the Bushmen often perform (rehearse) their ritually stylized storytelling, including interjections and gestures, the Yanomamo improvise their words. This unpredictability complicates the matter of self-correction, i.e., staying on the underlying rhythm. A common observation in traces of the "shouting matches" is the double-onset in which a syllable or onset begins at one appropriate point (timed either from a preceding stress-peak or on the shared rhythm) and then rebegins timed from the other. I have marked two of these in the bottom Yanomamo trace but they can be found in other two-person talk. Almost all of the talk sound represented by the charts above is the overlapped voices of two speakers. I have bracketed the syllable-onset points of each speaker--one above the trace, the other below.

hospitality) begin with displays of ferocity and end with ferocious chest-pounding duels. But they also know that a "mistake" in protocol behavior (i.e. in making the organizational distinctions) can almost instantly precipitate a deadly spear thrust and mayhem. If the underlying shared organizing rhythm of their shouting match is lost, self-correction disappears and the relationship is terminated. At this point the distinction between the "rules" and the "game" (which delineates the "reality") is lost. That condition, in my paradigm, engenders pathology.

What, then, is emotion? Is it the feeling expressed by the shouters? The intimacy following the chest-pounding? The fear that follows the dissolution of the "rules"? The anxiety that someone will err and throw the spear? The inner biochemical configuration? Can the feelings be disentangled?

I am not posing these questions to challenge emotion research but to call attention to the complexity of the emotion-immunity matter. I will return to this below.

Laughter at a Movie

The tracing in Figures 6 and 7 are made from a tape recording made by Carl Jones who sat with his tape recorder in the audience at many screenings in different theaters and at different times of a single comic movie, *All of Me*. The tracing here is of a single "joke" and the following audience laughter.

In the movie a central character is told that she is fatally ill and will die soon. (The comedy revolves around a mistake in her plan to transfer her "soul" to another person.) Shortly after she is told she will soon die, there are the following lines:

> Got a cigarette? (sigh)
>   You don't smoke!
> Can't hurt now.

> (laughter)

I have written the words over their representation in the trace at the top of Fig. 6. The second trace in Fig. 6 is a larger trace of the words alone. This trace was made from the sound track of a videocassette of the movie to eliminate audience sounds and acoustical distortion. I have also noted the presence of the underlying rhythm and the now-familiar interval between one speaker's stress-peak and the follwing speaker's onset.

In this talk the underlying rhythm is not the usual conversational 10 cps but is, instead, 7 1/2 cps. (Similar two brain rhythms (around 10 cps and 7 1/2 cps, known respectively as alpha and theta rhythms) have long been recognized and were formally reported by Brazier in 1960.) I have found this 7 1/2 cps rhythm in the recorded speech of radio announcers, onstage actors, a Yanomamo shouting at others to help him sweep the plaza for the feast, a New Guinea man calling to his ancestors, and even the stuttering rate of stutters. I once called this a "performance" rhythm. But that does not adequately distinguish it since both the Bushmen and the Yanomamo are "performing" in the examples above. I do not fully understand the occasion or the context which requires the 7 1/2 rhythm, but I have not found any interaction in which one rhythm

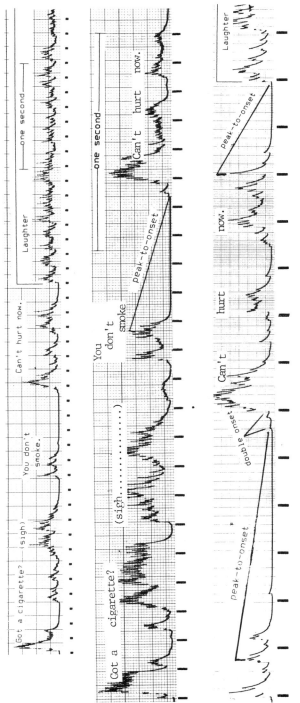

Figure 6. Laughing at a movie joke. The top and bottom traces are from a cassette taperecording made from a seat in the audience at an ordinary motion picture theater showing of All of Me. The middle trace was made from a videocassette of the same movie and has, of course, no audience laughter. The underlying rhythm is ±71/2 cps. which is found in "performed" talk by actors, radio announcers, etc. Although the rhythm persists across the entire interaction in the top trace, the second and third traces show the usual deviation-correction process found in all interaction or conversation. The bottom trace shows in detail the process by which the comedienne's "punch line" is sound-shaped such that the audience laughter is entrained onto the original rhythm train of the actress. Without this "feed forward," which is called "timing" in the theater, the audience would laugh out-of-synch with the actors–and, perhaps, each other. None of these rhythm-maintaining processes can be in the explicit awareness of the actors or audience, but participation in group activities in which all participants share the same rhythm produces good feeling everywhere in the world. In the present case the "fun" of the moviegoers is attributed to the "funny" joke.

or the other was not shared. I also observe that three beats of the 7 1/2 rhythm (.4 sec.) equals two of the .2 sec. syllable beats.

In the first chart of Fig. 6 the chart travel was set at 5 mm/sec so that the entire sequence of three utterances and the laughter are visible on a single line and I have added only the words and laughter that it represents.

In the second trace I have displayed only the trace of the talk and I have "magnified" it (chart travel of 10 mm/sec) for easier measurement. To eliminate theater noise this trace was made from a videocassette tape of the movie which, of course, has no theater laughter on it. In this chart we can make these observations:

1. The underlying rhythm is now 7 1/2 cps.
2. The onset of the first syllable of the second utterance ("You don't smoke.") begins two rhythm units after the stress-peak of the preceeding utterance (which ends with an audible inspiration-expiration sigh). This resets the underlying train so that the second utterance proceeds on a 7 1/2 rhythm train which is out-of-phase with that of the first speaker. When the third utterance ("Can't hurt now.") begins there is a double onset. I have indicated it. The first start of the onset is appropriately timed from the preceeding stress peak (marked with a curved line). It begins 5 rhythm units after the preceeding stress peak. The second half of the double onset (5 mm later on the chart) is on the speaker's original rhythm train - and the out-of-phase shift has been "corrected". I have projected the original rhythm across the out-of-phase segment with dots.

Now we can look at the third chart of Fig. 6 where the theater sound is used and where the time relationship between the punch-line ("Can't hurt now") and the following laughter can be measured.

According to the peak-to-onset "rule" the laughter should begin rhythmically timed from the preceeding stress-peak of "now". It does, indeed, begin precisely at that point. But the comedienne has stretched her "punch line" ("Can't hurt now.") such that her last stress-peak (in fact the last two high points on the chart) are on the original underlying rhythm. I cannot understand how the word "now" can have two such sound peaks, and I cannot recognize them by listening to the recorded sound. But they are clearly on the trace. The end result is that the audience laughter is both timed from the stress-peak and on the original rhythm. That is, the timing of the punch-line corrected for the out-of-phase response *in advance*.

The movie joke-laughter event parallels the two preceeding (Bushman and Yanomamo) interactional events in these ways:
-   A group of people come together and do a culturally defined same thing at the same time in a precisely organized way.
-   The event requires all participants to share an underlying rhythm and to participate in continuous self-correction to maintain the sharing of the rhythm. And all participants appear to be competent to engage in the process without explicity knowing what they are doing.
-   The occasion engenders positive feelings.

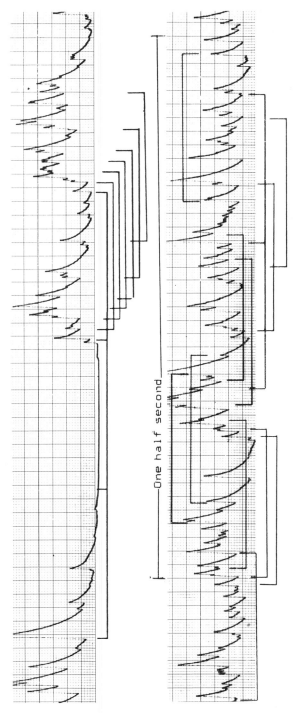

Figure 7. Laughter. The preceding figure (6) showed the rhythm of two people in a comic movie and the timing of the laughter following the "joke." These charts are much magnified traces of 1) the rhythmic relation of the laughter to the joke (top chart) and 2) the internal regularities within the sound of the laughter itself (both charts). The brackets represent one rhythm-unit (7 1/2 cps) and almost all onsets are precisely spaced one rhythm-unit from a preceding onset or peak (in laughter, as in shouting, onsets and peaks are almost simultaneous). I point out these regularities as evidence of precise organization within a theater audience—a co-participation in a shared organization. Although the members of the audience do not laugh in simultaneous synchrony, the traces show an unexpected regularity or organization in the audience behavior that is, as yet, unstudied.

Mechanically Generated Speech

Our library has a device which allows blind students to insert a typed or printed page and, after some whirring and beeping, to hear an artifical "voice" read the words. The words are phonetically clear enough to understand, but the blind student who intoduced me to the machine said that it was so fatiguing to listen to that she rarely used it. The two traces in Figure 8 are randomly selected slices of such speech. By using the "averaging" procedure described above a 10 cps rhythm emerges but, when this rhythm is best-fitted to the trace, some interesting observations are possible.

Although, at first glance, the onsets in this trace seem no more precisely matched or unmatched to the underlying rhythm than those in the other data, there is no "self-correction" involved. There is only "better than random" rhythm-onset fit. That is, there is no human "inner logic" that offsets some or many of the mismatches, there is only, presumably, a machine accomodation. When human speak there is an implicit listener who must be accomodated by pauses for recognition signals, by intonational patterns which signal inner relationships, emphases, phrase relationships, and ends-of-sentences. A machine cannot (or does not) do this. Thus the rhythm variations of the machine carry no information about either the talk or the speaker. (Precisely these aspects, however, are included in Clynes' (1983,1986) microstructure theories and applications to music performance that enable a computer now to perform with a high degree of composer specific musicality, as is evident from recordings included with these publications. But this has not yet been accomplished for poetry or speech.)

One important aspect of this, which was mentioned above, is the matter of minimal syllable timing. In human speech *motor* syllables require a minimum time slot and onsets begin on fixed points of entrainment (as state modulated), either on the underlying fixed rhythm or spaced from a stress-peak. This interval, in turn, has its counterpart in the human "listening rhythm". In the traces in Fig. 8 there is evidence that mechanically generated syllable onsets are independent of and therefore do not continuously accomodate this human "listening-valence". This would require the listener to make a quick, unaccustomed, and perhaps fatiguing compensation or continuously to infer flawed words from the larger sentence context. It is known that the comprehension of speech is impaired as speech rates are varied by speeding up or slowing down the tape travel rate on playback machines. (Humans tend to speed up or slow down their apparent rate of speech by putting more or less language onto each motor syllable - turning "how are you?" into "hiya", or prolonging voicing.) This is, I think, an example of rhythm mismatch or disorganization (between speaker and listener) which engenders fatigue for the listener. While fatigue is not classed as an emotion, it is certainly a state which is subjectively described and which is engendered by rhythmic disorganization. I have circled places where successive (possible) syllable onsets are less than the required .2 sec. apart.

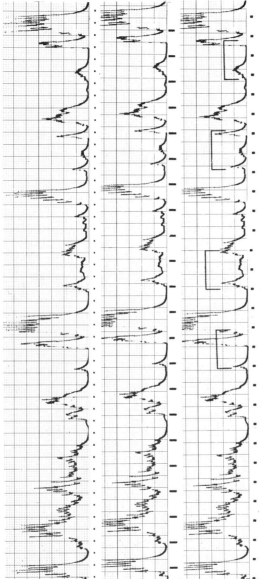

Figure 8. Electronically Generated Speech. Each of the three chart traces of electronically generated speech has been best-fitted to a rhythm: The top trace is fitted to a rhythm derived by the non-mathematical "averaging" procedure. Since it fits quite well across the entire trace, it is unrelated to any known speech-related or brain rhythm. The middle trace is best-fitted to the "performance" rhythm of Figure 6, (in case the 16 cps of the top trace is a double "performance" rhythm). The fit is poor. The bottom trace is fitted to a 10 cps rhythm. The fit between the upswings (onsets?) on the trace and the marked rhythm would not be impossible if the trace were of a conversation except that there are no peak-to-onset relationships to account for the deviations. The most unusual and "inhuman" evidence in the trace is the frequency of onset-like upswings spaced more closely than .2 sec. This would surely affect the comprehensibility of the speech. I have marked such places on the bottom trace.

Summary and Discussion

I have demonstrated in this paper that:

1. A fixed rhythm of either 10 cps or 7 1/2 cps underlies the motor syllable onsets of talk in interaction.

2. The motor syllable onsets of *behaved* talk do not always coincide with the fixed rhythm and I have called the behaved rhythm a modulation of the fixed rhythm.

3. The fixed rhythm can be found by "averaging" the onset train using a procedure that I have described.

4. When one speaker follows another, or interjects syllables into another's talk flow, the second speaker's onsets are entrained by the first speaker's vocal stress peaks. The following or interjecting speaker will being (i.e. onset) a nearly exact number of rhythm units or beats after the entraining stress peak.

5. Since the stress peak is language-determined and only fortuitously related to onsets or the underlying rhythm, the second or interjecting speaker's talk will not be on the underlying rhythm of the preceeding speaker.

6. In the interpersonal talk displayed here as chart tracings, the management of the talk interplay shows several possible conjoint self-correcting procedures for maintaining the integrity of the shared underlying fixed rhythm despite the intermittent deflections: double onsets, the shouted onsets of the Yanomamo, the "mmm" sounds without stress peaks of the Bushmen, the "feed forward" placement of stress peaks of the comedienne.

It is, then, clearly inferrable from these data that these micro-events embrace a variety of items of different "logical types", on different levels of organization" 1) an inferrable underlying fixed rhythm of biological origin, 2) a performed onset rhythm of unpredictable, individual origin, 3) stress peaks of language (cultural) original and 4) a self-correcting process which maintains an overall relational integrity between or among participants. The multi-level interaction is highly and precisely organized and outside the explicit awareness of the participants. There is an exchange or sharing of information that references or contributes to the meaning of the language-encoded material riding on top of it (which is not a concern of this paper), and there is the cumulative state-sharing which is felt as the "state of the interpersonal relationship" - i.e. how one feels about the conversation and/or the other person.

Since the participants necessarily have a "feeling sense" of the interaction (and will recall it by remembering-recognizing the "feeling-tone" before the event itself according to the research cited below), I have proposed that the variable relationships between the fixed and the performed rhythms represent 1) an encoding of the "states" of the interactants, 2) a process by which the states of the interactants are shared. I have, indeed, defined communication at this level, as "state sharing".

In explicity social contexts it could be said, analogously, that people in conversation share information and "feel good" when they agree (i.e. feel the same way about the shared information).

Related Research

Clynes (1973, 1977) asked subjects in several countries to express a series of imagined or fantasied emotions by pressing them on a key or button (see also Clynes, this volume). He used seven emotions, each of which was expressed 50 times (following appropriately spaced clicks on a stimulus tape). The key was linked to a transducer and thence to two pens which drew curves representing the downward and horizontal (toward or away from) pressures on the button. The curves were also stored in computer memory. Then the transients were computer-averaged for each emotion expressed by each person. He found 1) that the averaged curves for each emotion were distinctively different, 2) that the curves for the same emotion were the same across all subjects, regardless of culture. Clynes inferred from this that there are space-time forms or algorithms in the human brain which enabled a precise human expression-identification match (a "key-lock" fit). In research into music, Clynes (e.g. 1986) also found that each composer and each musical style had characteristic underlying pulses, and found a precise microstructure matrix to represent and generate these. He further demonstrated that the emotion curves were also recognizable in other expressive forms such as paintings - in which "love" motifs (e.g. "madonna and child" paintings) were expressed by smooth, rounded shapes (resembling the sentic curve for love) whereas "anger" motifs used abrupt peaking shapes (resembling the sentic curve for anger).

There are parallels between the research described here and the Clynes sentic and musical microstructure research. First, the individual, unaveraged curves are slight variants of the averaged curves. In my research language, the averaged or "ideal" curves are the fixed and universally (biological) shared comparators and the individual expressions are individually "state modulated". Second, the underlying "carrier" or comparator is not a recognizable emotion but a space-time form. The recognizably expressed behavior is, in a social or interpersonal contexts, an emotion. There are, then, three levels of organization or concern: 1) the abstract algorithm in the brain, 2) the curve which expressively implies the algorithm, and 3) the behavior that is called an expression of an emotion. In my research there are oscillations in the brain which pace motor syllable onsets, behaved modulations of the fixed oscillation which represent state information, and perceived feelings resulting from the sharing (or failure to share) the progressive levels of organization (the underlying "premises") in human interaction.

Clynes cannot "explain", but can only attempt to identify the process by which an expressed space-time form by the brain becomes perceived as an emotion. A space-time form, a curve, or a line (on paper or in music) itself is not an emotion but, in an appropriate context is experienced-perceived as one. And I cannot "explain" how the micro-relationships discoverable in vocal activity can be experienced as emotions in appropriate contexts. But the following research reports imply that this, indeed, happens.

In work on the recognition of emotion from vocal cues, Johnson, Emde, Scherer, and Klinnert (1986) an actress spoke the same sentence, "The green book is lying on the table", so as to give "clear vocal expressions" of each of four common discrete emotions: joy, sadness, anger, and fear. It was not surprising that the 23 judges were 100% accurate in distinguishing (forced choice) the emotions on hearing the recorded speech. It was not surprising that the accuracy fell to near chance when the words were synthesized by a Moog synthesizer (although the report does not describe how the synthesizer differentiated the emotions). But it was most surprising to the researchers to find a high accuracy in recognizing the emotions when the sentences were electronically fragmented and random-spliced or when they were played *backward*.

Those of us who work in the area of micro-analysis of human behavior are aware of the highly precise, organized "world" of events below explicit awareness which lies between biochemical or neuronal activity and explicity observable packaged behaviors. We are also aware that such "imperceptible" events may reach observers only as intuition or feelings. No one denies that significance of intuition or feelings in influencing or determining behavior. But, until fairly recently, the organized processes underlying these matters have been out of reach of quantitative research methods - as access to disease and immunity processes were limited before the microscope revealed the underlying world of complex organization and process.

There is another line of emotion research that has proposed that feelings, emotions, or states are the primary indexing categories for memory or recall (Fischer 1971, Tart 1972, Clynes, 1980, Gray 1982, Bower 1982). The commonality among these is the observation that the recall or memory of an experience is enhanced or facilitated when a person is in the same "feeling state" he was in at the experience. Fischer called it "state dependent recall". Tart wrote of "state specificity". Bower wrote that "Memories acquired in one state are accessible mainly in that state but are not available for recall in an alternate state". Both Bower and Gray believed that emotions blend like colors "with a few primary emotions that can be mixed in various proportions to create other emotions". This is consistent with the "finite inventory of emotions" view of Darwin, Clynes, Ekman, Plutchik and others, and it is at least not contradictory with the view developed here: that humans continuously experience a flux of states which become shared in interaction and therefore are a primary defining (and indexing) quality of experience itself.

In this picture, states need not be emotions writ small nor are emotions aggregated, amplified, or organized states. The matter is, like all of life-related phenomena, likely to be better represented as networks or relationship in which nodal points of experience are tagged by concomitant (shared) states. The "meaning" of states, then, is not specific (as we attempt to attach specific meaning to emotions) but are as diverse as the interwoven networks of relationship that are the stuff and the experience of life itself.

This leads, finally, to my opinion that the immunologist could be misled by the word emotion which appears in many guises or transforms in differing contexts. I would prefer a taxonomy of processes from which the possible diversity of emotion related phenomena would emerge. Substantive taxonomies can become a priori premises - useful for common discourse but potentially misleading to science since labelling interferes with our recognition and understanding of self-correcting processes. Labelling may also allow an illusion of sharing: married couples may agree that "love" describes their feelings for each other; Americans may agree that they live in a "democracy", etc. But if these implied premises are only semantically shared, the reality that is progressively constructed on these illusory premises can be progressively pathological. Pathology, then, begins with an underlying and undetected lie (or its equivalent in biological processes) in which the subsequent processes - the sequelae - become progressively flawed. Hence the state, feeling, or emotional concomitants are progressively cumulative and negative. It is this process which, I believe, intrudes on those complex arrangements called "the immune system". The following research supports this.

Kiecolt-Glaser et al. (1987) found evidence that marital distress is "caused" by intensity of attachment, not vice versa. In my research, as I have described it here, increased "communication" will surely increase "marital distress" when the underlying premises of marriage itself are not shared - i.e. when the pretense or illusion of label-based intimacy (sharing) generates increasing pathology in relationship. This contradicts the facile and popular assumption that interpersonal problems will be ameliorated by *more* communication or interaction. If the underlying premises are not shared, greater "intensity of attachment" (i.e. more communication) will surely worsen the relationship. The same research of Kiecolt-Glaser reported that "marital disruption is the single most powerful socio-demographic predictor of stress-related physical illness". Blood samples from women in unsatisfactory marriages showed weaker immune responses than that from women in satisfactory relationships.

In the April/May 1987 issue of Brain/Mind Bulletin an article titled "Depression to become Epidemic?" surveyed recent sociological and psychiatric reports on the increase of depression. Everyone concerned looked for "the complex of causes ranging from genes to environment". I suggest that the front page of every newspaper reflects the steadily growing uncertainty about fundamental (shared) premises. Sociologists call it 'anomie'. Added to this is the increase in 'communication' which inevitably - epidemically - diffuses the underlying state concomitants across interacting populations with even less detectability than the spread of a virus. We recognize the epidemic quality of national excitement, anger, fear, or mourning. But to look for a "cause" may be less relevant than to understand the process of emotional epidemiology inherent in interaction or communication. If emotions affect immunity, the search for a blamable and curable "cause" of immune dysfunction may be fruitless. The "cause" may have its roots in a natural human process in which the self-correcting capability is invisibly flawed.

References

Asch, T., and Chagnon, N., 1968, "The Feast," Distributor: Documentary Educational Resources.

Bateson, Gregory, 1971, Introduction *The Natural History of an Interview,* University of Chicago Library Microfilm Collection of Manuscrips in Cultural Anthropology, series 15, Nos. 95-98.

Benedict, Ruth, 1934, "Patterns of Culture", Houghton Mifflin, Boston.

Benedict, Ruth, 1946, "The Chrysanthemum and the Sword: Patterns of Japanese Culture," Houghton Mifflin, Boston.

Bower, Gordon, 1982, Mood and Memory, *American Psychologist* 36(2):129-148.

Bower, Gordon, et al., 1982, *Journal of Experimental Psychology: General* 110(4):451-473.

Brain/Mind Bulletin, Vol.7 No.6. (Special issue concerning feeling-tone research of Wm. Gray and Paul Violette.) 1982.

Brain/Mind Bulletin Vol.12 No.8. 1987.

Brazier, Mary, 1960, Long-Persisting Electrical Traces in the Brain of Man and Their Possible Relationship to Higher Nervous Activity, *in* "The Moscow Colloquium on

Electroencephalography of Higher Nervous Activity," H. H. Jasper and G. D. Smirnov, eds., *EEG Journal Supplement* 13:347-358.

Byers, Paul, 1972, "From Biological Rhythm to Cultural Pattern: A Study of Minimal Units," (unpublished doctoral dissertation, Columbia University).

Byers, Paul, 1976, Biological rhythms as information channels in interpersonal communication behavior, *in* : "Perspectives in Ethology II," P. P. G. Bateson and P. H. Klopfer, eds., Plenum, New York. *also in:* 1979, "Nonverbal Communication: Readings with Commentary," (2nd edition), Shirley Weitz, ed., Oxford University Press, New York.

Chagnon, N., 1968, "Yanomamo: The Fierce People," Holt, Rinehart and Winston, New York.

Clynes, M. Sentics: biocybernetics of emotion communication, Annals of the New York Academy of Science, vol. 220, Art, 3:55-131, 1973.

Clynes, Manfred, 1977, "Sentics: The Touch of Emotions," Doubleday Anchor, New York.

Clynes, Manfred, 1980, The Communication of Emotion: Theory of Sentics, in: "Theories of Emotion," R. Plutchik and H. Kellerman, eds., Academic Press, New York.

Clynes, M. Expressive Microstructure in Music, linked to Living Qualities, in Studies of Music Performance, J. Sundberg (ed.), Publication of Royal Swedish Academy of Music No. 39, pp, 76-181. Stockholm.

Clynes, Manfred, 1986, Music Beyond the Score, *Communication & Cognition*, 19(2):169-194.

Coberly, L., 1972, "An Interactional Analysis of Ten Curing Ceremonies," (M.A. thesis, Columbia University).

Fischer, Roland, 1971, The "Flashback": Arousal - Statebound Recall of Experience, *Journal of Psychedelic Drugs* 2:31-38.

Goldman-Eisler, Frieda, 1956, The determinants of the rate of speech output and their mutual relations, *Journal of Psychosomatic Research* 1:137-43.

Johnson, W. F., et al., 1986, Recognition of Emotion from Vocal Cues, *Arch. Gen. Psychiatry*, 43:280:283.

Kiecolt-Glaser, J., et al., 1987, Marital Quality, Marital Disruption, and Immune Function, *Psychosomatic Medicine* 49:13-14.

Lindsley, D. B., 1961, The Reticular Activation System and Perceptual Integration, in "Electrical Stimulation of the Brain," D. F. Sheer, ed. University of Texas Press, Austin.

Marshall, F., 1959, "The Harmless People," Knopf, New York.

Stetson, R. H., 1951, "Motor Phonetics: A Study of Speech Movements in Action," Published for Oberlin College by North-Holland Publishing Co., Amsterdam.

Tart, Charles, 1972, States of Consciousness and State Specific Sciences, *Science* 176:1203-10.

Round Table and Two Informal Presentations

edited by
Ted Melnechuk

Helicon Foundation and UCSD
Department of Neuroscience

Clynes: To chair this final session, I now introduce my old friend Theodore Melnechuk, of the University of California San Diego. Ted is a poet and composer who for 25 years has also worked as an interdisciplinary networker and scholar in neuroscience. I don't know anybody who is so knowledgeable in so many subfields of neuroscience without himself having been involved in the research. I'm happy to turn the panel over the Ted.

Melnechuk: I want to make a brief statement on the style and content of our session. As to its style, here is a short poem by Dr. Orpheus called "The Session":

> By accident, anarchists
> summond a senate.
> Disorder was called.
> No one would second
> · unanimous motions
> to challenge credentials.
> Delegates tabled
> the question of voting
> to fix an agenda.
> Volunteer chairman
> lobbied for vetoes
> of all but impeachment
> Adjourning at random,
> they marched out amok
> to an anthem noise.

Now that's what we're *not* going to do. What we *will* do is have a break in the middle so that the session has two halves. This will symbolize the several antinomies this conference is trying to bridge—normal and abnormal behavior, psychology and neuroscience, and human and animal research.

As to content, we're lucky. The conference organizers and I have persuaded two guests to enrich our deliberations with bonus talks, one in each half of this session. The questions and answers specific to these informal presentations will surely lead panel and audience members to discuss other issues relevant to the conference theme. I count especially on the graduate students in the audience to ask sharp questions.

Let us begin with a short informal talk by Dr. Larry Stettner, Professor of Psychology at Wayne State University.

Facial Expression of Emotion

Larry Stettner

Stettner: Thank you, Ted I do want to say a few words about the kind of information concerning emotion we can get from the face and how we can use that information. This is an old issue in psychology with a checkered history in terms of how psychology has treated this information. It's been very dramatic for me because when I began studying psychology I "learned" that there is no reliable information on the face about emotion ...that it was just like verbal language, so that if I went to some other part of the world I couldn't expect to understand anything about what people were feeling from looking at their faces any more than I could understand their language. Furthermore, it was idiosyncratic from person to person and simply looking at a person's face without knowing that person or the context would yield no reliable information. I "learned" that from introductory psychology textbooks and none of my professors felt it was necessary to correct that impression.

And a lot of psychologists learned that and believed that, sad to say, for a long period of time, despite the fact that in their everyday life, of course, they did something else. Maybe at some other time, in another place, it would be possible to focus on the split in all psychologists between their psychological, scientific selves and their everyday interactions with the world and how well those two match or don't match up, and what the implications are. But eventually, through a circuitous route through ethology and animal behavior, I became interested in primate communication signals and then in human communication signals, based on incidental observations which I was doing. The naivete of this is embarrassing, but I guess I'm fairly shameless about it now. I was astonished to find in doing naturalistic observational studies of parents and children that my students and I could make very reliable judgements, and agree on, what was going on emotionally. Because I had "learned" so well that you couldn't learn from the face, we were mystified.

On what basis were we agreeing that this parent is happy while he's playing with the kid and this one's bored and this one's angry? How could we know? We didn't even know who these people were. It became fairly clear that it was the face that was giving us the primary cues, along with body actions, and so I became interested in the face for the information that was there. Of course, around that time, the work of Paul Ekman and Sylvan Tomkins and Cal Izard of facial expression was beginning to be promulgated. I became interested in looking at just exactly what information is available in the face, under what conditions. I want to talk about two of the research projects that I've been involved with and briefly indicate my conceptualization of what information is in the face and the fact that a) there is a tremendous amount of information, and b) there are complexities in interpreting the information in the face. I can now look back and understand why some people might have concluded that there's no reliable information in the face.

Of the two research projects, one has to do with smiles and their meaning. It grew out of an interest in joy and in positive smotional expression. As most psychologists know, it's easy to find functional explanations for fear and anger, but why is there joy? What function does it serve? Dr. Plutchik was one of the few authors I could find who wrote that there's a function for joy - it's a functional system, just like fear and anxiety and so on, and Carol Izard had written likewise. I was interested then in whether there are individual differences in the expression of joy. How much commonality is there from an objective, ethological point of view... and that gets you into smiles. At once, you realize that one of the problems or challenges or beauties in smiles is that they occur in many other situations besides joy or happy situations. If you want to use facial expression as an indicator of what people are feeling or attempting to communicate or how they're responding, you will run up against the problems that smiles will often mislead you.

If you use the kind of coding that a lot of people use in non-verbal interaction studies, which is relatively precise, you establish major categories, one of which is the smile. But if you use it as a single category, you are unfortunately introducing a lot of noise into your system because smiles have different functions. Although smiles could be genuine expressions of happiness, they could be attempts to mask other negative emotions, they could be appeasement signals, they could be social regulation signals, and so on and so forth. One needs to look at the structure of the smiles themselves and fortunately you can build upon the work of Darwin and then Paul Ekman. We now have molecular coding schemes — a facial action coding system — based on the anatomical possibilities of the face. Such approaches permit us to look at the structure and form of various smiles as cues to their functions, which is what I have been doing for four or five years. We have been asking, is there a relationship between the structure and function of smiles? Can we assess function from the various structural features of the smiles? By structural I mean anatomical: the various muscle groups and their patterning. Are the patterns meaningful or random variations of noise?

Our first challenge was this: We know there is a very wide variety of interpretations that people put on smiles but is there really enough variety in the physical form of a smile to carry all this variety of meaning? If there are only five or six different types of forms, but there are forty different interpretations, then we know that the cue is really context. So if a person smiles in one situation — for instance, after being reprimanded by a superior - we might interpret that as an impotent smile or a fearful smile, because we know the context. That very same smile might be interpreted as a flirtatious smile if that person had just entered a restaurant and looked at someone attractive. We can put all these various interpretations on a smile, but how much information is only in the form?

But, the face tends to be interpreted as a whole from a perceptual point of view;

Darwin talks about this in some of his early work on the face. At the same time, Shand was trying to figure out the extent to which the facial muscles can move independently. He was starting to work out the basic anatomical variations in the face. He wanted to see whether people could knit their eyebrows without affecting the mouth, etc. What he had to do, in order to just make such judgements, was to cover the eyebrows while the person was knitting them and have the person judge the mouth because, if you can see the mouth (even though it doesn't move with the eyebrows), you tend to see the mouth corners coming down even though they have not moved.

So a change in one area of the face tends to lead to a perceptual difference in interpretation of other areas of the face. There are little demonstrations you can do: you can draw a downward mouth with either angry eyes or sad eyes and people will judge the mouth to be either angry or sad. So, I would argue that psychologically it's not only the lip corners and the naso-labial crease and cheeks, but also the eyes, because eyes are part of the smile, as Darwin described. Even if we delimit the smile to those areas that are really involved in "the smile" we still have many possible variations and we have to include things like other eyebrow movements, the position of the brows, and most importantly, the effect of other lip actions. At the lip corners, there are many muscles that can pull on the lips simultaneously in different directions. It's really important, when interpreting smiles, to understand how the whole face works.

The face, by and large, has very little or no reciprocal inhibition. You don't have antagonistic muscles in the sense that if one is activated the other is inhibited. There can be simultaneous activation of muscles and what you get then is a result of the forces. You can in fact pull your lip corners up while at the same time another set of muscles is pulling them down. Or you can pull them up and another set of muscles will be pulling laterally, and so on. Therefore blends of fear and happiness, or sadness and happiness, or anger and happiness or whatever, can be expressed dynamically as a result of the forces. You can see that there are, I won't say an infinity, I'll say an indefinitely large number of positions that the lips can take. You have the basic smile which is zygomatic major, combined with various possible effects on the lip corners, as well as the eyes and brows. And because the visual message is not static, it's temporal patterning also gives information. Clearly, there are a large number of structural variations in smiles. Now that is not to say that context hasn't a role. I'm sure context has a very big role. But there's also a very big role for structure, so that form of a smile can give you much information about what type of smile it is. I've done some studies just to show that there's some common agreement in the interpretation of smiles (comparable to agreement found with the classic basic emotional expressions). We were successful, in our first try, in differentiating eleven different types of smiles. They are happy smiles, false/phony smiles, sad smiles, loving smiles, contemptuous smiles, sceptical smiles, smug smiles, puzzled smiles, shy smiles, coy smiles (coy/flirtatious as opposed to coy/shy), and excited vehicle smiles, as we call it, "the roller coaster smile", when somebody is showing happiness, excitement, and fear all at the same time.

Melnechuk: Please show us one.

Stettner: I'll do "loving".

Melnechuk: While we're in a loving mood, you've got about five minutes. Speaking temporally what about the change of the smile in time?

Stettner: Our estimate is exclusive of temporal parameters. Paul Ekman in his book "Telling Lies" has 18 different types of smiles, and we pretty much agree on the ones where we overlap, but he includes a couple of others that are social regulation smiles, smiles that really don't have a specific meaning in terms of an inference about an emotional state, but only in terms of social regulation: for example, an acknowledgement that you said something and I've processed it, and now I'm smiling to let you know that I'm ready to let you say the next thing. One of the broader issues, if you're interested in specific interpretations, is the issue of genuine smiles, natural smiles, versus controlled smiles or smiles altered in one way or another. My data suggests that human beings are extremely good at detecting the difference between a genuine smile and a smile that's altered in any of a number of different ways. Another issue is whether people can detect a happy smile when they have to contrast it to other smiles? It turned out they can, because in our matrix of four examples of 12 different types of smiles, none of the other smiles was ever judged to be a happy smile with anything *near* the frequency of the happy smile. The only one that was at all close was the false smile. But only about 30% of the false smiles were judged real, whereas 82% of the happy smiles were seen as happy. So I think humans have a very strong perceptual ability to detect happy or genuine smiles.

Clynes: Are you doing this with static pictures?

Stettner: Yes.

Clynes: If you did it with dynamic ones, you'd probably get even higher success rates.

Stettner: Definitely. The static picture is definitely an impoverished stimulus.

Clynes: How do you know, in the static picture, which moment to choose?

Stettner: There are very specific features that you can look for. Paul Ekman's latest work on controlled smiles of various kinds fits in very well with what we're finding: there are criteria, and I think people are sensitive to them. To decide the moment was the most complicated part of the study. The moments were actually frozen mements from video tapes. We *a priori* set criteria for the prototypes for the different kinds, based on our observations, - and then we had professional actors move specific facial muscles in specific configurations. We videotaped that entire session, then went through the tapes and got the one frame that came closest to the prototypes we had specified. So if we specified for example a fear smile, the brows raised and knitted together, the eyelids raised to the maximum, the lips stretched laterally, the jaw dropped, and the zygomatic was activated, all simultaneously.

Clynes: How did you get the specifications?

Stettner: Oh, how did we *generate* those?

Melnechuk: How did you know what should be there?

Stettner: We generated those hypotheses in three different ways. First, we just used hypotheses based on blends; that is, we assumed that if you had sad brows, and upturned lip corners, that would be a sad smile. So we went to the Darwinian prototypes and some of those were based on blends. Second, some were based on empirical induction from looking at newspapers and magazines for smiles where we knew the context. Third were some really truly ad hoc observations. It was a grab bag of different ways, giving us twelve we felt pretty good about. Eleven of the twelve work; the one that didn't work was the nervous smile. I think it didn't work because we had static portrayals.

Clynes: You say "we"; you had a number of people who were judging these criteria?

Stettner: Yes. I and two graduate students who developed the criteria. Then we picked single frames from the video tape and showed those to 8 judges, to see if they agreed.

Melnechuk: It is modified by culture. I'm thinking of the work of Eibl-Eiblsfeldt, for example; or the fact that the Japanese smile when embarassed. Of course not only they do. Have you been working only with American culture?

Stettner: We're working with the American culture, but we want to do cross-cultural work, because I have no idea of the generality of our findings, although I have some guesses about this. You mentioned Eibl; our coy smile has features almost identical to the features of the coy expressions that he has described cross-culturally. So that one of ours probably has some cultural universality. But we have no data on that. This is something that we're just starting to do.

Clynes: Well, I'm not at all surprised that you found this high precision and discriminability. I think it's wonderful. It accords very well with the kind of findings we've been getting from dynamic expressions of emotion when generating emotion through repeated touch expression. We have also found the *need* for smiling as part of the total gestalt of the emotion, particularly in love and in joy. We see that a little smile during love is very important. It's harder to do that *little* smile than it is to do a social smile. When you do it, it locks in with that feeling, and then that smile is not really so much a dynamic one anymore, but persists during the entire state of love, as you do a number of expressions. You have, I wouldn't say exactly a fixed smile, but a steady smile. In the phase of joy there is also a smile, which is slightly different, but we find that in reverence there is no smile. So the gestalt of these things includes movement, dynamic processes and the state as well, and what movement you would take is a complex question, if you are constrained to take a static cross-section. Of course, that is precisely what great painters have to do, and have done so superlatively well, at times. So it might actually be worthwhile to compare their choices, in order to arrive at your "standards".

Stettner: One question which I was going to ask but which you have partially answered, is about what is going on in people's faces while they are making your sentic movements, and the extent to which you incorporate that into your system. What you are saying is that you do incorporate that.

Clynes: Automatically. People can't help themselves.

Stettner: I couldn't imagine doing those movements without moving my face.

Clynes: But you don't make a new facial movement with every finger pressure expression. It becomes a steady thing. Just as in grief, for example there's a tendency to move your head down, to one side, and you wouldn't want to smile during grief. All that is part of the nature ...

Stettner: This is something that you initally observe as you train people in movements and you see that there are body and facial postures that go along with that. But is this something that you now try to incorporate in your training? If you see someone doing something incompatible, do you then say, this may not be working because you are not doing the right thing with your face?

Clynes: We can use this information on the integral aspects of the dynamic and static effects involving different parts of the body to improve not only the speed of learning to do the cycle well but also the intensity and quality or purity of the emotion. We know what the natural gestalt of an emotion is, and it is so particular for specific emotions. For instance, in reverence, now, if you do a movement for reverence like this, if you just put your thumb like that, or do this, or do that as you express reverence it ruins the reverence completely. It's gone, the whole feeling is gone. It's as if you were using your smiles with a slight distortion. The nervous system is tuned to these shapes, in some way that we do not know. That is of course, a most important and interesting question, which can be pursued from the genetic angle when we know a little more of how the genes control these patterns. At the moment, this is still beyond the capacity of genetic inquiry.

Melnechuk: If I can pick upon your words about genes to refer back to a point that Larry made earlier that seemed almost a challenge to the evolutionary minded amongst us. Dr. Plutchik spoke on the survival value of smiles. I think you comment on this too, Marvin in reflecting on Manfred's work, that the rewarding value of your own child's first smile at your is enormous, and I imagine part of its survival value is that bonding occurs. Do you have any further thoughts on that?

Minksy: I was just thinking of a friend of mine in college who became virtually sociophobic. He complained that people could tell what he was thinking whenever he tried to tell a lie or otherwise be devious. He was very uncomfortable because he felt that people could always tell when he was masking something. I told him that it was because of his fooling smile, and he said "What?". All of his roommates agreed that whenever he said something that wasn't true he was smiling out of one side of his face. It was quite a relief to him that they weren't reading his mind. He wouldn't have survived in a competitive society.

Plutchik: I have little difficulty grasping the initial staring point of that type of study, as I tried it myself sometime back in the fifties. I actually did something along the same lines, in which, instead of labeling the series of facial expressions in advance with my labels, I simply collected a group of geometric patterns. One of the patterns was a U-shaped pattern, an other was an inverted U pattern, and another pattern was a straight line or an ellipse and so on, and I took it for each part of the face separately, and then got judges to tell what the patterns meant to them. Which I think avoids the problem that I perceive.

Stettner: These were human faces.

Plutchik: Yes, human faces.

Minsky: You asked a subject to look at one of these patterns, make a face for it and ...

Plutchik: No, no. It was simply to look and describe what emotion people thought was represented.

Stettner: What did the faces took like?

Minksy: Like what emotion was in the geometric pattern?

Plutchik: I had three parts of the face, the forehead, the eye patterns, and the mouth patterns. There was a fair amount of consistency in what the judges did. The problem that I have is that when you say there are twelve smiles, or eighteen smiles, I think what you are saying is that there are lots of variations in facial patterns as a whole. So it is like a conditional probability situation in which the interpretation of a partially open mouth is dependent on what you are doing with your forehead or eyes. And I don't think that it is quite fair to say that you are then dealing with smiles. You see, if we go back to the evolutionary view which Ted brought up, people like Andrews and others have pointed out that mouth patterns of a number of different sorts do convey information. Just as I said yesterday, they represent communications and intentions of various kinds and for the most part of the ethologists tell us there are three such intentions that are communicated by mouth patterns, and I don't really care whether you call it a smile or something else. You can open your mouth in several different ways. One of these types of patterns is what you would call an appeasement expression, and it is the kind of a smile that is not exactly a smile, and I suppose with a subtle facial coding system, you would find that is a little different than something else. But in addition to appeasement, a second thing that smiles represent is affiliation. Certain types of open mouth patterns tend to bring people closer, and that is the bonding that you mentioned, Ted, particularly with regard to parent-child relations. The third major thing the ethologists tell us is that open mouth patterns can represent is threat. So what we get, is really three interacting patterns — affiliation, appeasement, and threat, which are all represented by what you do with your mouth, and the interpretation that an animal or human gives to this is dependent, in part, upon context and what the rest of the face is doing, but these patterns can be described in approximate ways in probabilistic terms.

Minsky: On the issue of whether it is the mouth we're talking about or the subset of expressions that people call smiles, I think they can be divided into two different subjects.

Plutchik: The word smile is a very loose term. People can open their mouths and turn their lips up somewhat and they will call it a smile. They can keep their mouthes closed and turn it up and call it a smile. They can open their mouth and pull it to the side and call it a smile. They can open their mouth and open it relatively wide and call it a smile. Now these are all smiles of sort, but they really communicate different information.

Stettner: Well sure.

Lewis: But even if you take your three categories, which are different phenomenologically, you can think of them all as bonding techniques. Some are direct, and some are indirect, but trying to manage the same goal. The appeasement smile certainly does that. The affiliative smile does not have to be devious or indirect and the threat smile may also defend against the severance of bonds.

Scott: From an evolutionary point of view, this implies that whatever you are talking about has some sort of a function. I think that what Dr. Lewis has said is quite insightful because it implies a broad general function of smiling. That would be backed up by the developmental evidence, because babies smiles are not differentiated in all these different ways, and it must primarily have that function of bonding. Thus, I think you can think of this as having a primary function which is then differentiated into many other important things.

Clynes: From an evolutionary point of view there is another interesting thing. Notice that it is not possible to laugh without first smiling. First there is a little smile, and then you laugh, and as you finish laughter, you end up with a little smile. Laughter is a higher evolutionary thing than smiling, so that here there is a recapitulation of the evolutionary chain of events in the pattern itself. Laughter is akin to smiling but is another development.

Lewis: I'm puzzled by something that Manfred just said and I just want to know, do animals smile?

Zivin: Primates retract their lips and show their teeth. Perhaps it functions as a smile (as it's associated with affiliative behaviors).

Lewis: I had the fantasy that smiling and laughter both were more or less uniquely human.

Panksepp: How about tail wagging, Paul?

Melnechuk: Primates will lure you to the cage and then throw excrement at you, and then smile.

Lewis: That's a triumphant laugh!

Zivin: An important paper on the evolution of the human smile and laugh is by Van Hooff (in Hinde, R.A. (Ed.), *Non-verbal Communication.* Cambridge: Cambridge U. Press, 1972, 209-241). He shows by contextual analyses that there are two higher primate displays of non-threatening excited playfulness, the "relaxed open-mouth display" and of submissive affiliation, the "silent bared-teeth display." He argues that these two converged over evolution in humans to form components of a display of varying intensity, with a smile less intense that a laugh. So we're back to the question of what must be present, to say that it is the emotion you think of as indicated by the word smile. Apes do a movement that contextually suggests thay may be feeling some of the social tension that humans may feel when they laugh.

Lewis: But we are so infected with bonding. From whatever I've understood, we've got it lifelong.

Panksepp: Lots of other species have it lifelong too...

Stettner: If you get to know baboons, you look for lip smacking in situations in which you would look for smiles in humans. It has a lot of varied functions: it's appeasement, it's also reassurance, and in a tense situation, it helps reduce the tensions. I think that the form of smiling from nonhuman primates to humans has changed dramatically.

Lewis: Let me put it another way. I think we're the only species in which the baby is born into a whole context of morality. The very way you treat the baby, the way you pick the baby up, those are all now inscribed in the culture, and every culture has a morality. That's what we're born into, which I think is different from what animals have.

Melnechuk: I recall a neurological finding that certain brain strokes will eliminate the capacity to do the false, or what I call the flight attendant's smile, but leave intact the capacity to smile spontaneously. It may be that the stroke has wiped out the cortical intentional controlled smile but has left some lower neural mechanism of smiling.

Panksepp: I think the neurological evidence certainly indicates that laughter and smiling are very primitive processes, emerging from the brain stem level. People having demyelinating diseases in the midbrain start to show spontaneous releases of emotional fixed action patterns. For instance, they go into crying spells and laughter spells. The two typically go together: a person who shows one will begin to show the other. So those two sides of the social coin seem to be imprinted at brain stem level, which suggests, to me anyway, that other mammals should possess the same funda-mental process although the species-typical expression may well be different. I think that the tail wag is certainly related to the smile, but if you're walking on all fours it may not be as informative to move your face as to move your tail — which may be what your companions are looking at. Maybe even humans shift their butts back and fourth a little when they are laughing.

Melnechuk: Only if they're cheerleaders. Dr. Clynes discovered an alternative form of laughter that is close to your tail wag, because it involves finger wiggle. Manfred please tell them about it.

Clynes: I don't think it has that much relevance to this discussion, but may I just say before I do that, that babies actually start to smile before they laugh, as far as I know, so they may also be giving an indication that laughter, evolution-wise, is really later than the smile. And a second comment, to emphasize the importance symmetry in certain kinds of smiles. The meaning of a smile is radically changed if there's an asymmetry in the smile. A truly loving smile is symmetrical. In the sentic cycle experience you learn to expect there's something wrong if a person produces an asymmetric smile.

To come to Ted's point, I don't see any relevance here.

Melnechuk: I see the relevance. Jaak said that the tail wag can express...

Clynes: The tail wag?... OK, but this is not like a tail wag, because a tail wag's a natural thing. Now we have done something *unnatural* ... we have done something

Melnechuk: Unspeakable.

Clynes: Unspeakable. Yes. Unvoicable. We have changed the laughter pattern of humanity and made it kind of inhuman, but using our brain. I asked myself, "What is the laughter pattern?" It consists of a breathing pattern plus a voice pattern. Now sentic theory says, as a result of many observations, that it doesn't matter which motor output you use for a particular emotionally-expressive dynamic form, i.e. you can substitute another motor output as long as you keep the same dynamic form. So, we made a prediction, in the sense of hard science, that you can take away the usual motor pattern from the laughter, and substitute an arbitrary other one, provided that other one has enough flexibility .. to go fast enough for the "haha". So, for example, the nearest thing was... well, I'll do it now if you like, so.

Dr. Clynes demonstrates silent laughter by silently mouthing "haha" while tapping with a finger in time with the syllables.

Melnechuk: You could have fooled me.

Clynes: And sure enough the prediction came true: While doing this I have the same sense of funniness ... and what is that? This sense of funniness comes out of laughter, and only if my substitute goes at the right rate, then I feel exactly the same thing. And your eyes will water, and all the rest of it. You get the same enjoyment, except for the sound; but it's unnatural. But that very thing proves that one can predict a *new* phenomenon of this kind. We can displace a tension into some other form of muscular tension ...

Liebowitz: You don't look like you've displaced it; you just look like you've added something on.

Melnechuk: Well, he didn't make the sound.

Clynes: I displaced the vocal motor output and added on this other thing, in place of it.

Liebowitz: You were making a vocal motor output ...

Panksepp: It was like whispering laughter.

Liebowitz: You weren't quite, you were making a vocal motor output.

Clynes: You still have to do the same breathing pattern. It is not a voiced laughter and the breathing pattern makes some sound that does not sound like laughter at all. There are two patterns involved, breathing and the voiced sound. We just took the latter one of these and substituted for it another muscle activity, finger pressure say. And *only* when the chosen muscle output activity has the same repetition rate as the "haha's", does the sense of funniness lock in. Without such muscle output, in addition to the breathing there is no funniness. That is the coherence priniciple which is involved in this prediction of a new, biologically based, emotionally expressive pattern for laughter. In a similar way the natural tension in the back of the neck which is part of yawning can be arbitrarily replaced by another tension elsewhere in the body. There are many different kinds of laughter, so you modulate. There is happy laughter, or malicious, or sardonic, etc.... These are sentic modulations of the basic pattern, using the expressive forms of the emotion to modulate the laughter pattern.

Liebowitz: The other issue that comes up with smiling and laughing is that it's not always communicaive. People can smile and laugh by themselves with certain emotions...

Lewis: It might be communicative even if one is literally along, because we carry in our heads all sorts of symbols of other people. Who knows who's there when you're alone?

Liebowitz: But there's another way to think about it, rather than in a communicative way, and that is really just in an expressive way, that it's really almost an overflow of the activity of certain brain circuits when you feel in a certain emotional state.

Clynes: I call that "auto-communicative".

Liebowitz: And if somebody, say they fall in love, they're feeling very happy. Now they can have this great grin on their faces when they're with the ...

Lewis: Yes, that's what I meant...

Liebowitz: ... and the smile and laughter in that sense is really an overflow of the emotional and chemical arousal that's ...

Minsky: Either that or else you could call it communication in a stupid form. The presence of the other person is only a minor physiological feature.

Zivin: While we're talking about subdividing the phenomenon, we should mention something that's probably occurred to everyone at this table who has worked on expression. What do we need to know beyond the behavioral form in order to be comfortable that the emotion that we think is being expressed is in fact present? That's been the problem all the way through the work on facial expressions of emotion: to get independent confirming evidence that what's happening on the face is tied in any way to what we, in common language/lay-psychological theory, *think* is happening on the inside. And there certainly is enormous controversy in the field now as to whether cognition, and cognition of what sort, and when, is necessary, in emotion. Dr. Plutchik, for example has a very specific position where appraisal of the stimulus has to occur to kick off the state. There are folks in the field who would say, "No, that's not necessary", ... but its methodologically absolutely untapped. The best we've been able to do is to have people report what they think they're feeling when they do this on their face. But it's a *terrible* methodological problem. I'm very sensitive to it because I'm trying to measure any physiology that might give us a clue to differentiate between states. Paul Ekman has one paper that (Ekman, P., Levenson, A.W., and Friesen, W.V. *Science,* 1983, 221: 1208-1210) slightly suggests that there are some gross patterns that differentiate positive and negative or activating/de-activating states. These measures are of face *makers*. I'm starting to look at whether or not we can pick up any physiologic pattern differences in people *perceiving* — not making, but perceiving — facial expressions in someone else, in a natural situation.

Melnechuk: How do you measure?

Zivin: Using what Ekman did. He got the greatest differentiation on finger skin temperature plus heart rate. I'm also doing EMG because I'm measuring tonus, because as I'll say a little later in the second mini-topic, emotions involve posture. I'm also measuring breathing and skin electrical resistance, with the interpersonal situation on videotape.

Melnechuk: Graduate students, any questions?

Audience: For your stimulus, you put the picture up and then you're going to have EMG for a minute, for a second?

Zivin: I'm lucky to be using a sleep lab as a natural setting. I have as subjects men who have come in to be evaluated on sleep difficulties like sleep, apnea ... They've been wired up for physiological measurements since early morning and they take brief naps all day. After their second nap, an actor posing as another middle-aged patient walks in. He gives one expression, and goes into a few seconds patter that can lead him to another expression, and then a few seconds patter that can lead him into a third expression. The order of expressions is varied across subjects. We are looking at what responses we get within the first 30 seconds after each expression. I'm just piloting now.

Audience: That almost seems to me to be too long.

Zivin: It probably is.

Audience: The Ekman study wasn't half a minute, where they had the actors pose and took peripheral measures.

Zivin: Yes, Ekman had them hold the pose for 6 sec. I don't remember how long after the pose he still looked for effects. In theory, we would allow a "window" of 30 sec. after the expression is made in which to look for any effect. In practice, things change so fast during conversational interactions that, when we tract what's happening between the actor and the subject, it makes sense only to use only the first 4 - 8 sec. of that window. We know when the expression was made in relation to the polygraph measurements because the actor presses a button in his sleeve that feeds a signal to the polygraph when he makes each expression.

Melnechuk: I'm glad you raised the issue of temporal distinctions because it raises a point that I was troubled by during the meeting. You've measured the duration of emotional expression as a matter of seconds. Then there are moods that may last minutes and hours, and attitudes that may be measured in months and years, and then there are traits that may be measured in years and lifetimes. Yet the word "emotion" has been used for all of them. As I listened to you for two days, I was trying to tell what the duration was of what you were talking about. Anybody want to comment on that?

Minsky: Probably there are different brain centers involved. On the methodological question, I think psychology has gotten used to the idea that subjective things are hard to measure, and a lot of people forget that this is just bad luck, because brain cells are only half a micron and synapses are smaller than that. In a hundred years there'll be this magnetic thing and you put your head in it, like the instrument used on Spock's brain in the latest *Star Trek* film. Then you'll see which brain centers light up and the methodology will be trivial. So, it's all right to think about it, but you shouldn't feel too uncomfortable that the methodology of measuring emotions is obscure, because we're in the Middle Ages of psychology and we don't have electricity yet, so to speak.

Liebowitz: I think you can better study short-range emotion than these long-term patterns. The long term patterns are part of something called personality. It's only very recently that people have begun to try to break those down in terms of short-range emotional dispositions and then look at personalities and see what the sum total is. That's one of the thrusts of psychopharmacology, actually. There are the short-term modifications but very few people have looked at the long-term effects of psychopharmacological interventions - what happens over six months and what long-term modifications there are.

Lewis: If we think in the context of bonding, we can think of emotions as life-long. On occasion, when we invite their expression in the laboratory, it's of short duration for the experiment that we perform, but love, I should think, would be regarded, at least in thie species, as life-long.

Melnechuk: Since you can be angry at someone you love, you've now introduced another kind of distinction. Yesterday, Marvin mentioned that a colleague of his, Roger Schank at Yale, divided congnitive scientists into types - the "neats" and the "scruffys" - and I've noticed that we have amongst us at this table what I'll call "lumpers" and "splitters". Thus we have one group, especially in animal studies who claim that there are four fundamental emotions. Plutchik has eight. Clynes has around ten. The other lists we know of by Izard etc. list on the order of ten fundamental emotions. On the other hand, others amoung us have distinguished guilt from shame, and we have seen that anxiety alone has at least three types, pharmacologically dissected. We have seen that guilt can be dissected into aspects of feeling appalled, feeling blameworthy, feeling obliged or responsible. Now shame has shyness, embarassment in the cluster. What I'm getting at is the old problem of should we be lumpers and look, like the physicists, for four forces that reduce to one, or should we be splitters and look at the thesaurus and see that there are hundreds of names of different emotions. And what are the principles of deriving compound molecular emotions from atomic fundamental emotions? Some of you have said that they're additive. I think you said, Bob, they add up to a compound derived by addition. I know Clynes has said that the expression of melancholy is compound, the first half of which is, I think, love, and the second half of which is grief. So he has a theory that you can temporally combine emotions in their expression. Will anybody here give me rules for handling the obvious multiplicity of subtle human emotions and somehow reconcile that with the claim of essentially only ... four ... or not many more basic emotions?

Panksepp: I think both sides have truth in what they say. There has to be some lumping initially. If you don't lump, you don't know how to split complex things. So my approach is minimalist, based solely in terms of what solid empirical evidence can support. If we can agree on the basic ones, we have the possibility of proceeding with more empirical rigor than if we start with too extensive a list. For four basic affective substrates one could construct an enormous amount of affective diversity. There are various possibilities. You can interact them, you can add them, you can subtract them, and perhaps you can come to one million eight hundred thousand different varieties, especially when you add the complexity of a cortex on top of the basic potential.

Minsky: I've an objection to that. It's time to come out of the Middle Ages. You can't add processes. You should study computer science and take it with a great grain of salt. For example, nostalgia isn't love plus grief. Nostalgia is probably using some type of memory retrieval mechanism to get a recollection, to put it in short-term memory, then turn on another emotion to process it in a certain way and put it back. I'm saying the language of addition, multiplication, and so forth that comes from the disgusting statistical psychology of the 1930's to '50's should be abandoned and you should not add, you should patch, you should call, you should stack, you should cash. There are several hundred words to replace this word add. I think the trouble is that we are still in the world of adding and subtracting, and you have to clean all that out.

You cannot add two processes. In a parallel computer you can have two brain centres running, but I bet they *won't* run. You want a little theory of what the emotions do, and I think you should stop saying sadness. You should say sadness, but you have to have some theory too. It doesn't matter if it is wrong about what sadness does to memory and to representations.

Panksepp: I think you need to know the hardware though. I believe that we will understand the hardware sometime and this is really the only kind of evidence which will lead to a substantive science of emotions, although many may shun the approach since the evidence is so hard to come by.

Minksy: But in the meantime you have to make up hardware, because making up adding is just as bad.

Panksepp: But there is excitation and inhibition in the nervous system. Excitation is a basic function of the nervous system, and no one would disagree with that. Excitation added to excitation in common parlance is addition. If I take an angry animal, and I further irritate it, I will get a super angry animal as opposed to a mildly irritated animal. This is an addition.

Melnechuk: But it's not necessarily linear addition.

Scott: Hundreds of emotions have been described in human beings. If you look at those, the way they are defined is by the context. For instance, you can't think of what awe would be like without looking at some grand mountain or ocean, or something like that. You can't identify certain feelings, except in a particular context, and what you have tried to do in getting at these fundamental emotions is to get emotional states that can be recognized per se; ... in other words, that are not dependent upon the contextual mileu in which they occur. Then the theory would be that the other emotions — these hundreds of emotions that people have described — are really variations on, or perhaps combinations of, these fundamental things, which are associated with particular situations, and in that way you can get an orderly arrangement of emotional phenomena, which also lends itself, as Jaak has pointed out, to physiological analysis, while the other does not.

Melnechuk: It is the combination procedure that worries me. I haven't seen a pyramidal linkage of the few to the many.

Panksepp: I have a suspicion that it may be located in language cortex largely. When the language cortex is looking at brain processes which are "combining" — for lack of a better word — in various ways, it attaches a label to it, and we find this infinity emerging from simplicity due to a host of minor variations, like the minor variations on a smile, which we have already discussed. From a biomedical perspective, if we take patient populations with emotional disorders, I think it is very useful to focus on what is basic and how can we understand those underlying processes. Unless we understand the basic nature of emotionality biochemically at this point, we won't have a deep knowledge of emotionality, and we won't be able to manipulate these things medically in effective ways.

Audience: How much of this is linguistic then? If the Normans had not conquered the Britons and doubled the number of English words, would we have half the number of emotions?

Liebowitz: In terms of what Jaak was talking about, looking at the fundamental states, I think ... is a very useful thing for studying psychopathology, to try to get down to certain core vulnerabilities, and determine whether some state is a panic attack, or whether it is extreme hypersensitivity to criticism, or whether it is too much autonomous mood liability of one type or another. Those things are probably going to be basic, and psychopharmacology provides one method of teasing out among the apparent heterogeneity, things that you could then study temporally, and cross-sectionally and biochemically and neurophysiologically, to try to detect some core vulnerabilities.

Melnechuk: I would like to second the thrust of what you say in that my experience has been that each level or approach has passionate advocates, outstanding champions, like yourself, of what you are up to, who necessarily must think that is the best thing to do. It certainly is for you, but looked at socially, it takes all kinds, and the rest of the disciplines can't be idle while they wait for you to make your fundamental discoveries. They've got to go ahead at their levels too. Psychology may be valid in its own terms, as Skinner was even though he didn't care what physiological mechanism connected stimulus to response; it could have been spaghetti, as far as he was concerned. Yet he made some important discoveries, such as intermittent reinforcement, which were not correlated with brain mechanisms. Meanwhile, people were finding out remarkable things about the brain, at the organ level, regional level, circuit level, cell cluster level, cell level, organelle level, macromolecular level, small molecule level, and ionic level, and some day maybe even at the quark level, for all I know. And that is all right. We all have to work in parallel.

Panksepp: I agree with everything you say. Maybe I was responding to Marvin's statement that we are in the Middle Ages, when we are perhaps even more primitive, in the Dark Ages, even in Stone Ages, and how do we get out of those stone ages? Marvin's point, I believe, was we get out of it theoretically, while my perspective is that we will get out of it empirically, but I think the two need to go hand in hand, since you will not have good empirical data unless you have good theory, but if you just have theory that doesn't lead to observable consequences, it will be sterile.

Zivin: I would like to throw in a third element in the search, between theory and observation; namely a search for plausible constraints on what should limit the theory and what should limit the empirical search. This solution occurred to me: that whatever we are looking for should make evolutionary sense. Therefore it should be tied to some fundamental survival relevance and inclusive fitness features. That can be used to limit us from getting so multiplicative we can't focus.

Minsky: You have to be careful in the case of human intelligence, because what happened, I think, is that a couple of million years ago, what evolved was a way to manage more memory than other animals could have. This had a big survival advantage, and it lead to increasing the size of the brain very rapidly, and this was such a survival advantage that a lot of the things that came along with it will probably not be understood if you are too evolutionary, because they are bugs. If you have a big new machine, it is going to be full of things that are not adaptive, and so I would cut off evolutionary analysis at about half-a-million years ago, and go very easy on saying we won't accept this unless it has some purpose, because it hasn't been debugged yet. The generation time of man got longer, and his rate of evolution slowed down, and that's why we go crazy.

Zivin: Let me try to be a little bit more sophisticated about what we mean by evolutionarily making sense. To say "Because it exists, it must have a function, and what's the function?" is simplistic. This is the know-nothing, stupid social Darwinism. That was not what I was suggesting that we do, but rather to look at what are simple systems, features, that could have evolved by transmissions of genes through behaviors and populations.

Minsky: You will probably find that there are emotional things which are ridiculous and the reason we survived is that we learned to control them, and we are socialized.

Audience: There is a function of emotions that we have not really talked about yet, namely energy discharge. I bring it up because when Dr. Clynes was speaking last night, he described that these emotional states which are generated can be exhibited only for so long; for instance, you can cry for only so long. Then, there is the possibility that there is some other state inside us, such as when you work well at the end of the day you have more energy. Maybe emotion is energy release, and the other state that you described, where you get energy, is something different, or are there emotions which are energy-releasing emotions, and others that are energy-generating?

Melnechuk: The notion of energy release is a Freudian idea that implies we are somehow like steam-engines. I think it is merely metaphorical, and should be examined hard, as to whether it described anything real.

Clynes: Yes, mental energy is more than a one-dimensional kind of thing. The word energy is improperly applied, we think we know what we are talking about, but we really don't, because it has multiple dimensions. What I was trying to say yesterday was that there are different types, and if I used the word energy, I should really have given names for the different ones. Those that work neurotically, and those that are driven through creative impulse. And the specific emotions favor these differently, for want of a better word, energies. This is the very core of the problem of how to link the psychoanalytic viewpoint with the kind of findings that we find through the repeated expression of emotions and the generation of emotions, in what we call a generalized form without cognitive causes. With generalised emotion we can affect the energy level of a person strongly and very specifically. We want to generate anger, we can do that. We generate anger, and a dog comes along and we kick him without any reason. Or, we generate love, and there is a different kind of energy.

Minsky: I think the problem with "energy" is that if you inhibit or destroy a certain brain center or activate another, an animal will do something a hundred thousand times, as though it had energy...

Lewis: Yes, but perhaps the thrust of the question you raised may be understood in this way: and that is, yes there is energy discharge in emotions, we can all experience that we are releasing something. But if we also think of energy as a communicative function, then what we are releasing may involve us in a feedback that will energize us. So when Manfred feels much better after he has done a hard day's work, maybe his superego has had a nice little boost from having communicated well with other people and with his own internal ....

Clynes: I think the concept of mental energy is a very important question. The word energy itself, as related to physics is already a misnomer, because we have been associating it with the old physics where there was force. Energy in today's physics is a way for particles to change their state of motion, so they move around in space differently, without the anthropomorphic concept of forcefulness, and effort. There is no *effort* in nature, except in persons (and other living beings). Mental energy and what we call our "physical energy" is also how much *effort* goes into doing things. Parodoxically the more energy, the less effort! We were talking about emotions as having long-term effects. The diurnal cycle very much affects the level of energy. It is the quality of experience, and also the mixtures. If you have a mixed emotion, and I completely agree with Marvin about emotions not being additive - when we first did these forms people said, why don't you do mixed emotions and add two parts of joy and three parts of anger, and so on, - it's total nonsense, because qualities are not additive in the expression; but nature seems to have solved the problem by a *sequential* thing, telescoping incomplete forms together.... thus melanchlody is expressed by first love, and then sadness, together giving you that melancholy effect. It's still a unit, a single expression, a lock and key type of thing and it has a different energy. If the thing is like a lock and key, you cannot change the lock linearly, and you cannot add a key to another key, but you can chain them together (no pun intended).

Minsky: But you can think of it as a compound expression, or a grammatical construction, and all communication after a certain point has to be sequential, because people are not good parallel processors.

Clynes: Well, how does that relate to the energy level?

Minksy: I don't understand why you use the term energy among scientists. It's the way to communicate with people about feelings, but you said "for want of a better word" and I bristle because there are hundreds of better words.

Clynes: Yes, give us some.

Minsky: They take too long. It just depends on what you are trying to do. If you are trying to say why somebody persists in an activity, then you have to make up a little theory of why you would ever stop an activity, and what we know is that nervous systems don't stop activities just because they run out of things. On the whole, they stop because there are inhibitory brain centers, like those which evolved to stop sexual activity after a certain point. If you take that brain center out, you can go on forever. It's not a matter of running out of energy.

Melnechuk: Is there anyone specializing in that?

Minsky: Presumably it would be illegal.

Scott: I have a comment, and this brings up a fundamental function of emotions, which we often forget about. That is, think about what would happen if human beings did not have emotions; presumably you would react like a machine. You would give one quick reaction to a stimulus. Once the stimulus was gone, there would be no further reason for reacting; What emotion does is, it permits an organism to keep on reacting for a long, long period to brief situation or stimulus or some kind of a change. One thing that goes along with this is that you feel that you are energetic. Energy in this sense is not energy in the sense of physics, but a feeling. In other words, it is one aspect of emotions that no one has really talked about here.

Minsky: It is a feeling of conviction for some.

Melnechuk: Some of the recent comments, including Dr. Panksepp's final comment, and things that Marvin said, raise (especially in the sense of humor) the issue of whether emotions and thoughts are in fact distinct. Dr. Panksepp, whose decorticated animals keep on expressing emotions, could say that emotions do not need cortical processes, although emotions may be elaborated or modified cortically. On the other hand, the existence of humor shows that at least in humans, perhaps only in that species but perhaps in others, too, an emotion may be a cortical-limbic thing that is not dissectable. It seems to me that humor is a highly evolved sense.

Panksepp: I think that humor obviously requires a lot of cortical processing but laughter does not. I think that the basic program for laughter emerges from play circuitry, and it is in play when children laugh most. As they run around, chasing each other, catching each other, getting away, they are laughing all the time, but if someone snaps a finger or an airplane goes by, all that laughter disappears as soon as you have to start thinking about the situation. Rats play in the same way. As soon as something intrusive occurs, they stop playing. If you look at animals playing, they almost appear to be tickling each other and the easiest way to get laughter (to awake the basic biological substrates of humor) is to tickle a child. My suspicion is that if human children were born without a neocortex, they would still laugh if you tickled them, even though they would never understand a joke.

Melnechuk: But you need the cortex for humor, and that is a real emotion, the feeling of amusement. It is as much a feeling as any one I have heard today. In that case then , it isn't only subcortical.

Panksepp: Well, I want to hold out the possibility that the feeling of mirth — the feeling good when one laughs — comes from elsewhere than the cortex. At present, we don't know where in the brain it emerges. Although I think we can be fairly certain that getting the point of the joke emerges from the cortex, I suspect that the affective feelings aroused by laughter arise elsewhere. Without a cortex, the human understanding of humor may be lost, but not the basic joy of play. Perhaps the cortex provides only one gateway to the joy circuitry which is active in laughter.

Minsky: But perthaps the cortex elaborates the feelings ...

Panksepp: Maybe. Play is the main situation in which joy and laughter occur (and it seems that even in human children that is the case — the more laughter, the more joy there is in a play situation). And then when you take away practically all of the neocortex of neonatal rats and they subsequently play normally during juvenile life, I would assume they are feeling pretty good about it still, so the feeling good about it does not seem to require a cortex.

Minksy: In my new book *Society of Mind* , there is a theory of humor. I wonder if you would like it, because the theory is that it's an extremely negative emotion, and this is what is funny about it. Humor connects with play and shame. Namely, you treat something humorously in order to build Freudian Censors against it. That is, if you learn something, and it is not real, or if you have a joke. The point of a joke is that something is taken with a wrong meaning, and then you want to put that in a memory ... a special memory, to remember that is the wrong thing to do. All jokes are about mistakes, if you look carefully. To identify humor with joy, I think it is fooling you too. It may feel like joy, but what is happening is building a negative memory of remember, don't do this again. Tickling is extremely unpleasant, but again it is masked as a positive thing.

Panksepp: Perhaps I carried it too far ... but you know, eons and eons of human children would disagree with you ...

Minsky: That's right, and that is because, it masks itself. It is like a deepest Freudian thing. The pleasantness of humor is to hide from you that it is a repressive phenomenon ...

Melnechuk: Others wish to comment.

From the Audience: If tickling is unpleasant, would't you have to exert work to get it going? If it is inherently rewarding in primates, how can you say it is unpleasant?

Minsky: Laughing teaches people *not* to do something. It doesn't teach them to do something.

Audience: But a moment ago, you said that tickling was inherently unpleasant ...

Panksepp: I think both are happening in the play situation. I think play is a reality-testing principle in the brain. You have to go out into the environment and see how far you can go, and play will take you to the edge of your knowledge or of your environment where things are not funny anymore, are not joyous anymore. And you learn that you have to back off from that point. So I think I can agree with both perspectives.

Melnechuk: Can I comment with a citation of a very interesting scholar named Gershon Legman. He is a scholar of pornography and of dirty limericks and such forms. Amongst his many wonderful works are two volumes of a book entitles " *The Rationale of the Dirty Joke*" - Volume One has two thousand dirty jokes, with where he collected them, "heard in a men's room" or "told by a UCSD undergraduate coed" and so forth. The jokes are printed in italics, embedded in a Freudian analysis of what they really mean, so you have the obvious surface content. The second volume, subtitled "No laughing Matter," contains two thousand more dirty jokes. Every dirty joke that I ever heard but one is in those two volumes. Legman says we laugh at what makes us anxious, which is I believe a generalization of what you said, Helen. Do you think that is a reasonable analysis?

Lewis: Yes, the lovely thing about Freud's joke book if you read it carefully, as I did recently, is that it becomes very clear that what he was describing (leaving aside what he said theoretically) is that laughter relieves humiliation, and that it is shared laughter that relieves humilation. If you tell a joke and the other person does not get it, it's no joke. But that whole notion that's what jokes are for, that they nicely relieve hurt ...

Minsky: But they also teach you what not to do.

Lewis: Well yes, you can use them that way, but again, what you have learned in laughter, if you arrive at it, is that you and that other person really can get together, and that both together can understand humiliation, and that it is not so terrible, and so on.

Minsky: Well, I think there are many sides, but another side of shared laughter is telling somebody what they should be hurt about if I really meant it.

Lewis: Of course, that's why it is so difficult. Sometimes ridicule is gentle, and then one can respond to it and take a lesson from it, but the minute it gets mean ...

Minksy: The reason I emphasize this is that I think something happened to psychology since Behaviorism, which is that we don't study what people don't do. Freud is almost the last person to mention repression, because the experimenters and their methodology are weak on it. You can watch behavior, but you can't explain what non-stimulus the animal non-reaction to is not doing something else, and that's why I think humor has been so poorly studied. Humor is the main way of communicating what not to do, and telling people which sensors and repressors to build. I disagree with you if you think humor is very joyous and so forth, for I think there is a sinister element to that joy. It is constraining and teaching us to stay in our place.

Clynes: The disagreement we have is quite a radical one here: because I disagree about the nature of laughter with you. I think laughter to be a healthy thing. I agree with you about the nature of jokes. Freud wrote a book on the nature of jokes. He did not write a book on the nature of laughter. I think the construction of jokes is most often a way of releasing hidden aggression, but I think that to be a misuse of the natural gift of laughter. It is a derisive use of laughter, whereas I consider the natural gift of laughter to be nature's arrow from appearance to reality. It involves an apparent mistake: the mistake is suddenly discovered to be part of a larger order, and one laughs with a sense of discovery. The derisive humor and laughter is an inversion of this paradigm, and in a sense a perversion of it: cf, Schadenfreude.

Minsky: I absolutely agree, but I feel the natural place for humans is swinging among the branches, and I don't think "healthy" and "natural" are the same thing. I'm against both.

Clynes: Why are we laughing at this now?

Minsky: To keep people from thinking things I don't want them to ...

Clynes: Because of discovery ... It's a sudden discovery.

Melnechuk: We have a procedural issue. I announced at the beginning that we would have two parts, separated by a break. But this is rolling along so beautifully, I hate to break it. One way would be for people to go out individually.

Lewis: Could we have a very short break?

Melnechuk: OK.

Melnechuk: Now for part three of the session. Part two was the break, and obviously a lot of interesting discussion happened then in another format. Now we are going to have another colleague willing to give a brief summary of main points. We have Dr. Gail Zivin, who is a professor of Psychiatry and Human Behavior at Jefferson Medical College in Philadelphia. Gail, why don't you give us your theme and do 15 minutes.

Effective Features of Facial Signals

Gail Zivin

Zivin: My theme in this current work is the search for the basic signal features of expressive behaviors. These would include, but not be limited to, emotional expressions. (One also expresses attitudes, moods, intentions, motivations). I am trying to bring some order to the question of what information we pick out of a movement or position, when it means something.

There are a few working assumptions to guide my search for these basic features: (1) These features are found singly or in combinations in the most basic, most survival-relevant, and cross-culturally-distributed social signals. "Most basic" means being tied to the simplest organization of fundamental social relationships, such as mother-infant, first-born-next born, or mates. (2) The features are universal across humans, other primates, and possibly other mammals. (I'm assuming that some elemental recognition of and reaction to these features is innate, but that's not a necessary assumption for this early phase of the search). (3) The features reflect, in social signals, simple but universal and physically compelling aspects of physical reality. Examples of these simple aspects are up-down, near-far, fast-slow, toward-away, expanding-shrinking, open-closed. (4) There is a small finite set of these. I'm just at the beginning of the search for ways to constrain the listing of possible features, and that's what brought me to this conference: I believe that some of these features are what are being read and responded to in other's emotional expressions. (Once there are multiple lines of theoretical constraint on the list of features, the dimensions composing the features can be empirically tested by factor analyses of characterizations of mammalian displays).

My previous empirical work on two human signals led to my realizing that we needed to know what components of features made those two signals effective. It took several years to realize that no one had asked that about the effective components of all human displays. I'll tell you briefly about those two human signals — which I believe to be displays, that is, selected by evolution to be signals and therefore "innate". Around 1974, inspired by finding behavioral indications of monkey self-confidence during serious observations at our zoo's monkey island, I found similar postural cues in preschool children. Very detailed observations of faces, postures, and contexts showed that human preschoolers showed two opposite signals, which I called the Plus and the Minus, that were significantly correlated with, respectively, winning or losing a conflict (Zivin, G. *Social Science Information*, 1977, 16, 715-730). I'll do them for you; you'll recongnize them immediately. You see the Plus in statues going back to ancient Greece through portraits of past university presidents. I'll show you an exaggerated form so you'll have time to focus on it. Adults usually do it very subtly — faster, with fewer components, and camouflaged by context: adults will present themselves as superior or competent, rather than have overt conflicts. That subtlety starts by age 10 (Zivin, G. *Child Development*, 1977, 4B, 1314-1321). In the full Plus "face" the chin lifts, brows are raised in the middle, eyes open and make contact, the mouth can be doing almost anything, and the posture is up, erect and open. If I throw this gesture in while I am doing something else, even just talking to you (demonstrates), I can give you the impression that I'm quite competent and know what I'm doing.

Lewis: We used to call it stuck-up.

Zivin: Yes, "stuck up," "haughty". The fellow who wrote the *Dress for Success* books, Malloy, reported an experiment at a lecture. I have no idea whether the methodology was adequate, but it makes an interesting illustration. He was interested in clothes as determining the impression made on employers by employees in the white collar world. He dressed blue collar people in the clothes he recommends and upper middle class people in his idea of blue collar clothes, posed them for photos, accompanied the photos with identical resumes, and asked propspective employers to evaluate these candidates. Of course, he got the results he expected, with much more confidence in the "well dressed" people as more intelligent, reliable, etc. I was interested in the poses. All the "well dressed" were posed in the Plus "face," while the others were posed in slouches.

Back to the other signal. It is just the motoric and situational opposite of the Plus. That is significant because it follows the Principle of Antithesis that Darwin posited for biological, non-arbitrary signals (Darwin, C. *The Expression of the Emotions in Man and*

Animals (1872). Chicago: University of Chicago Press, 1965). That principle says that oppositely motivated, and thus oppositely meaning, signals will be the motor inverse of each other, for example moving toward and moving away from something. The Minus "face" has lowered chin, slightly furrowed brows, broken eye contact, and collapsed shoulder posture (demonstrates). You get the impression the person feels like crying. It's not surprising that the person who makes this is likely to lose a conflict or, in adults, give an impression of inadequacy. Adults tend much less frequently to make this gesture in non-extreme circumstances, but they do have duals of Plus "face" vs. impassive during impression-making challenges. We traced the increased subtlety in form and context, and the changes in types of conflicts, from 2-1/2-year-olds through a 45-year-old (Hottenstein, M. P. *An Exploration of the Relationship between Age, Social Status, and* Facial *Gesturing*. Unpublished doctoral dissertation, University of Pennsylvania, 1977; Zivin,G. In R. S. Feldman (Ed.), *Development of Non-Verbal Behavior in Children*. New York: Springer-Verlag, 1982, 63-98). But it's so prevalent that it's wonderful to watch acquaintances make Plus "faces" at each other when they meet at some event like intermission at the ballet.

Melnechuk: Does it work for picking horses?

Zivin: For finding a really confident and assertive horse? It might, if you knew the right horse signal components to look for. But that gets us back to my earlier question: Are there universal signal features for universal situations - across mammals - and if so, what are they? It seems to me that the Plus and Minus "faces" convey the signal features of open and ready for outside contact vs. closed and unready. And it seems that this is mainly carried by chin level and supporting shoulder posture. It's the chin that stays present while, with subtlety, the other components drop out.

Audience: Gail, have you done any observations in singles bars or where any situational courtship behaviors are occuring?

Zivin: I have not looked at situations that would be courtship. Though I guess it would be appropriate for males and not females during initial impression-making in our middle-class subculture.

Liebowitz: Have you ever tried to program people to behave differently and see what the subjective effects are? For instance, my social phobics. They always seem to feel that they are faking. Have you ever tried suggesting that they get their chin an inch and a half higher, and see what happens?

Zivin: I haven't but early on, I wanted to do a demonstration program with kids who were having social problems in school, to teach the ones who look like they are inviting the piranhas to pick on them, to just change from minus to plus. In fact, frequency of plus does correlate with preference and hierarchy. People who do this more are perceived as the leaders and are more liked. I have that data on the all age groups. I thought we could change some losers into winners. I could not get clearence to manipulate kids in that way. I could not get Human Subjects Committee approval.

Liebowitz: But could you do it in people who come for clinical help

Zivin: Yes, I could have, but I just didn't try.

Melnechuk: Someone in the audience has a point?

Audience: Well, I'd like to question the assumption that there is a win-lose continuum. This is too much of a simplification. It seems to me that a critical question is how open or closed I am to an interaction.

Zivin: You are questioning all the assumptions loaded into the words "win" and "lose" and suggesting that being open vs. closed might be closer to what is more fundamentally going on in situations that we have labeled as types of conflict or impression-making. I'm very glad for that question because I agree with its point that win-lose are cultural interpretations that are less fundamental than being open or closed and because it reminds me to be more careful by emphasizing that any observational category, even if its instances are carefully operationalized, as our types of win and loss were, is just a label applied to behaviors that look similar according to some criteria which may or may not fit a subcultural definition - and whose subcultural definition may or may not correlate with a more fundamental, biological dimension. That's why the signals were named "Plus" and "Minus," not "win" and "lose"-although "A" and "B" would have been still less loaded. But there is historical and cross-cultural evidence (Spiegal, J. P. and Machotka, P. *Messages of the Body*. New York: Free Press, 1974) that these particular open or closed gestures are found in people and poses that are considered superior.

Melnechuk: Is it because they look taller? Remember, when we were kids, the ones who were competent were way up there. And it may be that seeing Plus returns you to that level. By the way, while my chin is up, you have only five more minutes.

Zivin: I think the question is on the right track. Let me see if there is anything else that might be interesting that I have not yet mentioned. Do people really respond to these signals or is it just our research team's impression? We wanted to know this. We took videotapes of people who are naturally doing this, and edited the videotapes so that subjects saw the beginning of a challenging conversation, stopped before the outcome, and they saw matched conversations where you did not have these faces at the beginning. They were asked to predict what would happen. There were too few that were technically good enough to have a sample large enough for statistical significance, the majority of the predictions in the right direction.

What are some of the physiological mechanisms that may be involved that link seeing these signals to winning or losing or making an impression? One thing that occurred to me was, it is affecting the reaction system: if you are wired to perceive something, shouldn't you be wired to have some kind of reaction to it? That led to doing the physiological study I mentioned earlier, but before I got there I was able to measure only behavior from the videotapes. We measured the latencies of response of the kids in conflict, after they saw a Plus face versus a Minus face. If they have just seen a Plus face, it takes twice as long to move a muscle and three times as long to do something combative, than if they have just seen a Minus face (Zivin, 1982, Op.Cit.).

So it seems to me that there is some evidence that there is something going on in the reaction system when one perceives these two different gestures. What is affected in the reaction system? That question led to the physiological study: I wanted to see if there was quieting, physiologically (eg. EMG), in the people who see this guy come in and make a Plus "face".

Panksepp: There are other behavioral situations where that same posture occurs in an exaggerated form-in laughter. People often hold their chins up when they laugh, and laughter seems to be a common sign of victory. And the entire bearing of the body can be very high, whenever one wins. When there is a competetive situation, especially among kids, and if they get the last "lick" in, they are really delighted, and there is generally laughter on the winning side.

Audience: You have mentioned cross-cultural diversities and we know that in Turkish there is that comparable ultimate denial of an upward head movement. One throws one's head up and back and makes that little hissy noise. If a Turk does that you can't go further at all in an interaction.

Melenchuk: Gail, could you reword that for the tape?

Zivin: There is a Turkish example of a similar movement which has superiority attached to it. It is not openness for continued contact but it is kind of indication of "I've just maybe stopped you." Is that a reasonable paraphrase? And so it captures the element of having won, maybe not necessarily the openness to continue the interaction.

Audience: Prior to this movement, do both people in the dyad have a neutral posture, or is there a continual up and down, and then only the last gesture, as if it were a closing gesture?

Zivin: They can be doing anything before, and it's usually the first one who does the Plus or the Minus that predicts the outcome.

Audience: In the down face, do the eyes come up prior to the head or just the head?

Zivin: No, the eyes coming up would be really something very different.

Audience: Thinking of the Eibl-Eibesfeldt work, is it the flirting kind of glance?

Zivin: If the eyes came up first it *would* be coy, but the Minus is not coy. It's just the opposite. It has no ambivalence, it's all off.

Liebowitz: I remember Diana Fossey used to talk about how you approach a gorilla. What you do is you look down. If you look up and stare at it, that's too much of a provocation. This seems to be a parallel.

Zivin: Yes, also with baboons. If you want to get your car smashed driving through the game preserves in Kenya, just stare at them.

Melnechuk: A colleague, who studies monkey colonies and their communication patterns told me he never gets a ticket when he is caught on the highway because he gives the primate submission signal. The cop gives him hell but never a ticket.

Liebowitz: People walking around the "main line" (i.e., in Philadelphia) walk around like this all the time.

Melnechuk: Like a pro cleaving the waves. I've seen it but I hadn"t known what I was seeing.

Audience: Are you postulating a causal relationship between the posture and the message? Could it not be the other way around? Posture might be the consequence of social acceptance or respect. How do you know that the causal connection is in the direction that you say?

Zivin: I really can't say because I haven't got, and I dont see how to get, data on kids young enough, before they've started a sense of themselves. My early conversation with ethologist W. John Smith was about signs of monkey self-esteem, and I first started wondering about such behavior as a dependent variable of self-esteem. That's how all this started more than 12 years ago. So I certainly think there is a probable link, and its likely to be a spiral relation both of gesture causing acceptance and of social acceptance causing the feeling that leads to the gesture.

Audience: Would you see the same person give Plus faces to one person and Minus faces to another?

Zivin: That's an excellent question. I haven't found an adequately controlled comparison across settings, but what I can tell you is, when we coded the semester's worth of tape on people of all ages in peer settings, we found that folks tended to make one face more than the other regardless of what sample setting we had them in. One can do both depending upon the relationship, but there are behavioral habits that make a person more prone to do one rather than the other. Especially as you get older, it becomes automatized as an element in self presentation. It becomes relatively independent of the specific person you are interacting with. It becomes a part of how you collect yourself when you're showing yourself.

Melnechuk: I remember the film of Chaplin called *"The Great Dictator"*. A famous scene has Hitler in one barber chair and Mussolini in the other. And Hitler pumps himself higher, and Mussolini pumps himself higher still, and so forth back and forth, till they are up against the ceiling.

Minsky: I like the idea that its a perspective of height, because you might ask how does a child know who is an adult and who is the child? Then the naive idea is that it is height, but size invariance is a problem: when somebody is far away, they'll look smaller; however, the chin angle will be invariant. If a tall person is so far away that you can barely see him, you'll still see under the chin.

Zivin: Well, we now know from Michael Lewis' work that it's not height that kids use for discriminating. He used midgets and kids, and two or three years olds acted emotionally differently to adult midgets and to same size kids.

Minsky: That wrecks that theory.

Melnechuk: Perhaps one of the reasons people used to, and apparantly still do, pick on older women with osteoporosis and the widow's hunch, is that it keeps the chin down permanently. It may be another stigma. There are born losers. You can see that because their chins are down.

Minsky: Culturally speaking, traditional Japanese bow. The depth of your bow shows the depth of your respect. So when two Japanese meet, they dont always bow equally. The person who has the higher position will bow less than the person with lesser position.

Clynes: This problem brings up the question of posture, and how posture can indicate many frozen emotional states. I think we have been neglecting that aspect of the conference's theme.

Melnechuk: You designed the conference.

Clynes: There are all these what we call "virtual body images" of the specific emotions. Sometimes these get frozen, and schools of techniques have developed (such as Feldenkrais) whose purpose is to get rid of these no longer conscious postural memories of past emotions which also effect the immediate communication. One senses not just by this Plus/Minus dichotomy that you pointed out but by many vairations that a person has in walking, in the shoulders, and all the rest of it. And we immediately sense these as personality things. However these can be rectified, and then this is also therapeutic. A whole line of therapies have evolved that relate to the body images, which of course also can be linked back to childhood as well.

Lewis: I wonder whether Marvin would agree with me that perhaps what was being referred to as the Japanese making distinctions between depths of bowing clearly has some kind of monkey forerunner. Maybe that's the part of the baggage that in an evolutionary sense we may be carrying with us from our primate heritage that we may someday be able to do without.

Audience: You may call it baggage, but I think it has great value, for "dress for success" situations, where a person can assume an important victory by keeping the chin up.

Melnechuk: I always try to leave looking like that.

Minsky: Going back to your comment, Helen, about whether it is "baggage", well , it's even embedded in our verbalizations. You look up to someone that you admire. Now you can't look up unless you are down. And you also look down on people who aren't up to your standards, and you can't look down unless you are up. So even our language attests to these positions of your head.

Liebowitz: And when someone is down, we tell them to keep their chin up.

Melnechuk: William Condon in Boston filmed mother-child interactions and co-worker interactions and then, by very minute analysis over years, was able to show that with newborns, mother's speech choreographs the only apparently random motions of the baby, which in fact are in exact synchrony with the phoneme boundaries of the mother's speech. He also showed that co-workers, or anybody in a dyadic situation, even if there is a rank difference, tend to reflect the posture of the other. So you'll commonly find that if someone folds his arms during a talk, the other soon folds his arms. If someone crosses his legs, the other one soon crosses his legs. There is a nonverbal mirroring going on beside whatever is happening at the verbal level. When you see the film the monkey-see, monkey-do mirroring is hilarious.

Lewis: And that is in a benign atmosphere. I mean it is mothers and babies and co-workers, and nobody is fighting with anybody else. My point about baggage was that maybe we have carried along with us so much of the primate heritage of aggression that we obviously can do with less.

Clynes: Yes, as humans we do have the unique advantage that we can sit around here and talk about emotion (and talk about talking about emotion): to look at our baggage and see what is missing and what might be too much. But can we and should we modify that baggage we inherited? Cultures seem to extract various penalties for suppressions and attempted modifications, in balance for their enhancements. As Marvin implied, we cannot know scientifically either what is natural or what is healthy in social terms. Mental health, and even the concept of mental health, is inseparable from social structure of which we have little scientific understanding. Yet understanding emotions and their cognitive substrates seems to offer a way towards increasing that understanding - beyond early attempts to reduce them all in effect to sexual manifestations, important though these are.

Man can not only sit around a table and talk about emotion; he can consider them in an abstract or "Apollonian" way (rather than a Dionysian bacchanale) and incorporate them in art and in music where they can be kept on "ice" for generations to come. Looking at them in this way, their cognitive substrates can lead to a measure of wisdom of which man alone among animals is capable, and a corresponding freedom from enslavement to them. Though we carry our baggage and cannot be freed from it, we alone among animals can *deliberately* choose to transform its content to give meaning, affecting many, in the future as well as in the present, through symphonies, through incorporation in religious thought - and also through destructive war and holocaust.

In the long run, the emotions may well prove to be our most valuable and most dangerous baggage. We need to study this baggage - what is in it and how did it get packed? It is too late to live in innocence. Through such study we may yet avoid accumulating greater guilt and destruction, and perhaps some day, even regain a measure of innocence on a higher level.

Melnechuk: Perhaps with that, we have arrived at the time not to march out amok but to dance out in harmony, with our chins up, smiling.

BIOGRAPHICAL SKETCHES

Helen Block Lewis, 1914 -1987

Helen Block Lewis had not yet completed revisions on the transcript of her presentation when she died this past January 18th. Accordingly, we have include her presentation, verbatim, as she gave it on September 26, 1986. We took the liberty of including reference citations, as best as we were able. Her presentation was a resourceful look at the past and future of a field that she had helped develop. Helen was a sensitive interpreter of the human condition, and a brilliant integrator of diverse fields of knowledge. Perhaps her major contribution was the re-interpretation of psychoanalytic theory in the modern conceptual structure of emotions. In her 1971 book "Shame and Guilt in Neurosis" she traced the manner in which emotions emerged within the therapeutic interaction. More recently, in the two volumed "Freud and Modern Psychology," she updated psychoanalytic theory within the context of modern findings in experimental psychology. Helen Block Lewis was a bridge builder between disciplines. At the end, she was also the energetic editor of <u>Psychoanalytic Psychology</u> and Emeritus Professor of Psychology at Yale University. She was a person of insight and vision. We shall miss her.

Robert Plutchik is Professor at the Department of Psychiatry, Albert Einstein School of Medicine. He has helped foster the current renaissance in the study of emotions through his research, theorizing and advocacy of more work in this important area. His work has bridged animal and human research, basic experimental work and clinical applications. His synthesis of the field as well as theoretical perspective has been summarized most comprehensively in "Emotion: A Psychoevolutionary Synthesis" (1980, Harper & Row), and most recently in collaboration with Henry Kellerman pulled the field together in a four volume series on "Emotion: Theory, Research, and Experience" of which the last volume is concerned with Emotions and Psychotherapy. His most recent personal work has also been devoted to the analysis of emotions in the clinical situation, but he concurrently continues to explore the basic biological issues, his most recent inquiries being into the genetic basis of emotions.

John Paul Scott is Emeritus Regents Professor of Psychology at Bowling Green State University. He received his doctorate in biology from the University of Chicago, and spent most of his research career, before coming to Bowling Green, at the Jackson Labs, Bar Harbor, Maine, where he established an intensive research program analyzing the genetic components of behavior in dogs. The analysis of different canine temperaments led him to focus on the basic nature of emotionality, with a special focus on critical periods of early development. Much of his recent work has focussed on the nature of aggression and the separation response in dogs. He has a steady publication record of major contributions in these and related areas since 1936, and presently he his working on comprehensive survey of social behavior. He helped found the Animal Behavior Society and was instrumental in the formation of the International Society for Research on Aggression (ISRA) in 1972. Most recently, he has been instrumental in promoting the study of warfare by the ISRA and has helped create and disseminate knowledge about this aspect of the human dilemma.

Jaak Panksepp is Distinguished Research Professor in the Department of Psychology at Bowling Green State University. He did his graduate work at the University of Massachusetts in physiological psychology and pursued postdoctoral work in feeding and nutrition at the University of Sussex and in sleep physiology at the Worcester Foundation for Experimental Psychology. His present research is devoted to the analysis of hypothalamic, limbic and neurochemical mechanisms of emotional behaviors, with a current focus on understanding how the separation response, social bonding, social play and fear are organized in the brain. His past work in hypothalamic mechanisms of energy balance control was supported by a NIMH Research Scientist Development Award. He is author on over 150 research articles and reviews which deal primarily with brain control of motivated behaviors. He is co-editor of "The Handbook of the Hypothalamus" series. His general research orientation is that a detailed understanding of basic emotional systems at the neural level will highlight the nature and genesis of emotional disorders in humans.

Michael Liebowitz received his medical training at Yale University and is currently Director of the Anxiety Disorders Clinical the New York State Psychiatric Institute, Professor of Clinical Psychiatry at Columbia University and Assistant Attending Psychiatrist at Columbia-Prebyterian Medical Center. During the past decade has been in the forefront of research on the evaluation of pharmacotherapeutic maneuvers in the treatment of panic attacks, social phobias and other personality disorders which can arise from emotional imbalances. His work is helping revolutionize our thinking about the medical treatment of emotional ailments. He has published more than a 150 articles in the area, and has contributed a popularized synopsis of psychobiological work in the area entitled "The Chemistry of Love."

Manfred Clynes, now Research Professor of Neuropsychology, and Sugden Fellow at Queen's College at the University of Melbourne (he has a D. Sc. in Neuroscience, Univ. of Melbourne, M.S., Juilliard School of Music and did graduate work at Princeton University), in work spanning two decades, has discovered biologically given temporal shapes, genetically preserved, through which specific emotions are transmitted and generated, and a number of biologic principles that describe their function (sentics). he has shown how they apply to music, and the arts, as well as in personal communication. From these a simple and effective therapeutic method has evolved, sentic cycles, that uses an easily learned touch artform. Recently he has advanced our understanding of the language of music and cognitive science by finding two principles of unconscious musical thought, operating on the microstructure of music, that give life to the "dead" musical notes of a score. In the 1960's, as a neurophysiologist at the Rockland State Hospital in New York, he discovered the law of unidirectional rate sensitivity of biologic channels of communication. As inventor, his 40 patents include the CAT computer that enabled Event Related Potentials of the brain to be widely studied in the 1960's and 70's. A concert pianist of international repute, but also poet and humanist, he has performed throughout the world and studied with Pablo Casals and Sascha Gorodnitzki. He now performs only on rare cherished occasions.

Marvin Minksy is Donner Professor of Electrical Engineering at MIT, and is one of the foremost thinkers in the field of artificial intelligence. Educated at Harvard and Princeton, and a member of the National Academy of Science, his teachers included John van Neumann, and later Warren McCulloch for whom he has particular admiration. As a guiding light he has headed the Artificial Intelligence Laboratory at MIT for many years, and his laboratory has inseminated the field with fertile thoughts and thinkers. His view has been that the processes of thinking are not appropriately modelled by logical paradigms. As a consequence, his work has become increasingly concerned with cognitive psychology and with emotions, culminating with a recent seminal contribution, "The Society of Mind" (1987). In this work he takes the radical view that thinking involves a very large number of quasi-independent agents loosely and hierarchically cooperating but without a single continuing overriding entity. Expanding his earlier work with K-lines and the Perceptron he provides challenging new concepts on how the brain and also computers may need to function in order to accomplish what we so easily call thinking. And emotions, in this view, appear as aids to thinking.

Theodore Melnechuk, although not a laboratory scientist, has been a key facilitator of emerging scientific disciplines for a long time. The recent emergence of neuroscience as one of the most rapidly growing and vigorous fields of science was promoted, in no small measure, by his networking at the Neurosciences Study Program in Boston during the sixties. He was the founding editor (1963-1972) of the Neurosciences Research Program Bulletin, as well as co-editor of the first major modern compendium of neuroscience research, "The Neurosciences, A Study Program." He has helped organize numerous conferences on leading-edge topics in neuro- and psycho-biological research. Most recently, his advocacy of psychoneuroimmunology has helped that area to become a prominent field of inquiry. He has made numerous contributions to the neuroscience community and has written extensively in health related areas. He has also helped scientists keep a perspective on their labors through the humor and light verse of Dr. Orpheus, whose reflections have graced the pages of many scientific journals. Presently Ted is Planning and Editorial Consultant at Helicon Foundation and is affiliated with the Department of Neurosciences, School of Medicine, University of California, San Diego.

Paul Byers teaches anthropological communication and structural research methods at Teachers College, Columbia University. He first described the rhythm-sharing underlying human (and monkey) interaction in 1972 and continues to explore the biological processes involved in human relations. He believes, following the work of Gregory Bateson and the Palo Alto group, that the processes found in the microanalysis of dyadic or group interaction have formal characteristics at all levels of organization. The paper in this volume is his first attempt to suggest the implications of his research for other disciplines.

During the round-table discussion Gail Zivin and Larry Stettner summarized their work on ethological aspects of human emotions.

Larry Stettner is Professor of Psychology at Wayne State University. His earlier research focussed on brain mechanisms of avian learning, and he has made the transition into the study of human ethology, with a focus on a rigorous analysis of smiling in various contexts. Most recently, his laboratory has been focussing on analyzing changes in this response as a function of depression.

Gail Zivin is Professor of Psychiatry and Human Behavior at the Jefferson Medical College. Her work has focussed on the development of expressive behaviors in children, how humans use facial gestures to indicate social rank, as well how such gestures reflect the outcome of social encounters. She is one of the founders of the International Society for Human Ethology.

AUTHOR INDEX

SUBJECT INDEX